Descartes' Philosophy Interpreted
According to the Order of Reasons

Volume I

The Soul and God

MARTIAL GUEROULT

Descartes' Philosophy Interpreted According to the Order of Reasons

Volume I

The Soul
and God

Translated by
Roger Ariew

With the Assistance of
Robert Ariew *and* Alan Donagan

University of Minnesota Press, Minneapolis

This work was supported by a grant
from the Translations Program of the
National Endowment for the Humanities,
an independent federal agency.

English translation © 1984 by Roger Ariew (based on 2nd ed.).
Originally published as
Descartes selon l'ordre des raisons, vol. I, *l'âme et Dieu,*
1st ed. Copyright © 1952 by Editions Montaigne.
2nd ed. Copyright © 1968 by Editions Montaigne.
All rights reserved.
Published by the University of Minnesota Press,
2037 University Avenue Southeast, Minneapolis, MN 55414
Printed in the United States of America.

Library of Congress Cataloging in Publication Data

Guéroult, Martial.
  Descartes' philosophy interpreted according to the
  order of reasons.

  Translation of: Descartes selon l'ordre des raisons.
  Contents: v. 1. The soul and God.
  1. Descartes, René, 1596-1650. I. Title.
B1875.G813   1983   194   83-21771
ISBN 0-8166-1255-2
ISBN 0-8166-1256-0 (pbk.)

The University of Minnesota
is an equal-opportunity
educator and employer.

Contents of
Volumes I and II

Contents
Volume I
The Soul and God
(The First Five Meditations)

Chapter IV. The Cogito: Priority of Knowledge of Soul over Knowledge of Body   75

Chapter V. The First Proof of God's Existence by Effects   103

Acknowledgments

I would like to thank the numerous people and institutions without whom this work might not have been possible: the National Endowment for the Humanities' Translations Program and Susan Mango, its able and efficient director; my two consultants and readers, Robert Ariew and Alan Donagan; the many historians of seventeenth-century philosophical thought who have given much support and encouragement to the project, Lesley Cohen, Edwin Curley, Daniel Garber, Marjorie Grene, Michael Hooker, and Margaret Wilson; Virginia Polytechnic Institute and State University's Department of Philosophy, Center for Programs in the Humanities, and Center for the Study of Science in Society for their word-processing and secretarial help; Lindsay Waters and the editorial staff of the University of Minnesota Press; and most importantly, Susan Andriette Ariew, for the countless hours of reading, rereading, and proofreading the manuscript.

Introduction

Martial Gueroult's *Descartes selon l'ordre des raisons*[1] is one of the great masterpieces of Cartesian scholarship. Its effect on French Cartesian studies has been profound, radically transforming the methodology for understanding Descartes. As Yvon Belaval phrases it in his lengthy critical guide to Gueroult's *Descartes,* "were we to contest it page per page, it would hold up as an incontestable monument of thinking, which is often subtle without becoming overly clever, always powerful, and always building. But it does more. It renews our view, not so much by a new interpretation . . . as by a redressing of perspectives."[2]

Gueroult's *Descartes* is the product of a doctrine about how one ought to understand Descartes, prescribed by Descartes himself. From the beginning, in the Preface to the *Meditations,* Descartes relates that he has no expectation of approval from a wide audience; he is not looking for casual readers, but for the few who will meditate seriously with him. To meditate seriously is, for Descartes, to link propositions with the rigor of a geometer, to worry about the order and sequence of reasons, and not to quibble about single conclusions by themselves.[3] But, according to Gueroult, no one has yet paid attention to Descartes' advice: ". . . of the enormous number of commentators, critics, and historians who, during three centuries, have occupied themselves with Descartes, there is not one, it seems, who has obeyed his imperious counsel. None of them, even those who believe they follow a systematic method, like Hamelin, do much more than pick holes in the texts."[4] They follow the order of topics, an order that Descartes has rejected because it distorts the order and linkage of reasons; to follow the order of topics is to consider each problem separately, although Descartes did not consider them separately (to consider the Cogito in Descartes, freedom in Descartes, thought in Descartes, God in Descartes, etc.). "And it is not rash to think that a divergence so radical between the method recommended by the philosopher and the method of those who have commented on him could have regrettable consequences in interpreting his work."[5] Gueroult repeats this general criticism of Cartesian scholarship in his reviews of Anglo-American Cartesian studies. For instance, in an article entitled "Descartes pionnier (Un Descartes au goût britannique),"[6] Gueroult develops a criticism of Norman Kemp Smith's interpretation of Descartes, which he had already accused (in an anonymous review)[7] of having treated the Cartesian problems separately, of having broken the unity of Cartesian thought: "Instead of going about it Descartes' way, he goes about it his own way, breaking into a thousand little pieces the marvelous entity [about] which Descartes told us . . . that the least thing removed from it or the least thing added to it carries with it its complete ruin."[8]

Gueroult's doctrine about how one ought to understand Descartes is itself derived from a larger conception about what it is to do the history of philosophy, which, according to Gueroult, is neither to do history without concern for the philosophical truth the doctrines may express, nor to do philosophy detached from the tradition that shapes it.[9] According to Gueroult, philosophy cannot isolate itself from history any more than the history of philosophy can isolate itself from philosophy; the historian of philosophy finds himself torn between the contrary tendencies of ceasing to be a philosopher and detaching himself from history. The most radical form of the first tendency is the wish to consider philosophies not as eternal truths, but as contingent historical events explained by historical, sociological, and psychological factors; Gueroult polemicizes against these "psychologists" in "The History of Philosophy as a Philosophical Problem" and in "De la méthode prescrite par Descartes pour comprendre sa philosophie" (he concentrates, in the latter, on the problems with interpreting Descartes as the "psychologists" do). The second tendency has the consequence that "throughout history, philosophy has never ceased to do violence to its history."[10]

The tendency to do philosophy apart from its history is evident in the Anglo-American analytic tradition; and curiously, it is most evident in the case of analytic writings about Descartes. Descartes, one of the absolutely pivotal figures in the history of philosophy, has often been the whipping boy of the Anglo-American analytic tradition; numerous studies within the tradition have attributed positions to Descartes that he did not hold historically, in order to refute the positions (sometimes the attribution comes as the myth behind the philosopher's writings, and sometimes it comes as a philosophical reconstruction, or what the philosopher ought to have held; regardless, one can easily argue that G. E. Moore, Gilbert Ryle, Norman Malcom, J. L. Austin, and others, have been guilty of attributing to Descartes positions that he did not hold, in order to refute them). It is to Descartes' credit that he was not buried by this, but that he withstood the unfavorable readings; these readings brought about fresh studies resulting in greater admiration for the Cartesian corpus (here one can point to the recent work of Margaret Wilson, and others,[11] which makes some use of Gueroult's *Descartes*). It is not an exaggeration to assert that, until recently, Anglo-American writings about Descartes were either ahistorical critiques in the analytic tradition (as above) or historical commentaries (for example, Boyce Gibson and Norman Kemp Smith's commentaries) reflecting the French Cartesian work of fifty years ago (E. Gilson and O. Hamelin, for example). One would hope that the publication of Gueroult's *Descartes* in English would be instrumental in the process of reestablishing Descartes in the English-speaking world as a philosopher to be studied in detail (instead of one to refute).

Given the state of Anglo-American Cartesian studies, it does not seem surprising that Gueroult's *Descartes* had not yet been translated. However, even that does not provide a sufficient explanation for its neglect, given the importance of the work: even the primary English-language bibliography of Cartesian studies, Gregor Stebba's *Bibliographia Cartesiana,* lauds it as "the most impressive of all systematic Descartes commentaries."[12] And in France, Ferdinand Alquié, Gueroult's great "psychologist" opponent (who thinks that Descartes' metaphysics is tied to Descartes' historical situation and the fact that Descartes has always had problems knowing where reality was, or distinguishing waking from sleeping states),[13] has written favorably about Gueroult's *Descartes:* "I recognize the legitimacy of Mr. Gueroult's project, I admire its strength, its novelty, the depth of its explanation, and I rejoice for the light it sheds on so many points, especially with respect to the *Sixth Meditation.*"[14] Moreover, Gueroult's *Descartes* is not an isolated work fashioned by an unknown scholar; Gueroult, a member of the Institut and professor at the Collège de France, wrote a series of essays on Descartes,[15] a monograph on Descartes' ontological argument,[16] an extremely important book on Leibniz,[17] a monumental three-volume study on Malebranche,[18] an equally monumental study on Spinoza[19] (Gueroult died before completing the third volume), as well as some other articles and books on the same philosophers and on Berkeley, Maimonides, and Fichte.[20] The only real explanation for the present neglect of Gueroult's work[21] in the English-speaking world has to point to the virtues of the work itself, to its depth, the subtlety of its thought, its richness, and its monumental nature, its length. Until now these virtues have made it almost impossible to study Gueroult's achievements without having a good command of the French language (and knowledge of Latin). In fact, these virtues continue to pose difficulties even after the problem of translation is resolved. For the English-speaking reader, Gueroult is almost as difficult in translation as he is in the original language.

Roger Ariew

Preface

One ought to mistrust the intellectual games that, under the pretext of discovering the deep meaning of a philosophy, begin by neglecting its precise meaning"; this maxim of Victor Delbos was ours constantly while we were writing the present work. It subordinates "comprehension" to "explanation."

In fact, it is possible to imagine having comprehended something without being able to explain it, when, believing ourselves to understand something else, we merely understand ourselves in that respect. This illusion always arises when whim and fancy come to the understanding. A vivid and impatient imagination is satisfied that, rather than trap itself into the tight links of a text, finds in the text the opportunity to take free flight, needing only to return from time to time and perch upon some of the references strewn at the bottom of the pages. These generous effusions, proceeding by illumination rather than by strict analysis, can no doubt hit upon some truth here or there, but they do so by chance, like a moth striking the luminous globe around which it revolves. If they can procure for us the feeling of "comprehension," that is due to a transformed, romanticized doctrine, in which the transformation imposes foreign perspectives and a foreign environment upon the doctrine.

Doubtless the change of generations, constantly varying the light that illuminates works, at times accentuates the relief of some doctrines. But this play of light leaves the monument intact. It is otherwise with romanticized interpretations, which pervert form and content, like the virtuoso who would dare play Mozart in the style of Schumann, Chopin, or Ravel. We would say of such a person, "he has no taste for philosophy." And that is surely so if philosophy and its history amount to science. But then, the requirement of truth demands the respect for content and form, no less strictly than the requirement of taste ought to demand it, it seems, from anyone who would be tempted to see in philosophy a substitute for music or literature. However, the imagination, wishing to shatter the double barrier of truth and taste in order to be more at ease, sees in the call for authenticity, in the call to the text and its rigorous linkages, and its precise and thankless obscurities, an impertinence, a defiance to the mind, which, as we all know, is never really itself unless it contradicts the letter of the text. The "demon of philosophy" would not know what to do with a text.[1]

There certainly is a demon, but it is less certain that it is a demon of philosophy. Demons should not be trusted: they often pass for what they are not. As makers of tales and deniers *(Ich bin der Geist der stets verneint!),* the truth and the text mean little to them. However, it is in the text, and not within their phantoms, that philosophy, which is not a vain delirium, attempts to discover the key to the enigma proposed to it by the work of the great geniuses. And this text has to be explained.

Historians have two techniques at their disposal for this: textual criticism itself and analysis of structures. For Descartes' philosophy, textual criticism (problems of sources, variations, evolutions, etc.) has been amply practiced: the remarkable works of Gilson, Gouhier, Laporte, and others are known by all. On the other hand, the analysis of structures has been little attempted. L. Brunschwicg has at times applied himself to it with the strength of mind one knows he possesses. But his point of view, governed by the apology for knowledge and for mathematical sciences, remains extrinsic. For him it is less a matter of laying bare the demonstrative and architectonic structures of the work, than to dissociate, as with a chemical reagent, two incompatible and hostile elements: the archaic and the living, to separate the wheat of modern scientific and creative thought, from the chaff of dead concepts, the heritage of the "grammatical"—in brief, to oppose the ideal Descartes to the real Descartes.

What we attempt here is the objective analysis of a work, in particular the *Meditations,* that contains the essentials of Cartesian metaphysics. The discovery of such structures is basic for the study of any philosophy, for it is by these structures that it deserves to be entitled *philosophy,* in contrast to fable, poem, spiritual or mystic elevation, general scientific theory, or metaphysical opinions. These structures have as common characteristics being demonstrative, whatever is the chosen path, whether rational or irrational. They always consist of a process of validation. This demonstration combines logical means with architectonic means. The architectonic is what draws the works of philosophy closer to the works of art. But the architectonic element of fine arts concerns the simple material possibility of the work and its action on the aesthetic sensibility of the subject. The architectonic element of the philosophical work attempts to incline or compel the intelligence of the subject to a judgment ratifying the truth of the doctrinal teaching.

Without elaborating on this question, which we later treat, it is suitable to note that Descartes, while excommunicating the history of philosophy, nevertheless has formulated here and there—particularly in his letter to Voetius—some excellent rules of good sense that ought to guide every historian: for example, the principle that "what is important and useful in the books of the superior intellects does not consist in such or such thoughts that one can extract from them; the precious fruit that they enclose ought to come from the whole body of the work."[2]

Descartes justly has a real horror of "unconnected thoughts." And it is clearly evident that, in what concerns him, the conflict of interpretations stems largely from attempts to split hairs about the text[3] and to proceed by disjoined references able to prove white or black at will. And this is more so since terms have different meanings—even opposite meanings—according to whether they are at this or that place in the chain of reasons. One only has to neglect place for aberrations to flow freely. Doubtless the diversities of interpretation may be defended by referring to the temperament of the interpreter, his existential situation, etc. "To each his own truth"; so be it. But the truth of the interpreting subject is all the same for us, except in the case of exceptional thinkers (Husserl, Brunschwicg, Jaspers, etc.), whose personal reactions we desire above all to know. With respect to the normal interpreter, it is Descartes' truth that we are seeking when we read a book on Descartes. As for Descartes' judgment on these contradictory views, it is extremely clear. For him they could only be false: "Every time that two persons have contrary judgments on one thing, it is certain that one of them is wrong. Moreover, neither of them has the truth, for if he had seen something clearly and distinctly, he could have proposed it to his adversary in such a manner that it would end up forcing his conviction."[4]

In spite of this, it remains true that each person proclaims that only his Descartes is the true one, with greater force accompanying the greater degree of falsification. And it is infinitely less probable that any interpreter would ever succeed in "forcing the conviction of his adversary" as wishes Descartes, for here we are concerned with a subject for which there is always the risk that the imagination obscures the view of the understanding. That is why it would be preferable, instead of claiming the truth exclusively for oneself, which is natural but derisive, to ask oneself about one's method and see whether it is suitable. We would thereby be posing for ourselves a Cartesian question, since, according to Descartes, a bad method would without fail cause us to deviate from the truth, while a good method would without fail bring us to it, except, of course, for the errors of application inherent in human nature.

And it seems that once the requirements of historical critique are satisfied, the better method is truly the analysis of the structures of the work. This analysis, which is recommended for all philosophies, is particularly needed here. Cartesian philosophy is intended to be rigorously demonstrative. Its author insists that he follows the order of the geometers, that there are no good demonstrations in philosophy that are not mathematical, and that his work cannot be understood by those who do not have a mathematical mind. It is therefore evident that we ought to force ourselves to understand this philosophy by its demonstrations, and these demonstrations, according to their mathematical spirit. We must therefore above all bare the *order of reasons* that is the sine qua non of the value of Descartes' doctrine in his own eyes. "I should not advise anyone" he writes, "to . . . read my book, except those who intend to meditate seriously with me. But those who, without worrying much about the sequence and linkage of my reasons *(rationum mearum seriem et nexum comprehendere non curantes),* amuse themselves with splitting hairs on each of the parts—as many do—those, I say, will not get much profit from reading this book."[5]

But this concern with the *nexus* and the *series rationum* does not appear in the work of most commentators. Even interpreters who, like Hamelin, appear to follow the order, see in Descartes only a biographical succession, and not a rational linkage, and in reality, they merely observe the simple chronological sequence of topics. Most of the other critics only consider the various topics separately or in succession: freedom in Descartes, thought in Descartes, God in Descartes, etc. This is evidently a way of doing things that is repugnant to the spirit and letter of Descartes' doctrine. "To proceed by topics," writes Descartes, "is only good for those whose reasons *are all unconnected;*[6] it is impossible "to construct good proofs"[7] in this way.

The exact restitution of the order will allow us to settle no less precisely the deep meaning of the doctrine and to discover aspects that are often ignored. Our intent, however, was not to come up with something new at all costs, but to be right. For us the banal is worth more than the novel, if the former is true and the latter is false. Our conclusions are for the most part in agreement with the traditional view of Descartes. We will rediscover here the Descartes who, having won five or six decisive intellectual battles, tells us that he is sure to win the two or three others necessary for accomplishing all his designs.[8] We will rediscover the thinker of granite who knows no other anguish than that of truth—assuming that one can call anguish the inflexible will for truth and the complete certainty of its discovery. We will not be doing him the harm of resolving him into inferiority complexes, guilt complexes, and other psychoanalytical categories, according to today's fashion. This powerful, solid, and geometric monument, like a Vauban fortress, will clearly not please all our contemporaries. Historical truth is what it is; we should not read history books if we find it shocking. Thus, we should take care not to disguise it in order to render it more pleasant. That is the advice Descartes gives us with respect to all truths, including the ones in which we are interested: "I can in no way approve of trying to deceive oneself by feeding on false imaginations [. . . .] That is why, seeing that it is a greater perfection to know the truth than to be ignorant of it, even when it is to our disadvantage, I conclude that it is better to be less cheerful and to have more knowledge. Thus it is not always the most cheerful person who has the most satisfied mind; on the contrary, great joys are usually sober and serious, and only the slightest and most passing joys are accompanied by laughter." [9]

Martial Gueroult

Descartes' Philosophy Interpreted
According to the Order of Reasons

Volume I

The Soul and God

CHAPTER I

Cartesian Metaphysics
and the Order of Reasons

1. The Unity of the System and the Indivisibility of Truth

There is, in Descartes' writings, a seminal idea that inspires his whole enterprise, which is expressed as early as 1628 in the *Rules for the Direction of the Mind:* it is that knowledge has impassable limits, founded on the limits of our intelligence, but that, within those limits, certainty is complete. From this a twofold requirement follows: part philosophical—one must seek to determine the limits of our intelligence;[1] part methodological—it is necessary beforehand to doubt everything, but not to doubt our intelligence. Hence it is the examination of intelligence that will permit us to discover how far the mind can reach: "If someone undertakes to examine all the truths human reason can attain, which, it seems to me, ought to be done at some time in his life by everyone who seriously strives to arrive at wisdom *(bona mens),* he will discover . . . that nothing can be known before intelligence, for it is from intelligence that things can be known, and not conversely."[2] The statement of this principle, which is formulated in *Meditation II* in the following manner—the Cogito is the first of known truths, the mind is easier to know than the body, for the mind knows itself without the body, but the body cannot know itself without the mind— ushers in the era of modern idealism and reverses the Scholastic point of view. Together with the rejection of all that is not certain in the eyes of intelligence, it shows incontestably, despite quibbles of detail, that as early as the *Rules* Descartes was aware of the need for methodological doubt, of the Cogito, and of the unity of knowledge.

But the problem of "the limits of our intelligence" that was first addressed in 1628, encompasses, along with the necessity of considering its own validity, the prior questioning of that validity itself, which is an aspect of the problem that will be treated in all of its fullness in the *Meditations,* by means of the device of the evil genius. The indubitable certainty of our intelligence, at first simply postulated in the *Rules,* will be required in its turn to furnish "its certificate of believability." It will therefore be called into question as long as that requirement is not met, and doubt will necessarily be heightened, at least provisionally, to the point at which it calls into question what "the nature of my mind" irresistibly makes me hold as certain.

On the other hand, once the problem is resolved, the truth of the ideas of our intelligence will be definitively established. By the solution of the problem of the objective validity of clear and distinct knowledge, metaphysics will permit the scruples of the savant to be satisfied, legitimating the universalization of the methods of mathematical physics that had until then yielded only partial successes.

Consequently, metaphysics as a universal science or as a systematic science constitutes one and the same whole; and from 1630 Descartes, declaring that without the knowledge of God and of himself he would never have been able to discover the foundations of physics, contemplated inserting in his treatise on physics one of the most metaphysical of theses, that of the free creation of eternal truths.[3] This thesis, in fact, cannot be denied unless the incomprehensibility of God is disregarded;[4] and the incomprehensibility of God, which is by no means his unknowability, and even less his irrationality, but rather "the formal reason of infinity,"[5] is indispensable if we are accurately to resolve the problem of the *foundation of truth* and of *the limits of our intelligence*. Infinity requires us, in fact, to conceive God as first truth, foundation of all the others: "It is a 'blasphemy' to say that the truth of something precedes the knowledge that God has of it . . . , for the existence of God is the first and most eternal of all the truths that can be, and is the truth whence all the others proceed."[6] On the other hand, the free creation of eternal truths involves the affirmation of the limits of our intelligence and forbids restricting the infinite to the finite necessities of our understanding. Thus infinity, by the extent to which it goes beyond my own reality and power, leaves no choice but to postulate outside my own reality and power a supreme "reason": God, the sole reason that establishes the objective validity of my intellectual faculty (by infinite omnipotence which, when properly understood, excludes the possibility of deceit) and reveals its limits as finite understanding.[7] To ignore the tight bond that links the leading conceptions of the *Rules* to the theory of the incomprehensibility of God, of which the doctrine of eternal truths is only one aspect, is to misunderstand the rational unity, continuity, and rigor that are the characteristic mark of Cartesian thought, and to make imagination prevail over understanding in its interpretation.

From the beginning, then, Cartesianism was engaged in an effort to construct a complete system of certain knowledge, at once both metaphysical and scientific, a system fundamentally different from the Aristotelian one, because it is wholly immanent in the mathematical certainty embodied in the clear and distinct intellect, but no less complete, and even stricter in its need for absolute rigor. The totality of this system is not at all an encyclopedia of material items of knowledge gathered effectively, but is the fundamental unity of *first principles* from which all possible certain knowledge flows.[8]

This explains both phases of the scientific career of Descartes and their contrast: before 1630, the search for precise solutions of particular problems of mathematics and mathematical physics; after 1630,[9] the abandonment of these inquiries and the construction of a vast system of universal science[10] in which detailed solutions and mathematical technique are absent.

The titles of the scientific works that followed the research in metaphysics, *The World* and *Principles of Philosophy,* are by themselves eloquent enough; they treat the vast outlines of the whole of science, grounding them on the deepest foundations of all certainty. It will be incumbent upon the journeymen savants who follow to discover detailed demonstrations and particular truths: "I do not promise to supply here exact proofs of everything I shall say," wrote Descartes in his *Treatise on Light,* "it suffices that I open up for you the road by which you will be able to discover them yourselves when you take the trouble to look for them."[11]

Nothing is therefore more systematic, for Descartes, than his own doctrine. It is, for him, a single block of certainty, without any cracks, in which everything is so arranged that no truth can be taken away without the whole collapsing: "I see that it is easy to make mistakes about the things I have written, for truth being indivisible, the least thing that is taken away from it or is added to it, falsifies it."[12]

Consequently, the method is nothing but a compilation of some simple procedures, from which it is possible, conformably to the order of reasons, in accordance with the indivisibility of truth, to derive before our eyes the absolutely certain knowledge originally present in the unity of *sapientia humana,* which embraces all the sciences "for they are all interconnected and interdependent,"[13] and which, "remaining always one and the same, however different the objects are to which it may be applied, is no more changed by these objects than is the light of the sun by the variety of the things it illuminates."[14] This luminous unity is present in me before I become aware of it; that is why the unconscious, presupposed by innateness, and by the principle that the soul always thinks, is not clouded consciousness. It is light in itself, already present in me as light, without however being perceived: "The reason why I believe that the soul always thinks is the same as that which makes me believe that light always shines, even though there are no eyes to see it."[15]

2. Rational Order and Order of Topics: Rational Order as Generator of the System and as Rule for Interpreting It

Philosophy cannot be scientifically constituted as a unified and monolithic block of certainty in conformity with the indivisibility of truth, unless it is established, like mathematics, by a rigorous chain of propositions according to the order of reasons. It must therefore break with the customary construction of traditional works, notably those inspired by doxography, which are divided into chapters each exhausting a topic of inquiry, purely and simply juxtaposed in a ritual order, in which nothing is necessarily connected: "The order consists solely in that the propositions laid down first must be known without the aid of those that follow, and that those that follow must be so arranged that they are shown to be true solely by the propositions that precede."[16] This order is radically opposed to the order of topics, not only because it is not the same, for it is necessary instead of being conventional, but because it dissociates as a whole each of the topics that were considered separately: God, soul, error, body, etc. In fact, one and the same topic contains different elements whose proof requires that they be distributed on different links of the chain, often far removed one from another: "It should be noted that in all my writings I do not follow the order of topics, but the order of reasons, that is to say that I do not say in a single place everything that could be said about a topic, for in that way I would not be able to give proper proofs, there being reasons that must be drawn from farther off than others. But in orderly reasoning, from the simpler to the more complex *(a facilioribus ad difficiliora)*, I make what deductions I can, first on one topic, then on another. This is in my opinion the true way to find and explain the truth. And as for the order of topics, it is only suitable for those whose reasons are all disconnected, for those who can say as much about one difficulty as about another."[17] The model philosophy will follow will no longer be the *Treatise of Philosophy* divided into chapters, or the *Summa,* with its questions and its articles, but the *Elements of Euclid.*[18]

These remarks, it appears, suggest the rule Descartes wished to see observed for understanding his doctrine. Since the certain, systematic whole is constituted by the orderly linkage of truths, no single truth of the system can be correctly interpreted without reference to the place it occupies in the order.[19] Since doubt radically rejects everything that has not been reintroduced to its place in the chain of truths, every objection that interposes, against a previously established truth, an element not appearing earlier as demonstrated in that chain, is by hypothesis null and void. *With respect to knowledge,* it is in that part of the chain from which it is excluded, an utter nullity. Thus one may see, for example, that all the objections advanced in the name of the body against the self-sufficiency of the soul posited in *Meditation II* in truth count for nothing; for the body does not figure among the links that need to be posited in knowledge before the soul is posited. It is impossible to contest the intertwined terms in a mathematical proof by reference to a term foreign to it, nor is it possible to suppose that in a series of reasons, each of which entails the succeeding one, the last, although depending on the others, could be used to challenge the positing of those preceding it.

For this same reason of order, one must take as beyond question that a thesis enunciated before another is a condition of that other; such is, for example, the case of the proof of God from effects that, preceding the ontological proof, must be held to be a condition of it, to the extent that the latter, detached from the former, loses all its validity. It is likewise because of considerations of order that Descartes thinks it necessary to treat "things that must be considered separately from others . . . in separate *Meditations*."[20] It suffices therefore to examine the grouping of the questions in each *Meditation* to know at once that they are inseparable and reside all together in the same place on the chain of reasons. It is highly significant, for example, that one finds the question of the essences of material things treated in the same *Meditation* as the ontological proof.[21] Finally, one must be able to explain why this or that question is treated before or after this or that other; for example, why the problem of error is treated after the proof by effects and before the ontological proof; why the ontological proof appears not only after *Meditation III*, but after *Meditation IV*, etc. Minor problems they may seem. In fact, they are fundamental problems; for in a geometry, to understand the reason for the order of its propositions is purely and simply to understand it.[22]

Thus philosophy is developed as a pure geometry, which owes all its certainty to the internal linkage of its reasons, without any reference to external reality. To invoke experience "according to common usage" against this or that reason in the chain is as pointless as to attempt to refute the demonstrated truths of geometry in the name of experience.[23]

3. Analytic Order and Synthetic Order

Descartes, it is true, distinguishes two orders, synthetic order and analytic order; and, according to whether it is a question of one or the other, situates the same doctrines in different places. In the *Discourse on Method* and the *Meditations*, where the order is analytic, the place of the ontological proof, for example, is not the same as in the geometrical exposition in the *Replies to Objections II*, nor as in the *Principles*, in which the order is synthetic. Of the two orders, which should decide? Descartes tells us which himself: it is the analytic order. Synthetic demonstration is not, in fact, the "true way," even in geometry; for although "it more effectively wrings the consent of a reader, however obstinate and opinionated as he may be," it "does not teach the method by which the result has been discovered." In metaphysics, where the primary notions, because of their remoteness from the senses, cannot be easily grasped, synthetic order is particularly inadequate.[24] The synthetic approach is therefore suited above all to presenting the totality of results already obtained by means of the method of discovery, in such a fashion that the reader can "comprehend it all at once."[25]

In this way, the *Principles* sets out systematically the organized body of science, but it does not include the deep justifications reserved for analytic works. In metaphysics above all, the analytic approach is the preferred one inasmuch as it alone permits, at the same time, both the arousal of attention and the detachment of the mind from the senses, to which, unlike the case in geometry, its deeper notions are not suited. That is why analytic demonstration in metaphysics assumes an aspect it does not possess in geometry, namely, that of *Meditations* that satisfy, not only the requirements of logic, but also such requirements of psychology as are proper to it.[26]

4. The Order of the *Meditations*

The consequence of the foregoing is that all interpretation of Cartesian metaphysics must rest above all on the little treatise of the *Meditations,* not because it contains the whole of philosophy (any more than the *Principles* contains the whole of science) but because it comprises the essential elements set forth according to their true justification.[27]

This observation has a threefold consequence. First, the *Objections and Replies,* the correspondence, and the synthetic expositions amount in the eyes of Descartes only to clarifications or further elaborations that can never serve to weaken, much less contradict, the teaching of the *Meditations.* The *Meditations* is constantly invoked by Descartes, now as a breviary, now as the necessary and truly demonstrative introduction to the whole of his philosophy. It is to it that the first part of the *Principles* expressly refers;[28] it is on it that he comments to the end of his life, without ever changing anything in it.[29]

Second, the metaphysical theories that Descartes has not deemed it necessary to expound in his *Meditations* are considered by him, whatever may be their importance and their depth, as appertaining, not to the "main points" of his teaching, but to its further implications or extensions. They have no place among the conditions indispensable to its certain demonstration and to its fundamental structure: "And that is why . . . I have purposely omitted many things throughout this treatise, because they call for the explanation of many others."[30] This preoccupation with order will explain why a doctrine as captivating as the doctrine of the eternal truths does not appear in the *Meditations,* nor in the other treatises, even though in 1630 Descartes announced to Mersenne his intention of expounding it in his *Physics.* This silence cannot be explained as prudent caution,[31] because that theory was, after all, very close to Duns Scotus' theory[32] and because it would be made public in 1641, when the *Meditations* and the first six *Objections and Replies* were to appear in one volume. On the other hand, it is evident that that conception, important as it is, does not belong among the fundamentals of his doctrine. As we have said, it is no more than a derivative aspect of one of his essential theses: the incomprehensibility of God. The elaboration of the analytic demonstration of the *Meditations* bears witness that it is not necessary for solving the three great problems to which those essential theses give rise: the problem of *the foundation of truth* (the objective validity of clear and distinct ideas), the problem of *the limits of our intelligence* (error and the human conditions of truth), and the problem of *the foundation of the natural sciences* (the foundation of mechanism, the separation of substances, the existence of bodies, the substantial union). But on the other hand, it provides a valuable complement to the thesis of the incomprehensibility of God (which grounds the proof from effects) and can serve to support the rejection of every consideration relating to divine finality. It confirms the limitation of our understanding. Finally, by radically separating God from the object of our sciences, it provides a certain assurance, in addition to the foregoing, of the self-sufficiency of those sciences,[33] which the perfect autonomy of extended substance had already guaranteed.

The third consequence is that, if the analytic order is the only one to provide a sound demonstration of Cartesian philosophy, if the *Meditations,* which is rigorously elaborated according to that order, alone enables us to grasp all at once the whole of Cartesian doctrine,[34] there is then no other way of understanding the *Meditations* itself than to place in evidence the order by which it alone demonstrates the truths it contains.[35]

However, there is some difficulty in perceiving that order, for Descartes has not always chosen to make it immediately perceptible to us. The *Meditations* is not, in effect, mere dry geometry, but the initiation of one soul by another soul acting as its guide. Furthermore, it is easy to confuse that order with the order of synthesis; and that contamination is almost unavoidable because of the comparisons one does not fail to make with texts that are governed by the synthetic order. However, this confusion is nullifying, because the two orders are opposed. In fact, the order of analysis is the order of discovery, and thus it is the order of the *ratio cognoscendi:* it is determined according to the requirements of our certainty; and the linkage of conditions renders it possible. The synthetic order, on the other hand, is what is established between the results of science; these results are the truth of the thing. It is, therefore, the order of the *ratio essendi*, the one according to which things are related in themselves, with respect to their real dependence. Now it is evident that the conditions that make possible an assured knowledge of the truth are different from the conditions that in themselves bring it about that things are or exist, and that the linkage of the items of my knowledge is not the linkage of realities to which those items correspond. Descartes sums this up with: "each thing must be considered in a different order according to whether it is referred to the order of our knowledge or to the order of real existence."[36] And so, according to analytic order, one begins with the certain knowledge of my self, which, as first truth for the subject (Cogito), is for me the first principle; in turn this first item of knowledge makes possible the knowledge of the existence of God, that is to say, the knowledge that the idea of perfection has an objective validity, which in turn makes possible, according to their respective limits, the knowledge of the objective validity of clear and distinct ideas, and then the knowledge of the objective validity of obscure and confused ideas. One is dealing with a line that is never deflected, going always from the simpler to the more complex *(a facilioribus ad difficiliora),* and in which God is no more than one link among others in a chain of knowledge. One rises from conditions to conditions, gradually exhausting the contents of one's soul, legitimating at each stage a new species of knowledge, and determining, where possible, its limits.[37]

If, on the other hand, one adopts the point of view of the order of things according to their real existence, the first reality for me (Cogito) is subordinated to the first reality in itself (God), as real cause of all the things from which one descends once more to the various works of creation: myself, essences, existence of bodies, distinction and union of soul and body. The most perfect example of synthetic deduction is furnished by the *Geometrical Summary in the Second Replies,* in which the analytic passage from the Cogito to God is not even mentioned, in which the notion of God as creator of all things allows the inference to the existence of all things and to the real distinction between soul and body.[38] The existence of God as first cause of all realities is its first principle in the order of synthesis *(ratio essendi),* just as the knowledge of my self as first condition of the possibility of all the other items of certain knowledge is its first principle according to the order of analysis *(ratio cognoscendi).* Since the knowledge of God thus made possible is itself demonstrated as the first item of knowledge that is *valid* for a thing outside me, knowledge of God is therefore established as the foundation of *validity* for all other knowledge; and hence it appears, but only from this point of view, as being also a principle according to the order of analysis.

Confusion of the analytic and synthetic orders is an ever present danger. In effect, analytic demonstration, which adopts the point of view of the *ratio cognoscendi,* and which consists in discovering true *items of knowledge* in such a fashion that they appear to us as necessary and certain, results in placing outside myself the *realities* that tend to be set, from the point of view of their *ratio essendi,* according to the synthetic order of their dependence in themselves. Since the order of the conditions of my certainty, which is not at all that of the real dependence of things,[39] refers to that real dependence just as knowledge refers to its object, nothing is easier than to have those realities thus interfere with and interrupt the process of demonstration. From that result severe confusions, which are the source of serious errors of interpretation and unjustified objections concerning the validity of the proofs.[40]

The object of the pages following will be, by constant reference to the analytic order of reasons, to arrive at an interpretation as scrupulous as possible of what, in the words of Descartes, constitute "the main points" of his philosophy.[41]

But has not Descartes himself warned us not to go too deeply into his *Meditations?* "One must not ponder at length about these *Meditations* and on the questions of metaphysics," he advises us, "nor is it necessary to trouble oneself to comment on them; and much less is it necessary, as some have attempted, to go more deeply into them than the author himself has done; he has treated them at a depth sufficient for an introduction."⁴² Indeed, in Descartes' mind, this warning is not specifically against the *Meditations* but against metaphysics itself, to which the *Meditations* is wholly devoted. In fact metaphysics, to the extent that it is an introduction, should not deflect us from that to which it is an introduction, that is, from knowledge of nature and from the mastery of our passions, "from physics and from sensible things," for that is its "principal subject matter,"⁴³ according to Descartes. One must first of all make oneself master of the universe, and, as Corneille says, "master of oneself as of the universe." We see Descartes repeat the same advice to Elizabeth and to Chanut for Queen Christina, insisting more specifically on the importance of the concerns of life, which must come before mathematics and physics, much more indeed than these in turn must come before metaphysics. Having only to deal with notions of pure understanding, metaphysics turns us away from using understanding together with imagination, that is to say from mathematics and physics, and even more from the concerns of life, which add the use of the senses to the use of understanding and imagination. Descartes also intimates that he sets aside no more than a few hours a day for matters concerning both the imagination and the understanding, and a very few hours a year on those concerning the understanding alone.⁴⁴

It is perhaps also necessary to be careful not to take such statements too literally, even though they are related to Descartes' deep desire to make of his doctrine, not an exercise of pure speculation, but an instrument of wisdom, or more precisely of happiness, which is always within reach of each of us in our life. With respect to things of this sort one must make allowances for the character of his correspondents: here a very young man, there a woman, who is, according to him, qualified, like all women, more for the concerns of life than for mathematical and metaphysical speculations. Moreover, these reservations in no way argue that the whole of metaphysics be included in the *Meditations*. It is therefore legitimate and even necessary to delve into the *Meditations,* not more deeply than its author has done, but if possible in the same way as he himself has done, if one intends to penetrate the metaphysics he has deduced there, which constitutes the key to all his doctrine. And this task is allowable to all those whose aim is to devote to metaphysics more than a few hours each year.

CHAPTER II

Doubt and the Evil Genius

1. The Point of View of the *Rules* and the Point of View of the *Meditations*

The *Meditations* unfolds in conformity with the rules of a method requiring us to follow the necessary linkage of reasons. Consequently, it seems it should come under the jurisdiction of that method, whose validity has already been constituted before it. On the other hand, the conclusions to which the *Meditations* leads us would be without force if the validity of that method were not firmly established. But this validity can only be founded by the *Meditations* itself, which constitutes the highest philosophy. From this it appears that the enterprise can only succeed by revealing an ultimate foundation that, while derived from the method, possesses intrinsic evidence such that, once attained, it appears as valid by itself, independently of the process by which it has been attained.

The point of view of the *Meditations* can therefore only be rigorously defined in contrast with the point of view of this method, considered in isolation, that the *Meditations* must employ and establish at the same time.

This method is revealed to us by the *Rules* (to which the *Discourse on Method* refers implicitly). The special character of the *Rules* is that the work of science is not related in it to any other principle except the human faculty of knowledge. No doubt many metaphysical theses can be perceived in it already: for example, the reduction of the material world to extension and movement; the real distinction between extension and thought; the theory of imagination and corporeal faculty; the link between doubt and the criterion of evidence; the relation between the Cogito and God's existence—*Sum, ergo Deus est,* etc.[1] Nonetheless, these conceptions appear only as examples, not as points of support. The method is presented as having a validity independent of metaphysics and as founded immediately on the inherent certainty of human reason in its original authentic manifestation, meaning mathematics.

This special character has led some authors, Natorp especially,[2] to think that Descartes had begun a kind of theory of knowledge related to the critique; they believed to have found in this a way, among others, to bring Descartes nearer to Kant. For Descartes, science would rest on the human faculty of knowledge, and the external intrusion of metaphysical questions would have transformed and distorted the first presentation of the true problem. In the *Rules* Descartes deals only with the mental. In the *Meditations* there appears another Descartes who raises some old questions.

The above conception does not deal fully with the concerns of our philosopher. In truth, the *Rules* is situated at the point at which the method is being formulated, but at which the problems that will be treated by that method have not yet arisen. They will arise once this method has been absolutely generalized, that is as soon as, vigorously putting to work the principle of not accepting anything as true that is not absolutely evident, Descartes poses the question of the validity of the mathematical evidence that was first considered by him as self-sufficient, without any other justification—in brief, when he asks himself how we are authorized to have faith in the evidence of clear and distinct ideas themselves.

Thus the two main questions that require the deep philosophical process of the *Meditations* are posed:

1) Can we judge validly that an idea, even if it is supposed true, corresponds with something real—in brief, does the reality external to me respond to the internal requirements of the understanding? This question is imposed forcefully on Descartes as soon as he begins to deal with a complete physics of the universe, instead of isolated questions of physics—in brief, once he rises to the mechanistic conception of extension and movement. In fact, this conception was the only one that responded to the requirements of clearness and distinctness of the understanding. However, does the universe conform to these requirements? From this the fundamental problem results: By what right can we conclude from true essences to existences outside these essences? Is what is valid for the former valid for the latter?

2) Another question is superimposed on the first. It concerns not only whether existing things correspond to the truth that I perceive in essences, but whether my clear and distinct ideas themselves are essences—in brief, whether what I affirm, in the name of reason, is truly the expression of an objective universal reason, and not the expression of necessities inherent to my subjective nature—whether the links I establish between these ideas have an objective validity, or whether they are valid only within the limited sphere of my self.

This second question is itself specified in two ways:

i) Is it possible that I be deceived even in what I call the intuition of ideas?

ii) If this question is resolved negatively, if one can be assured that what we know as intuition is true, can I be assured that it will remain true when I cease to have an intuition of it—that when I recall an idea captured by intuition or properties I have demonstrated, will this idea and these properties always be true, having remained immutable while I was no longer thinking of them? In brief, does there correspond to the conservation of items of knowledge in the extrarational faculty of memory, which all deduction presupposes (since all deduction takes place in time), a conservation, outside of me, of the truth in itself?

The affirmative reply to these various questions requires all of

Descartes' metaphysics. It is only because of such a reply that science, according to Descartes, is legitimated. Far from supposing that a methodological idealism can suffice, Descartes has never admitted that the human mind can define and posit the reality of things by virtue of its own proper necessities. He has never thought it possible to rest certainty on the human mind alone, whose imperfection he senses. In this way he differs completely from Kant, whom he resembles, on the other hand, when he poses the question of the objective validity of our a priori knowledge.

2. Characteristics of Methodological Doubt

The appearance of metaphysical questions is conditioned, as we have just seen, by the concern to establish certainty in an unshakeable fashion by pushing the investigation to its limit, meaning by putting to the test even the certainty of mathematics, from which the universal method arose. Thus, in order to end up with complete certainty, Descartes wishes to examine the whole sphere of certainty. He does not wish merely to have an illusion of certainty, to have blind faith in a certainty that is not itself controlled—in brief, in a certainty that is not certain by itself—not knowing whether this certainty is established and in what way it is established. Not to rely on a certainty before having required from it "its certificate of believability," meaning before having submitted it as a whole to a critique, and to examine the entire sphere of certainty, are two traits of Cartesian philosophy that incontestably draw it nearer to Kantian philosophy.[3]

And, if we wish to end up with complete certainty, we must not admit in ourselves anything that is not absolutely certain—in other words, we must doubt everything that is not certain with absolute certainty, and also we must absolutely exclude from ourselves everything that is stricken by doubt.

From this a threefold necessity arises:

1) The necessity for preliminary doubt.

2) The necessity to exclude nothing from doubt as long as doubt is not radically impossible.

3) The necessity to treat provisionally as false the things touched by doubt—which carries the necessity to reject them entirely.

There corresponds to this threefold necessity three characteristics of Cartesian doubt: it is *methodological,* it is *universal,* and it is *radical.*

Moreover, the methodological characteristic makes it a simple instrument for founding the certainty of knowledge, that is, the dogmatism of science. This results in a fourth characteristic: Cartesian doubt is *provisional.*

3. The First Stage of Methodological Doubt in *Meditation I*

Meditation I applies this doubt.

After having defined the aim: "certain and indubitable" knowledge, it indicates the means: hyperbolic doubt, which completely rejects everything not assured, whatever the degree of doubt. The preparation for this doubt consists, not in the censure of various opinions, but in the critique of their principle, a principle that will involve them all in its ruin, and this principle is that knowledge comes from the senses.[4] From this point on, an exhaustive process begins, which extends doubt far beyond the sphere of sensible objects.

This process, which goes from the complex to the simple, is accomplished in accordance with the order. The senses deceive us. Sensible perceptions are perhaps only dreams. But dreams are imaginary only because they arbitrarily combine simpler and more general elements: eyes, hands, heads, bodies, etc. These elements can only appear as real since, not being composite, they escape the possible arbitrariness of composition. However, these constitutive elements are themselves composite; they can therefore be arbitrarily composite, and consequently, imaginary, and therefore dubious. From this stems the necessity to rise to the level of the elements of these elements: shape, number, quantity, magnitude, space, time, etc. We then end up with absolutely "simple and general" natures, that, not being composite, escape, by definition, any possible arbitrariness of composition, and consequently, any doubt. We rejoin here the plane of the *Rules,* according to which mathematics is an absolutely certain science because it deals with simple and general objects.[5]

We ought to note that analysis also allows sensible quality (color, for example)[6] as one of the unbreakable constituents of our representations. Sensible quality cannot be fictitious, and its simplicity also renders it indubitable for us. Analysis gives the same status to sensation, the simple, primitive notion that will be the foundation of the psychology of *man* properly speaking. Descartes therefore implicitly divides ideas into two categories: composite (adventitious or artificial) ideas and simple ideas—the latter being sensible or intellectual (innate). All composite ideas are suspect, for they can all be artificial *(factitiae* or *fictae).* All ideas that are unbreakable, or simple natures, whether they are intellectual or sensible, are necessarily indubitable, because they cannot be artificial. They are the first notions, or immediate givens, that will later be revealed as innate.[7] For now, only the simple intellectual natures are retained—sensation will not be introduced into the chain of reasons until *Meditation VI.* That is because, although sensation is a simple nature, as is the idea of the understanding, sensation is less absolute than it, for the understanding can be without sensation, but sensation cannot be without the understanding. The order indicates therefore that the idea of the understanding must be first considered alone. Moreover, the indubitable character of each sensation taken apart in no way compromises the conclusion relative to the deceptive character of sensible knowledge, since this knowledge is only constituted by the combination of sensations. And this combination can always be considered as fictitious.

4. The Second Stage of Methodological Doubt in
Meditation I

As one might have already noticed, the question of truth has changed along the way. At first it consisted in knowing whether an external reality corresponded to our ideas; now it consists in the truth of things considered in their own reality, "without having to take great care to ascertain whether they are in nature or not."[8] But the order of analysis legitimates this passage, which is so surprising at first. By breaking up the images into the simple and general elements rendering them possible, one rises from fact to rule, meaning from given representations to necessary, universal conditions of all possible representations, which are therefore valid for all representations, imaginary as well as real. In this way we pass from the sphere of existence to the sphere of the possible, including all *conceivable* existence. It is true that a square has four sides, even if it does not exist in nature, for, whether the square exists or not, it remains no less true that it could not have more or fewer than four sides. Thus the result of the first phase of the analysis is to cast doubt on the particular content of representations and to subtract from this doubt the necessary conditions of all possible representations. Nevertheless, in this case these conditions are in no way formal conditions. They are certain conditions only insofar as they are ultimate constituents, therefore necessary constituents—in brief, to the extent of their simplicity. It is precisely their simplicity that excludes them from natural doubt, even though it is their function as condition of all possible representations that allows the affirmation of their intrinsic truth, setting aside their relation to an external existence.

Working out the principle of breaking up the complex into the simple, we are not allowed to rise to a level of elements simpler than these unbreakable elements, which, insofar as they are fundamental mathematical notions, constitute the content of our understanding. And the impossibility of doubting, which stems from the impossibility of pushing farther the breaking up of elements, is confirmed by the natural certainty that we attribute to them, that allows them to escape all the *natural reasons for doubt* —what sensible objects cannot do. On the one hand, *"the nature of my mind* is such that I cannot help believing them true while I am conceiving them clearly and distinctly";[9] on the other hand, it is because "they treat only of these very simple and general things," that "arithmetic, geometry, and other sciences of the same nature [. . .] contain something certain and indubitable," in contrast with "physics, astronomy, medicine, and all other sciences, which are very doubtful and uncertain, given that they depend upon the consideration of composite things."[10]

Since certainty naturally clings to these notions and since the method of breaking up of elements confirms the legitimacy of this natural certainty—if it were needed to do so—the *Meditations,* proceeding strictly according to the order, must neglect or avoid the supposed natural reasons for doubt that the more popular works *(Discourse, Principles)* invoke against mathematics. Thus, it also neglects the argument drawn from the paralogisms that are sometimes committed by mathematicians: these false reasonings can make me doubt my ability to reach these certain notions, but not the notions themselves, since by nature they cannot be doubtful, and since it is confirmed that in this case we have substituted some obscure and confused notions for them.[11] Moreover, they avoid the doubt drawn from the illusion of dreams, which are capable of deceiving us about existences, but not about mathematical notions, for whether I am awake or asleep, two and three add up to five, and the square can never have more than four sides.[12]

We therefore cannot see how the philosopher could obtain something simpler and more indubitable than these mathematical notions, if reflection cannot rise from the natural plane to the metaphysical plane, attacking the validity that our mind attributes to them necessarily "by nature." This reflection arises out of the confrontation of certainty with an old metaphysical opinion "received through hearsay," which is enough to shake it up, without our being able to draw from the content of these notions anything that could guarantee their claim to certainty. This opinion concerns the vague idea of an infinitely powerful God who would thus possess the power to deceive us in everything. Our will, drawing inspiration from this small doubt, then rejects entirely from certainty everything that intelligence naturally proposes as certain.[13]

The act of voluntarily rejecting as false everything of which generally I am not certain testifies to the intervention of my free will,[14] which not only suspends the affirmative judgment, but transforms it into a negative judgment, in order to keep myself from a positive judgment. This passage, from the plane of the nature of my mind to the metaphysical plane transcending it and putting it into question, allows the appearance of a discontinuity in the process of exhaustive doubt that renders extremely manifest the intervention of my free will. If we can rise above the sphere of our finite understanding, in order to strike down as a block the validity of the notions it presents as necessary and certain, it is because we can make use of a superior power, which is infinite relative to our understanding and capable of making an attempt against nature. This is an attempt against nature, because it ends up radically excluding from knowledge and certainty what "by the nature of my mind" completely repulses such an exclusion. This superior power is that of my will.[15]

Thus, infinity in its double aspect: divine, as the infinity of divine omnipotence, and human, as the infinity of my will, renders possible the passage from hyperbolic doubt based on natural reasons to hyperbolic doubt based on a metaphysical reason. By passing from universal doubt based on natural reasons to universal metaphysical doubt, the understanding is compelled to justify, if it can, the natural certainty it has of its ideas. The following problem arises out of this: Is what constitutes, for my understanding, the condition of the possibility of all representations, meaning of everything conceivable for me, ipso facto the condition of possibility of everything real in itself? Is the possible for my intelligence a true possible, an essence? That is what *naturally* I am necessarily brought to think, but what *metaphysically* is as yet by no means established.

By combining itself with the notion of a deceiving God who is infinitely powerful and the principle of possible doubt with respect to clear and distinct ideas, the action of the infinite will gives rise to the fiction of the evil genius that establishes a method of research allowing one to reject from knowledge what can be doubted with as small a degree of doubt as possible, that is to say, permitting me to reject outside my mind, as I would the false, what could have remained within it under the heading of simply doubtful. The voluntary and methodological character of this fiction is highlighted by its dual quality as problem-solving device and as psychological tool: in making possible an operation of the will that must be carried out against the habits and temptations of the probable, it is a psychological tool;[16] as giving shape to the principle that ordains the treatment of the doubtful as false, it is the analogue of these fictive constructions of geometry or astronomy that allow one to accomplish calculations and demonstrations, and to exclude doubtful notions for the benefit of certain notions.[17] But above all, this voluntary fiction, installing falsity provisionally, but peremptorily, even at the core of divine infinity, gives to doubt an absolutely universal scope. It reduces to one the set of various reasons for doubting our faculties of knowledge. Deriving support from it, the will can, through its indivisible act of freedom, radically reject outside of me everything I cannot but accept as knowledge. This radical doubt, which is the suspension of all judgment on everything, announces a categorical attitude of the philosophizing subject by its unitary and total character. It is radical because it requires a radical doubt in order to have a complete certainty. Descartes wishes to pose the problem of certainty in its fullest extent. On this point he resembles Kant, who would judge it necessary, in order to reform reason, to institute a critique that involves the whole faculty of knowledge, instead of censuring some particular doctrines.[18] But he differs from Kant in that, for him, a metaphysical hypothesis allows him to pose the problem, and metaphysical knowledge allows him to resolve it; he also differs from Kant in that the foundation of the validity of my knowledge cannot be discovered within my mind, but outside it.

The first absolute certainty immediately emerges from this total and radical doubt. There is, in fact, something that even metaphysical doubt cannot reach: the internal condition of the act of doubting, a condition inherent in it, that is, the existence of my thought—"I doubt, I think, therefore I am."[19] Thus metaphysical doubt is exorcised by reference to the conditions for doubt, as was the hyperbolic doubt based on natural doubts, but each in a very different way. For if I cannot naturally doubt mathematical notions, it is because the condition that renders doubt possible—namely, composition—is absent from them. The impossibility of doubting is here based on the nature of the object offered to thought, and certainty accrues to this object. On the other hand, if I cannot metaphysically doubt my thought, it is because its existence must always be affirmed in doubt as a necessary condition for this mental operation, such that it suffices for one to doubt in order not to be able to doubt the thought that doubts.[20] The impossibility of doubting is based here on the nature of the very act of doubting, and the necessary presence in it of its sine qua non condition: the thinking subject. Certainty therefore accrues uniquely to the subject. In this way one knows that the problem of the certainty of objects remains whole.

5. Various Kinds of Hyperbolic Doubts

The passage to the first absolute certainty was rendered possible by: 1) working up various kinds of doubts; 2) using the hypothesis or fiction of the evil genius; and 3) calling on the principle of breaking up the objects of natural doubt and having recourse to the internal condition that renders possible the very act of doubting for the subject.

1) Methodological and systematic doubt, which is fictive and proceeds not from things but from the resolution to doubt, differs from true doubt which results from the nature of things and can engender skepticism.[21] It is because of its systematic and generalized character that it deserves the name *hyperbolic,* in accordance with its etymology: from *hyperbole,* excess; in rhetoric it designates a figure by which one gives the object in consideration a higher degree of something, whether positive or negative, it does not possess in actuality. Similarly, there is a twofold principle of this doubt: treat as *absolutely false* what is merely *doubtful,* reject *universally,* as *always* deceptive what could have deceived me *sometimes;* this responds perfectly to the meaning of the word hyperbolic, by accomplishing the hyperbolic leap in two different senses. There are therefore as many degrees of hyperbolic doubt as there are degrees of generalization of doubt, and as there are categories of objects, which are in themselves less and less naturally doubtful and yet are excluded.

The universal doubt extended to sensible knowledge—by virtue of the errors of the senses—is less hyperbolic than the one extended to mathematical knowledge, under the pretext of the paralogisms to which one can fall prey (according to the argument of the *Discourse);* these two doubts are less hyperbolic than the one that, being based on the illusion of dreams, dares to strike at sensible ideas and mathematical ideas with one blow. The most hyperbolic doubt of all is the one based on the hypothesis of the evil genius, because, being absolutely universal, it attacks what the dream argument could not have attacked, namely, the intrinsic objective validity of clear and distinct ideas. In fact, considered independently of this hypothesis, whether I am dreaming or awake, mathematical properties keep their own truth. They do not keep it, on the other hand, if God willingly deceives me with respect to them: then, whether I am awake or dreaming, they have the same falsity. Descartes, in fact, grants to all doubts having a methodological character a hyperbolic quality;[22] but he distinguishes among them those he considers more universal: doubts based on the illusion of dream and doubts based on the hypothesis of the evil genius.[23]

2) The doubt based on the evil genius occupies a place by itself, insofar as it alone rests on a *metaphysical* opinion, and not on natural reasons for doubt, that is, on doubts raised by errors or illusions that are produced naturally (errors of the senses, deliriums of madmen, illusion of dreams). From this it derives its name, *metaphysical* doubt. Not only is it not suggested by nature (either by our mind alone, or by our composite substance), but it is contrary to the *"nature of our mind,"* which spontaneously considers clear and distinct ideas as indubitable.

3) When one wishes to exorcise hyperbolic doubts based on natural reasons for doubt,[24] the method consists in seeking what escapes the *material condition for doubt,* namely the simple, given that doubt can only be directed at a fiction and that all fiction is composite. One therefore infers the certain from the simple. When one wishes to exorcise metaphysical doubt, the method consists in seeking the *formal condition* for doubt in general, a condition that, being necessarily posited as real by doubt itself, necessarily escapes it. Since indubitability is the necessary character of the simple, absolute indubitability entails absolute simplicity; we then infer from the certain to the simple, simplicity no less evidently arising from the generative process, in any case.

6. The Problem of the Evil Genius

The hypothesis of the great deceiver, or the fiction of the evil genius, which constitutes the instrument of metaphysical doubt, poses a problem—that of its origin or of its foundation. Is it based, at least in part, on the nature of things, having its roots in some truths of Cartesian philosophy? Or is it, on the contrary, an artifice entirely alien to these truths, such that once these truths are discovered they radically abolish the pretext in whose name it was invoked?

In the first case one conceives[25] that the hypothesis is based on the true nature of divine omnipotence, and one relates it, along with the doctrine of eternal truths, to the consequences implied by this omnipotence taken in itself. The idea of a universal deception, of which God would be the author, would then not be a fiction entirely excluded by the nature of God, but one of the possibilities originally open to his omnipotence. However, God, who is good, would have freely chosen to limit his omnipotence by his goodness, and since deception is an evil, he would have chosen to be veracious. The refutation of the hypothesis of God's deception would not therefore be rightly accomplished by the proof of his omnipotence, but only by recourse to his goodness. The opposition between the evil genius and the veracious God then appears as the reflection of a kind of conflict between his power and his goodness, between his power and his will: God being capable of deceiving us, but not wanting to. From this stems the identification of the roots of this hypothesis with the theory of eternal truths: God was as free to deceive us as he was free to create truths other than those we recognize, to the extent that it could have been true that the sum of the angles of a triangle were not equal to two right angles, and *two* plus *three* not equal to *five*. God's power would thus conceal in its foundation something irrational and anarchical. The conflict between omnipotence and goodness would exhibit a certain tragic character, well designed to seduce the imagination. One draws from this the ideas of a certain pessimism and a certain anxiety tied to the mystery of our origin, etc.[26]

In the second case one conceives that the hypothesis could not be based on the true nature of divine omnipotence, for divine omnipotence necessarily suppresses the hypothesis. One can hold goodness as the sole argument capable of establishing divine veracity only by misunderstanding the nature of this omnipotence. Consequently, God's goodness could not limit his omnipotence. Moreover, since God's omnipotence is by nature capable of freely instituting truths other than those that have been created, while it is incapable to deceive by its nature, there is no common ground between the theory of eternal truths and the hypothesis of the evil genius; the former is based on the true nature of things, while the latter is a pure and simple fiction that renders possible the real or fictional misunderstanding of that nature.

Descartes' texts, when consulted as a whole, affirm that the second interpretation is the only possible interpretation.[27]

Certainly, the positing of the problem of the validity of the ideas of our understanding involves the possibility of defining the limits of this understanding *(limites ingenii definire,* as in the title of the *Rules),* at the same time that it involves putting into doubt the natural certainties that refer, by means of the hypothesis of the evil genius, to the vague notion of divine infinity, in opposition with the finiteness of our being; and in this way, one can be tempted to establish a link between this hypothesis and the theory of eternal truths.

But, in the first place, if this hypothesis had the same foundation as the theory, it would rest on true knowledge of God's omnipotence, as the other does. It would therefore be irrefutable metaphysically by the true concept of this omnipotence; it could only be avoided morally, by an appeal to God's goodness limiting its own power. And Descartes expressly excludes this possibility. Goodness, no doubt, excludes deception, but omnipotence excludes it no less: "We can see that it is impossible for God to be a deceiver, as long as we consider that the form or essence of deception is a nonbeing toward which the Supreme Being can never incline."[28] Goodness, rather than limiting omnipotence, agrees with it, for deception is fashioned from powerlessness as well as from malice: "Wanting to deceive, far from being a mark of potency *(potentia),* is a mark not only of malice, but of weakness *(imbecilitas).*"[29] Omnipotence itself excludes malice.[30] The refutation, already acquired on the ontological plane, would be simply confirmed on the moral plane, on the supposition that God's goodness was on a moral plane in God, instead of on an ontological plane, or even simply distinct from it—a distinction that Descartes rejects.

Consequently, the hypothesis of a deceiving God is not based on the "mystery of our origins" but on the misconception that we have of our author and of his omnipotence.[31] Once I understand this omnipotence clearly and distinctly, I conceive by one and the same reason that it has created me freely along with the eternal truths, for it is the necessary author of all being, and that it could not have deceived me, nor have wanted to deceive me, for it cannot be the author of nonbeing.

The principle that establishes the doctrine of the eternal truths is that "nothing can exist in any way not dependent on God." This principle includes the negation of the inverse principle: "It is evident that it is no less repugnant to assume that falsity or imperfection as such is derived from God, as that truth or perfection is derived from nothingness."[32] And it is on this latter principle that the hypothesis of a deceiving God rests. Therefore, if the theory of eternal truths is true, the hypothesis of a deceiving God is false. Since the principle of the former is the negation of the principle of the latter, we must conclude that the doctrine of eternal truths entails in a mathematical fashion the refutation of the hypothesis of the evil genius.

Thus the doctrine of the eternal truths rests on the knowledge of the true God and true omnipotence, while the fiction of the evil genius is based on the conception of a false God and is permitted only insofar as the true God is only "known confusedly."[33] It is not based on the knowledge of his idea, but only on an *opinion* with respect to his nature: "I have long held in my soul an opinion that there is a God who has created everything,"[34] an opinion that has come to me "through hearsay."[35] This opinion is precisely that of the theologians of *Objections II* and *VI,* who attempt to establish from the Scriptures—by means of an equivocation, in any case—that God, who is omnipotent, "the Supreme Lord of everything, can dispose of anything as he sees fit," and consequently, "He can be a great deceiver."[36] And Descartes specifies that these "opinions," which are the antithesis of knowledge, precisely misunderstand the true nature of omnipotence. By their substitution of the word for the object, the finite for the infinite, they lead insidiously toward atheism.[37] In fact, what is atheism, but the extreme limiting of the reality and omnipotence of God? And to attribute to God the power to deceive us, under the pretext that he is omnipotent, is to limit in fact his real omnipotence, on account of the *word,* thinking that omnipotence is capable of inclining toward nothingness. From this follows the conclusion that the atheist, more than anyone else, will think that God is a deceiver, for "the less powerful he will conceive the author of his being, the greater will be his occasions for doubting whether he may not be of such an imperfect nature as to be deceived in matters that appear most evident to him."[38]

Therefore, when setting aside opinion for true knowledge, the word for the thing, when truly carrying to infinity the incomprehensible omnipotence of God, as we must, we ought to conclude at the same time that he is not free to deceive us and that he is the free creator of eternal truths. That is why, once the true nature of God's omnipotence is discovered, the difficulty will be reversed; the problem will no longer be to demonstrate that God cannot always deceive me *(Meditation III),* but to demonstrate how it is possible that I am sometimes deceived *(Meditation IV).* And this more so, since the fact that I am sometimes deceived can be used to justify the hypothesis that he always deceives me.[39]

It is argued that the hypothesis of the evil genius can only come to the mind of a philosopher who, like Descartes, does not constrain God to the necessity of eternal truths. Is not the first condition for admitting that God has the freedom to deceive us the positing in him the primacy of free will with respect to what we call truth? If God himself sustains the true, is it not impossible ever to conceive that he could produce the false? In truth, this reasoning assumes what is in question, namely, that the hypothesis of a deceiving God is not an "opinion" but a concept based in reasons. However, this topic concerns an opinion that we do not hold by natural light, but that we have received "through hearsay"; it can therefore accommodate all these absurdities. And the facts prove that it can accommodate them, for we could have rejected the theory of eternal truths and have accepted the hypothesis of the deceiving God. Such is the case with the theologians of *Objections VI.* No doubt this is an absurdity, since it professes at the same time that God necessarily sustains the true and that he is free to create the false. But it is just as absurd to base the freedom to deceive on the freedom to create the true, since that is to conclude that being can engender nonbeing by the fact that it can produce only being and that it is free to produce any kind of being it wishes.

Since omnipotence renders deception impossible, it is evident that goodness, which itself excludes it, in no way limits omnipotence. Therefore God's omnipotence could not give refuge to a radical irrationality, nor could it exhibit a tragic foundation. Of the two reasons that exclude deception, the only decisive one is the metaphysical reason, which is based on the true nature of omnipotence. Goodness gives to it alone a precarious certainty in this regard. In fact, is not what I call "good or bad" so by virtue of the notions that God has freely imposed on my limited understanding? Could not God have instituted by decree another "good" that would justify the very essence of deception?[40] The argument based on the metaphysical reality of the true escapes this relativity. Certainly God could have freely created truths other than the ones that are given to me as such, for he could have created other beings, but he could not have created deception, which is neither another truth nor another being, but the absence of truth and the absence of being, and is therefore excluded from creation by the Supreme Being. Thus, although nothing proves that deception cannot be another good, one different from the one I understand,[41] it is evident that it cannot be another truth, since it is destructive of any possible truth. In addition, the vicious circle traditionally brought up against reasoning that goes from evidence to divine veracity and then justifies evidence from veracity could not be resolved by distinguishing the moral plane (God's goodness) from the intellectual plane (evidence).[42] For, although the truth of a reason and the goodness of a volition are situated on two different planes, that does not prevent the truth of this reason from being intrinsically illusory, and therefore radically worthless for the philosopher—on pain of circularity—if God's malice wished to render rational evidence deceptive.

However, although the true nature of God's omnipotence is the deep basis for the necessary divine veracity, goodness is not, in this case, a less useful and even less indispensable foundation.[43] First, we have to appeal to it, at least provisionally, as long as we have not reached a clear and distinct knowledge of omnipotence. In addition, it must remain linked to the argument about omnipotence after we are able to give the latter the place it deserves. In fact, by revealing the impossibility for God to incline toward nothingness, the clear and distinct concept of omnipotence guarantees the reality of everything that exists in creation, and consequently, the truth of everything real in our ideas. But the work of God is not only reality, it is also "assemblages" and "dispositions" of realities; and the necessity for God to create only the necessarily true real does not, in addition, guarantee that the disposition of real things cannot lead us into error. Thus falsity can exist for creatures, even though God, who creates only being, has never directed himself toward nothingness. From this arises the necessity to find a supplementary guarantee in God, one that allows us to affirm that his veracity extends equally to the *disposition* of realities. This guarantee is given to us only through the goodness of God who, refusing to deceive us, disposes the realities consequently. This foundation of veracity with respect to finality is a principle without which Cartesianism could not establish the fundamental truth, within the limits that are circumscribed by the sphere of our "nature," of sensible quality, of our instincts, and of our passions.[44]

However, this appeal to divine goodness, required in this case by the nature of the question, since it no longer concerns the guarantee of a *truth,* properly speaking, in the created work, but concerns a *utility,* does not place us at a different plane from God, other than at the plane of his omnipotence. Goodness, in fact, is reduced to omnipotence in the end. The good is reciprocal with being, by virtue of the identity of the transcendental predicates, evil with defect, nonbeing with impotency.[45] Thus it is not by virtue of the *created* true and the good that universal deception can be excluded, but in virtue of God's infinity itself—meaning with respect to the plenitude of his *uncreated* being—that reveals the idea of the perfect present in me.

The double function assumed by divine omnipotence—to refute the hypothesis of the great deceiver and to establish the doctrine of eternal truths—is related to the extremely original Cartesian theory of possibility[46] and to one of its fundamental distinctions, of the impossible and possible in itself (for the omnipotent God) on the one hand, and of the impossible and possible for our understanding, on the other hand. This distinction, which is of extreme importance, since it conditions the conception of the substantial union, is subverted by the confusion of considering as a single doctrine the theory of eternal truths and the hypothesis of the evil genius, both conceived as equally based on the nature of divine omnipotence. In fact, with respect to this omnipotence, the former is a truth and the latter an absurdity.

CHAPTER III

The Cogito: Knowledge of My Existence and Knowledge of My Nature

1. The Truth of the Cogito and Mathematical Truth

The Cogito, by which my understanding reestablishes within universal doubt a firm, unshakable point against the fiction of the evil genius, posits relative to the order of reasons a first reason that, by terminating the chain of uncertainties, dominates the chain of certainties. This first certainty, which is confined within itself, in no way destroys universal doubt outside of itself; it introduces an *exception* to it. It introduces an exception *of fact,* since universal doubt, which is based on the evil genius, remains as rule; yet it is also *necessary,* since we are constrained to conceive that what we are verifying in this case cannot be otherwise. This necessity certifies its rationality.

By furnishing some evidence appropriate to an indubitable truth, the Cogito allows one to consider everything that possesses comparable evidence in the same way. It therefore imparts, by furnishing an external mark of the true,[1] a pragmatic means to constitute science; but it is incapable of establishing it in the full sense of the word, since it leaves open the question of rule.

The Cogito is but an exception to the rule of universal doubt imposed by the fiction of the evil genius, because in reality the Cogito naturally falls outside the sphere of this rule. Universal doubt would apply only to what the I affirmed as an existential or essential truth valid outside of itself. Here the I affirms only itself: the object posited is nothing but the subject. By this exact coincidence between my thought and existence—reduced to the existence of the subject—the knowledge of an unshakable and, at the same time, existential truth is acquired, since it relates immediately to a given intellectual existence and since it includes the immediate actualization of the necessary relations, "in order to think, one must exist," which establishes the indissolubility of the bond between existence and thought.[2] From the fact that I am certain of both the content of my assertion—"I think therefore I am"—and of the certainty I attribute to it—for it is impossible that I am deceived when I say that I necessarily exist if I am thinking—I acquire a certainty of my certainty that is infinitely superior to the initial certainty of mathematical propositions, which have certainty with respect to their content, but lose metaphysically the certainty of this certainty as soon as the evil genius is evoked.[3]

But how can this superior certainty dominate the certainty of mathematics, since, despite its rationality, it is altogether different, being confined within the subject while the latter bears on objects—mathematical statements?

The answer is that mathematical essences are only considered insofar as they are ideas or thoughts that find in the Cogito their ultimate condition of possibility, and it is in virtue of the relation of subordination necessarily instituted by the order of reasons between the Cogito as simple absolute nature, and mathematical ideas, as simple natures relative to it. The twofold characteristic of greater simplicity and more elevated function in the order of the conditions of my knowledge works in favor of the Cogito with respect to mathematical truths, in the same way that it would work in favor of the latter with respect to the simplest sensible elements.

First, mathematical notions only condition the representations with respect to their possible content; they themselves constitute a content, namely, the necessary content of all possible representations, the necessary elements from which all these representations are *constituted.* They can therefore, in this way, possess only a relative simplicity and generality, this necessary content (extension and the multiplicity of shapes and possible relations) in itself offering some diversity and complexity. The Cogito, on the other hand, abstracts away any content; it has therefore an absolute simplicity. And certainty grows in direct proportion to simplicity. As the process goes from conditions to conditions, from the complex to the simple, doubt tends to be less and less pressing and natural, so that it finally becomes "light and metaphysical," and it requires a maximum effort of will when it attains the region of mathematical ideas whose relative simplicity and generality would escape the natural doubt relative to complex and particular things. It must therefore completely vanish and make way for complete certainty, that is, something certain in itself, once the chain of reasons reaches an ultimate term that is absolutely simple and universal (the Cogito), and that dominates it: the Cogito and all the truths of connection—that things that have been created cannot have never been created, for example—have such clarity and *simplicity,* says Descartes, that it suffices for us to think of them in order for their truth to be manifest, so much so that it suffices to doubt them in order that they be true, since one must think them in order to doubt them.[4]

On the one hand, the mathematical contents are posited immediately as the conditions or *elements* of possible *things* (and not simply as the conditions for *my thinking* of these things; and I do not know whether the conditions that I perceive in my thought are effectively conditions of things in themselves, or simply conditions necessary in me of representations without any objective validity. On the other hand, the Cogito raises me to the ultimate condition of the possibility of all my representations, and not to the conditions of the possibility of the content of these representations. This characteristic is affirmed by the fact that the Cogito is instituted by beginning with the doubt that abstracts away the contents themselves in order to allow only the fact of its representation or its thought to remain; it is not instituted by beginning with the thought of something. From this it follows that the reality posited in this case, meaning the reality of my thought, is completely based in the function that this thought assumes as the condition for all possible representation, whatever its content.[5] Its validity therefore becomes incontestable. On the one hand, we have reached the "most simple and general" element, meaning consciousness, which is always identical and indivisible, abstracting away any diversity or complexity of its contents; and on the other hand, we have reached the ultimate condition, for, although we can abstract away the contents of thought, it is impossible to abstract away my thought, which must remain as condition of representation in general, whatever its content. In the same way that we can deny sensible knowledge without denying the ideas of the understanding, we can deny the ideas of the understanding without denying the Cogito, but not reciprocally. "The only thing that cannot be separated from Me . . . is that I am a thinking thing."[6]

2. The Order and Necessary Positing of the Existence of the Self and Its Nature

Thus returned to its place in the chain of reasons, the Cogito can be sheltered from aberrant interpretations.

First, its fundamental role with respect to mathematical truths is no longer in question: it establishes them by being the necessary condition as rule, in the same way that they would establish the sensible representations by their title of sine qua non condition. Second, as the ultimate term in the series of conditions of representation, it shows its necessity from without, because it is impossible for the understanding to abstract away the final condition—namely, the thinking self—just as the immediate apprehension of the principle "in order to think, one *must* exist" reveals it from within. Third, being that which remains when the rest is abstracted away, but without which the rest cannot subsist, and which cannot be abstracted away, it is a substance, according to the epistemological definition of the term, meaning insofar as it has a simple, absolute nature, *primo per se,* concrete and complete.[7]

The order of reasons therefore authorizes Descartes, beginning with *Meditation II,* to draw from the thinking self affirmed as substance, all the consequences required for the march of science, on the condition that one is restricted to the epistemological sense of the word substance, without infringing on the metaphysical sense, which alone can ultimately confer to it divine veracity, to which is reserved the privilege of investing our clear and distinct ideas with objective validity.

Fourth, the fact that the Cogito finds in its characteristic of most simple and most general ultimate nature the deep justification of certainty that we are constrained to give to it, proves that the reality it entails is not that of my personal concrete self,[8] but that of my thinking self in general, as universal condition of all possible knowledge.

Doubtless the Cogito, as a substance—in the epistemological sense—is, according to Cartesian terminology, something "concrete," and something complete. But this term ought not seduce us, since Descartes merely uses the term in order to express the characteristic of substance to be self-sufficient and to be capable of being thought clearly and distinctly separately from other things.[9]

The term is similarly attributed to extension. In this way, though apprehended in an immediate experience, and though it is a singular reality and not a universal concept of all ways of thinking,[10] the thinking being captured in the Cogito—without being an abstraction deprived of reality—is only an abstract being, in the strict sense of the word, since its self-sufficiency is only affirmed through its ability to be conceived clearly and distinctly *as a whole (totum)* apart from everything else, and to be posited as the ultimate residue of a process of elimination.[11] It is thus opposed to a real concrete; to Leibnizian substance, for example, whose self-sufficiency is disclosed, on the contrary, by its ability to sum up the infinity of its predicates, to be the reason for their integration, such that, far from being proven a substance by the possibility of being thought without them, it is only a substance by its express and necessary reference to them, insofar as it is revealed as the formula that accounts for their series.

However, one must not confuse the criterion that allows us to know that a thing is a substance *(quod),* meaning concrete and complete, with the definition of what is *(quid)* a complete or substantial thing; and Descartes specifies that "by a complete thing I understand nothing more than a substance endowed with forms or attributes that are sufficient to let me know that it is a substance."[12]

That is why knowing a thing as substance is not knowing the substance itself. Substance, being substance only through the properties, forms, and attributes it renders possible, and manifesting itself through them, is known by them; a substance without attributes cannot be known to me—the more attributes it has the better I can know it, and reciprocally. Thus, when one abstracts away the modes of conceiving—by opposing to them thought as substance, properly speaking, meaning what remains under the change of accidents and what depends only on itself—far from acquiring in this manner a complete knowledge of the thing, we diminish the knowledge we can have of it.[13]

We ought to abstract substance from its modes only provisionally, simply with the view to *distinguishing it* from them, in order to authenticate it as substance, without ceasing to relate them to it.[14] Further, the concept of substance cannot be thought clearly and distinctly if one abstracts away the concept of accident, for what has no modes cannot be substance, substantiality cannot exist without accidentality and vice versa: the relation between the two terms is necessary and reciprocal in this case.[15] On the other hand, although no accident can be thought of without substance, substance can always be thought of without *this* or *that* of its accidents: the relation between the two terms is then still necessary, but is unilateral. Also, when what is at stake is only the recognition of what properly constitutes the substance in a complex, meaning what remains under its changing modes— or, what comes to the same thing, its principal attribute—I cannot do so except by seeking for what, in this complex, can be conceived clearly and distinctly without having to think of the rest.[16]

Consequently, when what is at stake is not instituting the first scientific truth that is affirmable with certainty, as is now the case, but looking at scientific thought as it exists in reality outside the first presentation of the science I now have (with which my future science will later attempt to be integrated as a certain truth, in any case) substance must be conceived as not being able to exist without its modes. In fact, science will later teach me that my thought has some modes, and then, referring to divine veracity, that God can create and preserve separately the things that I conceive clearly and distinctly as really distinct, but not those that I conceive as simply *modally* distinct.[17] Although this later distinction has a basis in things, it is a fact of my mind, of my "reasoned reason," and it does not correspond to an effective separation between things.[18]

But with respect to the Cogito, taken as the beginning of metaphysics, we are dealing with, not a thinking thing, which can be outside of what my thought represents to me as actually indubitable, but only with what I can affirm, at this point on the chain of reasons, as being a certain *truth* for my science. And what I can affirm then as scientifically certain, is only my own existence as pure intelligence. One therefore is dealing only with an abstract being here, since this pure intelligence has been affirmed only as the one thing that I could not abstract away in myself, after having abstracted away everything else.

This abstract being is a real being, and within its kind, the most real that can be, since this pure intelligence includes and conditions the reality of all my modes of thought, and since it is found within them, whatever their complexity. Similarly, extension is a real being because it involves the reality of all material bodies, however complex. This maximum of reality establishes the maximum of universality. Simplicity is, in fact, necessarily linked with universality, for the character of the simplest nature is to find itself in all composites.[19] And what is found in every composite, without itself being composite, is, as we have seen, the most certain. That is why Descartes said that arithmetic and geometry, insofar as they treat only extremely simple and general things, contain something certain and indubitable.[20] And, we have seen that the Cogito was for me still yet more simple and more general, and more certain than these things. If the Cogito were not immediately for me the most abstract and most universal being, it would not be the most real nor the most simple, and it would be incapable of establishing science. In fact, I find this simple and real, abstract and universal being in a complex, concrete (in the usual sense), individual, etc., self. Hence, it is bound to happen that I confuse it with the latter as soon as I lose track of the linkage of reasons. This confusion is easily engendered since it gains authority from the frequently stressed oppositions between axioms (for example, *in order to think, one must exist)* and general propositions *(everything that thinks is)* on the one hand, and the Cogito as the intuition of a singular reality and an existence—mine—on the other hand. But this singular reality is the reality of a simple nature possessing the universality proper to singular rational essences; and my existence is affirmed only insofar as it is reduced to the being of this singular nature, that is, to pure intelligence, the ultimate condition of everything I know or believe to know. That is the existence of my pure self, which has nothing in common with my individual, personal, concrete self, which can only be captured empirically, and not by a purely intellectual intuition. Actually, this concrete individual self *does not exist for my science.* Only what I can affirm with complete evidence and certainty exists for it, and is real and certain for it. And at the present stage, relative to the order, I can legitimately affirm nothing other than my self insofar as it thinks and it is only pure intellect.

It is therefore not surprising that, since the existence that has been posited in all certainty as first truth is uniquely what could have been posited, by abstraction of the rest, as the simplest among them and as a purely intelligent nature, this nature possesses the generality that Descartes attributes to all *primitive notions.*[21] It is not even a finite self in general, but a self in general: "It is an intellectual nature," specifies the *Summary of the Meditations.*[22] And Descartes adds for Silhon that "by spending sufficient time on this meditation, one acquires little by little a very clear, and so to speak, intuitive knowledge of the *intellectual nature in general*; this is the idea that, considered without limitation, represents God to us, and considered as limited, is the idea of an angel or of a human soul."[23]

Since I posit, in the Cogito, the certainty of my being only to the extent that I perceive myself simply as *intellectual nature, meaning* reason, soul, or thought, apart from any of its accidents (whether I am thinking this or that, the true, the false, the obscure and the confused, the clear and the distinct; whether I am doubting, imagining, sensing, willing, or conceiving; whether my thought is attentive or not, quick or slow, etc.), it appears that the self posited here as indubitable is this self common to all men, the specific form establishing the difference between man and animal (namely reason), but not establishing any difference between men, that is, not containing the principle of their individual difference.[24] That is why Descartes can state that reason is "complete in each and every person," and also state that reason or intelligence constitutes me totally *(totum)*, for it is the whole essence of my substance.[25]

The expression "little by little" that we lift from the letter to Silhon must not lead one to believe that we rise discursively from the Cogito as a particular truth to an approximative generality similar to the generality of the dialecticians' universals.[26] The letter is concerned with "meditating" meaning "reflecting," in order to attain, "so to speak," the *intuition* of a *nature*. And this reflection is entailed by the constitutive process of the Cogito: it is not sufficient to discover the certainty that I exist, one must also discover *what I rightly affirm when I affirm my existence.* Lacking this clear and distinct knowledge, I risk including in this existence elements that must be excluded from scientific affirmation, meaning legitimate elements relative to the reasons. From this arises a new meditation that cannot be truly dissociated from the first, since it completes it. This meditation will reveal to me that the affirmed existence is, and cannot be other than, the existence of my pure intelligence constituting the whole *(totum)* of my thinking being. In this way, I will also soon know that I ought to posit intellectual nature as constituting my *nature.* When, having pursued my meditations, I come to know that what is necessary for me is necessarily true for things, I will have perceived that this nature is in itself my essence, and the essence of every thinking substance. I will have then attained, "so to speak," the intuition of the intellectual nature in general whose properties are necessarily imposed on all intellectual natures. This is "so to speak" because the intuition that I have is in reality the intuition of my intellectual nature, whose universal validity I perceive. The universal validity of intellectual nature thus perceived does not diminish its singularity. However general a nature may be, it is always a singular thing that I capture by intuition. For example, in geometry, the triangle that my understanding captures before its particular imaginative realization is a singular mathematical being that has characteristic properties that are exclusive of the properties of the other mathematical beings. And I have a distinct intuition of them. However, this triangle is a general thing.[27] The worst error would be to dispute its *reality* on this ground,[28] and to judge as real only the particular (and not singular) triangle that the imagination presents to me under some sensible aspects, thereby endowing it with the status of concrete being to the eyes of nonmathematicians. It is therefore conceivable, and even unavoidable, that nonphilosophers, meaning those who remain estranged from the spirit of geometry, as Descartes has expressly told us, confuse the self of rigorous science, which is legitimately affirmable, an intellectual essence having necessary and universal properties, with the "concrete" self of the psychology of common sense—the self that is pure intelligence, whose rational intuition was rendered possible by a rigorous process, with the self that is above all the self of imagination and sensation, which daily experience reveals to us "without any elaborate preparation," as states Gassendi.[29] We understand that meditations burdening us with such "elaborate preparation" must be constructed "little by little." They are "painful and laborious,"[30] for they are exercised against my imaginative and sensible faculties, from which I must abstract myself in order to release what is alone legitimately affirmable relative to the rigor of science. They end up with a disconcerting result for nonphilosophers, who do not conceive any self other than the empirical self. From this arises the necessity of meditating at length in order to familiarize oneself with these new and strange items of knowledge.[31]

3. The Cogito Is Not the First Given of an Introspective Psychology, but the Necessary Truth of a Science of Pure Understanding

The necessity that Descartes affirms of an "elaborate preparation" for setting out the Cogito as it should be set out, that is to say, with that "metaphysical certainty [. . .] which is all that is in question here,"[32] brings to light its status of rational scientific truth and reveals that it has nothing in common with a simple act of self-consciousness, of psychological origin, within the power of anybody whatever. It differs from this, not only by its modality (necessity), but also by its content, insofar as it affirms only a pure intellect, an essence detached from everything that would mask it from natural consciousness, and which is affirmable as actual only insofar as it is perceived as the sine qua non condition of the possibility of all knowledge. It is consequently impossible to subscribe to the following valuation: "Consciousness of the self is neither the appearance of a new object for consciousness, nor the emergence in me of a pure or transcendental self, but an awareness of one's consciousness. Cogito does not signify 'Cogito me cogitantem,' but simply Cogito; only this Cogito is now full of necessity, as it were."[33] This language would perhaps have been accepted by Gassendi—except for the remark about necessity—but not by Descartes.

In addition, Descartes understands by *metaphysical* certainty no more than *scientific* certainty, that is, a certainty established rigorously as a true certainty, an evidence experienced as a true evidence. Metaphysics is, in effect, nothing more than another science such as mathematics or physics. It differs from them only insofar as its objects are taken wholly by pure understanding, excluding any other faculty; while the objects of mathematics and physics are also taken by pure understanding, but they require the concurrence of the imagination (construction *in concreto)* and sensible experience, insofar as it bears on the pure natures of materal existing things and their combinations.[34] In fact, experience can teach us about existence by itself. But the difference of object does not change anything with respect to the essence of science, which remains "always one and the same, no matter how varied are the objects to which it applies."[35] Metaphysical certainty and evidence are of the same nature as the certainty and evidence of mathematics and physics, but are more rigorous, for they are absolutely indubitable: they are the certainty and evidence established as such—in brief, they are second-power certainty and evidence (certainty of certainty, evidence of evidence—it is evident that it is impossible that the evidence of the Cogito be deceitful), and they are soon to be carried to the third power (by divine warrant). In this book we use the term *science,* and not the term *metaphysics,* since the latter may hide from today's reader the sense of a discipline "more certain than mathematics" that Descartes gives to this term. Thus we use the expression, *my* science, to denote that the truths necessary for my understanding cannot be affirmed originally as having outside of me a validity for things in themselves. It is because of *Meditation III* that *my* science will later become *the* science, and that the truths of my science will be held as the truths of things.[36]

4. The Nature of the Self as Thought; the Nature of the Self as Pure Intelligence; the Possibility and Legitimacy of This Twofold Knowledge According to the Order

Obtained as it is from the analysis of the givens of knowledge, which are the necessary universal condition of representation in general, the Cogito posits the self as being essentially the intellectual power to know: *"Mens, sive animus, sive ratio, sive intellectus.'*[37] Will, in spite of its infinity, is posited only as a mode of this intellect; this power can subsist without will, while will cannot subsist without it.[38] Thus the position of the existence of my thinking self *(quod)* leads directly, according to the order, to knowledge of its nature *(quid).*[39]

This knowledge exhibits two aspects.

First, Descartes places in evidence that this nature is purely spiritual, since it can only be thought apart from the body. In this way is introduced the notion of the substance of the soul as pure thought, heterogeneous with the substance of the body, a notion that will become the truth of the thing when, after *Meditation III,* the knowledge that I have of myself will be invested with objective validity—in brief, when the clear and distinct idea of my soul will be perceived as an essence. Second, Descartes places in evidence its purely intellectual nature, which leads him to distinguish it from what is not pure intelligence in the soul. In this way is introduced the notion of modes of the thinking substance that also will be converted into the truth of the thing later on.

If the knowledge of the various properties of my soul (knowing, willing, judging, desiring, sensing, etc.) is obtained, in the same fashion as the knowledge of its existence, by an immediate reflection of consciousness on itself,[40] the knowledge of its nature—and later on, the right and necessity to attribute to it the modes that I can discover in it in fact and that "it seems to me" it possesses—is acquired by a rigorous methodical process that consists of reflecting on the conditions that render possible the knowledge of its existence as thought in general—*in brief, by a reflection on my first reflection.* In other words, the examination of the reasons that have rendered possible the position of my existence as thinking self in the certainty of knowledge, allows me to acquire, with equal certainty, the science of its nature by responding to the question: "What am I, I who exists?"[41]

In fact, the knowledge that I am a thinking thing, being the first (the first indubitable truth of science), could not have been conditioned by another: the first known thing cannot depend on things that are yet unknown and that consequently are assumed to be nothing.[42] Its knowledge therefore could not have depended upon the things that are the object of imagination, that involve the bodies whose existence is unknown to me (rejected outside certain knowledge as doubtful, the doubtful being assimilated with the false), and that are consequently annulled.[43] In this way I understand, on the one hand, that if I want to know myself, according to the order of reasons, I must know myself through pure understanding and not through the imagination that speaks to me only of the body; and, on the other hand, I must know myself as being simply and uniquely, meaning essentially, pure thought *(intellectus).* By reflecting on the process that has allowed me to know rationally, with respect to the order, that I exist, I have been able to draw from this very process a complex conclusion, in part relative to a mode of knowledge that has allowed me to posit the existence of my soul, in part relative to the very nature of this soul. Since the knowledge of my existence can only be strictly intellectual, my nature can only be conceived as pure intelligence, and consequently, as pure mind. The order of reasons has constrained me to pass from the fact that the position of the existence of my thinking self is in no way conditioned by corporeal elements or objects of the imagination, to the two affirmations that nothing imaginative belongs to my pure essence and that nothing corporeal can be included in the true knowledge that I have of my nature: "It is extremely certain that this notion and knowledge I have of myself, thus precisely taken, does not depend on things whose existence is not yet known to me; and consequently, and for even stronger reasons, it does not depend on any of the things I can picture or invent in my imagination."[44] And that is why "I know for certain that nothing of what I can understand by means of my imagination belongs *to the knowledge I have of myself* and that it is necessary to recall the mind *from this way of conceiving* in order that it may be able to know *its nature* with perfect distinctness."[45]

I have reached a dual conclusion. In fact, I have learned *what I am:* I am a mind, meaning something thinking, exclusive of every corporeal element; and I have learned what is the nature of this mind: it is essentially an intelligence, by itself exclusive of the imagination and of the senses. In this way, the true meaning of the words *mens, animus, intellectus, ratio,* which were until then unknown to me, become known to me.[46] I now know that these different terms must be equated, since they all designate one and the same principle, intelligence, which by itself constitutes the one and only condition of the possibility of my knowledge in general.

By reflecting on the conditions that have rendered possible the certain knowledge of my existence, I have elucidated the clear and distinct idea of my own nature. But I have also produced other ideas in me, namely, those of the conditions that have rendered possible this first idea for me. I perceived clearly and distinctly that I cannot know my own nature except by setting aside imagination and senses. From this I see immediately that the conditions rendering possible the clear and distinct idea of my nature are identical to the conditions rendering possible the clear and distinct knowledge of my own existence. But was it not precisely because, in fact, I acquired for myself the clear and distinct knowledge of my nature by knowing myself simply as a thinking thing that I learned in all certainty that I existed (as thought)?

I thus immediately perceived that in order to have knowledge of my nature I must have simultaneously accomplished two proceedings, which, although different, are in fact but one. In fact, I had to posit myself as a mind, that is, as something incorporeal; and moreover, I had to posit my mind as pure intelligence—which is not the same thing, for could not philosophers have posited the essence of the pure mind elsewhere than in pure intelligence, for example, in will or sensation?

But it is impossible that I posit myself as incorporeal without positing myself as purely intellectual, at the same time. In fact, if I could not have posited the being of my self except by excluding everything corporeal from its idea and if I were thus constrained to conceive a real distinction between my soul and body, it is because I could not know my own nature except by turning away from what seems to involve the body in me, namely, imagination and senses. Thus I could not posit myself as incorporeal without positing myself as purely intellectual. Moreover, since I cannot *know* myself except through intelligence, I see immediately that I *am only* intelligence; and because I *am only* intelligence, intelligence alone, and not imagination and senses, is capable of allowing me *to know* what I am. That is why I must conclude that imagination and senses are alien to the nature of my mind, while intelligence, which alone is required in order to understand it, belongs to it alone.

Is that to say that intelligence must exclude imagination and senses from my nature in the same way that it excludes body itself from it? No, for imagination and sensations are grasped directly in my mind as thoughts, while body is outside the mind and is unknown to me. Imagination and senses must therefore be related to the soul insofar as they cannot be understood without it. They can therefore not be excluded from it in the same way that the body is excluded from it; but, being alien to its nature, they can be related to it only as contingent properties, at least with respect to that in which they differ from intelligence.[47] They are modes of my soul, and there is only a modal difference between my soul and them.

Finally, given that pure intelligence is perceived as constituting the whole nature of my mind, since it alone is capable of letting us know it, we conceive that the other faculties (sensing, desiring, judging, willing, etc.), which are no more capable than imagination of letting us know this nature (because of what distinguishes them from pure intelligence), do not belong to my mind any more than imagination belongs to it, and that consequently they are also only contingent properties.[48]

5. Reflection on the Conditions of the Cogito as First Truth; Deduction of the Notions of Real and Modal Distinction; Theory of Modes

The rational necessity that has constrained us, in order to attain the clear and distinct idea of our nature beginning with the Cogito, to exclude from it, in very different ways, body on the one hand, and nonintellectual faculties on the other, has not resulted in allowing me to know what I am. It has in addition brought me to the knowledge of the real distinction and the modal distinction. It has thus given me clear and distinct knowledge of the technique that allows me to determine these two kinds of distinctions.[49] It has promoted these various items of knowledge to the level of certain truths within my science.

In fact, to perceive that I cannot with absolute evidence conceive what I am except by excluding from myself, by means of metaphysical doubt, everything except thought, is also to perceive that the determination of a thing as a self-sufficient nature requires that one be able to exclude from it everything left over after thus rendering knowledge of it clear and distinct. At the same time, what defines the concept of real distinction as *criterion* of all substantiality is discovered. Further, to perceive that, while in order to conceive my nature clearly and distinctly, I can and must exclude imagination, senses, and other faculties from it, and that it yet is impossible for me to exclude from these faculties which I know immediately by my thought, that same thought which indubitably constitutes my nature, is to discover at the same time the modal distinction and the *criterion* of the accidents of substance.

The genetic demonstration of this twofold distinction is accomplished, as is that of the nature of my soul, by a reflection on the conditions that have rendered possible the certain knowledge of the existence of my thinking self.

These ideas therefore appear as possessing the same certainty as the Cogito, since their knowledge is drawn directly from the knowledge I have of it. They are, consequently, absolutely certain *for me* (even though I do not yet know whether they are truths of things).

Their demonstration involves a twofold segregation, established by the intersection of the evil genius and the Cogito: everything that can be negated by means of the evil genius is excluded from the soul; everything that cannot, and in this way is proven to be inseparable from the Cogito, to which even metaphysical doubt succumbs,[50] is included in it, like the soul itself. Thus the evil genius negates everything that is corporeal, however small, for this negation does not negate anything of my thought.[51] As for the faculties of my soul that I discover in me to be alien to the pure essence of my thought, it cannot negate them, even though they do not properly belong to my nature, for although this nature can be known without them, they are *thoughts,* nevertheless, that can no more be denied than my soul, without which they cannot exist. In fact, if it is very certain that *what* I doubt, *what* I imagine, sense, will, etc., can be negated by doubt, it is no less certain that I cannot doubt that I doubt, imagine, sense, will, and that none of these faculties can be negated, since from the moment that they are, they are inseparable from the being of my thinking self. We rediscover in them the essential characteristics of thought, that is, the property of being posited as true once I try to doubt them and to reduce them to seeming falsities: "It is extremely certain that *it seems to me* that I see light, hear sound, sense heat; that cannot be false, and it is what is properly called sensing; and that is precisely nothing else but thinking."[52] Thus the principle of segregation that is entirely negative with respect to the body is tied to a positive principle with respect to the nonintellectual faculties of my mind, since it requires relating them to it necessarily, inasmuch as, though it reveals them as contingent relative to it, it reveals them at the same time as inseparable from it, once I notice that they *in fact* exist in it.

This method of segregation is considered by Descartes to be the great novelty of the *Second Meditation.*[53]

Although tightly bound to the real distinction between the soul and body, the modal distinction between intelligence as constituting the nature of the soul and the contingent faculties (accidents) is altogether different. By not perceiving this difference, Gassendi encumbered himself with pseudodifficulties, concluding that the nonintellectual faculties must be rejected from the soul in the same way as was the body, in such a way that a portion of the soul is amputated—and also that Descartes contradicts himself by referring sensation and imagination to the soul.[54]

But if intelligence or the principle of thought as "first act" or "principal form of man" is what soul amounts to, the word refers not to a part, but to the unity and whole, thought having no parts, but becoming diversified into a plurality of functions,[55] although remaining indivisible.

Moreover, that the nonintellectual faculties are contingent with respect to what constitutes the nature of the soul, cannot exclude them from it, since they cannot exist except by participating in this nature.[56]

However, the notion of modes and their distinction from substance is not always perfectly clear. We become particularly aware of this when the necessities of our mind acquire an objective validity by virtue of divine veracity. Thus, declaring in *Meditation VI* that it is sufficient that I can *conceive* a thing clearly and distinctly without another in order to be certain that the first is distinct from the second, "because they can be posited separately, at least by God's omnipotence,"[57] and affirming that I can conceive myself clearly and distinctly as a whole *(totum)* without the faculties of imagining and sensing, and that consequently, these faculties are modes,[58] Descartes concludes that God could have me exist without them: although modes cannot *exist* without substance, substance can *exist* without them. This conclusion is confirmed at the beginning of the same *Meditation,* where it is stated that imagination being in no way necessary to my nature or my essence, that is, the essence of my mind, no doubt I could remain always the same as I am now, even if I were to have none."[59] This conclusion is extended to all the modes and for any substance, since imagination and sensation are expressly paralleled with the modes of the body—shapes, movement, etc.[60] The conclusion is therefore as valid for extended substance as for thinking substance: one and the other could have been created without any of their modes.

That is a thesis that seems to be in opposition to the affirmation that there is no substantiality without accidentality. But such a difficulty can only be a verbal difficulty. Certainly, if the definition of substantiality necessarily includes accidentality, God, when creating a substance, could not create it without modes; otherwise, he would not be creating a substance. But it is not necessary that God create a substance. Since essences can be conceived clearly and distinctly without modes, he can create them without making of them a substance, in the sense of a being that is subject to some accidents.

However, have we not stated that any substance must have modes by which we know it and that a substance without modes would be unable to be known? And what is unable to be known cannot be the object of a clear and distinct idea. Thus it would be impossible to conceive that God could have created a substance without modes, because of the clear and distinct idea that we would have of this. Nevertheless, it is not stated that these "attributes, properties, or forms" by which we know substance are only modes—although Descartes speaks only of accidents to Clerselier (cf. above)—for substance has essential and necessary properties that are not accidents. For example, extension has the property of being extended in length, width, and depth, and of being divisible. Such attributes, and even the *principal attribute* alone, would be sufficient to allow us to know a substance that is devoid of modes.

The true difficulty is elsewhere. Descartes extends to all the modes the conclusions that he has drawn with respect to imagination and sensation. And no doubt it is evident that thinking substance can be created without these modes, or that these faculties can be conceived as modes, that is, that thought can be conceived clearly and distinctly without them. In fact, they belong so little to essential thought that they could not have come to it except by the violence that our thinking substance suffers from the fact of its union, a union contrary to its nature, with an adverse nature from which it is *really* separated. The exclusion of these modes outside the essence of the soul therefore appears tied to the exclusion of the body outside the soul. That is why the soul is posited as radically incorporeal. Thus the position of the modal distinction is, in this case, tied to the position of the real distinction and in some ways is dominated by it. But there are other modes than imagination and sensation, namely, the clear and distinct ideas and will. The attribution of mode to will is given implicitly in article 53 of the first part of the *Principles:* "Thus, for example, we cannot conceive shape except as an extended thing; thus imagination, sensation, and will so depend on a thinking thing that we cannot conceive them without it. But, on the other hand, we can conceive extension without shape or without motion, and the thinking thing without imagination or sensation and so forth with the rest."[61] The expression *"and so forth for the rest"* can only refer to will, although it seems that Descartes had shied away from stating this explicitly.[62] It goes without saying that if the essence of my thought is pure intellect, will is not part of it. God could therefore have created a mind without will.

Moreover, it is evident that in this case, what allows the exclusion of sensation and imagination from the pure essence of thought, and what renders these into modes, cannot also serve as foundation to reject will and clear and distinct ideas from modes. The distinction of these modes with respect to the essence of thought can owe absolutely nothing to the real distinction between the body and soul and to the alteration that this essence suffers by its union with an adverse nature. Pure minds (angels), devoid of bodies, have ideas and will. The modal distinction cannot be linked with the real distinction.

Do not the clear and distinct ideas arise from my intellect alone, an intellect that is separate from a body? Is it not of the essence of a pure intelligence to have clear and distinct ideas? What would a pure intelligence created by God without any ideas be? And can he not create it without ideas, since I conceive substance clearly and distinctly separate from its modes? There remains here no foundation for the distinction between mode and substance other than the classical criterion of variability, the only criterion valid for extension. While ideas change, the intellect remains identical to itself in the same way that extension remains identical to itself while shapes change.

But cannot the criterion be valid for will, since this power remains while volitions change? Certainly, as Descartes remarks, will is nothing other than volitions, but could one not say as much for intelligence—it is nothing other than ideas? Hence by what right can one think of will as a mode, and the self as a purely intelligent thing? Why do we not institute the self as a willing thing? Although I can easily conceive that God could create an intelligence without imagination and sensation, can I as easily conceive that he could create a mind without will? That, in fact, is "what we experience as coming directly from the soul [...], what seems to depend only on it,"⁶³ and what is a facet of our mind, of which the understanding is the other facet: *"Volitio et intellectio differunt tantum ut actio et passio ejusdem substantiae."* ⁶⁴ Thus all the kinds of thought are brought back to two kinds that seem symmetric: understanding and will.⁶⁵ No doubt my will is conditioned by my understanding, "for it is certain that we cannot will anything without perceiving by the same means that we will it," but on the other hand, "we scarcely *(vix)* ever understand anything without having some volition at the same time."⁶⁶ Moreover, will is nobler than understanding;⁶⁷ it is the most noble of our faculties, the only faculty that is infinite in me as it is in God and the faculty by which I resemble God.⁶⁸ How can what is finite in me—understanding—have as mode something nobler and infinite—will?

And do not the *Principles* open up another path that, if always followed everywhere, would have led to the proposition, *I have free will, therefore I exist?* Even if we are always deceived, Descartes states, "we still experience in us a freedom such that, anytime we wish, we can abstain from accepting as a belief things that we do not know well."⁶⁹ The immediate certainty of my existence results from this, because *we cannot doubt without existing.*⁷⁰ In brief, "I doubt, therefore I am." Doubt, meaning the free act by which I suspend all judgment, makes me perceive the freedom of my will as undeniably existing while I doubt everything. "That which we perceived directly" and "that which we cannot doubt during so general a suspension is as certain as anything we can ever know." "Free will can [therefore] be counted as one of our common notions."⁷¹ From this it seems to follow that it is not the certainty of my intellect that leads to the certainty of my free will.

It is noteworthy that this sequence is found only in the first part of *Principles.* Everywhere else *(Meditations, Replies to Objections, Discourse),* the certainty of my existence is not attested to by the consciousness of my freedom within doubt, through the formula, *I doubt therefore I am,* but by the fact of the representation (whether true or false), whatever the judgment brought to the thing represented, according to the formula: "Even if he deceives me, I think, therefore I exist."⁷² It is true that in the *Search for Truth,* my existence is attested to by doubt: "It is certain that you are doubting, and it is true that you who are doubting exist." But the fact of doubting is used insofar as it implies the *knowledge* of the fact that I am doubting, and not the *free act* of doubting: "You exist and you know that you exist, and you know this because you know that you are doubting."[73] This formulation is therefore in the same family as that of the *Meditations,* the *Replies to the Objections,* and the *Discourse.*

From what does this special character of the Cogito in the *Principles* arise? It arises from the fact that there we are dealing with physics, and not metaphysics. The task of the first part of the *Principles* is to supply the future physicist quickly with the metaphysical notions that are indispensable for blazing the path of the new science. And the first requirement on which the initial possibility of the scientific revolution hangs is an act of free will by which the physicist will reject all acquired prejudices and will decide to accept nothing that is not proposed to him by natural light alone. From this arises the need to awake in him a consciousness of the decisive role played by the act of judgment, on which the true and the false depend entirely. That is why the Cogito is presented as a function of judgment, meaning free will, and only secondarily from the point of view of the intellect by which I gain knowledge of this free will and which constitutes the essence of the substance of which this will is but a mode.[74] On the other hand, the *Meditations* is concerned with metaphysics; and its primary principle is that of the foundation of the objective validity of our knowledge. That is why the Cogito is not based on my freedom to doubt, but on the fact that I think or I know. The indifference of the *Principles* to the problem of the objective validity of ideas is denoted later on by the subsidiary role played by the a posteriori proof of God's existence, a proof that is of capital importance to the *Meditations,* since it is through it alone that this problem will be resolved.

But even in the *Principles* the voluntarist formula does not supplant the formula of the *Meditations*—I must necessarily posit myself as existing because I cannot doubt without thinking or think without existing.[75] In fact the demonstration that supports the Cogito necessarily involves the primacy of knowledge. All that I can assert at this point on the chain of reasons is that I represent myself as free when I doubt, but I cannot know whether effectively I am so. On the other hand, I know in all certainty that it is sufficient that I represent it to myself, meaning it is sufficient that I think in order to exist. Descartes replies to Gassendi, who objects that the certainty of existence can be inferred from any of my actions,[76] that Gassendi misunderstands him, for none of these actions is certain, none has the required metaphysical certainty that is at stake here, except thought.[77] Finally, any action in us is ours only to the extent that we have knowledge (or passion) of it.[78] No doubt it has been observed that if the understanding conditions any volition, the will conditions intellection, in return. But this is only approximately: *vix.* That is what occurs most frequently, in fact, but not always, nor necessarily. Intellection is, on the contrary, an absolute, necessary condition of any volition. For there is nothing in me whose existence can be affirmed that must not first be known. And what I conceive clearly and distinctly as being the condition in my soul of all the rest must be really—on the supposition that my rational thought has an incontestable objective validity—held to be the independent foundation, hence the substantial foundation, of all the other faculties.[79] It is therefore idealism, the assertion that the inference from knowledge to being is valid, which, by virtue of the order, constrains Descartes, even though he acknowledges elsewhere the eminent nature of will, to confer on will the status of mode even though it is infinite, and the substance of which it is a mode is finite. The rigorous genetic process from which I have drawn, at the same time, the certainty of my existence and the knowledge of my nature imparts a geometric rigor to this conclusion that the essence of my thought is only *intellectus sive ratio,* because this rational faculty of knowledge is the *only* faculty that it is impossible for me to deny within the hypothesis of the evil genius. My will is only the consciousness I have of willing. One can doubt that I am willing and affirm that my will, my effort, is but an illusion, state that it only *seems* that I will, in the same way that it *seems* that I sense or imagine; but, in any case, one cannot doubt that I think that I will. And it is starting with this certainty with respect to my thought that one can later draw out the certainty that I have concerning the faculties I *seem* to possess. In this way the principle that we have called Descartes' voluntarism is necessarily limited: will no more belongs to the thinking essence that constitutes me than movement belongs to the essence of extension.[80]

6. Intelligence as Essence of Substance; Intelligence as Mode; the Two *Quids*

These relations between modes and the essence of substance explain that pure intellect appears twice, in two different ways: as essence of the thinking substance and as mode of this substance. As essence of substance, pure intellect is present in all modes of thought, even in those that are the most alien to it, such as imagination, sensation, and will, for these modes must necessarily be related to "the intelligent substance" since "they embrace some type of intellection."[81] But insofar as the intelligent substance cannot, because of the presence in it of these non-purely-intellectual modes, always appear to itself as a pure intelligence relative to its essence, it becomes an accidental manifestation in it, and it must, on this account, take its place as accident with the other non-purely-intellectual modes. From this stems the two definitions of the thinking thing, according to whether one understands by the *quid* the essence of the substance or quiddity, properly speaking: *"Res cogitans, id est mens, sive animus, sive intellectus, sive ratio",*[82] or the substance including its accidents:[83] *"Res cogitans, quid est hoc? nempe dubitans, intelligens, affirmans, negans, volens, nolens, imaginans quoque sentiens."*[84]

Since pure intelligence appears as a mode, not by virtue of its nature, but because of the other modes that are foreign to the true essence of substance and that sometimes mask its pure expression, it follows that the manifestation of pure intelligence is contingent, but pure intelligence itself is not contingent, in contrast with all the other modes that are contingent with respect to substance. That is why, when Descartes enumerates the modes that are such that I can conceive the thinking substance clearly and distinctly without them, he mentions imagination, sensation, and will, but not intelligence. From this it appears again that the intellect is the principal attribute among all the attributes that the thinking substance possesses, meaning, "the one that constitutes its nature and essence, and on whom the others depend."[85] All the others depend on it since, as we have seen, they cannot belong to it except by embracing some type of intellection; and moreover, when substance is manifested by means of them and not by means of pure intellect, it does not cease to be conceived as pure intellect in itself, since they are in it only by means of this kind of intellection.

The confusion of these two *quid*s would immediately falsify the doctrine.

Yet no mistake is easier to make. In fact, as I know more attributes of a substance, the better I know the substance, and as I perceive more attributes of a thinking substance, the better I know it. That is why, after having enumerated the modes, *dubitans, intelligens, affirmans,* etc., Descartes concludes: "As a result I begin to know what I am *(quisnam sim)* with a little more clarity and distinctness than before."[86] There is only a short step from this and the conclusion, Hamelin's conclusion for example, that the *true definition* of thought is ordinary psychological consciousness in its widest sense and that the first *quid* is to be reduced to the second,[87] instead of basing the second in the first, as Descartes does.

Certainly, the definition by enumeration of modes is a *true definition*; it is the most immediately accessible, and it designates without ambiguity the thing in question. Thus it figures at the head of the definitions of the *Geometric Appendix to the Replies to Objections II* and at the beginning of the *Principles* (art. 9). But detached from what links it to the definition of essence and what gives it a rational character instead of its empirical character, it is only a definition *quid nominis.*[88] The *real definition* is the one that, detached because of the scientific *apparatus* of the Cogito, announces the essence of the thing—in this case, pure intelligence insofar as it establishes the legitimate attribution of the various modes to the substance they manifest and insofar as it is confirmed as the first absolute condition of all psychological consciousness, whether purely intellectual or not. To have consciousness is to know, and to know is merely to understand or to grasp *(comprehendere, intelligere).* If I know that I exist *(quod),* it is because I know what *(quid)* I am: namely, thinking; if I know that I am thinking, it is because I *understand* that it is *necessary* that I think since I err, doubt, deny, etc.; if I know that I am once I think, it is because I *understand* that it is *necessary* that I exist once I think. All knowledge, being intellection, involves a necessity: I only know myself as pure thought because I *understand* that it is *necessary* that I exclude from my being everything that is not pure intelligence, etc. It is the same for the knowledge of all things other than myself. We will see that if I know the wax, that if I perceive a man under a moving hat and overcoat in the street, it is because I understand *(comprehendo, intelligo)*[89] that that is the wax and that that is a man. I could not have known *that* that thing is *(quod)*, without understanding that it is truly itself, and therefore without first knowing *what* it is *(quid)*. And I know what it is by conceiving clearly and distinctly that it is really separate from everything else, that is, by *understanding* that it *necessarily* excludes all other things from itself; for example, I conceive that wax necessarily excludes from its substance what defines the substance of iron or stone.[90] The faculty of knowledge, consciousness in its essence, is—and the analysis of the piece of wax will confirm this—an understanding that constitutes for myself, by means of clear and distinct ideas that are in it from all time, what I posit as known.

Descartes legitimates the attribution of nonintellectual modes to intellectual consciousness from the fact that he perceives in them an intellection that renders necessary their attribution to thought for me. Transforming the nominal definition of thought (by the enumeration of its empirically certified modes) into a demonstrated theorem, Descartes makes progress in the clear and distinct science of the mind. He reconstructs ordinary (psychological) consciousness with all its modes beginning with its essence, pure intelligence, in the same way that he will reconstruct the material world beginning with its essence, pure extension or geometric extension. From this one sees an unfolding of reality, for as we shall see, essence being everywhere identical to existence, the existing things are nothing more than the actuality of their essential realities and their combinations. In the same way that the existence of the self is already only affirmable as actuality of the pure thinking essence, or intelligence, the existence of matter will only be affirmable as actuality of purely extended essence, or geometric extension. Finally, there will be a being whose "nature" will be fashioned from the mixture of the two others.

And this unfolding of essential reality as a single existing reality goes clearly against common sense, which is imbued with imagination and sensation. Common sense has as much difficulty in conceiving that the reality of the self is *completely* reduced to pure intelligence as it has difficulty in conceiving that the reality of the matter outside us is *completely* reduced to pure geometric extension.

The result of the confusion between the two *quid*s is fatal. In effect, by substituting ordinary psychological consciousness for mathematico-rational intelligence, as the essence of thought, we are led to see in the Cartesian knowledge of self only a pure and simple introspection based on our attentiveness (that was already Victor Cousin's interpretation), and we are led to see the *Meditations* as solely an intellectual biography, an account, the history of an experience, etc. We are brought in this way to see the Descartes of the *Meditations* as a psychologist. To do so would be to confuse necessary and sufficient conditions. For, if freedom of autonomous judgment detached from all prejudice and attentiveness are the sine qua non conditions of the discovery of the true, they are no more sufficient conditions for this than for mathematics. Montaigne had recognized this. In addition, a rational apparatus is needed, meaning the notion and adherence to the order that mathematics give us, and the application of precepts that the *Rules* has thought indispensable to formulate. One is brought, in addition, to subordinate the main thing to the accessory thing, the basic doctrine to the literary presentation, because of the charge imposed on the philosopher by the necessity to persuade a rebellious reader captured by imagination. Thus the spirit of Cartesianism is finally destroyed at its roots, a spirit that is not psychological but geometrical—thus a psychologism without rigor and without vigor is substituted for it.

Certainly since the subject is myself, no instrument is possible other than reflection on oneself. Moreover, the doctrine does contain great psychological wealth. The spirit of geometry does not exclude for Descartes the spirit of finesse, the psychological sense.[91] But psychology is nonapodictic, and the *Meditations* is a linkage of completely apodictic truths. Psychology thus serves a rational speculation; reflection is required by an order that also requires mathematical enquiry. What is at stake is not only to observe and to relate what happens in me, but to attain the essence of my self—which exceeds the ability of any psychology—and to account, by means of this essence, for everything that is discovered in my soul according to the order, and also, above all, to determine the limits of my mind, to establish the objective validity of my ideas, and in this way, to establish the objective validity of science. Doubtless, finally, the method itself has been discovered by a reflection on the spontaneous proceedings of my mind in the search for truth,[92] and it is not imposed on it externally and from on high as a canon, a pure logic expressing an ideal order in itself independent of the fact of my knowledge, which would subsist even if my original consciousness, indeed every thinking being whatever, should cease to exist. In this way Descartes represents a tendency opposite to Leibniz's, and Husserl would have reproached him with psychologism for this—as would have Kant.[93] But what I discover by means of this reflection on my mind are rational necessities inherent in my intellectual essence; and this return to the laws of my essence considered as deciding the structure of my mind itself has nothing to do with psychology, even if the logic that flows from it is tarnished by psychologism.

7. The Process of Internal Demonstration of the Various Notions of Distinction

One ought not confuse the genetic process that, beginning with the Cogito, allows the ideas of real distinction and modal distinction to be acquired, and allows their validity as certain scientific truths to be established, with the process of drawing the real distinction or the modal distinction from the direct intuition of the ideas of things. For example, I can draw directly the real distinction between thought and extension from the fact that I perceive in these ideas that one of them includes indivisibility and the other divisibility, and that consequently they radically exclude one another;[94] thus I can also demonstrate that I have the clear and distinct idea of a thing as substance because I can conceive it clearly and distinctly while abstracting it from everything else. But these proceedings and their legitimate use presuppose that I am already in possession of clear and distinct ideas of substantiality, of real distinction and of modal distinction, that I know that they are truths which are valid for my science, and that I know the criteria allowing their recognition and the conditions making possible their knowledge. However, I lack these items of knowledge, and the process begun by *Meditation II* has as its consequence getting me to know them and validating them as truths of science.

Certainly, these truths are in me before the light of my mind reveals them, for "internal consciousness always precedes the acquisition,"[95] and the reality of my understanding precedes the science that I could have taken from it. But insofar as they are outside my science, they are unknown and therefore they do not allow me to reach the known. Thus in order to know them, meaning in order to posit them in my science, I needed to start from the one thing that was first known to me, namely, that I am *(quod).* I then produced in me, in the light of nature, the idea of my nature *(quid),* and then through this, the ideas of substantiality, and of real and modal distinction, and discovered finally the conditions that render possible the knowledge of these ideas. Thus the discovery of the properties of the clear and distinct idea of my soul and of other subsequent ideas (substantiality, modality) has been rendered possible in me by the knowledge of the conditions that have themselves rendered possible the production of the idea of my nature in the light of my mind, exactly as, in geometry, the subsequent properties of a figure can be perceived by reflecting on the conditions that have rendered possible its generation or construction. And this analytic method is completely different from the one that consists in drawing from the intuition of the completely constituted figure the necessary properties it could include.

8. Conditions of the Subjective Validity of the Knowledge of the Nature of the Self

To what extent can the rigorous process that has just been set forth allow the attainment of true knowledge of the nature of the soul?

This is a twofold problem. First, it concerns knowing whether I can establish, within a science so constituted, that this science itself—meaning, for my own understanding isolated from the rest—this knowledge, can present itself legitimately as being necessarily the knowledge of my whole nature, and not simply a partial knowledge that does not authorize me to restrict the definition of this whole to my thought only.

Second, it concerns knowing whether the knowledge of my nature, such that the understanding represents it to myself as complete, possesses an objective validity, meaning whether in myself my nature is reducible to what my science represents to me necessarily—in brief, whether in itself it is reducible to my thought.

These two distinct problems sometimes interfere in the discussions that Descartes holds with his opponents; they have often been badly distinguished by the commentators. This is because, although they are extremely different, they can be condensed into the formulation of a single objection: is it certain that the nature of my soul is reducible only to thought?

In fact, if the science that I have just acquired from my soul does not have any objective validity, or if one cannot establish that it has any, I cannot affirm that my thought constitutes *in itself* the whole of the nature of my soul, even if my understanding is required, by virtue of the chain of reasons, to represent it to me as constituting this whole; in brief, I am not authorized to exclude from *the thinking thing in itself* the body that I exclude from *the knowledge that I have given myself of it*. And moreover, if the science that I have of the nature of my soul as pure thought cannot be legitimately posited within this science as the knowledge of the whole of my nature, I am not authorized to exclude from *the idea of the thinking thing* the body I have abstracted in order to obtain an independent knowledge of the idea. The first case concerns the right I have to exclude the body from the thinking thing, and the second case concerns the right I have to exclude it from the idea that my science has given me of it. The first case concerns an external problem: Must what is valid, according to the order of reasons, be held as the truth of the thing? The second case concerns an internal problem: Is the conclusion I have drawn been justified effectively by the order of reasons whose linkage constitutes my science?

In *Meditation II* Descartes replies succinctly and without the least ambiguity to these questions. On the one hand, it is incontestable that science has proceeded rigorously and that from its perspective, we are authorized, even required, to conclude that thought alone constitutes my entire nature.[96] On the other hand, it is no less incontestable that I do not absolutely know yet if my science has an objective validity. Better yet, I am required, given that the evil genius still reigns, to consider provisionally that it has none, such that I cannot yet know whether in itself the nature of the soul does not contain, besides thought, other constitutive elements that are unknown to me.[97]

First of all, considering the validity of the theory from the perspective of science or the order of reasons, its conclusion could have been contested. For, from what I am assured of being because I think thus, while yet I deny the body, it would follow simply that I can acquire some knowledge of myself without any knowledge of the body, and not that this "knowledge is complete and entire so that I am assured that I am not deceived when I exclude the body from my essence."[98] Similarly, from the fact that I can think clearly and distinctly about such and such a property of a right triangle by abstracting away another property that the triangle holds, I cannot affirm that the essence of the right triangle is reducible to the single property that I am considering and that the property I am negating by abstraction is excluded from it.[99]

Descartes replies that in order to know that two things exclude each other, meaning that there is a real distinction between them, it is necessary to know them as complete, but not to know them completely. No doubt, to know something completely is sometimes possible, but it is always impossible for me to know that this knowledge is complete, for my power to know would have to equal God's infinite power for me to be certain that "God has put no more in this thing other than what my understanding knows."[100] On the other hand, I can know something as complete, and I can have the certainty that this knowledge is such, if I can conceive this thing *clearly and distinctly* while denying everything else from it. The comparison with a single, separate property of a right triangle is utterly inadequate, because this property is not something complete, because it cannot be understood clearly and distinctly if one separates it from the right triangle, and because the triangle itself cannot be clearly and distinctly known if one denies this property of it. On the contrary, since I conceive my nature very clearly and distinctly by denying the body and everything belonging to the body from my nature, while it is impossible for me to deny thought, it is legitimate to conclude that the nature of my soul is constituted only by thought.[101] One must therefore distinguish between *abstraction of the mind* that renders inadequate, obscure, and confused a complete idea by restricting thought to the consideration of one of its parts, and *exclusion,* which, separating a complete idea from what does not belong to it, allows one, on the contrary, to have a clear and distinct idea of it.[102] "There is a great difference between *abstraction* and *exclusion.* If I said simply that the idea I have of my soul does not represent it to me as dependent on the body and identified with it, this would be merely an abstraction, from which I could form only a negative argument, which would be unsound. But I say that this idea represents it to me as a substance that can exist even though everything belonging to body would be excluded from it; from this I form a positive argument and conclude that it can exist without the body."[103] And the knowledge that one thing excludes another can be obtained in different ways. It can be obtained by the intuition of one of its fundamental properties that is the negation of a fundamental property of the other thing. Thus "the exclusion of extension can be clearly seen in the nature of the soul, from the fact that one cannot think of half of a thinking thing."[104] But it can be acquired also, which is the case in _Meditation II_, by the necessary process that has rendered possible the knowledge of the thing considered. The possibility to negate the corporeal thing without anything of my soul being destroyed, and the necessity to negate it in order that we can arrive at the knowledge of the nature of this soul, together prove, not just that I can acquire some knowledge of my soul without any knowledge of the body, but that the body must be excluded from my nature in order that I could truly know my soul, and that thus I know my nature as having to exclude the body, and as complete, when it is reduced to my thought without my body. "It seems to me very clear that the idea I have of a thinking substance is complete in this sense [meaning because I can conceive it alone and deny all other things of which I have ideas of it—M. G.] and that I have no other idea that is prior to it in my mind and that is joined to it in such a way that I cannot conceive them while denying the one of the other."[105]

It is therefore indubitable that my science can legitimately claim to know in an absolutely adequate way the nature of my soul as pure intelligence. This conclusion is confirmed by the consequences that the _Rules_ drew from the implications of the method. The process of elimination that has allowed me to attain the Cogito, in fact, has left only an absolutely simple residue that is incapable of being broken up; it is, moreover, the first reason, and consequently, it is the simplest of all the simple natures. And a simple nature cannot contain in itself anything other than what I know of it; otherwise, it would no longer be simple, but composite. It must be known completely, or not at all.[106] Therefore, once I know this simple nature that constitutes _the essence of the soul,_ I know it completely. This in no way means that I have a complete knowledge of the _soul:_ on the contrary, there are a multitude of properties in it that I do not yet know, and that perhaps I will never know. But it means that I have a complete knowledge of its _essence,_ which is plainly revealed to me as such and which no longer hides from me what it is: it is thought, purely and simply. In this way, I know in advance that all the unknown properties that it includes in itself cannot not include thought and must exclude everything foreign to thought. I therefore do not have a complete knowledge of my soul, but a complete knowledge of its nature as such.

9. Conditions of the Objective Validity of the Self. Objective Validity of the Knowledge of the Existence of My Self; the Merely Subjective Validity of the Knowledge of the Nature of Self at the Level of the Cogito

As for the objective validity of this knowledge, Descartes himself declares it null, for the moment, and declares that its truth resides only in the internal necessity of science. *only subjective*

The rational link that attaches the representation I construct for myself of the nature of the soul to the position of the Cogito as first reason, gives this representation in and for my thought a complete necessity and a certainty equal to the certainty of the Cogito itself. As it is certain that I exist for myself, it is certain that my thought cannot escape the necessities involved in the position of its own existence and which concern its own nature. It can no more subtract itself from their affirmation than from the affirmation of self. There is therefore no other science of the nature of my soul possible for my understanding than the one just developed.

However, although this science is as certain as the Cogito for my understanding, it has certainty only within it, that is, for my self enclosed within itself. One sees in this way the introduction of a fundamental distinction between the two truths that the Cogito brings to me linked to one another. Although it furnishes me the knowledge of my existence *(quod)* and at the same time the knowledge of my nature *(quid)*, these two items of knowledge each involve an extremely different order of certainty. The first is not only certain for me, but it already possesses a full objective validity, for it suffices that I *think* that I exist to know that I exist *in myself*. The second has only a purely subjective validity as of now, for the fact that *I think of myself as being by nature* pure thought in no way implies that *I am exclusively in myself a nature* that thinks. I only know that the *necessity* to represent my own nature to myself in this way exists in myself as certainly as I exist and as certainly that I can posit this existence only insofar as I think.

The science of my nature, while calling for the rigorous certainty of a perfectly rational science, therefore remains purely subjective as long as I have not established that, in its rationality, I have captured the truth of *the thing itself* whose nature I *represent* to myself. It is absolutely certain that the subject cannot represent his own nature to himself other than according to this science. But when I speak of *my nature,* I understand by this the essential reality of the subject such that it exists *in itself.* And nothing guarantees me that my subject possesses *in itself* the nature that it is necessarily constrained to attribute to itself:[107] "to belong to my essence and to belong to the knowledge I have of myself are two completely different things."[108] In other words, the science that I have thus obtained is absolutely necessary and certain, like the Cogito, but I do not yet know whether this science has *an objective validity,* and if, in itself, *in essence,* I am as I represent myself to be. That is why Descartes does not fail to emphasize that his conclusions have no validity except within the system of reasons that he has just developed: "I am now admitting nothing except what is necessarily true; I am, therefore, speaking precisely *(praecise tantum)*, only a thing that thinks."[109] That is *for me* the only valid residue, the one remaining when one has "rejected everything that can be rendered even slightly doubtful by the arguments that I have just now offered, so that there will remain only what alone is certain and indubitable."[110] But in order to have rejected from my certain knowledge all the things that are in this way unknown—for by definition what is rejected outside knowledge is unknown—I cannot say whether these unknown things are *"in rei veritate"*[111] different in themselves from the self that I know. How could I know this since I do not know them? "I know nothing of this; I am not discussing this now, since I can only pass judgment on things that are known to me."[112]

Truly, this observation involves two different interpretations, one restricted, and the other general, which basically are both present in the thought of the philosopher.

1) I do not know the body. How could I affirm validly that it is or it is not different from myself? Once I know the body, I shall be able to know whether its nature is in itself exclusive from mine.

This natural interpretation is a minor consideration. What is here in question is the nature of the self that I know, not the nature of the body that I do not know. And if I know that the nature of my self is radically different from the nature of body, I cannot suppose that the nature of body, which I do not yet know, can be the same as the nature of the self, for the nature of the self could not be different from the nature of body if the reciprocal were not true. Yet, it suffices for me to know the nature of my self in order to know, ipso facto, that the nature of body must exclude that nature of self, since the two exclusions are only two complementary aspects of one and the same incompatibility. And do I not have a clear and distinct knowledge of the nature of my self? As a result, am I not already, with complete certainty, obliged to exclude the nature of body from it and to assert that the nature of body, even though it is unknown to me, must necessarily be different from mine? But that is precisely the obligation that Descartes contests. The argument can have sense only if it places into question the objective validity of the knowledge I have of my own nature.

2) Certainly I know myself as having a nature that excludes the nature of body—in other words, in order to know myself, I must exclude body from myself. But can I assure that *"in veritate rei"* I am as I represent myself to my consciousness, *in veritate rationum?* That consequently, *in itself,* my nature is different from the nature of body? For that, I have to have known that my consciousness has an objective validity. But that is precisely what I do not know. And I can only speak about what I have indubitable knowledge of; therefore, for now, I do not know whether *in itself,* the

essence of my self is really different from that of body: "I know nothing of this; I am not discussing this now, since I can only pass judgment on things that are known to me." Truly, it is the objective validity of my knowledge that is put into question here.

The Replies to the Objections brings forth the literal details necessary with respect to this: "It is not true that I assumed something I did not know; for, on the contrary, because I did not know whether body was the same as mind or not, I made no assumption about this, but only treated the mind, until finally, in *Meditation VI,* I not only proposed, but demonstrated very clearly, that mind was really distinct from body."[113] Consequently, if I have the right to exclude body from my science, meaning from the knowledge of *the clear and distinct idea of my nature,* I do not yet have the right to exclude body from *the very nature* of my self. In order to exclude it legitimately from the thinking thing in itself, in the same way that I exclude it from the idea I have of it, I must demonstrate that the necessity of my thought is the very necessity of things. Therefore, what is *an exclusion with respect to my idea* is yet only *a simple abstraction with respect to the thing:* "Because I have said in one place, that while the soul doubts the existence of all material things, it knows itself precisely, *praecise tantum,* only as an immaterial substance; and seven or eight lines lower down, in order to show that by these words, *praecise tantum,* I do not mean an entire exclusion or negation, but only an abstraction of material things, I said that, in spite of that, I was not sure that there was nothing corporeal in the soul, even though nothing of the kind was known in it; my opponents are so unjust to me that they wish to persuade the reader that by saying *praecise tantum,* I wished to exclude the body, and that I have thus contradicted myself afterwards by saying that I did not wish to exclude it."[114] From this one sees that what is *exclusion* from the point of view of science can only be *abstraction* from the point of view of the thing. Thus the words *exclusion* and *abstraction* have different meanings according to whether one takes as point of view the truth of science or the truth of the thing.[115]

But if the truth that I have demonstrated has validity only for myself, the nature of my self possibly being entirely different from what I know, have we not spoken and deduced for nothing? That is a question that comes naturally to Arnauld's mind: "But he himself admits that, by the argument he proposed in his treatise, on the *Method,* the proof has proceeded only so far as to exclude from the nature of the mind everything that is corporeal and dependent on body, and not with respect to the truth of the thing, but only following the order of his thought and his reasoning—meaning that nothing was known to him to belong to his essence, beyond the fact that he **was a** thing that thinks. Hence, it is evident from this reply that the argument is still at the same place it was, etc."[116]

It is incontestable that the demonstration is not completed. In order for it to be completed, I will have to prove that the clear and distinct idea I have of my nature is an essence, meaning that it responds to the constitutive nature of the thing such as God has instituted; in brief, I will have to establish the objective validity of science: "Therefore . . . the problem whose solution he promises us remains in its entirety . . . namely, how it follows from the fact that he does not know anything else belonging to his essence except the fact that he is a thing that thinks, that there is nothing else that belongs to his essence."[117] This demonstration will be furnished in *Meditation III,* by means of the demonstration of divine veracity.[118]

The fact that the science of my nature has still only a purely subjective validity, however, does not diminish its own certainty in any way, since it is entirely evident and necessary. It is just that we will need to find a means of conferring on this certain science the objective validity that it still lacks.

Moreover, to have established that *for my science* it is necessary that it be so is a first result which is considerable and indispensable. From now on, it is certain that, in order to contest this truth, one would have to refuse to recognize an objective validity to every possible rational human science. Already and from now on, the question is enclosed in an alternative that excludes all the objections based on properties that I could not know, for only one of the two alternatives is viable: either human science as knowledge of truth of things is possible, in which case, that thought constitutes by itself the whole essence of my soul, is a truth of things, or else the proof that the truths of my science are truths of things and that an objectively valid, rational human science is possible would never be able to be administered, in which case we would no doubt never be able to prove definitively that, in itself, the nature of the soul really excludes the body, but we would also never be able to prove the contrary, either. We would purely and simply have recourse to the deep chasm of absolute skepticism, in this respect.

Besides, since it is necessary to proceed in an orderly manner beginning from the first indubitable certainty, and since the latter resides in the certainty of the existence of my thinking self, and in the subjective knowledge that I acquire of its nature in this way, it is impossible to constitute a science that is objectively certain, other than by beginning with a science that is subjectively certain; and if an objective science ever becomes possible, it will have to arise, in accordance with the order, from within the necessities of my subjective science itself.

The following is therefore incontestable from now on: first, I know at least something of my soul, since I know with certainty, if not all its properties, at least some of them;[119] second, I know it apart from the body—that its nature is known clearly and distinctly only by excluding the body; for that reason I necessarily represent it to myself as constituted by my thought alone; that it is impossible to argue in any way against the internal certainty of this knowledge; and that since the latter sums up all the science that is certain and possible at the present stage of the inquiry, the objections addressed to it could not be drawn from any science whatever, but from the unknown, that is, from a lack of knowledge; and that these objections are therefore null a priori, as is this unknown rejected as outside my knowledge. Certainly there are properties still unknown in me,[120] properties that may even remain unknown forever.[121] But they would not prevent me from knowing what is my soul,[122] in the same way that "if there were several properties in a triangle that no mathematician would ever know, they would not prevent one from knowing what is a triangle."[123] Moreover, I am assured from now on—if this science is valid—that these unknown properties cannot be repugnant to the ideas that this science has given me about the nature of my soul and that if even I discovered properties in my soul that would be repugnant to it, they would not be arising from its nature but from its composition with an adverse nature.[124] It is equally impossible, for any conceivable rational human science, that the knowledge I have of my nature and of the properties that I actually perceive can be deduced from unknown properties that can be in me, since knowledge of the former necessarily precedes knowledge of the latter in the order of reasons:[125] "it is certain that the knowledge of my being thus taken precisely in no way depends on things whose existence is yet unknown to me."[126] Therefore my soul is definitely posited as independent from these unknown properties, from now on, *for my science*. And that alone suffices. Science has to account only for itself. It must preoccupy itself with nothing other than what is necessarily inscribed, according to the order of reasons, in the sphere of certainty that is the sphere of complete certainty for me. Similarly, in geometry one cannot argue against demonstrated properties from unknown and undemonstrated properties; one does not worry about knowing whether things correspond objectively with the properties thus demonstrated, but only about the dependence of reasons that allows one to pass from the certain knowledge of one notion to the certain knowledge of another.

In philosophical science, however, it will happen that a reason will be seized at one point on the chain—the veracious God who will suddenly invest the truths obtained according to the order of reasons with an objective validity. That is where the superiority of this science over geometry resides: it is capable of drawing the demonstration of its own objective validity from itself, a validity that geometry postulates for itself, without having established it and without even having put it into question. In the same way that the Cogito, in opposition with geometric truth, immediately drew the certainty of its certainty from its content, philosophical science, by means of its internal development, will draw from the subjective necessity imposed by the order of reasons, the objective validity that will sublimate it as the truth of the thing. And, certainly, philosophical science will be wholly transformed in this way, since it will be completely metamorphosed as the truth of the thing; but in itself, in its internal certainty, it will suffer no modification, no more than in geometry the body of truths already demonstrated is modified by the addition of a new truth, discovered by virtue of the bond that links it to prior truths.

10. The Absolute Identity of Consciousness and of the Consciousness of Consciousness in the Cogito. The Cogito, an Indivisible Intuition of a Singular Thought

By abstracting away everything that is not simply pure thought in me, I allowed my mind to focus on itself and only on itself. This process of analysis and abstraction is to be identified with the process of reflection, because reflection, being only the attention of the soul restricted to itself, can only occur by abstracting away what is not purely soul. It was natural that this process ended up with the Cogito as reflective knowledge: *mens in se conversa*.[127] It was equally inevitable that, pushed to the extreme, it ended up with the Cogito as pure intellection, since it belongs to the definition of the reflection with which the soul could not have dealings, except with it alone.[128] Finally this reflection, like all attentiveness, is no more than the concentration of the whole capacity of intelligence on a single point that then becomes the sharp focus of light, the other points ceasing, or almost ceasing, to receive the light, and finding themselves rejected in the night, meaning in a void of knowledge.[129]

But in order to be conscious of one's thought, must one not first think, and then think that one is thinking? "But how can you be conscious, since to be conscious is to think? And, in order to think that you are conscious, you must go on to another thought; and thus you no longer are thinking of the thing you were thinking earlier; and thus you are not conscious that you are thinking, but of having thought."[130] My thought before the Cogito is doomed to escape irretrievably the actual intuition of itself in the Cogito, and the Cogito is then no more than a mirage.

Descartes' reply to this objection, whose origin stems from the Sophists, at first appears as an ad hominem reply, that only half reveals the thought of the philosopher, at least as it is reported to us by Burman, his interlocutor.

"To be conscious," he replies, "is to think and to reflect on one's thoughts; but it is false that this reflection cannot occur while the previous thought is there, since the soul can think of several things at the same time, persevere in its thought, reflect on its thoughts as often as it likes, and be conscious of each of them in this way." Descartes therefore seems to agree that thinking and thinking that one is thinking are two really different things, and that the consciousness of the Cogito, as reflective consciousness, can only be saved by the possibility of thinking two really distinct things at the same time. Moreover, this "at the same time" itself would be some time of greater or lesser duration, and not rigorously an instant. That is the reason for the two correlative propositions: a) "It is false that thought occurs instantaneously, since all our actions are in time, and I can be said to be continuing to persevere in the same thought for some time"; and b) "It is not true that our mind can only think of one thing at a time; no doubt it cannot think of many things at the same time, but it can still conceive more than one—for example, I am now conceiving and I am thinking at the same time that I am speaking and that I am eating."[131] Similarly, an eye can see several things during the same instant.

If these texts were held literally, the problem would not be resolved. For if the reflective consciousness of the Cogito is only explicable insofar as we can think several thoughts at the same time, and if consequently we recognize that the Cogito has the character of complex, and not simple thought—if it is several thoughts at the same time—its certainty is ipso facto compromised. Its certainty was absolute, in fact, only because it was given as noncomposite, simple, and unitary, a thought separated from others, self-sufficient, and because of this, grasped in an instantaneous intuition, which is itself indivisible. Moreoever, Descartes observes that in optics if I can see several objects at the same time, it is because I see them confusedly, for in order to see an object clearly and *distinctly,* one must, on the contrary, concentrate all one's vision on it alone.[132] And he tells us that it is the same for thought. The more the light of the mind is dispersed on a greater number of objects at the same time, the more confused is the knowledge; on the other hand, the more it concentrates on a smaller number, the more distinct is the knowledge.[133] That is what one could call the principle of conservation of the same quantity of thought, a principle to which Malebranche will accord an important role.[134]

Consequently, it is possible to think several thoughts at the same time, but on the condition that the thought is confused. The Cogito would therefore be a relatively confused thought, in this case. Besides, since the intuition of a single particular thought is always clearer than the knowledge of several, the Cogito, as the knowledge of several thoughts at the same time, would be less clear and distinct than the thought on which it reflects, which is not double, but simple; and generally, reflective or philosophical consciousness would be less distinct by a degree than nonreflective consciousness—which is contrary to the hypothesis. The Cogito, being an absolutely clear and distinct thought, can therefore be only the intuition of a single thought, and not the confused knowledge of several. Science, having clear and distinct ideas as object, must, in fact, always insure that the mind has only a single thought at each instant, and not several.[135] That is why science requires *perspicacity* first, "which consists in grasping the distinct intuition of each thing *(res singulas distincte intuendo).*"[136] It requires "one to become accustomed to embrace by thought such simple things so few at a time that one thinks one never knows anything of which one does not have an intuition as distinct as the intuition one knows most distinctly of all"[137]— for example, the movement at the same time of the extremities of a stick or the indivisible instant in which the weight raises one side of a balance and lowers the other.[138] And it is evident that my thought cannot embrace anything so simple and so unique as my single thought itself, and that the Cogito, which is preeminently a scientific truth, since it is the first and fundamental scientific truth, could not escape the condition that governs the scientific knowledge of all truth.

It is true that science also has as object to conceive distinctly, as much as possible, several things at the same time *(plura simul quantum fieri potest distincte concipere).*[139] Science is less the isolated knowledge of each link than the knowledge of their linkage.[140] Deduction, although constructed from singular intuitions, aims at this linkage. And science, in addition to perspicacity, requires *shrewdness,* which is the art of discovering the links between several terms. Since it claims clear and distinct knowledge of a multitude, it would not be satisfied with memory for joining past intuitions with present intuitions because remembered intuitions are neither intuitions nor items of evidence. From this stems the process of repeated enumerations designed to suppress time and substitute for memory the actual vision of all the items of evidence perceived at the same time in their rationality.[141] This is a process whose success is conceivable only because in themselves all the truths are linked together outside time, at every instant. But if an intuition can grasp clearly and distinctly several things at the same time, there would be no reason to refuse to see the Cogito as a clear and distinct intuition of several thoughts at the same time.

There remains, however, the task of resolving a seemingly serious contradiction between the definition of the conditions of clear and distinct knowledge and the definition of science. Can the necessity for all clear and distinct knowledge to be the intuition of a single object at one instant be reconciled with the definition of science as clear and distinct knowledge of a multitude of objects at the same instant? Surely that can be done if the result of science is precisely, after having isolated each nature, to discover the rational link that reduces the plurality to the singular unity of their *ratio.* The mind is not dispersed once it captures the absolute nature that, at a *single point,* delivers to it the secret of an infinity of cases. In brief, the indivisibility of truth[142] establishes the single intuition of all truths, which is only the intuition of a single truth.[143] No doubt, this single intuition of the whole set at an instant remains just an ideal for man, memory and the movement of thought in time never being completely reduced to zero by the repetition of long series of terms.[144] Still, the indivisibility of the whole is equivalent for completed science to the indivisibility of each singular lower reason of incompleted science, in the same way that the indivisibility of the instant as elementary time corresponds to the indivisibility of eternity, which is beyond time.[145] And the vision of the multitude in clear and distinct intuition is possible only when the multiple reabsorbs itself in a superior indivisible unity, which is then the true singular object of the intuition.

The solution of this apparent contradiction leads us again to conclude that, within these conditions, the Cogito could not be the clear and distinct knowledge of several thoughts. In fact, a result of the above is that science can only know distinctly several things at the same time after having known them separately, clearly, and distinctly, and after having discovered their rational link, in order to reduce them finally to an indivisible unity by means of this link, such that the knowledge of this ordered plurality becomes an instantaneous and indivisible intuition of a singular thing, as was each of the successive items of knowledge of the relative natures taken one at a time.[146]

Consequently, the Cogito cannot be clear and distinct knowledge of several thoughts at the same time except by a decomposition that allows one to grasp by a distinct intuition each of the ideas it encompasses and their link, ending up with an instantaneous intuition of the singular reason that would establish their indivisible unity beyond their plurality. But this cannot amount to anything: the Cogito is itself the final element that is unable to be broken up, the element on which the analysis rests definitively; it is therefore necessarily a simple and singular thought immediately grasped as such in an instantaneous and indivisible intuition.

Thus, in virtue of the assimilation established by Descartes between the spiritual light and material light, in virtue of the *Dioptrics,* in virtue of the scientific—meaning completely clear and distinct— character of the Cogito, in virtue of the completely indefeasible conditions of all clear and distinct knowledge—and we are concerned, in this case, with the most clear and most distinct knowledge of all—the Cogito, as reflective consciousness, must be a radically simple and unitary thought, not the vision of two different thoughts at the same time. The "I think that I think" that characterizes the reflexivity of the Cogito therefore does not imply any internal duality between my thought insofar as it is *thought* by my thought, and my thought insofar as it *thinks* my thought. Within the Cogito, consciousness and consciousness of consciousness are identical. From this it results that there is no difference between the thought that precedes the Cogito and the Cogito itself, between (nonreflective) consciousness and (reflective) consciousness of consciousness. It is therefore not necessary to conceive that my antecedent thought perseveres in time—in the sense that one understands by this that it continues into the following thought—in order that the following thought is assured, in the Cogito, of effectively thinking the true thought, such as it was in the preceding thought, and such as it is naturally when I do not expressly think that I am thinking.

This philosophical reply, which consists in refuting the objection by means of the identity of the subject and proper object of all thought, has been formulated by Descartes on another occasion, when replying to Bourdin: "The first thought, whatever it is, by which we perceive something, does not differ more from the second, by which we perceive that we have already perceived it, than this second differs from a third, by which we perceive that we have already perceived that we have perceived it."[147]

Spinoza, and above all Fichte, would reply in the same way, by positing the identity of the idea with the idea of the idea, or the identity of the thought with the thought of the thought.[148] And this reply amounts to saying that there is no real difference between the thought and the thought of the thought, but only a difference of reason.

Burman's objection implicitly converts thought into a thing, introducing a real distinction between the thought on which one reflects and the reflecting thought, a real distinction that is allowable only between thought and body, or generally, between two different substances.[149] And it is evident that there is no difference of this kind between the thought and the thought of the thought. No doubt there are differences between them. The definition of consciousness itself implies this difference: "to be conscious is to think and to reflect on one's thoughts."[150] Similarly, one can note that "since the action by which one believes is different from the one by which one knows that one believes, the two actions often occur one without the other."[151] Philosophy or science, which is only reflective consciousness, is itself different from the ignorance that is the absence of reflection. Further, philosophy is often absent from the human mind, which remains most of the time in a state of unreflectiveness. Moreover, it is impossible to deny the fundamental identity between what is explicitly in science and what is implicitly in our ignorant minds. That is why science or Cartesian philosophy can, in spite of its novelty, appear simultaneously as something "very ancient, since nature itself has engraved and printed it on our minds."[152] Hence, once this science is revealed to us, it imposes on us, in spite of ourselves, the consciousness that we possessed it already from all time.[153] That is because the difference between the degrees of consciousness of a single thought do not make it different thoughts. Thus my belief, with or without the express consciousness that I believe, remains the same belief. The difference between nonreflective thought and reflective thought is not, in fact, a difference in itself, but only a difference for my thought. And "a distinction constructed by thought" is neither a real distinction nor a modal distinction, but a distinction of reason.[154]

Then, in what does this difference consist that, although a distinction of reason, is an important difference, since it separates philosophy from nonphilosophy, science from nonscience, and the Cogito from ordinary thought? It is completely based, as we have seen, on the abstraction of everything that is not properly my own thought, which allows to concentrate the light of our mind on it alone. Thus my thought appears in a maximum light that renders it distinctly explicit for me as consciousness of self. One can therefore state, with respect to this, that it is the thought that perseveres through time (which is not to say that this perseverence does not imply as many creative acts and as many distinct founding institutions as there are instants in this duration); but this thought is here at its most luminous point, instead of being obscure and confused, as it was before abstraction and attentive concentration. From this it also results that within the Cogito the thought of the thought is but one thought and not two thoughts, for, borrowing a comparison inspired by the *Dioptrics,* an object may be illuminated twice as much, or seen twice as well, due to the fact that one has concentrated twice as much light on it, but this object remains one, and does not become two objects. Thus, reflection on oneself must not be understood as an act by which thought, tearing away from itself, then turns on itself in order to contemplate itself from the outside, as if dividing itself in two; reflection must be understood as an operation by which thought detaches itself from what is not itself's (by means of abstraction), in order to restrict its field of vision to itself alone.[155] "To turn one's sight on oneself" is for Descartes a metaphor designating the concentration of all my light on a sharp point—myself—such that I *myself become better illuminated* and consequently *become clearer to myself.* There is no real division into two things, but a better vision of what I am by a condensation of my own light. That is why the consciousness of consciousness, immediately perceiving that "internal consciousness always precedes its acquisition,"[156] already encloses the knowledge that expressly constitutes the latter. It perceives that the light was already there. This type of reflectivity will be Spinoza's.

The reply to Burman that one can have several thoughts at the same time and that thought is not accomplished in an instant, perhaps may be reconciled with the contrary assertion of the *Rules* that there is only one distinct thought per instant and that clear and distinct thoughts are accomplished in an instant. Has not Descartes declared, in his physics, that no movement is accomplished in an instant, but that all movements are composed of elementary, instantaneous, therefore nontemporal movements?[157] The same concepts preside on the true science of physical things and the science of clear and distinct thought. The *Rules* seems to testify that thought is, like movement, amenable to notions inspired by analytic geometry, in contrast with our current perceptions of things, but intended to account for them. The indivisible instants of elementary movements, whose summation imparts real movement, meaning temporal movement, do not each admit of any assignable course and are ultimately rests;[158] in the same fashion, the instantaneous intuitions, whose sum constitutes my thought in time, are nontemporal rests that are to be contrasted with "the continuous movement of thought,"[159] which is "always temporal like my actions." That is why, according to this point of view, several apparently contradictory languages are possible, in the same way that several languages are possible in physics with respect to movement. First, my thought appears as a continuous duration that is infinitely divisible; but in concentrating itself on itself by means of attention and abstraction, it perceives itself as intelligence, a pure light grasped by an instantaneous, indivisible, nontemporal intuition. It sees that time is essentially foreign to its constitutive act.[160] Repeating this intuition, my thought can make the Cogito persevere through time. God creates my existence at each indivisible instant, and this continual repetition of these indivisible creative acts gives rise to the duration of my existence, a duration that I represent to myself as length, an indefinitely divisible quantity. Similarly, God creates an indivisible elementary movement at each instant, and by continually repeating this creation, he gives rise to what I represent to myself as a temporal movement describing an infinitely divisible course. And similarly, my thought in time is a summation of instantaneous, indivisible, nontemporal intuitions.

The passage to the Cogito is consequently only the free establishment, in my instantaneous intuition, of a thought (my consciousness) that is identical to the previous thought (nonreflective), but more distinct than it. However, this identity does not prevent the previous thought from being entirely abolished, since duration is identical to existence and since the past is no longer. Certainly, I can, in the very instant in which I institute the Cogito, evoke the previous thought through memory—which, because of a lack of spiritual concentration, would not expressly be perceived as such. For I can think of several things at the same instant, once I am not thinking them absolutely distinctly. But this comparison through memory clearly does not belong to the Cogito itself, which is a clear and distinct intuition, and which is only so because of the singularity of what it knows actually. I know myself in this present instant as existing insofar as I think, and *I necessarily conceive in this way that my nature can be nothing other than pure consciousness. I therefore know in this way that, in the previous instant, my consciousness could not be anything other than the one I represent to myself actually as necessarily constituting my whole nature.* I therefore do not need to preserve my previous (nonreflective) consciousness in order to know that it is the same consciousness that I represent to myself actually as constituting my being.

Such is at least the necessary condition of the Cogito in this location on the chain of reasons, which like all scientific chains in the process of being forged, requires that each link be an intuition separate from a singular thing.

11. Applications in the *Principles,* with respect to the Determination of Particular Substances, of the Rules of Real and Modal Distinctions Deduced in *Meditation II;* Particular Material Substances and Particular Spiritual Substances

The knowledge of the nature of my soul as pure intelligence, the second truth established according to the order of reasons, has allowed me to discover, in all certainty, the conditions that render possible the clear and distinct knowledge of the essence of a substance and thus to establish the universally valid *criterium* of all substantiality—or what comes to the same thing, to discover the real distinction—and to discover also at the same time the *criterium* of the accident. The use of these criteria for the determination of thought and extension as substances and for their real distinction, as well as for the attribution of their respective modes, does not occur until much later in the chain of reasons, during *Meditation VI,* when what is at stake is to prove the real distinction between soul and body, once the necessities of our understanding have been reendowed with their objective validity, and the truths of my science have been transformed into the truth of the thing (since *Meditation III).*

But does not the rule of the determination of substantiality include more than that? Since it is capable of allowing us to discover any substantiality, any real distinction, must we not affirm that there is actually substance and real distinction everywhere the rule is applicable? In addition to the clear and distinct knowledge of universal substances, thought and extension, does it not impart the means to make pronouncements that are no less clear and distinct, no less indubitable and certain, on particular substances as such, whether physical or psychical—in brief, to perceive real distinctions between a *multitude* of particular physical substances, as well as between a *multitude* of individual psychical substances?

However, this application and the formulation of this application are not evoked in the *Meditations,* which is devoted to metaphysics only and which has no other task than to establish the real distinction between the soul and body, and to establish rigorously the knowledge of the substantiality of the *res cogitans* and of the *res extensa.*

But the problem ought to be necessarily posed once one is no longer dealing with pure metaphysics but with physics, meaning a science whose primary mission is to account for the different substances that are located in the material world. That is precisely the object of the *Principles,* which deals with "examining generally how the whole universe is composed; then, particularly, what is the nature of this earth and all the bodies that are found commonly around it, such as air, water, fire, the loadstone, and other minerals."[161] This is the task that occupies the second, third, and fourth parts of the work. The first part, which announces the truths of metaphysics, not in and for themselves as in the *Meditations,* but only as principles that allow the establishment of physical science, could not fail to envision the *criterium* of substantiality from the point of view of the eventual determination of the particular physical substances that constitute the central object of the inquiry, even though there exists, in reality, but a single extended substance of which they are but modes. And, by means of a natural parallel, it also poses the problem of particular psychical substances (individual souls), even though this problem does not fit in the sequence.

The process that serves to establish the substantiality of a being by excluding elements that can and must be separated from it, outside its idea, in order that we may conceive it clearly and distinctly, is then presented without ambiguity as allowing one to pass from the conception of created universal substances, *thought* and *extension,* to the conception of created particular substances, whether they are individual souls or different bodies (wax, stone, wood, etc.)

With respect to bodies, we can conceive of such substances when we can think each of them clearly and distinctly, by excluding the rest of extended substance from their idea. For example, what establishes in me the singular substance of a body, such as wax or stone, is that I can think clearly and distinctly of this part of extension by excluding all the other parts from it: "Two substances are really distinct from one another from the sole fact that we can conceive the one clearly and distinctly without thinking of the other. . . . That is why from the fact that we all now have the idea of an extended and corporeal substance, although we do not yet know clearly whether such a thing exists in the world, we can conclude that it may exist, because we have an idea of it, and in case it does exist, whatever portion we can demarcate [in it—M. G.] by our thought must be really distinct from its other parts."[162] In brief, the exclusion of one of the two parts of the extension that we can each think of clearly and distinctly, by means of this exclusion, itself establishes a real distinction between these two parts, which constitutes them as substances in our eyes. For "real distinction is properly speaking found between two or more substances."[163] The determination of particular material substances therefore closely imitates the determination of universal substances (intellectual nature in general, extension): we conceive the latter as substances in virtue of their reciprocal exclusion, which allows us to think them clearly and distinctly, and in the same way we conceive really distinct substances in extended substance when we can think them clearly and distinctly as extended beings by exclusion from the rest of universally extended substance. Under these conditions, a certain mode of the universal substance of bodies, itself diversified by an infinity of lower modes, may be considered as a substance in contrast with the other modes of this substance that we reject outside it, in order to have a clear and distinct knowledge of it.

Thus wax and stone are simple modes of extension, on the one hand, but on the other hand, each of these modes (for example, wax, an extended mode considered as the unity of various modes or properties that are the properties of wax) appears as a substance with respect to the rest of extension. In fact, we can think of wax clearly and distinctly by excluding all other modalities of extension from it, meaning all the "geometric variations" that do not belong to it, and that belong to stone, iron, wood, etc. Each of these substantial modes appears as really separated from the other, a stable element that accounts for, without resort to the rest of extended substance, the various lower modalities that are related to it as something identical and permanent, which we call a substance. Thus we understand by the substance *wax* the subsistence of a particular mode of extension, under the various lower geometric variations that constitute the properties of wax (degree of hardness and elasticity, malleability, coefficient of liquifaction, weight, a stable relation between the variation of the different shapes stemming from the variation of physical actions exerted on the body, etc.). This mode, which is immutable under all these changes, limits the sphere of these changes, the degree of their possible amplitude, etc. The set of these changing lower modes is related to the substance wax, which is an immutable mode, in the same way that the modes of extension in general are related to the extended substance. They cannot be conceived without it, but it can be conceived without them, being the *quid proprium* that I always recognize behind their metamorphoses. And, of course, I cannot know the wax without these changing properties by which it reveals itself. But I can know it through these, only because I understand through it that these properties are its properties and that they express it.

As the immutability of a mode of extension that can present lower modifications, the substance of wax is nothing more than the subsistence of a certain quantity of extension under the diversity of its geometric aspects. In brief, the unity and identity of a physical body, by which we identify it as being such a substance, is the capacity it possesses to preserve *a same quantity* under various aspects, adding in length what it loses in width or depth, and inversely: "The one and same body, retaining the same size, may be extended in many different ways, sometimes being greater in length and less in width or depth, and sometimes, on the contrary, being greater in width and less in length."[164] The particular substance of a body is therefore nothing more than a *numerical invariant,* which thus renders it independent from the rest and which constitutes it as a principle of explanation autonomous from the various aspects it assumes. This conception is the basis of the Cartesian theory of molecules or corpuscles, and of the Malebranchian theory of "configurations" and "shapes." It is an extremely modern conception, which is the seed of the theory of specific weight.[165] One sees that, in spite of the archaic vocabulary, we are miles away from Scholasticism.

In this way the apparent contrast between articles 63 and 64 of the *Principles* is explained. According to article 63, I have a distinct notion of extension insofar as I conceive it as substance of bodies. According to article 64, I can also conceive it distinctly as a mode or attribute of the particular substance of a body, for example, when I consider that the same body with the same magnitude can be extended in various ways. Then if I conceive these various modes of extension by separating them from the particular substance of which they are modes, I cease to have a distinct conception of them, taking them as things subsisting in themselves and confusing the idea we ought to have of substance with the idea we ought to have of its properties.[166] Article 63 is concerned with universal substances, particularly extension. Article 64 is concerned with particular substances of various kinds of bodies. In the first case the modes of extension are explained by the universal extended substance. In the second case, the various modes of extension that wax can take are explained by the substance, wax. It is the constitutive numerical invariant of the substance, wax, that makes us be able to think it clearly and distinctly apart from the other modes of extension and that, accounting for all the geometric modalities which it can include, allows me to understand them and at the same time to understand wax—therefore to know wax—on which they are dependent and which remains immutable under their transformations. If, on the contrary, we consider them apart from this substance, we would believe that they could subsist without it, although they are subordinate to this invariant that makes them what they are. We would then be confusing the idea that we ought to have of the substance, wax, and the idea of its properties. That is the error of the empiricists who reduce wax to its external properties. They believe that they know wax only by its changing properties (by the sensible changes that are the obscure expression, in my composite nature, of its real geometric variations), when it is through the knowledge of the geometric invariant, which remains in spite of the changes in its variable forms and coordinates them, that it is possible for us to recognize it as identical, and consequently, to know it as wax.

One finds in this indistinct application of the concept of substance to created universal substances—extension and thought—as well as to particular extended substances that are modes in reality, but that are thinkable clearly and distinctly in abstraction from the other modes, the same absence of univocity as in the indistinct application of this concept to God, as well as to extension (and thought). In reality, God is alone worthy of substantiality, because he is the only being to be self-conceived in the full sense of the word, the only being to cause itself and to sustain itself. He can forgo extension, while extension cannot forgo him. However, a created substance, although it is unable to be conceived absolutely by itself, since it depends on God, which causes and sustains it, does not need any other created substance to exist and to be conceived. It can therefore be conceived without its modes, but they cannot be conceived without it. It can therefore, in this manner, be conceived by itself and be given the title of second-order substantiality.[167] Moreover, the particular substances could not be substances in the sense in which extension is, for they are modes of it, and they cannot be conceived without it, while it can be conceived without them. But they can be given a third-order substantiality, insofar as being modes, they have no need of other modes of the universal substance to which they are related, in order to be conceived clearly and distinctly.

According to the *Principles,* it seems that one can go in this way up to the individual substance of each soul; and Descartes expressly establishes an exact parallel between the determination of particular material substances, beginning with extended substance, and the determination of psychical substances, beginning with the thinking substance. What establishes this individual substantiality for my knowledge, he asserts, is the possibility that I have to think of my soul excluding any other thought from it, in the same way that I have been able to exclude extension from it: *"Similarly* because each perceives in himself that he thinks and that in thinking he can exclude *all other substance,* whether *thinking* or extended, from himself or from his soul, we can *also* conclude that each of us, thus considered, is *really* distinct *from all other thinking substance* and all other corporeal substance."[168]

Thus in the same way that I conceive, clearly and distinctly, wax, wood, or stone as different physical substances, by excluding the rest from the proper and invariable extension of each (actually conserving the same total quantity of magnitude under the variations of magnitude in the three dimensions), I conceive the individual soul as a distinct substance really distinct from any other psychical substance, by excluding it from everything that, relating to thinking substance in general, does not belong to its own thought and that can be excluded from it without rendering obsure and confused the knowledge I have of it. Correlatively, articles 63 and 64 are concerned with thought as well as extension. If I have a distinct notion of thinking insofar as I conceive it as constituting the nature of the soul, I can also conceive it distinctly as a mode or attribute of the particular substance of a soul when I consider that a soul can have various thoughts. Then, if I conceive these various thoughts by separating them from the particular substance of which they are modes, I cease to have a distinct conception of them by taking them as things that remain by themselves—thus confusing the idea that we ought to have of the substance with the idea that we ought to have of its properties.[169] Thus we see Descartes describe the substance of wax and the substance of the soul in the same way: "Everything falling within the domain of taste, smell, sight, touch, and hearing is changed, and yet *the same wax remains.* . . ." Whatever are the infinite variations of extension the imagination teaches us that the wax can receive, "it is *the same* [*wax*—M. G.] that I see, that I touch, that I imagine, and it is *the same* that I knew from the beginning."[170] "The human soul . . . is a pure substance, for even if all its accidents change, as for example if it conceives of certain things, wills others, and senses others, etc., it is always *the same soul.*"[171]

Article 63 is concerned with the thinking substance in general (as it is concerned with extended substance in general). Article 64 is concerned with particular thinking substances, namely, individual souls (as it is concerned with particular material substances, namely, the different kinds of bodies). In the first case, we account for all the possible modes of thought through the thinking substance in general; in the second case, all my possible thoughts are explained through my soul, as an individual substance, exclusive of all other individual substance. Descartes' reflection, which we have already explained, is then illuminated anew: "By spending sufficient time on this meditation [on the Cogito], one acquires little by little a very clear, and so to speak, intuitive knowledge of the intellectual nature in general; this is the idea that, considered without limitation, represents God to us, and considered as limited, is the idea of an angel or a human soul."[172] We know our soul as individual substance by thinking it clearly and distinctly by exclusion of everything that, as intellectual nature, is not perceived as belonging to our own intellectual nature.

In this fashion arise the comparisons that Descartes sometimes draws between the soul and particular physical substances. Thus he declares to Mesland that "he places no other difference between the soul and its ideas than the difference between a piece of wax and the various shapes it can assume."[173] Moreover, there is a numerical invariant—or its equivalent—in each soul, namely, the conservation of the same quantity of thought through all the changes. We should note to what extent the theory of attentiveness is modeled on a physical theory: in the same fashion that all corporeal substance preserves the same quantity of extension, whether it is contracted or condensed, or whether it is dilated or rarified,[174] each spiritual substance, each soul, preserves the same quantity of thought, whether it is contracted or condensed by attention, whether it is dilated or rarified by distraction.[175]

However, although each corporeal substance has its own invariant of extension, Descartes has not asserted that the invariant of thought is not the same in each spiritual substance. He categorically asserts the contrary, in opposition to Spinoza and Leibniz (this is not merely an affectation of modesty; it emphasizes the decisive role of the method). For Descartes, every human mind has the same capacity for intelligence, and all differences arise from whether we employ it better or worse.[176] It is true that elsewhere he asserts that men are containers with different capacities and that some are so small that "a few drops of water are sufficient to fill them up." But there the subject is not souls alone, but souls united substantially with a body.[177]

However that may be, this parallel and analogy between individual psychical substances and particular substances of material bodies immediately raises some serious objections. To proceed from the concept of universal substance to the particularity of my individual substance seems to contradict the spirit of Cartesian philosophy and the legitimate process that begins with *my thought,* as a substance in the epistemic sense of the word, captured immediately in the Cogito. It is the same for the parallel between the relations of the extended substance and particular physical substances, with the relation of the thinking substance in general and my substance in particular. Other than that Descartes always goes from the particular to the universal, there is no analogy between the corporeal substances, which are not real substances, but perishable modes, and souls, which are genuine substances and, as such, naturally indestructible. A substance is what depends only on God, without the help of any other created thing; if my soul fits this definition, corporeal substances, which are only modes, exist only by their interdependence with the set of other modes on which their appearance and disappearance depend. The extended substance in general is the only corporeal being that depends only on God and that shares indestructibility, and hence substantiality, with my soul. That is what Descartes specifies in his *Summary of the Meditations:* "Generally all substances, meaning all things that cannot exist without being created by God, are by their nature incorruptible. . . . Body taken in general is a substance; that is why it does not perish. But the human body, however much it differs from other bodies, is only formed and composed by a certain configuration of members and by other similar accidents; whereas the human soul is not thus composed of accidents, but is a pure substance. . . . From this it follows that the human body may easily perish, but the mind or soul of man (I do not distinguish between these) is immortal by its own nature."[178]

One must note, however, that the case for material bodies, especially simple bodies, is not the same as the case for the human body; the physical world presents, in fact, a series of bodies that have the property of remaining the same *indefinitely* under the constant change of their aspects or their form. They therefore have some measure of the indestructibility of genuine substances *in fact.* That is why common opinion has given them the title of substance. Whether it is cold or hot, liquid or solid, wax *"remains"* and remains *"the same."* And if some agents can destroy it effectively by decomposing it, wax as a species *remains* in the universe. Which is to say that the simple bodies or molecules constituting the first elements, although arising from the division of extension, are perishable *as a rule,* conserving a true indestructibility *in fact.* There are therefore, in addition to genuine substances that are naturally unperishable (souls), things—namely, the various kinds of bodies—that, although naturally perishable, have a permanence in fact and an indestructibility sufficient for us to treat them as substances. And the determination of these substances is brought about according to the universal rule that allows us for certain to distinguish among our ideas those that are ideas of modes from those that are ideas of substances.

The method of the determination of substances by means of exclusion, a criterion of real separation, is drawn from a process by which, beginning from the Cogito, the rational science of my nature is constituted and is validated. This method is the process itself, clearly and distinctly perceived, expressly stated as a universal rule applicable to ideas, striving to discern which of our ideas represent substances and which represent modes.

And it is only insofar as particular material substances are justifiable according to this rule, in the same fashion as individual souls are, that the comparison can be instituted among them; and in this way the comparison is limited, leaving intact the fundamental difference that makes them opposite. In fact, the basis of the application of the rule is not the same in both cases. In the case of my soul, the rule was produced at the same time as it was applied, since I saw that it was impossible to posit myself as a certain truth in science without excluding from myself everything that was not pure thought. I perceived in this way that 1) I could not know myself and posit myself with certainty except by knowing myself and positing myself as self-sufficient, meaning as substance; 2) that it was necessary that everything known clearly and distinctly apart from the rest be substance ipso facto. My science having *ab ovo* annulled a priori everything not in me (by metaphysical doubt) there was nothing left for it posited outside me that I ought really exclude. I alone am known; I alone exist. Do there exist other substances outside of me, whether corporeal or spiritual, that I ought to exclude? I know not; I cannot speak of this, and I cannot presently oppose my being to theirs. I therefore attain a truly absolute self, which is absolutely pure at the same time, for it could not be posited except as pure intelligence. One sees how little this self is individual; for the "I" of the individual implies the "you" of the other, that *I exclude* from myself certainly, insofar as I posit myself as a substance, but that *I am positing,* at the same time (outside of myself). One sees by this to what extent Descartes is at the ends of a transcendental intersubjectivity. My self does not have to detach itself from a set to which it belongs. It is originally affirmable alone, *for science.* Nevertheless, I already know that *if ever there existed other spiritual beings,* I would have to exclude them from myself, as they have to exclude me from them.

If the *criterium* of real distinction, consisting in the possibility of knowing myself clearly and distinctly without thinking of the rest, cannot serve toward the determination of individuals as long as I do not know whether anything exists outside of me, on the other hand, once (divine veracity having guaranteed the objective validity of my clear and distinct ideas and the informational value of my sensations) I know that there really are other men outside of me, I would know them as individuals then, by excluding them from me, and by knowing that each of these souls is self-sufficient and excludes all other souls from itself as validly as I exclude them from myself.

But this reciprocal exclusion of individual spiritual substances in virtue of their self-sufficiency does not occur in virtue of a numerical invariant present in them, as it happens for corporeal substances, even if each of them has in itself this numerical invariant that constitutes the conservation of the same quantity of thought. Indispensable as a criterion of substantiality with respect to a divisible body within divisible extension, the numerical invariant has no role to play with respect to knowing or establishing indivisible substances that are in no way relatively autonomous parts of a divisible substance. I acknowledge these indivisible substances as substances, recognizing in them the principle of autonomy that I know in myself. The innate idea of spiritual substance, which is identical with the clear and distinct idea of my self, and which renders possible the perception of their existence outside of me as being that of intelligent substances, by allowing me to understand them, will be, in this case, the foundation of the application of the rule of reciprocal exclusion that allows their knowledge as individuals. The principle of permanence and identity, which constitutes the positive reality of substance, is not in fact, for souls, a simple numerical invariant given as a fact, for all thought, being unextended is without parts, and subtracted from quantity and number. It has an indivisible spiritual unity laying the foundation of a natural indestructibility, without which there is no real substance. Individual corporeal substances, having parts, are without intrinsic foundation, and if they are not destroyed, in fact they remain exposed to destruction by nature. If they subsist, it is not in virtue of themselves, but in virtue of the laws of physics and the play of the set of other modes. Thus, on the one hand, the subsistence of the numerical invariant allows one to think of such a body, as long as it persists, by excluding from it all the other modes that are distinct from it, and thus to conceive it as independent, meaning as substance; on the other hand, physics, by revealing that this persistence itself depends on the mechanical agreement of the set of modes of extended substance, assures that the independence of such corporeal substance with respect to the other modes is in the end only apparent. Nevertheless, the factual stability presented by the numerical invariants allows us to conceive the different kinds of bodies as substances and to treat them as if they were substances absolutely. But these are third-order substances, substances according to common opinion, not second-order substances, or substances rigorously.

Given the above, one understands that Descartes can reserve the title of substance *stricto sensu* to the individual souls that are naturally indestructible because of their indivisibility and to extended substance in general, which alone, and in contrast to particular corporeal substances, is naturally unperishable. Correlatively, he will accord real unity to the human body only to the extent that the latter is informed by a soul united to it. In itself it has only a precarious unity, subject to the renewal of its parts.[179]

In the *Principles* Descartes respects this difference, since a body (wax, for example) is said to be substance insofar as it is determined by our thought as *part* of the extended substance that is really distinct from *other parts,* while my soul is called substance insofar as it is determined by *all* thinking as excluding from itself *all other thinking substance* and can thus "be considered as really distinct from all other thinking substance."[180]

These texts from the *Principles* attest to the falsity of the theory of individual substance. Laporte's interpretation, which we have had to avoid, in a sense is explained by this real Cartesian difficulty, by the absence of a link between the concept of general substance and the concept of individual substance. The difficulty cannot be posited for extension. First, there are no true individual extended substances, but only bodies that behave like substances; these bodies, being only modes, are only specifications—they are modes of extension variously extended. But it is not the same for thought and, in certain respects, if one considers the thinking substance in general, the *res cogitans,* it appears as an abstraction with respect to individual substances, for these individual substances are not modes and contain something extra. Moreover, the way in which the Cogito was posited in the certainty of science implies necessarily that one has come upon something that resembles the Kantian "I think" or rather the Fichtean Self, in some respects. And in order to go from the self, as universal condition of all knowledge, to the concrete, individual self, one must *add* something. It is noteworthy that, in his philosophy, Fichte believes impossible the deduction of the individual concept from the finite Self in general: science can only posit a priori the reality of my finite self; one must have recourse to experience in order to determine this self as a concrete individual. As for Spinoza and Leibniz, they establish the individual substance only by setting aside this process belonging to Descartes, which is essentially a process of the critique and consists of positing the thinking self as the necessary residue of a series of eliminations.

The knowledge that we can have of the individual substance (whether material or spiritual) is far from being the first in the order of reasons. Although I capture myself originally only in the self that is mine and that consequently is individual, *in fact,* the Cogito, taken in itself, does not reveal to me that I am an individual substance: it reveals to me that I am a thinking self (identical in each). Indeed, there is no science except for the science of the mathematically necessary. It is therefore not sufficient that the "I" that pronounces the Cogito is at the same time a concrete individual *in fact,* in order that I have a science of this individual as such in this way. In fact, this "I" is also united to a body, but this body does not yet exist as rule for my science. A science of the self as an individual, a person, etc., cannot appear until I am conscious that it is *necessary* that I recognize myself as an individual. Thus I have the science of my own existence once I perceive that it is *impossible* that I do not exist the moment I am thinking and as long as I am thinking. The Cogito imposes on me, secondly, the necessary knowledge of myself as a purely intellectual nature (common to all men), since I perceive, by reflecting on my first reflection, that I know myself clearly and distinctly only by excluding from myself everything extended and everything that is related to extension in me. I see at the same time that in this way I clearly and distinctly know the nature of thought and extension only by their reciprocal exclusion. Thirdly, it is only by another reflection that I can conceive the possibility of a necessary knowledge of my self as an individual substance, by means of my capacity to conceive myself clearly and distinctly by excluding all other thinking substance from myself, because I do not yet know whether any such substance exists. I also perceive that I can know by means of a necessary and certain science a particular corporeal substance as such (using the very attenuated sense of the word *substance* applying to various particular bodies), when I can think of such a part of extension clearly and distinctly by excluding all other parts from it.

Let us add that the substantiality of individual souls and of particular bodies does not figure among the "main points" of the deduction that the *Meditations* takes as its task.

CHAPTER IV

The Cogito: Priority of Knowledge of Soul over Knowledge of Body

1. Immediate Evidence of This Priority in Virtue of the Order. Verification by the Analysis of the Piece of Wax

I exist as a thinking thing; that is the first indubitable truth in the order of reasons. My nature is no other than pure thought and pure intelligence, exclusive of all corporeal element; that is the second truth, flowing immediately from the first truth, according to the order. I therefore know myself, my existence and my essence, while, at the same time, body, rejected as outside of knowledge, and canceled by the evil genius, remains unknown to me in its existence and essence. From this I conclude that body is less easy to know than soul, since soul is known before it in the order of reasons.[1] That is the third truth.

This third truth, resulting immediately from the order, does not need to be demonstrated further. However, there is a great difference between being *convinced* and being *persuaded*.[2] Further, the third truth is a truth of pure understanding to which is opposed a persuasion stemming from my "nature," meaning from my soul united substantially with a body, experiencing through sensation that it composes a whole with it,[3] and deriving, from imagination, a tendency to believe that all my knowledge comes from the senses, that the bodies I can see, touch, feel, are captured directly in this way without the least help of intelligence—that they are known first and consequently better known than soul, which, being incorporeal, cannot not be sensed, touched, or felt, but only thought.[4] The truth therefore goes against "common sense," meaning a set of habits I acquired from birth, for which my nature (in the strict sense) is not directly responsible, but of which it is the indirect cause. And these prejudices draw strength from the power of corporeal impressions to confuse the soul, and the capacity that sensation has to move me and touch me more deeply than pure ideas.[5]

In order to refute this opinion definitively, it is therefore expedient to deliver a verification and to set aside for now the demonstration according to the order, in virtue of the necessary requirements of all valid certainty, to "let go the reins once more" and "allow my mind to roam," by allowing it to be situated provisionally *in the opponent's point of view*. Consequently, we proceed to consider one of these objects that "appear to be outside." We examine what it is about these sensible perceptions that makes them capable, reputedly, of delivering to me, by themselves, immediately, the knowledge of one of these objects.[6] That is the well-known analysis of the piece of wax.[7] It constitutes an anticipation of the general verification that the success of physics will bring to the entire set of metaphysical conclusions.[8]

This verification is decisive, for when following the order of reasons, I had established that the soul is known only by intelligence, having negated body and set aside imagination; and now the analysis of the knowledge of this supposedly given external thing reveals that, far from knowing the external thing through imagination (the soul is negated by the fact that intelligence is set aside), I know it only as an idea of the understanding, meaning through pure thought, having set aside all sensations.[9] Common sense is therefore beaten on its own ground: "That which I thought to see with my eyes I understand only through the faculty of understanding that resides in my mind. Bodies are not known insofar as they are seen or touched, but insofar as they are understood by thought."[10] In this way I know that, since body is known through the intermediary of the soul, knowledge of soul precedes knowledge of body, as the immediate precedes the mediated and the condition precedes what is conditioned. We rediscover here, by another means, the conclusion obtained directly by following the genetic order of reasons.

2. Different Aspects of This Priority

But one finds it considerably enriched and strengthened. First, the privileged position that common sense gives to the knowledge of things falling under imagination is not only abolished, but reversed. Since we conceive everything through intelligence, imagination cannot be of use without intelligence; something like the soul, which is captured only through intelligence, without ever falling under the senses, is confirmed as something more conceivable than any thing else, because of its purely intellectual nature.[11]

The fact that a thing falls under imagination and senses therefore does not constitute a virtue that renders it more easily knowable, but an imperfection that renders it infinitely less capable of being captured in the truth of its existence or essence. In fact, although the organ that allows me to know the existence of soul, namely, intelligence, gives me the soul itself, since it is not really distinct from it, in such a way that this knowledge is posited in all necessity as absolutely certain, the organ that gives me the knowledge of the existence of body, namely, imagination and sensation, not being really distinct from my thought, but from body, immediately gives me nothing more than the existence of my soul, and lets escape the body that it is supposed to allow me to know, by rejecting it outside the circle of the known. The existence of body is therefore a priori necessarily doubtful and is therefore annulled by the evil genius.

Moreover, although the organ that gives me knowledge of the existence of soul (intelligence) is the same organ that gives me clear and distinct knowledge of its essence, the organ that gives me the (problematic) knowledge of the existence of body (imagination and sense) is incapable of giving me knowledge of its essence, which cannot be known clearly and distinctly except through intelligence. From this it results that it is impossible that I am deceived with respect to the essence of soul by the knowledge I derive immediately from its existence, through the intellect, whereas I am necessarily deceived about the essence of body by the problematic knowledge that I derive from its existence, through imagination and sense. Consequently the soul, which is immediately certain of its existence, requires no effort in order to know its essence, since, in order to attain it, it does not need to disencumber itself of the deceptive veils drawn on its true nature by the organ that revealed its existence to it. On the other hand, with respect to the essence of body, I am required through an effort of imagination to lift the sensible habits that give us its existence, but that hide its true nature from us. From this one sees that, if knowledge of soul is more easily acquired than knowledge of body, that is not only because of its priority, but also because of its intrinsic nature; it is because, in opposition to the former, even with respect to its existence, it is radically outside the grasp of sensible knowledge.

But it is also richer, and consequently, it is more distinct. In fact, the more faculties through which I know problematically the existence of bodies, and the more faculties that allow me to know immediately and in all certainty that I exist, the more faculties I can relate to my self as its own modes. The more ways I picture myself as knowing bodies, the better I know myself.

Moreover, since there are infinitely more things in me than things that serve only to know bodies, I can indubitably attribute infinitely more properties to myself than I can attribute problematically to bodies. The absolutely certain knowledge I have of myself is therefore infinitely richer than the uncertain knowledge that I have of bodies.[12] This is an argument that Cartesians will take up again under the simplied form of *Replies to Objections V:* the more attributes of a substance one knows, the more one knows the substance; there is therefore nothing of which we know more attributes than our mind, for the more one knows of other things, the more things one can count in the mind, from the fact that it knows. Thus its nature is more known, meaning more distinctly known, than the nature of any other thing.[13]

This doctrine of the primacy of spiritual knowledge over corporeal knowledge is a most central thesis, since it accomplishes the destruction of certain fundamental principles of Scholasticism: for example, that material things are more easily known than spiritual things and known before them, that all knowledge comes from the senses, that the inference from being to knowledge is valid, and that it is better to know the *quod* before seeking to know the *quid*. By establishing that "the mind considered without the things one commonly attributes to the body is better known than the body without the mind"[14] Descartes introduces at a proper level in the order of reasons the principle stated by the *Rules:* "Nothing can be known before intelligence, for the knowledge of all things depends on intelligence, and not inversely."[15] In this way the principle of mathematism is established, that "the inference from knowledge to being is valid."[16] No doubt, at this point on the chain of reasons, the principle is established only with respect to a subjectively necessary science, whose objective validity is not yet assured. But the essential is already acquired, since, in order to deny the objective validity of this principle, one would have to deny it for all possible human science at the same time. Thus, simply because of the way in which the Cogito was posited, the traditional perspectives with respect to the conditions of any science have been reversed.

However, does not the way in which the demonstration of this principle was drawn beginning with the Cogito itself constitute a surprising paradox? The thesis that soul is more easily known than body is concluded from a reflection on the conditions that allow the deduction of the knowledge of my self as pure intelligence beginning with the Cogito itself, meaning the positing of my existence; Descartes teaches that now that I know *that I am* I have to know *what I am:*[17] "I do not yet know clearly enough what I am *(Quisnam sim ego ille),* I who am certain that I am *(qui jam necessario sum)."*[18] In this case, we are going from the *quod* to the *quid,* in conformity with the Scholastic rule that goes from a given existence to knowledge of essence.[19] Is it not paradoxical, under these conditions, to draw the inverse rule from the Cogito, a rule that prescribes always going from the *quid* to the *quod,* from knowledge to being? Or at least does not this indicate that a limit must be assigned to the range of application of the rule, not the knowledge of my mind, but the knowledge of things external to it? The rule of the scientific knowledge of external things would therefore be the inverse of the rule of the scientific knowledge of my self: the former would go from idea to thing and the latter from thing to idea.

Truly one could argue that the point of departure for the knowledge of my nature is not my existence, but an item of knowledge—the knowledge I have of my existence—and that besides, if I affirm my existence in all certainty, it is in virtue of the clear and distinct knowledge I have of it; thus the original affirmation of my existence puts into action the principle that the inference from knowledge to being is valid: "The inference from knowledge to being is valid because it is impossible for us to know something if it is not, in fact, as we know it, *that is to say, existent, if we conceive that it exists,* or that it is of this or that nature, if its nature is the only thing known."[20]

But this reply, which expresses the inescapable idealist character of all assertion with respect to internal or external things, does not reply to the difficulty considered here. When a scholastic asserts that the inference from being to knowledge is valid, he means that one must first *know* that something is *(quod)* in order then to know what it is *(quid);* and to suppose that I can know something only through sensible knowledge is to suppose that beginning with this knowledge and because of it I can bring myself to the intelligible knowledge of what the thing is.

The true meaning of the Cartesian formula is therefore its mathematical meaning, namely, that knowledge of existence is governed by knowledge of essence—that it is justifiable by means of it and not vice versa. That is precisely the formula that is inverted with respect to the existence and nature of soul.

This inversion is opposite to the way our knowledge of the existence of soul and body are given. From the fact that the existence of the soul is given immediately as a certain thing to my intelligence, the soul can, beginning with the knowledge of its existence, know itself in all certainty as being in essence pure intelligence; thus it seems that the inference from being to knowledge is valid. From the fact that the existence of bodies is given to me only through sensible knowledge affected by doubt, it is impossible to go from their existence, given so problematically, and attain certain knowledge of their essence as well as their existence; the inference from being to knowledge is invalid.

But the explanation of the paradox itself verifies that it is only an apparent paradox. The being given to me in the Cogito is nothing other than the light of knowledge, pure intelligence. If one knows the essence of mind beginning with its being, which seems to be given before this knowledge itself, it is because the being in question is nothing other than the essential condition of all knowledge; and it is by highlighting this ultimate condition of knowledge that I was able to posit the existence of this being. Thus, I can just as easily state, in this case, that I am going from being to knowledge, as I am going from knowledge to being, for here being and knowledge coincide, as subject and object also coincide. The certain fact of my existence has been posited only because I was thinking, and it is because I have been made aware that the positing of my existence was rendered possible by my pure thought that I was able to recognize it as the essence of my self.[21] The Cogito therefore includes in itself a passage from knowledge to being, and the knowledge of my essence starting from its being consists in explicitly recognizing that I know that I exist because I know. That is perhaps why I would cease to exist if I ceased to think.

Another consequence of this doctrine is that rational psychology appears as the first and easiest science, and must, in principle, occur before pure mathematics. In fact, it deals with what is first known by intelligence, that is, with intelligence itself, which is the condition of knowledge of mathematical notions. This psychology is completely different from the psychology of the soul united with the body, or psychology of passions, which deals with sensation and not clear ideas; this latter science is, in the sphere of science properly speaking, the most difficult discipline, being the last in the order of reasons and the most disconcerting for the understanding.[22] The relation between these two psychologies is therefore absolutely different from the relation of pure mathematics to physics. Far from being substantially separated from one another, these two latter sciences are both based on the clear and distinct idea of extension. That is why physics attempts to be identified with pure mathematics as much as possible, by radically eliminating the sensible element to which it occasionally has recourse.[23] Concrete psychology, on the other hand, does not cease to diverge in principle from rational psychology, since, far from eliminating the sensible element that is alien to it, it is based on it as the ultimate simple nature on which everything depends, and it attempts to rid it as much as possible of everything that the understanding can add to it as a prejudice or an interpretation that would render it inauthentic.[24]

3. Problems Raised by the Analysis of the Piece of Wax

The analysis of the piece of wax has appeared as a decisive and brilliant verification of the conclusions imposed by the order of reasons. However, this universally noted, classical, and apparently simple text is not without difficulties; it poses a certain number of problems that are more or less complicated.

a) Two Senses of the Word *difficult*

First, does not the general thesis confirmed by the analysis that soul is easier to know than body contradict the assertion, which Descartes repeats many times, that knowledge of soul, shackled by knowledge of body and sensation, because of its union with it, is at first extremely difficult? Does not the thesis also contradict the assertion that the *Meditations,* which attempts to discover this, requires a powerful effort of which few men are capable, a kind of twisting against the fold of our habits, against which will has to act in order to repel the prejudices that are occasionally caused by imagination? Is not the value of *Meditation II* to bring to philosophers, for the first time, an efficacious way to rid the idea of the soul of all the falsifications introduced to it by corporeal knowledge? Finally, is not such an effort, according to Descartes, more difficult than the effort of the mathematician and the physicist in discovering the essence of bodies and their true properties behind sensible qualities? For the mathematicians and physicists can find help in imagination while the metaphysician, who deals only with the pure ideas of the understanding, can have no dealings with it, unless he wishes to be misled.[25]

Such questions cannot be posed unless one neglects to distinguish between the order of rational knowledge and the order of common knowledge, between the plane of science and the plane of life. When Descartes states that knowledge of soul is the easiest knowledge, he means that it is easiest of the *scientific truths,* and the first item of knowledge in the order of science. He does not mean that science is easier than common knowledge. The passage from common sense to science is, in fact, the most difficult climb there is. But what I know by common sense is not the easiest knowledge, since it is not even knowledge, but nonscience. The words *easy* and *difficult* have opposite meanings depending upon whether one is situated on the plane of life and ignorance, or on the plane of intelligence and science. Life, which assures me that the soul is united to the body and which leads me to believe, by claims influenced by prejudices, that everything comes from body and that soul is corporeal, finds an almost insurmountable difficulty in accepting what is the first and most blinding of truths for the understanding—that soul is substantially distinct from body. Inversely, the truth taught by authentic sensation, that I am substantially united with a body, is the most difficult and final truth for the understanding, since for itself it is properly inconceivable in itself. We will later rediscover the same opposition with respect to God: in itself and according to the order of pure science, it is the easiest to know; but in fact and given man's condition, it is the most difficult, for in order to conceive it, we would have to set aside everything that we derive from our human nature, meaning the sensations on which we base our life. The unavoidable difficulty with the proof, in this case, arises from this.[26]

However, the only valid meaning of the word *difficult* is the one given to it in the *Meditations,* meaning in philosophical science. In some way it is the true or scientific meaning of the word. It concerns the truths that cannot be discovered until many others are discovered by means of their intermediaries, in virtue of more complex reasons.

b) The Impossibility of Reducing the Representation of the Wax to Sensations

Since the argument, whatever are its many consequences elsewhere, has no other aim, in this case, than to demonstrate that body is known by the intermediary of the soul, could not this aim have been met by considering imagination itself? Since body cannot be known except by perceptions, and perceptions are thoughts, is it not evident that body cannot be known except by thought? Will not Berkeley thus reduce ideas to things and things to ideas?

This path is unmanageable. In fact we have demonstrated that the soul was purely spiritual by proving that its nature was pure intelligence: we have recognized and confirmed in this way that imagination could not be explained by pure intelligence—that is, by the nature of the soul alone.

Therefore if we admitted that body is known only by imagination, we would be excluding a priori that it can only be known by pure intelligence; we would thus be upholding the opposite thesis. We deprive ourselves of the means to prove that the soul is an essence for us, in itself separate from body, exclusive of it, prior to it, and as such including the condition of its knowledge. From this one sees that it is impossible to establish that knowledge of body depends on knowledge of soul and comes after it, other than by proving that the soul is as pure intelligence exclusive of imagination, the condition of knowledge of body.

c) Understanding, the Necessary and Sufficient Condition of the Knowledge of the Nature of Body; the Necessary, but Not Sufficient Condition of the Knowledge of the Existence of Body

The idea of the understanding allows me to know *what is* wax *(quid),* but does it also allow me to know that wax exists *(quod)?* If not, can I generally conclude that knowledge of soul conditions knowledge of body? Ought I not be satisfied with concluding that it conditions the knowledge of its essence by the clear and distinct idea of extension that is innate in me? By what right do I add that it also conditions the knowledge of its existence, which is given to me immediately only by imagination and senses at the time that I am conscious that I exist?

In other words, the function that the understanding assumes would only explain one part of the knowledge of body; it could not take the place of the sensible function that must be preserved as the necessary condition of the knowledge of its existence.

In fact, if it is incontestable that the sensible function cannot be assumed by the understanding, which cannot itself teach us the existence of the thing, it is no less incontestable that imagination or senses cannot exercise their function (positing the existence of body) without the understanding, while the understanding can exercise its function (knowing essence) without imagination and senses. In fact, it is impossible for me to be conscious that something corporeal exists *(quod),* if I am not first conscious of what it is *(quid).* In brief, I cannot perceive that something exists, for example, the wax, if I do not recognize it as always one and the same, under its changing sensible covering, as being the thing whose *idea* I have, if I am not conscious of this idea as being the permanent condition of the knowledge of this thing, and in addition, as entailing the existence of the thing from the fact that it is endowed with the sensible qualities imposed on it. This necessary subordination of perception to the concept explains Descartes' assertion that intelligence alone, and not sense, knows. Moreover, it already entails the principle that the inference from knowledge to being (from essence to existence) is valid, a principle that is still limited, in *Meditation II,* to the sphere of a purely subjective validity. Extension, in fact, is only posited here as *an idea of my understanding* conditioning the possibility of *my consciousness of material object;* this is not yet in any way *an essence expressing the nature in itself of the substance* of material things and entailing the conditions of possibility *of material thing in itself.*

d) Physics and the Analysis of the Piece of Wax as Verifications

We have stated that physics constitutes a *verification* of the demonstration according to the analytic order of reasons. The analysis of the piece of wax is a similar verification since, in order to confirm the conclusions drawn from this order, it also has recourse to something physical—the piece of wax. However, there is a great difference between the two verifications. Physics brings forth a verification of the general conclusion of all the *Meditations;* it not only confirms that the idea of extension is a condition of our *knowledge of material things,* but that the nature of these things is in itself only extension; the success of pure mechanism in the explanation of the set of material phenomena verifies the fact that the soul is in itself a substance separated from corporeal substance, using a path other than the path of metaphysics, by proving that the substance of bodies excludes all spiritual element and is really separated from the substance of mind. The analysis of the piece of wax stays, on the contrary, as does all of *Meditation II,* strictly on the plane of subjective science. The object here is to confirm that soul is better known than body, that it excludes the latter from its knowledge, by establishing that the idea of extension, being a condition for *knowledge* of body as object, constitutes *for us* the essence of this object; from which it results that:

1) body, being known only through the idea of the understanding (the idea of extension), is known only through intelligence;

2) this idea, constituting *for us* the condition of possibility of the corporeal object subsisting as such, must *represent to us* extension as being its substance;

3) the sensible qualities must be excluded from *the representation that we have of substance.* But we do not yet know in this way, and we do not postulate as physics does, that extension is *in itself* the substance of bodies and that the sensible qualities are *in themselves actually excluded* from it. In fact, we do not know at this time whether the necessary conditions of our representation are essential truths at the same time, that is, conditions of the truth of things themselves.

e) The Question of Primary and Secondary Qualities

From this one sees that the analysis of the piece of wax does not have as consequence, or as object, to establish a doctrine of primary and secondary qualities, even though this doctrine is involved in it. In fact, we do not yet know whether bodies exist and whether we have the right to affirm that extension, whose idea conditions their knowledge, constitutes the essence of their substance; whether the soul is in itself really separated from body, as I necessarily conceive it in my science; and whether, consequently, sensible qualities are in themselves really excluded from the nature of body. I only know that these conclusions are necessary for me within the science that my understanding elaborates. These assertions will be legitimate only when we will have established the objective validity of this science. All that we are able to say is that we are certain from now on that if ever we were able to establish this validity, the true reality of bodies will be geometric extension, and their true knowledge the knowledge of the geometric determinations that constitute their properties. But this alone is assured (the question of the knowledge of the existence and true nature of bodies having been set aside): that knowledge of soul is necessarily easier than knowledge of bodies, because I know its existence and essence before the existence and essence of bodies and because it is a necessary condition of all possible true knowledge of bodies. The unique object of *Meditation II* is not to determine in what the true nature consists, nor even to determine the true knowledge of body, but to determine in what consists the true knowledge of soul and its true nature, at least with respect to the necessities of our understanding; it is, consequently, to discover that this knowledge is more easy than the knowledge of bodies, once one has set aside from it the ideas of sensible things that have been wrongly included in it: "that is all I intended to prove in *Meditation II,"* specifies Descartes.[27]

f) A New Aspect of Mathematical (Geometrical) Ideas; Reduction of Knowledge to Intellection; the Rational Ideas of Extended Things as Foundations of the Representation of the Object, but Not as Foundation of the Objective Validity of Representation

When breaking up the sensible representation I have of the piece of wax, I acquired from it a clear and distinct knowledge by the "perfect inspection" of the element or fundamental idea in it that comprises the whole condition of its knowledge as object. Descartes tells us with respect to the piece of wax that "what is important to notice here is that perception is not a vision, nor a touch, nor an imagination, and has never been that, even though it formerly appeared to be so; but it is solely *an inspection of the mind,* which can be imperfect and confused as it formerly was, or clear and distinct as it is at present, according to whether I attend more or less to the things which *are in it and of which it is composed."*[28] The analysis of the piece of wax therefore repeats, while conferring on it a new and higher sense, the result obtained in *Meditation I* by means of the breaking up of sensible representation into its most simple elements. The mathematical notions were then conceived as indubitable—recourse to the evil genius excepted— as constitutive elements of this representation that are incapable of being broken up, for where the simple is attained, fiction is impossible. But they also held their privileged position by virtue of appearing in this way, as the *condition of possibility of every represented object*—for whether these objects exist or not, whether I am awake or asleep, these notions subsist no less, as ultimate elements, the necessary conditions that render the objects possible.

However, insofar as these notions appear only as necessary conditions of the *content* of represented objects, and not as the formal conditions of the thought or representation of these objects, they become vulnerable to the doubt of the evil genius.

Here, on the contrary, the mathematical notion or idea of extension, which remains as a residue of the analysis of the composite,[29] receives its priority and its certainty from its participation with the absolute certainty (although subjective certainty) of the Cogito, as an idea of the understanding, conceived expressly as a thought of my soul. It participates in it by being perceived as assuming its part of the function that the latter assumes generally as *formal condition* of the possibility of all possible representation, the function from which the Cogito necessarily draws its indubitable character. In this way, but only in this way, the idea of extension escapes the doubt of the evil genius, for even if it is intrinsically false, that would not prevent it from necessarily governing my representation of the corporeal object and establishing its unity and permanence under the changing diversity of its sensible covering; neither would that prevent it from being known in this way prior to the sensible representation of the object, nor from investing its existence as an idea in my self with the existence of the Cogito. But the reality of extension, as essence or as existence, remains doubtful. The plane here is not the plane of *Meditation I,* but the plane of the Cogito. What is indubitable in this case is nothing more than the existence of my thought and the existence in it of a certain idea— the idea of extension.

On the other hand, the general function of the Cogito as condition of all possible knowledge is specified in the idea of extension that appears as a condition of all possible knowledge of *the external object as such.* One can regret that Descartes did not push his conclusion farther here, at least explicitly. Although the idea of extension appears here as the necessary condition of the representation of all material objects, it does not bring forth the sufficient condition of the representation of the object, wax, insofar as this object is differentiated from other material objects—wood, metal, water, etc. But it is beyond doubt that, in the same way as for the material object in general, the possibility of the representation of particular objects also requires innate ideas as foundation of their unity and permanence, which are in this case the ideas of certain geometric variations (the *figuras seu ideas* of the Rules), that allow me to recognize this or that body at each instant as being the same under the diversity of its sensible changes. What allows me to understand and recognize the particular substance of such bodies, wax, stone, etc., is that I have the idea of the subsistence of a certain mode of extension (the numerical invariant), which is in itself the subsistence of "the same quantity of magnitude"—under the diversity of changes that it assumes under the three dimensions.[30]

This analysis does not consist in demonstrating that the substance of bodies is pure extension—although this conclusion is included in the analysis—and this analysis does not consist in establishing simply that the idea of extension in general is a condition of pure perception of bodies. What the example aims at is what allows us to know *any* body whatsoever; wax, for example, is the idea of "something extended" *(extensum quid)* that "remains the same" under the diversity of variations of that thing, which is wax, and not wood or stone. This "something" is clearly not simply extension in general, that remains the same under the diversity of every kind of body, wax, wood, stone, etc., but a certain extended element that remains the same in the wax only, or in the wood only, etc., and that allows us to recognize the body as being always "this same wax that I knew from the beginning," in this way, and not wood or stone. This element is precisely the geometric invariant that Descartes defined in article 64 of the first part of the *Principles,* as we have seen; and this geometric invariant, contrasting with the endless apparent variations of extension that imagination presents to me, is knowable only by my understanding.[31]

Whether or not the innate intellectual notion that renders possible knowledge of wax is nothing other than this numerical invariant, it is clear, on the other hand, that the numerical invariant is in no way necessary in order to perceive wax, to know this notion clearly and distinctly, and even less to know it as the idea of a geometric invariant and to have its mathematical formula present to the mind. If that were not true, I would have to be a physicist in order to perceive wax, since only the physicist accedes to the science of this formula. It suffices that my understanding has an obscure and confused knowledge of it. Then, although knowing wax because of its rational idea, I do not notice this idea and do not attribute to it the foundation of my knowledge; on the contrary, I place the foundation of my knowledge in the sensible images that I relate to the existing wax as their cause. That is what is produced in the common man before any philosophy. The reader of the *Meditations* has a clearer and more distinct knowledge of this idea when he perceives it clearly and distinctly as a condition of possibility of the perception of the thing. But the physicist who is not content to perceive that the idea of a certain determination of extension is a condition of the perception of wax, can discover the mathematical formula of this numerical invariant, and rise to the clearest and most distinct knowledge of this innate idea. There are therefore several distinct possible degrees in the knowledge of the idea of the understanding that conditions the perception of the thing: "Perception . . . is solely an inspection of the mind, which can be imperfect and confused as it formerly was, or clear and distinct as it is at present, according to whether I attend more or less to the things which are in it and of which it is composed."[32]

The doctrine of innateness, of the idea of extension, and of all the ideas that, as concepts of the understanding, contain the principle of unity establishing the representation of various things, is already implied here, not only in virtue of the substantial autonomy of the thought requiring that all my thoughts come from my mind alone, but because of the role assumed by these ideas as necessary conditions of the sensible representation of all existing things. The remark by which Descartes ends the analysis of the piece of wax confirms this consequence. It concerns the internal necessary condition that allows me to represent—meaning to recognize outside of me—the existence of other men on the occasion of the perception of their sensible appearances. If it is possible for me to judge that coats, hats, etc., are men and not inert machines, it is because I have in me the ideas of thinking substance and of man, which I could never draw from sensible appearances alone. Moreover, these ideas, first known by me, allow me to *recognize,* in this case, that these things are men and not machines, because their appearances are presented in such a way that their interpretation or *intellection* is possible only through these ideas.[33] They are like the rules that render possible the permanent unity of each of these objects. One understands in this way why Cartesian terminology tends to substitute the term *to comprehend* for the term *to know: I comprehend the piece of wax.* . . . "I comprehend *(comprehendo)* solely by the power of my mind that which I believed I saw with my eyes, etc."[34] That is because we have just ascertained that the act of knowing is an act of knowing only because it is an act of intellection. It is intellection that allows me, by interpreting the sensible appearances, to perceive under the sensible appearances the idea of the known thing that is always similar to itself, in brief, *to recognize,* and thus *to comprehend,* the thing they signify. Physics, which allows me to know the universe in conformity with the true nature of things, is itself only an intellection of material objects, beginning with sensible "variations," which are referred to these geometric "variations" that they are incapable of having us grasp by themselves.[35] In other words, if I can know by sensible perception itself that such a thing exists *(quod),* it is because I was able to recognize what it is *(quid)* under its appearances; and I cannot comprehend what a thing is *(quid)* except by means of intelligence:[36] "What is it then in this piece of wax that we comprehend with such distinctness? Certainly it cannot be anything that I attained by the senses. . . . We must therefore agree that I cannot even conceive *what this piece of wax is* through my imagination and that *only my mind perceives it.*"[37]

To the extent that the idea of my understanding specifies as the foundation of the representation of the external object the function that the Cogito assumes, of rendering possible all representation in general, it is legitimate to establish a comparison between this idea and the Kantian category, insofar as, for Descartes, as for Kant, the concept of the understanding intervenes in order to render possible the knowledge of the object as such by establishing its substantial unity and permanence under sensible diversity. Clearly, with the exception of this characteristic, everything else separates the two philosophies since a concept is an innate idea for Descartes and not a simple a priori; for Descartes a concept is not a form deprived by itself of intuitive content, nor an element that is heterogeneous to space, nor an activity of the mind, nor a synthesis, nor a form empty of phenomena in general, but something expressing, on the contrary, the nature of the thing such as it is in itself directly in us, etc.

However, the most interesting difference is the one related to what makes them similar, for it testifies to the radical subjectivity in which Cartesian scientific philosophy remains, at this point on the chain of reasons. If the idea of the understanding renders possible an item of knowledge by establishing the *objectivity* of sensible representation, and if it introduces in it the principle of unity and substantiality that in this representation makes me recognize, meaning comprehend—therefore know—the object, *this foundation of objectivity* is in no way ipso facto *the foundation of the objective validity* of the representation. In fact, I do not yet know whether the representation of the object I have thus obtained corresponds to the thing outside me, for not only do I not know whether this thing exists,[38] but I also do not know whether its essence is in itself such as I conceive it clearly and distinctly, meaning, whether it is pure extension. Only the demonstration of God's existence will allow me to resolve the question. On the other hand, in Kantian philosophy, since the reality of external things, the object of science properly speaking, is only the reality of the phenomenon, the conditions of the possibility of my representation of the thing are ipso facto the conditions of the possibility of the thing itself, and thus, in this way, they have an objective validity. No doubt these things are but phenomena and not things in themselves; but the opposition between *realitas phenomenon*, based on the structure of the transcendental subject in general (universal subject), and the empirical appearance of the phenomenon, based on the particularity of the sensibilities of individual subjects, is sufficient to establish the opposition between common knowledge, which claims to attribute to things qualities they do not have, and science properly speaking, which discovers their real properties, meaning the truth in itself of physical phenomena.[39] From this one sees that, in Kantian philosophy, the constitutive function of the representation of external things as objects allows the attribution of an objective validity to the conditions that render it possible, and establishes legitimately the distinction between primary qualities (which for Kant are space, movement, impenetrability, and force)[40] and secondary qualities, while the Cartesian deduction is incapable of doing so at this stage. It does not allow one to know whether the sensible qualities ought to be excluded from the essence of material things, in the same way that my science excludes them, at this stage, from the *idea* that it necessarily constructs for itself of their true nature.

The conclusions relative to the essence of bodies therefore have the same destiny as those relative to the essence of the soul. I cannot affirm that the essence of soul is in itself such that I am constrained to represent it to myself (that is, as pure intelligence) in virtue of the necessary conditions of the knowledge of my soul beginning with the Cogito (I had to posit my thought, having abstracted away the rest—imagination and body) and, in the same way, I cannot affirm that the essence of bodies is in itself such that I am constrained necessarily to represent it to myself (that is, as pure extension) when I perceive that the idea of extension, which is innate in my understanding, is a necessary condition of the representation of external things, having abstracted away sensible qualities. In each case, the foundation allowing the attribution of an objective validity *(veritas rei)* to the truths of science is wanting. I remain enclosed within a purely subjective certainty. Here and there I obtain the conditions of possibility of my knowledge, and not the conditions for things—neither a *representation* of their nature nor the certainty that this *nature* is in itself theirs effectively.

g) The Impossibility of Assigning the Substance Composed of Soul and Body as the Source of the Geometric Idea of Extension in the Soul

Since the analysis of the piece of wax has served as verification for the demonstration that, for our science, soul is essentially distinct from body, known before it and known more easily than it, one can see how aberrant is the interpretation that consists in establishing the knowledge of extension as a clear and distinct idea innate only in my understanding, in the primitive innate idea of the union of soul and body, which is alien to pure understanding, under the pretext that one explains in this way how the understanding can have in itself an idea of extension, even though the essence of extension is completely repugnant to the essence of the mind.[41] In fact, if this were so, the pure idea of extension as inherent in pure intelligence would then not come before the primitive notion of the union of soul and body in the order. I would then not know the nature of body through the understanding alone, but I would know it first through the existing body itself, insofar as it is revealed to me as united to the soul. It would therefore be impossible to prove that knowledge of bodies depends on intelligence alone and that, consequently, knowledge of the soul alone precedes knowledge of body and is a condition of it.[42] In other words, we cannot see how the primitive notion of the union of soul and body could furnish the understanding alone a pure notion of extension such that it would necessarily reject outside of it everything that comes from imagination and sense, that is, generally, everything that is sensation or related to it—it would in fact derive its principle from a union with an existing body, meaning from sensation itself. One ought not think that a notion that rests on the union of soul and body, and is unintelligible for pure understanding, can serve to prove the substantial distinction between soul and body, which, precisely, is alone intelligible for this understanding, but is radically unthinkable from the point of view of sensation; one ought not think that the proof of the real distinction between soul and body rests on the proof of the existence of body and its union with soul, an absurdity that some commentators have not hesitated to reproach Descartes for holding, although, as we shall see, he has never committed this absurdity. Descartes has always stated, in keeping with his conception of the absolute separability of substances, that their union is incomprehensible for the understanding alone and that the understanding would never be able to know it by itself, in the same way that their separation is inconceivable for sensation, which by itself would never be able to admit it.[43]

Such an interpretation not only destroys the internal economy of Cartesian doctrine, but also ruins the essential principle it attempts to demonstrate from start to finish, that all items of knowledge proceed from the mind and not from the things outside of it, and that the inference from knowledge to being is valid. The fact that mathematical knowledge can find support in the imagination proves that it is "in harmony with the senses,"[44] but it does not prove that it stems from the presence of body substantially united hereditarily with my mind: "One might perhaps believe that a science is most subject to imagination when it considers only magnitudes, shapes, and movements; such a science is in no way based on such phantoms, but only on the clear and distinct notions of my mind."[45] I must conceive the myriogon by the understanding *alone* before attempting to represent it imaginatively to myself; and this attempt to render imagination concrete requires a painful prolonged effort, an effort that finally comes to nothing. It requires my understanding to turn itself, together with its idea, from within to without, toward something that, in this way, manifests itself as something alien to it.[46] The support that these ideas can find in imagination proves only that, in opposition to the notions of pure metaphysics—God, soul, etc.—they represent a reality which, actually constituting the nature of bodies, appears through the imaginative knowledge caused by the existence of these bodies and which reveals to us this nature by a "direct illustration."[47] In this way one understands that the imagination can render them more expressive and more lively (within some "narrow and strict limits"[48] within which it allows these ideas to become concrete), while it can only be an obstacle to the clear and distinct ideas of the nature of our soul and God, since what appears through it is contrary to their nature.

Moreover, it is impossible for a *clear and distinct idea* to be *introduced* in pure understanding by the substance composed of soul and body, for there is no common measure between one and the other, nor between pure idea and sensation (which belongs to the sphere of the substantial composite).[49] Attempting to justify this interpretation as an attempt to resolve the problem of knowing how I could represent to myself something entirely repugnant to my mind by means of an idea of my mind, is to assume a task that Descartes himself has considered as outside the grasp of all possible philosophy. The alternatives, "What the mind perceives is not extension, but then how can that represent extension? Or what it perceives is extension, but then how can that be inherent to the mind?"[50] cannot be posed for Descartes, because a first declaration of his philosophy is that the mind perceives in itself ideas that have the remarkable property of presenting themselves as reflecting in the mind what is outside it, or at least what is outside its idea. The constitutive property of the idea as such is to be *representative,* meaning to possess a content (an objective reality) by which what is outside it—meaning outside my mind—is presented to my mind in the manner of a picture.[51] The mind does not see the thing, but it sees a picture that it conceives as a simple picture; that is why the mind does not become the thing itself.[52] From this arises the necessity to seek whether what the mind sees in the picture actually corresponds with the reality of the thing. No doubt, one could ask oneself how it is that the mind perceives the picture as a copy and how a purely spiritual picture of what radically excludes the mind is possible. But these are questions that Descartes has not seen fit to ask or to resolve, because, according to him, they exceed the limits of our capabilities. This property of the idea to represent formal reality by its objective reality as a picture is the constitutive character that allows us to distinguish it immediately from other thoughts. It is a first given that is revealed to us by natural light,[53] before which every investigation stops. It could only be obscured by attempting a deeper explanation. It surely belongs to the set of notions so evident and so simple (such as doubting, thinking, existing, etc.) that are understood immediately by themselves, while not allowing us to know anything that exists.[54]

The problem for Descartes has never been to explain how the idea is originally posited as the representation of an object,[55] but to examine in what way I can have a clear and distinct representation of this object (the problem of method), and how I can prove that such an idea has an objective validity (the problem of the critique of knowledge and metaphysics). Since it is the distinctive property of the idea to represent something that is outside it, it is evident that the idea of extension, while not being extended itself, allows us to know what is extension: "And though geometric shapes are wholly corporeal, nevertheless one ought not think that the ideas by which we conceive them are also corporeal, when they do not fall under the imagination";[56] it is by means of the knowledge of the incompatibilities between ideas that I can know, assuming that my ideas can have objective validity, that their objects are incompatible in themselves and that extension in itself excludes thought. That is precisely what we will have to prove, that the incompatibilities I perceive between the ideas of things effectively reflect things that are in themselves incompatible.

One can, if one wishes, reproach Descartes for having voluntarily stopped his inquiry with this property of reflecting an object that is possessed by ideas, but that is not the same as to suppose that one is permitted to discover, in his philosophy, a solution to a problem that he did not pose and that is not to suppose that one can falsify this philosophy in order to attempt to resolve the problem. In *Meditation VI*, in his *Letter to Elizabeth* of 28 June 1643, and in his *Treatise on the Passions,* Descartes does not seek to conceive how pure intelligence can, in spite of its radical spirituality, receive in it the clear and distinct idea of extension, which excludes thought; he seeks to discover how these two substantial realities, which are really distinct and whose union is repugnant to the understanding, can necessarily appear to the understanding itself, under the constraint of sensation, as substantially united in my nature, in fact.

Now if we consider the texts on which an attempt to establish this interpretation has been made, we perceive that they do not concern the conditions of a priori knowledge of extended *essence* or the presence of this idea in the understanding alone, but the conditions of sensible perception of existing material extension, in brief, the conditions of knowledge of the *existence* of bodies. These texts are, in fact, all drawn from *Meditation VI* or from Part II of the *Principles* (article 1). And article 1 of Part II of the *Principles* demonstrates that God would be a deceiver if he were to lead us to believe that existing bodies cause sensations in us, "often stimulating" us to perceive clearly and distinctly material substance as existing, and to posit "external bodies" as being the "occasion" for us to form an idea of them, whereas in reality these bodies do not exist and their perception and the perception of material substance is in this case directly caused by God or by other nonextended beings. And this sensible perception of extension, by which I believe that bodies exist, has nothing to do with the knowledge of geometric essences that I perceive as true without knowing whether or not there exist bodies in nature that correspond to them. Perhaps sensation is an occasion for my mind to bring forth these innate ideas and to teach me through sensible coverings, but above all through the constraint it imposes on me, that there corresponds an existence to them in nature; but this would not prove that these ideas are innate in me because of the hereditary substantial union of this mind with a body. Otherwise, a pure mind, an angel for example, which by definition does not have in itself the primitive notion of the union of soul and body, would be radically deprived of any knowledge of extension. However Descartes teaches the contrary; for an angel, accidentally united to a human body and deprived of this notion, meaning sensation, would know clearly and distinctly the extension and movement of the body.[57]

It is the same for the texts of *Meditation VI.* The cause of objective reality that Descartes seeks there is not the clear and distinct idea of extension that refers to essence, but the sensible idea that refers to existence.[58] I conceive the real difference between the substance soul and the substance body because the understanding alone gives me the clear and distinct knowledge of the necessary incompatibility of their essences, and not because the existing body exercises a passion (sensation) on my soul that involves the action of something alien to me. That is why the concept of the real difference between the two substances does not authorize me to conclude that an extension exists outside of me; that is why God does not deceive me when, having himself implanted the clear and distinct idea of extension as exclusive of thought in my understanding, he also makes me represent to myself indefeasibly the sensible images of the existing thing as coming from the existing body itself, and not from him. For I know very well that there is a radical difference between the idea of the essences of things as eternal truths, the idea of which God is in me the immediate author, and the sensible representation of bodies existing outside me that I cannot know as such—meaning as existent—except through the causality they exercise on me. This causality and the passion that reveals it do not teach me that they are *external to me* for the understanding *by itself* is sufficient to teach me that they are so by nature. It teaches me that they *exist,* meaning that this alien power, of which my passion is the effect, *can* be attributed to them *since they are alien to me,* and *must* be attributed to them since God makes me believe it. Thus I know that *they exist,* since they act on me and do not merely stay in the realm of the possible; therefore I know in this way that they exist outside of me, since they cannot exist except in conformity with their own nature, which excludes mine.

In brief, this interpretation confuses the conditions of knowledge of the essence of bodies with the conditions of knowledge of their existence. And it is precisely this confusion that one discovers in the commentaries of those who wrongly reproach Descartes for having based his proof of the real distinction of body and soul on the existence of bodies and the substantial union of body with our soul.

h) The Order and Three Conditions of Knowledge

But these confusions have only been possible for the above commentators because they have not been attentive enough to considerations of the order. In fact, the order requires that, at three different places, three different kinds of conditions of knowledge be treated, ordered according to an irreversible relation of dependence:

1) *The condition of knowledge of the clear and distinct idea of body (Meditation II),* the exclusion outside *the idea* of body of everything that is not extended in order to obtain a clear and distinct idea of its nature.

2) *The condition of the clear and distinct knowledge of its essence,* the certainty that our clear and distinct idea of the nature of body has an objective validity—in brief, that the essence of body is in itself such that we conceive it in ourselves. Since this condition is known, we will be allowed to exclude from the substance of body in itself what we have excluded from the clear and distinct idea we had of it. The proof of this objective validity of our

clear and distinct ideas of bodies, rendered possible by *Meditation III*, will be given at the beginning of *Meditation IV* and during *Meditation VI*.

3) *Finally, the condition of the clear and distinct knowledge of the existence of bodies:* it resides in the immediate consciousness of the passion proper to sensation, which attests indubitably, in virtue of divine veracity, to the action of an alien power, which can only be the power of body.

It is impossible to demonstrate with certainty that bodies exist, if one has not first determined the conditions that render possible the certain knowledge of their essence; it is impossible to have a certain knowledge of their essence if one has not first determined the conditions that render possible the knowledge of their clear and distinct idea. Inversely, what renders possible the knowledge of existence as such is not what renders possible the knowledge of essence as such, nor the knowledge of the clear and distinct idea as such, etc. The Cartesian demonstration assumes these strict distinctions and their subordination according to the order. To misunderstand them, to reverse the order, is to fall into confusions from which aberrant interpretations arise. And one of the most serious of these confusions, as we shall see, is the confusion between the conditions of the clear and distinct knowledge of the nature of body and the conditions of the clear and distinct knowledge of its existence as such.

Moreover, the order of the conditions is not the same with respect to knowledge of the soul as with respect to knowledge of the body. With respect to the soul, the conditions of knowledge of its existence *(Cogito, ergo sum)* allow one to determine the conditions of the clear and distinct idea of its nature within my science *(Meditation II)*. The conditions of the certain knowledge of its essence—meaning what allows me to assure myself that what is necessarily valid for my clear and distinct idea is necessarily valid for the thing to which the idea refers—are realized at the same time as the conditions of the knowledge of the essence of bodies, by the proof of divine veracity *(Meditation III)* and the consequences one can draw from it *(Meditation VI)*.

Thus with respect to soul, we go from the knowledge of its existence to the clear and distinct idea of its nature, then from this idea to the conception of its essence as such, while with respect to body we go from the idea to the essence and then from the essence to the existence, the latter requiring a new factor (the passion proper to sensation).

i) Intersections with *Meditation VI*

The results of the analysis of the piece of wax with respect to the conditions of the sensible representation of the existing body will be rigorously cross-checked, in *Meditation VI*, by the articulations of the proof for the existence of body. In fact, as it is necessary, in order that *I have the sensible representation of the existing body,* that I *first* have the clear and distinct idea *of extension,* which is inherent in my understanding alone, exclusive of all sensible and imaginative element; similarly it is necessary, in order to prove that *bodies exist,* that I *first* know through the understanding alone, by a pure inspection of the mind, that *the substance of body as extension* is really distinct from the substance of soul and excludes from itself everything spiritual.[59] Thus, the knowledge of the essence of body renders possible, as sine qua non condition, the positing of its existence, in exactly the same fashion as the *knowledge of the clear and distinct idea* of its nature allows one to establish that this idea renders possible *the sensible representation* of its existence, in the domain of pure representation (in which one does not bother with knowing whether the body exists effectively or not). Here as there, one proceeds from the *quid* to the *quod.*

j) The Problem of the Conditions of Knowledge of the Nature of Soul and the Knowledge of the Nature of Body

The verification, toward which the analysis of the piece of wax proceeds, finally amounts to more than a simple verification, since it teaches us something above and beyond what it was supposed to confirm. Not only does it verify that the soul is pure intelligence, that it is radically distinct from body and is known before it, but it also teaches us that the knowledge of bodies consists essentially of the knowledge of the pure idea of extension—and it reveals to us the necessary conditions of the knowledge of its nature. And those conditions are exactly the same conditions that preside over the knowledge of the nature of soul, namely, the elimination of everything that comes from imagination and sense.

Because of this, one is baffled and led to a confusion that is at first difficult to resolve.

If in fact the conditions of knowledge of the nature of soul are the same as those governing the knowledge of the nature of body and if one can deduce these same conditions from the true nature of soul, must one not, since the same conditions must lead to the same consequences, conclude for body the same as we have concluded for soul? Since soul is discovered as pure intelligence, from the fact that it can only be known as intelligence, having abstracted away the imaginative and the sensible, must not the nature of body, which is known in exactly the same way, by pure intelligence, also be pure intelligence? Have we not posited this, by which body is essentially constituted for us, as a simple idea of our understanding alone? Then how can we end up at the same time in this manner with this altogether different conclusion that body is radically different from soul and is known after it?

In other words, how, after having posited the nature of body as based for me, in *an idea* of my understanding alone—as is the soul—can I conclude that the nature of body is reduced to *the extension* it represents (which in itself radically denies intelligence and idea) and is not reduced to this idea. This results in the following confusion: I posit that the nature of body radically excludes intelligence and is pure extension because it is known only by pure intelligence as an idea that, as such, radically excludes extension. The same exclusion of imagination and sense seems to require granting two different states to the nature of body: in the first state, which excludes the sensible and imaginative, it is an idea and it excludes extension; in the second state, for the same reason, it is only pure extension and excludes ideas.

This difficulty is real for the scrupulous reader; however, it is not a real difficulty for the doctrine.

The two opposite conclusions with respect to body are equally possible and legitimate according to whether one relates the conclusions resulting from the abstraction of the sensible to the form of the idea as consciousness, or to its representative content, meaning to the object that, within this idea, is represented as such to myself. When the object and the subject are identical, and the reality of the known thing is completely reduced to the reality of the knowing subject, the conclusion of the process of abstraction cannot be dual; that is, the thing as represented is completely identified with the idea or form represented—the thing is therefore pure intelligence itself: that is the case of the soul, in which the object is reduced to the knowing subject in the Cogito. In the opposite case, in which the object revealed to us by the idea is represented by the idea itself as irreducible to the very being of the idea, to the representing entity, and as exclusive of the nature of the knowing subject, the reduction accomplished by the abstraction of the sensible bares a duality of nature: the conditions of knowledge of the thing determine only the nature of the knowledge by which we represent it to ourselves, not the nature of the known thing, which, on the contrary, must be in conformity with the clear and distinct revelation that is given to us by the idea alone and that consequently must exclude the mind in this case. Thus the paradox disappears once one refers to the original nature of the idea that natural light announces within myself as a picture referring to an object that is reflected by this idea.

However, in both cases, with respect to the nature of soul or with respect to the nature of body, the same problem remains. I do not know whether what I represent necessarily to myself as constituting these natures effectively satisfies what they are in themselves—if the idea I have of them is an essence. No doubt, in what concerns the soul, it is absolutely certain that my own thought is identified with its existence, since it is through this thought that I know that I exist indubitably; but the conclusion that I could draw from this, namely, that the essence of my soul is identical to the nature of the knowledge that has allowed me to know its existence, even though it is entirely clear, distinct, and necessary for me, is not yet valid from the point of view of the truth of the thing in itself.

That is why the demonstration of the substance of the soul as pure intelligence does not precede the demonstration of the substance of body as pure extension in the order; the two demonstrations are one and the same consequence of one and the same truth, that what I know clearly and distinctly is such as I represent it to myself. And this truth itself results immediately from divine veracity, whose reign is attested to by the proof of the existence of God. These two demonstrations will both occur at the same place in *Meditation VI*. If, on the other hand, one is concerned with the simple knowledge of these two natures, the idea of the nature of soul must precede the idea of the nature of body in the order, for the first idea depends immediately on the first known thing, namely, the existence of my thinking self, while the second idea already assumes that I have the idea of my soul as an understanding possessing this idea.

Finally, one ought to note that if these two ideas give me the same certainty of the nature of their proper object, that is, a purely subjective certainty, one of them entails the objective certainty of the existence of its object, while the other entails its absolute ignorance. It is certain that I exist, and it is as certain that I conceive that I know body by means of the understanding alone and because of the idea that the understanding provides us as extended nature excluding intelligence; nevertheless, I am not assured in this way that its nature conforms to the idea I have of it and that body exists. I only know that I exist, since I am thinking this idea. Similarly, as certainly as I exist, I perceive that I know necessarily my soul by the understanding alone and that I know it necessarily as having a purely intellectual nature; but I am not assured by this that it has this nature in itself. Nevertheless, in opposition to what holds for body, I am assured that it exists, since my mind has been able to draw, from the indubitable knowledge of its existence, by inspecting the conditions that have rendered possible this first certainty, the certain knowledge for myself of its nature as pure intelligence.

Let us recall that what is at stake in the analysis of the piece of wax is not to seek in what the essence of body consists and even less to establish that body exists—both things that we cannot actually know—but what are the necessary conditions that render possible its representation as such. I then perceive that these conditions reside in an idea of my intellect alone, an intellect that must be posited as known first.

4. Two Modes of Segregation; Foreshadowing of the Doctrine of Composite Substance

As we have seen, one and the same process of segregation with respect to sensibles leads to different results, according to whether one relates it to the object that is identical to the knowing subject or to an object (extension) that the subject opposes as exclusive of it, in the idea that it constructs of it. In the first case we obtain the knowledge of soul as pure intelligence, and in the other, we obtain the knowledge of body as pure extension excluding intelligence.

The bifurcation of this process toward two different results shows that in fact we are dealing with two different segregations. With respect to the knowledge of the nature of soul, what is at stake is to dissociate it from the knowledge of the corporeal that has entangled itself with or substituted for the knowledge of the spiritual, which can never be anything other than intellectual. With respect to the knowledge of the nature of body, what is at stake is to eliminate from the knowledge of its essence what is related to the knowledge of its existence. The knowledge of body, unlike the knowledge of soul, is therefore not uniquely intellectual; it is intellectual only with respect to its essence—that is the only point of view that excludes the sensible. Its existence cannot be given to us by intelligence alone; it requires the senses at the same time. It is impossible to eliminate the sensible when what is at stake is the knowledge of existence. Certainly we do not yet know whether bodies have an existence and whether, consequently, the sensible allows us to know it; but we ought to think that if bodies exist, we would know them through the senses. On the other hand, intelligence alone allows us to know what the soul is and whether it exists; in what concerns the soul, the sensible must be radically eliminated from the knowledge of its essence as well as from the knowledge of its existence. That is how the superiority of the knowledge of the soul over the knowledge of the body is definitively established; that also renders its existence unproblematic. From this point of view, the radical exclusion of the sensible occurs only with respect to the soul.

But from another point of view, one can glimpse an entirely different perspective. As soon as the sensible qualities are perceived as sensations, meaning as facts of consciousness, and as soon as the faculty of sensing is perceived as a faculty of thought, the sensible recovers its place in the soul as a mode of thinking. And simultaneously, as soon as body is conceived as having a purely extended nature, meaning a nature exclusive of thought, the sensible qualities as sensations or spiritual phenomena must be radically excluded from it. Then the radical exclusion of the sensible is produced with respect to body, not with respect to soul. However, if sensible elements are attributed to the soul, they are not attributed to it as *sensible elements,* but as *representations* (ideas in general), which, while involving thought, cannot be without thought. Moreover, thought can be without them; thought is essentially intelligence, and by itself it is repugnant to the form of sensible faculty. With respect to this, *the sensible as sensible* appears to us again as radically excluded from the essence of soul, which is pure intelligence.[60]

We thus obtain a twofold exclusion and a twofold attribution. The sensible, as sensible, is radically excluded from the essence of soul, while it is, as representation, radically excluded from the essence of body. At the same time it must be related to soul as a representation, which supposes thought, while as a sensible, it is related to body, sensibles alone being capable of imparting their existence to us. The sensible therefore appears as something falling in between, excluded from both soul and body, but necessarily related to both; it is related to soul by the faculty of thinking that it entails, even though it is repugnant to its essence because of its content, and it is related to body as that without which one could never be given its existence, even though it is repugnant in itself to the nature of the latter.

One sees then that the sensible could have support only in a thing that would include both thought and extension in some way, and that at the same time would be radically excluded by both and would therefore be substantially different from them. Moreover, this thing would substantially unite on the plane of existence the form of thought with an obscure and confused content that is repugnant to its essence, that it cannot account for, and that concerns the existence of bodies.

By characterizing the thing in that way we have merely given an external and provisional definition of the substance composed of soul and body. Thus the complex relations of exclusion and attribution of the sensible with respect to both soul and body, which constitute in *Meditation II* the thread of the demonstration with respect to the primacy of knowledge of soul over knowledge of body, and the necessary nature that our science must assign to the one and the other, already seems to sketch the outlines of the theory of the substantial union of soul and body. From this we see that this conception is prepared for, and that far from being an outrageous final result of the system, as it has often been thought, on the contrary, it arises from its deepest parts. Moreover it is possible to perceive this only by following the analytic order of reasons, the order "by which the thing is discovered."

5. Content and Container of Consciousness: The Problem of the Principle of Evaluation of Contents

Even though the thinking self could only have been posited in all certainty by a process of abstraction, as condition of all possible representation, whatever is the content, it is not a formal self, but a self full of consciousness within which are all the contents. In fact, these contents are radically cut off from the external thing that has been cancelled by doubt; but, on the other hand, these contents cannot exist without consciousness itself. This conjunction is particularly favorable to the conception of the radical innateness of all the contents. In this way the self is necessarily represented to my understanding as a substantial reality whose ideas, with respect to their form and their content, are just modes—this reality being immediately captured by an intellectual intuition; this is a complete contrast to the Kantian conception of the Cogito in this respect, as we have seen.

First, the fact that the Cogito has been posited only by a process of elimination that tends to separate consciousness, as a condition of representation in general, from the contents it represents, also entails an important consideration—the possibility to distinguish in consciousness, as will be accomplished in *Meditation III,* ideas as modes of my thought "between which I recognize no difference or inequality" and for which the Cogito is sufficient to account, for "they all seem to arise from myself in the same fashion," and the representative contents (or objective realities) of these ideas, by which they are clearly "different from one another,"[61] and of which the Cogito is not capable of being their immediate source, since it is only the condition of knowledge in general, an abstraction of these contents having been accomplished.[62] We will then ask ourselves what is the origin of these contents: do they arise from me or from elsewhere? In order to reply to this question Descartes will appeal to the principle of causality, under the form: the minimum of the reality of the cause is equal to the reality of the effect; and he will evaluate the degree of reality or perfection of the contents and of my self itself. Since Descartes will reply to the question by showing that various contents (objective realities of the ideas), including those that may be produced by the self itself, have been introduced in reality by God himself, meaning by an external source, the scope of the substantiality of the thinking self will be somewhat reduced. It could only be maintained by the innateness that allows the content of ideas to remain as original modes of the self, even though they have been implanted in it from the outside. That is why, on the one hand, the self *is sufficient for itself,* but, on the other hand, as understanding or faculty of knowledge, it is receptive and *passive* with respect to the contents of the ideas that are imposed on it. There is an antinomy between the self-sufficiency of my substance, which leads to a spontaneity excluding all passivity and the passivity-receptivity arising from the action exercised on this substance by an external cause. That is the antinomy that Spinoza and Leibniz will attempt to resolve. But one can understand, in these conditions, why the self was able to conceive itself as substance by abstracting away its contents, and to perceive itself as subsisting and self-sufficient only as a condition of all possible representation, as "intellectual nature in general." No doubt, the abstraction of the contents and the doubt that strikes at their objective validity does not exclude them from my consciousness. Whether they are illusory or not, they are in my consciousness and they remain there. But the self does not establish the certainty of its being by thinking these contents (by thinking of something); the self establishes the certainty of its being by the thought that *thinking is necessary for all consciousness or thinking of the contents.* The substantiality of thought is thus established for science because of the thinking of thinking, not because of the thinking of contents. In this way substantial thought has similarities with the Kantian self, even though the Kantian self is only purely formal.

Second, the evaluation of the degree of reality or perfection of the contents and of myself, which all constitute the core of the proof of the existence of God by effects, will allow another problem to surface. The Cogito, which has been posited until then only as condition of the consciousness of the contents in general, meaning of their verification in me or their presence for me, has not been posited as the standard by which I can measure the degree of perfection of these contents and of the self itself. If this standard must be sought outside the self, how can one do this, and where can one find it? If it is only legitimate to discover it in the self, how can the Cogito, posited until now as simply the condition of consciousness in general, having abstracted away the contents, transform itself into a principle of the evaluation of the reality and perfection of these contents and of its own being at the same time? The task of the subsequent linkage of reasons will be to resolve this problem.

CHAPTER V

The First Proof of God's Existence by Effects

1. The Precariousness of the Actual Investigation of the Cogito: The Necessity for a New Threefold Investigation

The Cogito can now be viewed from a twofold point of view. As an indubitable truth revealed by the evidence, defined by intellectual clearness and distinctness, the criterion of truth, all the ideas that satisfy this criterion with the character of *true,* may be invested in it. That is the rule of evidence. Consequently, since we may consider as true everything these ideas teach us, the various sciences, mathematics, astronomy, physics, medicine, etc., can be constituted; and it would be sufficient, in order to constitute these sciences, that we consider their various ideas and link them according to the required order.

In addition, the intuition of the thinking self as the condition of everything else, while itself not being conditioned by anything, leads to substance epistemologically defined, meaning to a simple nature, *primo per se,* which constitutes the first link in the chain of certainties. Philosophical science can therefore begin from that, as long as it is constantly upheld by this first intuition of the thinking self, which necessarily escapes all possible deception. That is the "fixed and sure fulcrum" that will allow the world to be moved.[1]

But with respect to the validity of the evidence as criterion able to be used by the sciences, the certainty of the fact of the Cogito has in no way abolished the rule of the hypothesis of the evil genius. Since this hypothesis remains vigorous, the passage from the complete certainty of the Cogito to the complete certainty of the other clear and distinct ideas—with respect to the truth of the subject in itself as with respect to the truth of the object in itself—appears as a precarious and illegitimate extrapolation. Doubt ought to strike at the objective validity of these ideas as a rule. Therefore I cannot, as a rule, attribute to them any truth other than the one that defines the incontestable necessity by which our understanding imposes them on us; nothing allows me to affirm that what is necessarily valid for me is also necessarily valid for things. All that I presently know with an unshakable certainty is that the sciences constituted by the linkage of clear and distinct ideas are the only true sciences possible and valid for the human mind. But I cannot yet affirm that the human mind reaches the intrinsic truth of things through them.

With respect to philosophy itself, as it directly stems from the consideration of the Cogito, we have already admitted that its necessity rendered it as certain as the Cogito, but that we could not confer on it an objective validity that would surpass the affirmations allowed within the sphere described by the Cogito. This conclusion, which is valid for the sciences, properly speaking, is valid also for philosophical science, and the objective validity of the sciences cannot be assured until the objective validity of philosophical science is assured.

Moreover, the factual certainty of the Cogito itself constitutes within universal doubt an exception that is as uncontestable in fact as it is unjustified as a rule. That is why, once I detach myself from the actualized Cogito in order to render it objective with respect to myself, by situating it in the set of items of knowledge that my understanding has always reputed naturally as true, I rediscover it confronted, as these items of knowledge are, by the ever valid hypothesis of the evil genius. This hypothesis puts back the Cogito within the set of clear and distinct ideas, since the Cogito is, like them, a representation, the representation of a "spiritual thing" by which "I represent myself to myself."[2] It strips the Cogito of its privileged position. Thus, in spite of the fact of the Cogito, I am required to return to doubt, as the rule, meaning as the principle of universal deception erected from the beginning as an indefeasible rule of methodological inquiry. Consequently, an oscillation between the fact of the Cogito and the rule of the evil genius is produced, an oscillation between the factual certainty that I exist when I think and the absolute doubt that the hypothesis of the deceiving God maintains as a rule. This oscillation renders the certainty of the Cogito precarious and unsettled, and the certainty of the Cogito no longer appears absolute.[3] The certainty of the certainty that characterizes it seems to require a third-power certainty that would settle it definitively. In other words, if, as we have seen, degree of certainty is a function of degree of simplicity and absoluteness of reasons, the deficiency that the certainty of the Cogito still evinces seems to verify that it does not constitute the simplest and most absolute reason, and that it ought to be related to a simpler and higher reason.

In this way the question of the epistemological substantiality of the Cogito is brought into doubt. My thinking self was posited epistemologically as a substance insofar as it was self-sufficient. But it was posited as such for me insofar as I posit myself as independent from everything else. It is, therefore, at this point on the chain of reasons, not an absolute substance by itself, but a substance under the contingent condition that I am thinking—in brief, because of the fact that I am thinking at this instant of time: "The proposition 'I am, I exist' is necessarily true *every time* that I utter it or that I conceive it in my mind."[4] There is no certainty about my self except during separate instants of actual intuition that cannot maintain themselves and that can just as easily exist as not exist. Once I stop thinking of myself, I stop appearing to myself as existing. And it is inevitable that I would stop thinking of myself, "because I am of such nature that I cannot always have my mind directed on one thing"[5] and also because, in order to expand my science, during the next instant, I must turn my thought away from myself, in order to bring it to other objects.[6] My certainty, properly speaking, which was upheld by my actual intuition, therefore disappears in order to be replaced by the memory of my certainty and my intuition. And even a perfectly faithful recollection of my state of certainty is not the same as the state itself, no more than the recollection of the intuition is the same as the intuition itself, for it lacks the constraining power that would require me to be certain.[7] Since I no longer have the intuition that would render me certain of my certainty, I no longer see why I was and ought to have been certain. I am immediately seized by the doubt raised by the hypothesis of the deceiving God. Thus the certainty of my certainty, the privilege of the Cogito, is abolished in the recollection of my certainty. The Cogito then descends to the level of mathematical truths, meaning to the level of these ideas that are certain while one contemplates them,[8] but that, in spite of their clearness and distinctness, do not confirm by themselves the certainty of their certainty against the doubt with which the hypothesis of a deceiving God strikes them. And since the certainty of these truths would only be a prejudice for the atheist, the certainty of the Cogito also appears as only a prejudice.[9] In other words, at the same time as I said "I think, therefore I exist, but perhaps if I stopped thinking I would stop existing," I should say: "I think that I exist and I know that I know, because I am thinking that I think, but if I were to stop thinking that I think, ought I not inevitably stop thinking that I exist, stop knowing that I know, and consequently, stop being certain?" And inevitably I stop thinking that I think when, in order to expand science, I turn my thought away from myself in order to fix it on another thing. Thus, as long as the Cogito constitutes the only point of support for my science, science, meaning the chain of items of knowledge that are necessary for me, is impossible, since once my mind stops fixing on the Cogito in order to fix on something else, the point of support disappears in the darkness of universal doubt, carrying with it the whole chain of reasons.

It is clear that the higher reason that we must discover will have to escape from this precariousness and temporality, and will have to constitute an epistemological substantiality that will sustain itself entirely by itself, thus offering to knowledge an unshakable foundation of stone or clay. The certainty of the certainty will be restored, not as a fact but as a rule, not during the flash of some contingent instants, but for the universality of time, not just for a particular single truth (the Cogito), but for the universality of clear and distinct ideas. Such a reason will therefore entail the refutation of the hypothesis of the great deceiver. A twofold problem will therefore be resolved in this way: 1) the problem of the certainty of my self, the foundation of the subjective necessities that constitute the intrinsic necessities of all human sciences; 2) the problem concerning the objective validity of these subjective and intrinsic necessities.

Since subjective certainty, meaning the certainty of the Cogito, is itself put into question, if not in fact, at least in principle, by the subsistence of universal doubt as a rule, it will become certain only when the abolition of this right is restored in the certainty relative to the objective validity of the subjectively necessary truths. A reversal will then be produced: once this higher reason will have extinguished the universal doubt that unsettled my subjective certainty of fact, the necessity inherent in things will appear as a foundation of my internal necessities, and the necessities of my clear and distinct thought will be revealed as the direct expression of the necessity of things.[10]

From this one sees that God will be the higher link of the chain of certainties, that God will be finally posited as the sole foundation of science—instead of the Cogito, which will be conceived as only its starting point[11]—a foundation without which an atheist, satisfied with the Cogito, could not have a certain science.[12]

The aim of the investigation is therefore threefold, even though it is a single goal: 1) to restore the unsettled certainty of the Cogito by discovering the *ratio* that directs it; 2) to establish as a rule my subjective certainty and restore objective validity to all the necessities that the subject perceives in his clear and distinct ideas; 3) to prove the existence of the veracious God.

The path that this investigation must follow is indicated unambiguously by what excludes the Cogito from all possible doubt, meaning the accomplishing and actuality of its intuition above and beyond privileged instants. There is no progress possible unless, instead of starting from the Cogito as an initial point that one leaves in order to look elsewhere, turning the mind away from it in order to fix it on another object during the next instant, we never stop, even for an instant, to remain attached to it, always staying within the precise consciousness of ourselves, realized in the intuition that makes us certain.

As a result, the inquiry could not be pursued except by considering what the actual intuition of my self places constantly before my eyes.

2. Preliminaries. Review of Thoughts and Its Role.
The Twofold Intention Presiding over This Classification.
Elimination of Judgment. Order of Problems

If one reunites the two requirements, the requirement to preserve the certainty and the requirement to attain the goal, we see that 1) the mind should "look within itself,"[13] meaning it should explore the content of its consciousness, and that, 2) proceeding in this exploration to discover if there are thoughts having objective validity in it, it should limit the exploration to the examination of which of our thoughts are susceptible to become objectively valid, meaning, it should examine our *representations*. The mind will then seek in the actual intuition of the content of our thoughts, given with the actual intuition of the self, whether it finds internal characteristics *requiring* it to invest them with this validity.

From this results the necessity to enumerate and to classify preliminarily the various thoughts of my consciousness, in order to be able, without risking any omission or error, to determine them with respect to these two points of view. We must first discover which among them are such that the evil genius cannot strike at their proper content because their content, itself included in the being of my thinking self, does not understand anything surpassing the actual certainty of my Cogito, in brief, does not entail by itself the positing of any objective validity. We must then delimit the set of representative thoughts that are within the scope of the present inquiry, in order to eliminate all others.

These two preoccupations both inspire the review of thoughts that Descartes makes at this point. Certainly, the emphasis is placed on the first, which alone is expressly mentioned: "I must here divide all my thoughts into certain types and consider in which of these types there is, properly, truth or error"[14] (and exclude the types in which there is error). But the second preoccupation is no less present. We can see this clearly when the inquiry, properly speaking, begins, an inquiry that is expressly restricted to the set of previously determined representative thoughts or ideas: the inquiry will consist in "seeking if, among the things of which I possess an idea, there are some that exist outside of me."[15] The enumeration of thoughts will then give rise to two preliminary exclusions of different degrees: 1) the exclusion of all thoughts that, necessarily involving error or truth, are "capable of deceiving me"; 2) the exclusion of all thoughts that are not representative and thus that do not interest the inquiry in progress. If the first preoccupation goes before the second, and is the only one expressly indicated, that is because Descartes attributes the error of common sense—and also the error of philosophers inspired by common sense—with respect to the problem of the objective validity of our ideas, to the neglect of the discrimination between thoughts that cannot be deceptive and other thoughts. The legitimate path of science cannot be discovered if, first of all, the principle of this error is not denounced.

Let us consider this classification according to the two points of view that have been specified. Let us first consider its function relative to the precise selection of the elements of consciousness, in order to determine the one that alone will carry the whole inquiry. We then discover a first division between a group of thoughts "which are like images of things" and to which "alone the name *idea* properly applies" such as "the ideas of man, of chimera, of angel, of God, etc.," on the one hand, and another group of thoughts, wishing, fearing, affirming, denying, etc., which are not representations, but are properly constituted by something else added to the idea stemming from the action of the mind.[16] The inquiry will be carried forth for the first group, the group of *ideas*. No other kind of thought poses the problem of objective validity, since objective validity is not suitable except for a representative content. The representative content is what Descartes calls the "objective reality."[17] In fact, what would it mean for an idea to have such validity if it were not merely a simple modification of my consciousness, but also a representation of something outside it—a *res,* an essence or existence—by means of its content, in an effective and not illusory fashion, in such a way that it requires me to go beyond myself? For even in the case in which the idea simply represents myself to myself, the idea has no validity unless it represents to myself what the self is in itself, meaning independently from the representing thing as such.

The result of this classification is to put immediately outside of all consideration such things as desires, judgments, and will, which are not representations at all.

This preliminary limitation of the field of inquiry would already be sufficient in itself to place into evidence the impossibility for Descartes to reduce the idea of God to the consciousness of my infinite will, as some authors do,[18] since will is not an idea, meaning a "representation,"[19] and it has no "objective validity," so that it is expressly excluded from the category of thoughts in which the idea of God resides; in a general way, it is expressly excluded from the kinds of thoughts we will have to consider in order to reach God. On the contrary, it is the idea of God that will allow me to judge, in virtue of its representative content, to what degree and in what respects my will is infinite, as God's will is. Consequently, that is what will allow me to discover that, with respect to this standard, my will is in me insofar as "I am made in the image and likeness of God."[20]

Having cleared the terrain, there only remains to pursue the investigation methodically by examining according to the order and by degrees "the various ideas" in order to determine if there are some among them whose representative content (objective reality) constrains me to posit outside them, meaning outside me, a formal reality corresponding to them, in such a way that the objective validity of the idea can be established necessarily. That is how Descartes proceeds. However, he delays this enterprise for now.

In fact, the other preoccupation appears and points toward a different point of view in the classification. In this respect, thoughts are divided into two other groups: the group of thoughts that cannot give rise to either error or truth, and the group of thoughts that can give rise to "the occasion for failing." Ideas, affections, or willings (desires, appetites, etc.) belong to the first group;[21] judgments belong to the second group. This second group must therefore be excluded.[22] The justification for this exclusion therefore appears as a necessarily preliminary question, for before attempting another path, we ought to make sure that it is the only good path. We ought to prepare it by ridding it of the obstacle that common sense erects against it; common sense always follows the opposite path, the path in which all conclusions are based on judgments.

We would be establishing that the new path is trustworthy if we demonstrated that it is based on the rock or clay of an element of my consciousness that is in itself undubitable, while the path of common sense rests on the quicksand of the single element of my consciousness that is not trustworthy—judgment.

In fact, if we consider the various groups of thoughts that have been enumerated, we would see that ideas cannot by themselves admit to the least falsity, no more than will and desires can. For whether I imagine a chimera or a goat, whether I will or I desire something good or bad, it is no less true that I have an idea, that I will, and that I desire.[23] Therefore, any investigation that takes as support simply the being of these realities such as they are given immediately to my consciousness, without adding or subtracting anything from them, would necessarily be as certain as the Cogito with which these realities are intimately connected. Therefore the evil genius cannot deceive me when I perceive them and describe them. He can only deceive me when later, considering simply the content of these ideas, such as it is given inherently to my consciousness, I perceive, in the infinite content of one of these ideas, that it implies necessarily a real infinite cause outside of me and that it thus possesses an objective validity. And he will not be able to deceive me when, having settled this problem of objective validity and having demonstrated the existence of God, I perceive the infinity of my will in myself, and when, relating the clear and distinct idea of God given by *Meditation III,* I discover that I resemble God in some respect because of this will.[24]

It is not the same for judgment. Certainly, it seems that we can also say: "Whether I judge truly or falsely, it is no less true that I judge." In fact, judgment is a fact of consciousness, as is will, desire, or idea. But when stating that idea, desire, and will cannot by themselves deceive me, I am not situated from the point of view of the form of consciousness common to them, but from the point of view of their content, which differentiates them from each other as ideas, desires, or will.[25] And from this point of view I cannot assert for judgment what I assert for the other contents of thought. For the content of the idea of a chimera, or the content of a willing or a desire that renders it into a willing or a desire for this or for that, in itself does not contain anything false. It does not posit any objective validity. However, we can rely on the presence of this content viewed in its barren state without risking error. The proper content of judgment is nothing other than the affirmation or negation of the truth of an idea, meaning the acceptance or refusal of its objective validity. It therefore necessarily entails truth or error in actuality. An investigation that takes such affirmations as its starting point is therefore at the mercy of falsity. It is evident, in this way, that one cannot discover a solid terrain except in the parts of judgments that are indifferent to truth or falsity in actuality, meaning in their contents, with respect to which judgment will be practiced. In fact, it is by means of the analysis of these contents that we will be able to discover what justifies or disables the judgments we make about them.

This necessity is particularly evident with respect to the problem we are concerned with. What defines the idea is its property to appear as an image that is related to an object outside it.[26] What defines the objective validity of an idea is its property *to be effectively* the picture of an object outside of it, not simply *to present itself* as a picture. To attempt to settle the question of its objective validity beginning with judgment, which relates it effectively to this object, is to assume that the problem is resolved and to muddle completely the order of the questions. In fact, we cannot attribute definitively any objective validity to the idea in virtue of the judgment that has conferred objective validity upon the idea unless the judgment is legitimate. But we cannot know whether it is legitimate unless we have discovered that the idea effectively possesses this validity and that thus the judgment is authorized to affirm it. And we cannot discover this unless we can know that an object exists outside its idea and corresponds to it, which is what we do not yet know because of the hypothesis of the evil genius, and which is what we cannot see ourselves ever knowing, if it were not for some indefeasible revelations inherent in some content within the idea. It is therefore the objective validity recognized of the idea that must legitimate the judgment of objective validity and not the judgment of objective validity that must legitimate the objective validity of the idea. Otherwise, my judgment could only be arbitrary and the solution I could believe to have drawn from it, also necessarily arbitrary. Further, this arbitrary judgment would be false, so that the solution drawn from it would also necessarily be false: "In fact, the principal and most common error that can be encountered here consists in judging that the ideas in myself are similar to things outside of me; for certainly, if I considered the ideas as only modes or aspects of my thought, without intending to refer them to something external, they could hardly offer me a chance for a mistake."[27]

The path that supports itself on the one element of consciousness that cannot be trusted, meaning judgment, is a path that leads to the confusion of the problem of the objective validity of ideas with the problem of the truth of judgments, a path that ends up reversing the true order of the questions by treating the first problem using the second; this is the path of common sense. It is natural that it leads to failure. The precise determination of the errors that have led us there would allow us to perceive what we must do to discover another path, which will be the path of reason and science. We will have to reestablish the true order of the questions, to distinguish them instead of confusing them, which is possible only by first abstracting away the eminently fallible element that is the support for all the conceptions of commonsense consciousness.

However, the reestablishment of the true order is difficult to accomplish. In fact, if it is easy to cut from idea all the actions of the mind that are added to it, such as will, desire, etc., it is much more difficult to cut out the action of judgment, which seems to constitute a unity with it. Ideas present themselves as images referring themselves to objects outside them, and judgment is added to them to affirm them as *effectively* corresponding to this object; the two elements are different, but it is easy to confuse them, since ideas present themselves as being what judgment affirms they are. However, since truth and falsity consist precisely in relating effectively, whether legitimately or illegitimately, an idea to something outside it, truth and falsity belong to judgment alone, and do not belong to ideas that are in themselves neither true nor false. Moreover, the objective validity of the idea is this property of its content, independently from judgment, to be effectively related to the object to which it refers. The legitimacy of judgment, meaning the determination of its truth, therefore cannot be established except through the preliminary determination of the objective validity of the idea. And in *Meditation III* Descartes is concerned with establishing the truth, or more precisely, the objective validity of ideas, and not the truth and falsity of judgments. It must be determined whether there are in me ideas that have objective validity in all certainty. Consequently, we will have to seek in the being itself of these ideas, beyond any judgment of objectivity that may be brought upon them, inherent characteristic signs such that their correspondence with the ideated thing is not only possible, but necessary; and it is necessary of a necessity comparable to the necessity of the Cogito, meaning the necessity from which I can no more subtract myself than subtract myself from myself. Only then will we be able to pronounce on the legitimacy of the judgments of objectivity brought upon ideas, meaning on the truth or falsity of judgments. We will then be able to judge these judgments, in some way, and we will be able to acquire a certainty of their certainty when we will perceive that they are legitimate.

Since objective validity is a property of ideas, and not of judgments, truth being a property of judgments and not ideas, the problem of the objective validity of ideas and the problem of the truth of judgment are different problems and must be carefully distinguished.[28] Consequently, we will have to consider them separately, and hence to consider them in separate *Meditations,* since one must treat "things separate in separate *Meditations.*"[29] The first problem is treated in *Meditation III* and the second problem is treated in *Meditation IV.*

The order requires that the problem of objective validity is treated before the problem of the truth of judgments. In fact, from what precedes, we see that the determination of the objective validity of ideas is a condition of the verdict rendered on the truth of judgment. Moreover we note that psychologically—or more exactly, phenomenologically, for this entails a necessary relation—ideas can exist without the judgments we bring to them—in the same way that they can exist without sensation, desire, and will—but not inversely. This irreversible dependence of these various elements of consciousness with respect to ideas merely expresses the substantiality of intelligence, which is necessarily instituted by the Cogito, and which renders the faculties other than pure understanding as modes that are incapable of existing without the intellect, while the intellect can exist without them. The examination of ideas that constitute the content of the understanding in general must then precede the examination of judgment and, consequently, the examination of will entailed by judgment.

From this we see that psychological observation—or phenomenological description—certifies the independence of ideas with respect to the other modes of the mind and the thesis of the intellect as principal attribute of substance with respect to which the other faculties are only contingent modes. These two theses together impose the dissociation of the problem of the objective validity of ideas and the problem of the truth of judgment in order to subordinate the latter to the former according to the order. Finally, this dissociation announces the opposition between the understanding and the will that will be made explicit in *Meditation IV*.

The order of reasons that imposes this dissociation and subordination destroys the preliminary obstacle that common sense would oppose against the correct definition of the problem. In fact, by preventing the confusion of idea and judgment, of objective validity with formal truth, it averts the fundamental absurdity that consists in establishing the objective validity of ideas on the judgment of objectivity arbitrarily brought upon them. Since the determination of the intrinsic objective validity of ideas permits only legitimating judgment, two requirements can be immediately formulated: 1) the suspension of all judgment of objectivity as condition of possibility of the examination of objective validity, and 2) the determination of this validity by an inquiry into ideas themselves for the *reasons* leading one to recognize this idea as corresponding or not corresponding effectively to a thing outside me.

We already discern two degrees of error in the doctrine of common sense. Certainly common sense is mistaken in believing that our sensible ideas are the faithful reflection in me of things external, to which they resemble. But this error has its source in a higher error, namely that, not mistrusting judgment, which alone can be subject to falsity, it starts from a judgment of objectivity, in order to determine objective validity, although the only legitimate method is the inverse. We must not believe that common sense is mistaken when supposing generally that ideas represent things outside themselves, for that is the definition of idea itself, and if no idea corresponded with something outside itself, no idea could be positively true, and science would be impossible. But common sense is mistaken in supposing that *sensible* ideas reflect external things. It is not the principle of correspondence of the idea with what is ideated that should be condemned, it is the application that judgment makes of it here that should be condemned. That is the occasion for which our judgment commits "its principal and most common error," for commonly it applies this principle without reason or reflection. In any case, it applies this principle with the same lack of reflection and reason with which it applies the principle of causality, when it believes blindly that sensible things cause sensible ideas in me. Thus the error is not in the principles themselves, but in their illegitimate or unreflective applications.

The refutation of the thesis of common sense therefore has a dual scope: 1) an extremely general scope that aims at the method based on judgment, and 2) a narrower scope that aims at the conclusion of this method relative to the privilege of truth normally given to the sensible idea. The error of common sense relative to the objective validity that it attributes to sensible knowledge is illustrated by the consequences of the fundamental error of the method that confuses the objective validity of the idea and the truth of judgment, that places the center of gravity of the question in judgment, instead of placing it in the content of the idea considered in itself beyond judgment.

3. Review of Ideas and Its Role. Problem of the Origin and Problem of the Objective Validity of Ideas. Confusion of These Two Problems by Common Sense. Refutation of Common Sense

In order to refute his adversaries more thoroughly, Descartes begins by placing himself in their point of view, the point of view of common sense—that is, Descartes begins with blind judgments that they accept as indubitable evidences, without criticizing them. And the result of these judgments can be summarized as the belief that all our knowledge comes from *sensible ideas,* that these ideas are *faithful images* of external things, and that their *origin* is to be found in these external things.[30]

The refutation of this thesis consequently gives rise to a new enumeration and a new classification, not just between thoughts, but between ideas: there are three kinds of ideas, *innate ideas, artificial ideas,* and *adventitious ideas.*[31] This enumeration constitutes a preliminary operation, as did the enumeration of thoughts. It does not belong to the body of the inquiry; it is designed also to blaze the path.

This classification is accomplished from the point of view of the origin of ideas. However, the problem that it attempts to resolve is not the problem of their origin, but, as we know, the problem of their objective validity. Yet, since common sense believes it is capable of resolving the problem of objective validity by referring to the origin of the various ideas, which is assumed known, it is necessary to follow it in its domain, to classify ideas from the point of view of their apparent origin, and to concede provisionally the privilege of objective reality to adventitious ideas. Only adventitious ideas manifest themselves to common sense as drawing their origin from an action exercised on me by an external thing they supposedly represent. And common sense believes that *once they are produced by the external thing,* they are necessarily their faithful images. But this classification by origin, as conceived by common sense, does not concern the true origin of ideas, which remains unknown for now: "For perhaps I might persuade myself that all these ideas are of the kind I call alien and that come from the outside, or else that they are all innate in me, or else that they have all been invented by me."[32] This classification operates at the level of common sense consciousness and rests entirely on spontaneous judgments.

In order to destroy the thesis of common sense, Descartes considers it as a particular case of this unfortunate general method that consists in treating the problem of the objective validity of ideas beginning from judgments, instead of beginning from the other elements of consciousness that are above the realm of truth and falsity. The judgments that intervene here are of two kinds: 1) judgments about origin, and 2) judgments about objective validity, which consist in affirming, in virtue of the judgment of origin, the conformity of the idea as image or picture of the thing, of which it is a copy; this second judgment seems to flow from the first. Descartes' refutation consists in proving that these judgments are arbitrary and that the affirmations resulting from them relative to the privileged objective validity of adventitious ideas are not only arbitrary, but false.

The first judgment is supposedly first established on an appeal to nature, the unreasoned inclination that brings me to see the cause of my perception in external things. But experience teaches me that natural inclination deceives me with respect to the good; it can therefore deceive me with respect to the true. It then claims to be established on the constraint suffered by my will during perception. But I suffer the same constraint during dreams. Nothing therefore prevents me from conjecturing that there is a faculty in me that is yet unknown that produces in me the representation of external things and is opposed to my will in the same way that my natural inclinations can be opposed to it. This first judgment, the judgment about origin, is unjustified as a rule, even if it is not false in fact.[33]

The second judgment consists in affirming that the idea resembles the external thing because the external thing is its cause. But even if it were its cause, it would not necessarily be similar to it.[34] In fact, my reason allows me to think that the idea of the astronomical sun, which my reason draws from its innate ideas, is much more similar to the real sun, which would be the cause of my adventitious idea, than the adventitious idea would resemble its cause. The question of objective validity is not necessarily settled by the question of origin. The judgment of objective validity is therefore as unjustified as a rule as the judgment of origin upon which it rests is unjustified.[35] Thus, common sense proceeds arbitrarily with respect to the judgment of origin or of causality, as well as with respect to the judgment of full objective validity or resemblance of idea with what is ideated. The judgments of common sense, far from resting on "reasons" drawn from the nature of ideas, are incited by a "blind and rash impulse."[36]

This whole refutation shows that common sense finally leads to making these five errors:

1) It is mistaken in seeing images of external things in sensible ideas.

2) It is mistaken with regard to general method, by believing that it can resolve the problem of the objective validity of ideas by starting with judgments that attribute objective validity to them spontaneously.

3) It is mistaken in attempting to resolve the question of the *origin* of adventitious ideas by means of arbitrary judgment, which, even if it is not false in reality, is without foundation or guarantee for whomever asserts it.

4) It is mistaken in basing its judgment of *objective validity* on the judgment of *origin,* for, since the latter judgment is gratuitous, it engenders the gratuitousness of the judgment that follows from it.

5) It is mistaken in thinking that the judgment about origin always allows as a rule the judgment of objective validity. Certainly, an idea, which I know in all certainty to draw its origin from an external thing that it supposedly represents, has in this respect a certain objective validity, for there is incontestably a real thing outside itself to which it refers. But we are not assured by this that it allows us *to know it,* meaning that it gives us a "picture" that resembles it. And it is its conformity with what it represents that constitutes its proper objective validity, not the fact that it is truly produced by an external thing which it might not resemble. An innate idea, even though it does not arise from the causality exercised on me by the thing it represents, can have complete objective validity, meaning it can be the resembling image of the thing outside of me; at the same time, the adventitious idea, which is effectively caused in me by the action of the existing external thing, has no objective validity because, although it can testify to the existence of the thing, it leaves it completely unknown in itself. Thus, the innate idea of a triangle adequately represents the essence of the triangle, such as it is understood in the essence of extension outside my thought; the idea of the sun "drawn from astronomical notions, meaning certain notions innate in me," is similar or as similar as possible to the real sun outside of me. On the other hand, the ideas of sensible qualities, colors, odors, heat, etc., or the sensible idea of the sun, have only an objective validity reduced to almost nothing, since even if we supposed that they can be effectively related to things or to real extended properties outside of me, which are their cause in me, they are not their copies, and they do not allow

us to know the nature of this cause, which has nothing in common with them, since it is in itself of a geometric "variation."

4. The Linkage of the Two Problems with Respect to the Idea of God

This refutation highlights a number of important consequences.

First, judgments of origin are exposed to the same risks and uncertainties as judgments of objective validity. The former are judgments of *causality,* and the latter are judgments of *resemblance between the idea and what is ideated.* In other words, *the principle of causality and the principle of resemblance between the idea and what is ideated* are subject to the same conditions of legitimate applicability. With respect to either of them, in order to avoid error, it is necessary to practice *epoche* and to consider the contents themselves, such as they are, abstracted from judgments added upon them. *The principle of causality therefore enjoys no privilege, in this respect, relative to the principle of the correspondence between the idea and what is ideated.* It can therefore give rise to the most serious errors, as can the latter principle; common sense applies it as badly.

What some interpreters have believed, that the refutation of the thesis of common sense eliminated as false the principle of the correspondence of the idea with what is ideated, in order to leave nothing more than the principle of causality, is therefore completely mistaken. That they have consequently accused Descartes of having contradicted himself when he later seemingly had recourse to the latter thesis is then also mistaken.[37] Certainly Descartes has stated that "the principal and common error of judgment" consists in that "I judge the ideas in me similar or in conformity with the things outside of me,"[38] but he does not mean by that that it is always false that ideas can correspond effectively to what is ideated, but only that judgment often wrongly affirms this correspondence; similarly it happens that it often wrongly affirms, or at least it affirms without proof, that such things are the cause of my idea.

The error therefore always bears on the application of the principles, and not on the principles themselves. How can Descartes in fact deny the truth of the principle of the correspondence of the idea with the thing ideated since that principle is taught to us by natural light as is the principle of causality?[39] How is this possible since idea is defined by means of this principle?[40] And how is this possible since without this principle one cannot even define the notion of objective validity? To seek the solution of the problem of objective validity is to seek how it is possible to apply this principle legitimately, meaning to seek whether "among the things of which I have an idea, there are some existing outside of me."[41] This principle is therefore true in itself, as is the principle of causality; it is contestable only in its application. This applicability is rendered radically impossible by the artifice of the evil genius, which constrains the self to deny provisionally everything external to itself, whether existing or possible. But the principle remains available and ready to be used once the artifice is destroyed, or once it is demonstrated that something exists outside of me and that I am allowed to affirm that I know it, meaning to affirm that it is in my understanding as an objective reality, exactly as it is outside my understanding as a formal reality.

Second, the refutation underscores the complex relations that unify and distinguish the problem of the origin and the problem of the objective validity of the idea. In themselves, at first, the two problems appear as distinct, and although they can be linked to one another, as we shall soon see, it is unquestionable that common sense has established an arbitrary connection between them, in any case. The judgment of origin, as we have seen, cannot establish the judgment of objective validity, with respect to adventitious ideas. As a result, the *presumption of origin* cannot decide about the objective validity of the idea in advance. This is an important consequence, because it reduces to nothing, from the outset, the objections of all who contest the validity of the proofs for God's existence under the pretext that the idea of God is an artificial idea, meaning a "chimera" or an adventitious idea, meaning an idea "acquired through hearsay." In fact, how could the presumed origin of the idea matter, once we place ourselves uniquely before its content—meaning its objective reality—which remains the same regardless of our hypothesis concerning its origin?[42] If we perceive by an inspection of the mind that this content is of a perception such that it surpasses the power of our mind and that it could only have been placed in us by God himself, we would be required to refer the idea to God and to attribute objective validity to it, even if we had admitted at first that it was artificial (chimeric) or adventitious.

It is true that in this case we would have thus refuted the hypothesis that the idea of God was factitious or adventitious,[43] and that we would have resolved the problem of its origin. We would also have paradoxically resolved the problem of origin since, in seeking to resolve the problem of objective validity and, reciprocally, having discovered that God is the necessary cause and archetype of the idea I have of him, and that this idea necessarily has objective validity, I perceive that God is the cause of myself, and that this idea "is born and produced in me from the moment that I was created, as was the idea of myself."[44] Thus on a higher plane, the problem of origin rejoins the problem of objective validity, by the intermediary of the problem of the foundation of "my chief idea."[45] The foundation imparts the origin, and objective validity is established from the origin. This origin is not suspected on the plane of common consciousness, where all innate ideas, in contrast to sensible ideas, are said to "come from nothing other than my own nature."[46]

But how can the problem of the objective validity of idea necessarily be linked to the problem of its origin, with respect to the idea of God, since Descartes has demonstrated that the two problems were distinct and that one could not prove objective validity through the intermediary of origin? That is because origin was postulated and not demonstrated; what was contested was not its necessity, but whether it would be sufficient to settle the problem of origin in order to resolve the problem of objective validity. Hyperbolic doubt operates at this stage at two important points: 1) the existence of things outside of me (essences or existences), and 2) the possible conformity of my idea with such things—if they existed. And it is evident that there are no possible representations of such things if they did not exist. On the other hand, it is no less evident that I cannot be certain that my idea represents the thing from the fact that I would simply have proved that there are things outside me and that the things outside me are the cause (or occasion) of my ideas.

One sees thus that the problem of objective validity must necessarily become more complicated and become a dual problem. We will have to establish that there is something outside of me and also that an idea in me is necessarily related to that thing and allows me *to know* it, meaning, presents to me its *faithful copy*. It is this inevitable complication that links, on a higher plane, the problem of the origin of idea and the problem of its objective validity; in this case, it links the problem of the origin of the idea of God together with the problem of the objective validity of this idea because this idea, on account of its properties, will appear as the only idea that will allow both problems to be resolved at the same time. This will occur when, abstracting away all judgment—which by hypothesis can deceive—we place ourselves before the contents of ideas and ask ourselves whether there is at least one among them such that I am *required* to attribute to it the thing it represents as its origin and, also, to conceive that this thing *cannot* be different in itself from what my idea represents to myself. If I discover such a content, then I would be certain that *I know* effectively something outside of me by means of my idea. I would have proved *the existence* of something outside of me and the effective *knowledge* of this thing by means of my idea at the same time. The solution of the problem of the origin of my idea therefore appears to be the sine qua non condition of the solution of the problem of its objective validity. It is a sine qua non condition, and as such a preliminary condition, but it is not a sufficient condition, for in order to obtain the complete demonstration, we must place into evidence that in addition my idea has a character sui generis that allows me to affirm also that it must necessarily resemble the existing thing, which on the other hand, is certainly its cause.

Consequently, we see that the two principles, the principle of causality and the principle of correspondence of the idea with what is ideated, will each have a role to play in the demonstration of the objective validity of our ideas and, more precisely, in the *demonstration of the objective validity of my idea of God,* a demonstration that coincides, as we shall see, with the *demonstration of the existence of God.* Without the principle of causality, it would be impossible for me to attain the existence of God. Without the principle of the correspondence of the idea with what is ideated, it would be impossible to demonstrate that my idea of God is the image of his being and allows me to know him, since to prove that something is the effect of something else is not sufficient to establish that it resembles it. The "new path" that has remained hidden from common sense and from traditional philosophy, and that is the path Descartes wishes to pursue, will consist of finding the means to apply these two principles legitimately.

After the demonstration of God's existence, in which the problem of origin expressly intersects the problem of the objective validity of the idea, and in which the principle of causality collaborates with the principle of the correspondence between the idea and what is ideated, the problem of the origin of ideas and the problem of their objective validity will continue to remain both distinct and associated. Their distinction will appear with respect to clear and distinct ideas other than the idea of God (for example, mathematical ideas); in this case, the objective validity of ideas is established independently from the causality of existing objects that would be represented by these ideas, for it is based on God's veracity that is in us the immediate and permanent cause of their presence in our understanding. This distinction will also appear with respect to *sensible ideas.* In *Meditation VI* it will be established that they are effectively caused by material things existing outside us, but that these causes will be revealed not as exemplary causes, but as occasional causes; the result of this will therefore not be that my ideas are in conformity with these things nor that they allow us to know them. On the contrary, it will be demonstrated that they are different from them. They allow us to know their existence, not their nature, not their *quid.* Their objective validity will therefore be reduced to a *minimum,* since the thing that we know exists because of them remains unknown in itself. From this arises the distinction between two principles of objective validity:[47] the one relative to the knowledge of existence, which puts the principle of causality alone into play, and the other relative to the knowledge of essence, which also puts into play the principle of the correspondence of the idea with what is ideated. With respect to God, in which existence and essence coincide, the collaboration of these two principles is total. With respect to the Cogito, the case is very special, since its existence is given immediately to us without the intervention of causality and since, from the knowledge of its existence, we draw immediately in a necessary way the knowledge of its essence, without the intervention of the principle of the correspondence with what is ideated, because here the idea is confused with what is ideated. Nevertheless, once the problem of the objective validity of the knowledge that I derive about myself in this way is posited and once I happen to ask myself whether it reveals my existence in itself, and whether the necessities for my science are necessities of things, the problem of the correspondence of the idea with what is ideated intervenes again; even though what is ideated is "myself," it is posited as an *object* relative to representation, a spiritual thing having its nature in itself, with respect to which the question of knowing whether the representation is in conformity to it can be posed. From then on, the problem of the objective validity of the knowledge I derive of my nature in the Cogito is only a particular case of the problem of the objective validity of clear and distinct ideas of finite essences.

5. Conclusion of the Preliminaries

Although preliminary, this twofold classification of thoughts and ideas therefore gives rise to multiple results, as often happens with Cartesian analyses.

On the one hand, it allows one to delimit the domain of the inquiry by isolating the idea of all other thoughts and by putting them out of play; on the other hand—and this is the aim of the refutation of common sense—it allows one to sidestep in advance all the possible paths other than the path of true science. This refutation aims at excluding judgment, above all. This exclusion was already implied in the general classification of thoughts, which, eliminating all the elements of consciousness other than ideas, carried with it, ipso facto, the elimination of judgment. But no elimination is more difficult to realize than this one, for it has against it the prejudices and the habits of common sense that date from my childhood and incorporate the results of judgment into ideas. Moreover, since idea is announced to my consciousness as the picture of something outside it, it constantly solicits, merely by its presence in me, a formal judgment of objectivity that is difficult to dissociate from it.[48] To exclude judgment is therefore the first, but the most difficult requirement, for what is at stake is not only the delimitation of the inquiry by restricting it to the consideration of idea, but also that one has to be certain at the same time that what is isolated from other elements of consciousness is an idea and not a composite [entity] incorporating foreign elements with it. From this stems the necessity for a special effort to return it to its authentic nature, which almost necessarily escapes the irreflection of commonsense consciousness.

At the same time, we discover from within, with respect to my sensible knowledge, new reasons for doubt, which are distinct from the external reasons that appeared during *Meditation I,* when the process of methodological doubt was being developed. We then doubted sensible ideas because, being composite, they could be imaginary. The character of this global condemnation was not to distinguish the sensible idea from its affirmation in doubt, one and the other being indifferently excluded. Here, on the contrary, doubt is specified, because of the internal analysis that dissociates two elements in ideas—its representative content (its objective reality), which is indubitable,[49] and the objective reality that one adds to it arbitrarily and that results from an act of judgment, which is doubtful.[50] It is clear that this dissociation was unmanageable as long as the Cogito had not been acquired. Only the Cogito, by discovering for me everything that is able to be posited about my consciousness with respect to its existence and the existence of what is contained in it, cannot be contested; it alone can allow me to preserve in certain knowledge, knowledge invulnerable even to the most hyperbolic doubt, what is purely and simply perceived as contents existing in fact in my consciousness. The refutation of the theses of common sense has also allowed us to distinguish between the problem of the objective validity of ideas and the problem of the truth and falsity of judgments. Finally it has allowed us to dissociate the problem of the origin of ideas and the problem of their objective validity. And while giving the means to affirm that, even if the idea of God were chimeric, it would not be necessarily false because of it; it introduces the conception of the innateness of that idea.[51]

In the same way that, in *Meditation II,* the analysis of the piece of wax, presented as a simple verification in the domain of common sense of the results acquired according to the order, by means of the rational demonstration of the nature and primacy of my soul, enriched considerably the conclusion obtained, the refutation of the affirmations and methods of common sense, presented here not as a verification, but as a preliminary operation with respect to the rational demonstration, properly speaking, of the objective validity of ideas, gives rise to many results that impart to it an infinitely greater interest than the interest that is normally given to simple preliminaries.

6. The Main Point of the Investigation. Proof of the Objective Validity of Ideas and Proof of God's Existence: Intersection of the Two Designs

Once everything alien to ideas, properly speaking, and in particular judgments of objective validity brought upon ideas, is eliminated from them, the self is confronted with the internal panorama of its ideas, which are equal among themselves as pure and simple modifications of consciousness, but are different, on the other hand, with respect to their representative content, meaning, with respect to the objective reality they offer inherently to the mind.[52] The investigation, properly speaking, can start now. We will have to discover the means to attribute necessarily objective validity to some or all of these ideas, by considering their contents alone.

This investigation assumes at first a great complexity. In fact, it begins along two different axes.

On the one hand, if I doubted the objective validity of my clear and distinct ideas, that is because, in virtue of the fiction of the evil genius, I challenged the *natural* certainty that my understanding gave me of it. In order for these ideas all to recuperate ipso facto what the hypothesis had taken away from them, it would be sufficient for me to destroy this hypothesis. Consequently, I must prove that God exists, meaning I must prove that a perfect being that could not be a deceiver exists. In this way the objective validity naturally attributed to clear and distinct ideas by our understanding would be assured. As a result, the problem is stated as follows: "In order to remove it altogether [this reason for doubting that depends on a deceiving God—M. G.], I must examine whether there is a God as soon as the occasion presents itself, and if there is one, I must also examine whether he can be a deceiver; for without the knowledge of these two truths, I do not see how I can ever be certain of anything."[53] The most immediate goal of the investigation is therefore to prove that God exists. Only the consequence of this demonstration will allow the resolution of the problem of the objective validity of clear and distinct ideas. And this solution will then be valid for the *universality* of these ideas.

But if one reflects upon this, to prove that God exists from the idea that represents him to me, and to prove that he exists exactly as I represent him to myself, meaning as an absolutely perfect and veracious being, is to prove that the idea of God has an objective validity. In this latter perspective, it is no longer the problem of God's existence that is the key to the problem of objective validity, but, on the contrary, it is the latter problem that is the key to the former problem. The problem of the objective validity of ideas then appears as requiring direct treatment for itself, and we will need to find its solution without going through God, since we do not yet know whether God exists. Consequently it will be advisable to seek "whether among the things of which I have ideas there are some existing outside of me"[54] in such a way that, perceiving these things as not stemming from me, I am assured "of not being alone in the world"[55] and of receiving the ideas by which I represent these things from the things themselves. That is why, instead of "interrupting the order of thought that we have proposed for ourselves,"[56] in order to refute the concept of the evil genius and to restore the objective validity that our understanding attributes naturally to ideas, we will pursue the methodical inquiry according to the direction it has taken from the beginning, without deviation; in brief, we will have to discover, through an internal examination, whether the necessities understood by my intelligence are the necessities of things. We "will pass by degrees from the notions that I discover to be the most basic in my mind to those I can discover afterwards."[57] Then, having reduced the notions concerning the problem to be resolved to "ideas" alone, we will examine the different kinds of ideas one at a time, by degrees, in order to discover the ones that are such that I am required to recognize their objective validity, meaning that I am required to posit outside them and outside me a corresponding reality that would be their "archetype or source (*archetypus*)."[58] As a result we will succeed in resolving the problem for a single idea—the idea of God—and not for the set of ideas.

It is evident that this second perspective is completely different from the first. According to the first we are concerned with proving that God exists. According to the second, we are concerned in seeking whether there are ideas having objective validity. According to the first, the discovery of the existence of a veracious God has the consequence of restoring to *all* the clear and distinct ideas the objective validity of which they were deprived. And we are assured that this validity is restored to them indirectly, by the intermediacy of God, without having to penetrate directly into the basis of this proper objective validity, which is recognized for each of them. According to the second, the discovery in my soul that a certain idea possesses necessarily objective validity has the fortunate consequence of demonstrating that God exists, for this idea is precisely the idea of God. Further, the inquiry that is pursued in a fragmentary fashion, idea by idea, does not aim at a universal solution of the problem of the objective validity of ideas; it stops with the examination of whether "among the things of which I have an idea, there are *some* existing outside of me."[59] In effect, the result attained is so far from being universal that it allows me to attribute in all certainty the objective validity in question, to only *a single idea*. On the other hand, I do not attribute this to it extrinsically, but by capturing directly the basis for this validity—the infinity of its objective reality.

Thus, instead of an indirect, but universal and global, solution of the problem of objective validity, we arrive at a direct solution, giving the basic reason for this validity; but it is a fragmentary reason, valid finally for *a single* idea. According to the first perspective, the problem of the objective validity of ideas seems to be resolved "on the occasion" of the demonstration of the veracious God.[60] According to the second, the demonstration of the veracious God seems to be discovered "on the occasion" of the solution of the problem of the objective validity of ideas: I must examine "whether there is a God as soon as *the occasion presents itself"* and *"in order to have the occasion* to examine without interrupting the order of thoughts. . . ."[61] I must resolve methodically, according to the order of reasons (by "passing by degrees from the notions that I discover to be most basic in my mind to those I can discover afterwards"), the problem of the objective validity of my ideas.

Thus, the two investigations seem to follow altogether different lines, in their immediate goal, as well as in their method and their result.

But it happens that they come together again by an admirable convergence, to the extent that they are almost one and appear to be strictly complementary to one another.

On the one hand, the methodical examination of various kinds of ideas, with the view towards discovering whether there are some among them that present some characteristics requiring me to consider them as faithful pictures of a formal reality that they represent, ends up discovering that an idea has such characteristics, namely, the idea of God. This idea necessarily has objective validity because it has a content of such amplitude that I am required to posit the thing from which it stems and to which it "conforms"[62] outside of it and me. It then becomes established as "impressed" in me by God himself, being like "the worker's trademark on his work." Thus, I can conceive by it, that, in some fashion, I resemble God, and that I was created "in his image and likeness."[63] Since to demonstrate the objective validity of an idea is to prove that it resembles what is ideated, once I have established that my idea of God has this validity, I have established that it resembles God, and consequently myself, insofar as I am marked by his impression, I resemble God to the maximum degree to which a creature can resemble its infinite creator.

The inquiry that concerned the objective validity of ideas has therefore come to an end with the objective validity of one of them. I know indubitably that there exists at least one thing outside of me—God—and that I *know* that thing with perfect clarity and distinctness, meaning that my idea is the perfect copy of what this nature is in itself. Moreover, here as elsewhere, I was able to attain the certainty that the object of the idea exists *(quod)* by means of the knowledge of its nature *(quid)*—meaning from the perfection of the objective reality of the idea. But, on the other hand, the result of the inquiry can appear meager, since it allows me to render to *only one* of my ideas the objective validity that it has taken away from all of them.

But this unique idea is "the first and principal"[64] idea, namely, the idea of God; and everything changes at once, for:

1) Although the investigation directly concerning the problem of the demonstration of the existence of the veracious God seemed to have been set aside in order to examine the problem of the objective validity of ideas, I suddenly perceived that at the moment when it seemed that I was no longer thinking about it in some way—being absorbed with finding an idea that was effectively the resembling image of something outside of me—I discovered the full and complete solution to this problem. In fact, if the idea of God necessarily has objective validity, God exists necessarily once I have the idea of God, as object of this idea.

2) Moreover, once I ascertain that my investigation, by examining ideas one at a time, succeeds only in resolving positively the problem of the objective validity of ideas for only one idea, I perceive that, because of the consequences, I have discovered the universal solution of this problem. In fact, if God exists, since he is necessarily veracious, the hypothesis of the deceiving God and the fiction of the evil genius are destroyed immediately. The metaphysical doubt that struck at clear and distinct ideas is ipso facto necessarily abolished. Then, all these ideas, together and at once, necessarily regain their objective validity.[65]

3) Finally, if we reunited the two inquiries, so that we brought to the set

of clear and distinct ideas, which have been reinvested with their objective validity in an indirect fashion, the internal reason that constrains us necessarily to attribute directly this validity to the idea of God alone, we discover the internal principle that established this objective validity in all of them. Since in the case of the idea of God it is the infinite quantity of the objective reality of the idea that imposes necessarily objective validity, objective validity is evidently a function of the objective reality of the idea. Consequently, if divine veracity requires us to grant to clear and distinct ideas the objective validity that our understanding attributes to them spontaneously, that is because the objective reality of these ideas is in a sufficient quantity for our understanding to perceive them unavoidably as true. Truth and reality are synonymous. In this way one understands that when the quantity of objective reality of an idea becomes infinitely small such that the understanding can no longer determine whether it is greater than zero, or determine whether it belongs to being or nothingness, the understanding necessarily comes to doubt the reality of the idea—therefore its truth—and to strip it of any objective validity: such is the case of sensible ideas (heat, cold, etc.).

This intersection of the two perspectives is expressly called forth by Descartes since he states that 1) he pursues the direct examination of each idea from the point of view of its legitimate objective validity only "in order to have the occasion to examine [whether there is a God . . . and whether he can be a deceiver—M. G.],"[66] and 2) he wishes "to examine whether there is a God, as soon as the occasion presents itself" only in order "to be able to lift completely the light and metaphysical reason" that makes me doubt the objective validity of ideas.[67]

Thus, on the one hand, the proof of the existence of God appears as the means with respect to the solution of the problem of the objective validity of ideas; on the other hand, the inquiry toward proving the solution of the problem of the objective validity of ideas appears as the means with respect to the demonstration of the existence of God. However, in spite of this reciprocity, the original design was nothing more than the discovery of the solution to the problem of the objective validity of ideas and the ability thus to transform the necessary truths of science into truths of things. That this concern is predominant can be seen with more than enough evidence insofar as the only reason for Descartes to demonstrate that God exists as quickly as he can is to prove that the evil genius does not exist and that our clear and distinct ideas have certain objective validity.

7. God, *instar archetypi*

An important consequence with respect to God himself can be drawn from the above. In fact, since for Descartes to prove that an idea has objective validity is to prove that it is effectively the same as when it manifests itself in consciousness, meaning that it is effectively the exact image or "picture" of an original thing it represents and from which it proceeds, and since to demonstrate the existence of God is to demonstrate that our idea of God has an objective validity, then the whole aim of this demonstration is to establish that this idea is the faithful copy of the thing it represents, and that it is a "standard" or an "archetype."[68] It is therefore completely natural for Descartes to exhibit God, whose existence is to be proven as the prime cause of our ideas and as "a standard or archetype *(instar archetypi)* in which is formally contained all reality or perfection that is found only objectively or by representation in the idea."[69]

Thus the condition for administering the proof no more requires that the principle of correspondence of the idea with what is ideated be challenged for the benefit of the principle of causality than the conclusion of the proof requires as a rule the exclusion of the conception of a model and archetypic God, under the pretext that this proof only ends up, in all certainty, in positing God as an efficient cause.

The demonstration of God's existence is, with respect to this reply, the positive aspect of the destruction of the privileged position of objective validity that common sense gives to adventitious ideas, which is the negative aspect. Common sense affirms that the external thing is the cause of the sensible idea and resembles it. The refutation did not consist in denying that the truth of an idea was in conformity with what is ideated, nor in establishing that one ought to be satisfied with proving that it was its effect. The proof simply placed in evidence that common sense applied the principle of causality as illegitimately and arbitrarily as it applied the principle of the conformity of the idea to what is ideated, in this case, and that it was not sufficient to prove that the idea was caused by the thing it claimed to represent in order to demonstrate that it resembled it, in this way. It has therefore required, as a condition of demonstration of the objective validity of any idea, the legitimate application (meaning necessary and indubitable) *of both principles.* And among all our ideas, the idea of God presents itself as being the only idea to have the privilege of allowing such an application. In fact, its content is such that I am constrained, lest I should disown myself, to posit something outside it that is its cause and that resembles it essentially—even though I do not know it completely in this way (in the same way that the idea I have of a triangle resembles exactly the essence of the triangle, whose properties are not all known to me and probably would never become known to me).

8. The Axiom: The Effect Resembles the Cause

The necessary intervention of the principle of the correspondence of the idea with what is ideated is conditioned, according to the above, by the affirmation that it is not sufficient that a thing causes an idea for the thing to resemble it. But does not Descartes assert the contrary in the *Entretien avec Burman* when he states: "It is a true and common axiom that the effect resembles the cause"?[70] If that is so, is it then not sufficient to prove that God is the cause of his idea in me in order to know that this idea resembles him?

This axiom, however, is not applicable in the present case.

We must in fact distinguish three kinds of causalities: absolutely creative causality (God's causality), natural production (the generation of a father), and artificial production (the production of an architect constructing a house). The axiom in question is applicable in the second case, and even more so in the first case. In fact, when the cause is itself a being and a substance and it produces something by calling it into existence, meaning by creating it from nothing, such a thing must resemble its cause, because it must also be a substance, a being. It must have *at least* that resemblance with the Creator. As a result, every created thing, even a stone, is the image of God, in different degrees, with respect to the degree of reality that God has conferred on it. And, since God has given me a greater degree of reality than he has given the other beings, I must resemble him maximally.[71] We rediscover here the Neoplatonist idea that was dear to the theologians of the High Middle Ages, who saw in created nature the allegory of divinity and all created things as imitating, to a greater or lesser degree, the God from which they drew their existence. Descartes' expression in the second proof by effects follows from this: "*From the very fact that God has created me,* it is very credible that he has produced me, in some way, in his image and likeness."[72]

However, the axiom is not applicable in the third case (artificial production), the case of the architect constructing a house, because we are not here concerned with a creative cause, but a cause that "merely applies active things to passive things."[73] And the proof by the cause that impresses the idea on us is under the third case, since the idea is *a passion* in us *whose active cause we are concerned to discover.*[74] God is not posited here as the Creator of my being, but as the cause of the passion he exercises on my being when imprinting the idea of the infinite on it. Consequently, the discovery of the cause of the passion would not authorize us to posit this cause as resembling its effect. That is why, in *Meditation VI,* the certainty that the cause of our sensible perceptions, which are passions, is the body existing outside us, does not authorize us to posit this body as resembling the perception we have of it.

On the other hand, this axiom can be valid with respect to the second proof of God by effects, since we will discover God through this second proof not merely as the cause of the idea he impresses in me, but as the *creative* cause of this self marked by this idea. However, the application of this axiom will result from this proof and will not be a condition of it. I will prove that I resemble God from the fact that I have demonstrated that he exists necessarily as my Creator. More exactly, this creative causality will serve less to demonstrate than *to explain* this resemblance, which is already established between myself and God in virtue of the first proof by effects, in which the perfection of the objective reality of the idea of perfection guarantees its perfect conformity with the formal reality that is its cause. The expressions *"I must not think it strange that . . ."* and "from the very fact that he has created me, *it is very credible that . . ."*[75] follow from this.

9. God, Efficient Cause

The character of the causality that was put into play in the first proof by effects therefore confirms the necessity for the appeal to the principle of the correspondence of the idea with what is ideated, and the necessity of such a correspondence must be the principal object of a proof that aims at establishing the objective validity of an idea.

Numerous commentators, however, have reproached Descartes for having the conception of God as Standard and Archetype. They have seen in this a residue of Scholastic and realistic thought that would contradict the true Cartesian doctrine of God as free and efficient cause, as well as the idealistic inspiration constituting the originality of the proof. The former would consist in putting aside the principle of the correspondence of the idea with what is ideated as completely erroneous, for the benefit of the principle of causality that alone has the ability to conclude the demonstration. Has not Descartes characterized "the new way" as the way of "the equality *ad minimum* of the reality of the total efficient cause and its effect," a principle that is "manifest according to natural light,"[76] in contrast with the common way, which is the way of the "principal and most common error" consisting in "judging that the ideas in me are similar or in conformity with the things that are outside of me"?[77]

It is incontestable that this traditional interpretation seems impressive and that it encompasses a certain feeling of what largely constitutes the originality of Cartesian conception.

First, it is well known that in his proof Descartes abandons the property of the idea of being the picture of something external in order to consider only its representative content in its intrinsic reality. No doubt the property of being *representative* does not stop defining the content of the idea as such and does not stop distinguishing it from the form of ideas and other thoughts; the differences among contents of ideas remain based on the differences of objects represented, but this property appears as extrinsic with respect to *the reality* of the content, which alone intervenes as an element of the proof and which is something intrinsic, capable of *being measured.* Because of this ability of being measured, the content gives rise to an immediate and legitimate application of the principle of causality—which is itself defined in accordance with a formula of necessary equality *ad minimum* between two terms. Descartes, considering all our ideas as equal with respect to their form as ideas *(nullam inaequalitatem inter ipsas),* discovers them unequal *(valde diversas)* with respect to their objective reality;[78] the application of the principle of equality *ad minimum*[79] between the formal reality of the cause and the objective reality of the effect to these unequal contents allows for the resolution of the problem. In fact, if there is a content whose quantity of reality or perfection surpasses the quantity of formal reality of my self, we will be forced to assign to it a cause different from my self and, consequently, existing outside of it. And I perceive such an idea in my consciousness, the idea of God, whose objective reality has an infinite amplitude and surpasses infinitely the formal finite reality of my soul. It necessarily requires a cause that must possess *at least* a formal infinite reality, in order to be adequate, and consequently, it must exist outside of me. Therefore there necessarily exists outside of me a perfect and infinite being, the cause in me of the idea that I have of it—therefore God exists.[80]

Secondarily, one sees that this reasoning underscores in a new way the disdain of historians who, interpreting the texts of *Meditation IV* in an aberrant fashion, believe that my idea of the infinite derives its origin from the consciousness I have of the infinity of my will (according to Descartes). If it were thus, I would discover immediately, in myself, in the formal reality of my will, what can account for the objective reality of my idea of infinity; I would no longer need, then, to go outside of myself in order to discover the adequate necessary cause of this reality: I myself would be God—a thesis that will be Fichte's and that Descartes explicitly rejects.[81] Moreover the infinity of my will is not the infinity of my whole being, and my will itself is infinite only under a certain aspect.[82]

The whole argument would collapse if one could demonstrate that I am infinite and that consequently I would be capable of producing the idea of infinity by myself. Thus the objection that one has to foresee is that I am infinite without knowing it, being infinite by means of potential perfections that are in me without my being able to detect them through their actions. Can one not assert that I have some knowledge that is capable of increasing a little at a time until infinity? Can I not, in this way, someday acquire all the other perfections of divine nature? Is not the power that can acquire these perfections for me someday also capable of impressing their ideas in me actually? No; for the existence of this progress toward infinity proves that I am actually finite. The certainty of always being able to surpass whatever degree of perfection I have attained testifies to the fact that I am destined to remain finite. And the assumption that I have potential infinity in this way does not entail that I am capable of producing the objective being of the idea of infinity as an actual being, when a potential being is nothing.[83] On the contrary, aspiring toward the infinity that we lack supposes the objective reality of actual infinity;[84] and to assume that the idea of infinity arises from the faculty we have of amplifying all the created perfections in order to construct the idea of God in this way, is to assume that this faculty itself, which is the faculty of conceiving something greater, comes only from the one thing in us that is the idea of something greater, namely, from God himself.[85]

Finally, the affirmation of the content of the idea as objective reality imparts an extremely precise meaning to the notion of the positiveness of the idea of infinity. This idea is evidently positive because it is the idea of infinity insofar as it encloses the (objective) *reality* of the infinite; to attempt to draw it out of the finite would then appear as immediately absurd since that would be to attempt to draw objective *infinite reality* from a *finite reality*. From this the Cartesian reply to Gassendi's objection derives its whole force: "It is not true that we conceive the infinite through the negation of the finite, since on the contrary all limitation contains in itself the negation of the infinite."[86]

In conclusion, since my self is finite beyond question, and the idea of God entails an infinite (objective) reality, it is impossible to discover the sufficient cause of this idea elsewhere than in the formal reality of the infinite itself, meaning in God.

It is evident that, through this recourse to causality, God is posited not as the model to which the idea must bear resemblance, but as the reality of which its content must be the effect, without the necessity that this effect resembles this cause. Moreover, this apparent radical elimination of the concept of the conformity of the idea with what is ideated seems confirmed by a detail of the demonstration. That is how the ideas of men, animals, and angels conceived as being able to be drawn from the combination of ideas that do not resemble them, namely, the idea of corporeal things together with the idea of God. It is true that one would say that this explanatory hypothesis is valid only for a derived idea, whose content has its cause in the objective reality of a higher, nonderived idea that could not be conceived except as the effect of a formal reality outside it, which is its archetype. But this reply seems not to be expedient for all cases. Thus, with respect to the idea of extension, the cause of the objective reality of this idea, which we can conceive as residing in an eminent formal reality, is susceptible to being attributed to the formal reality of my thinking self.[87] But my self has no resemblance to extension; it is even that which is most dissimilar to it. Finally, when Descartes conceives that the objective truth of the idea of an extremely artificial machine, having no reality outside the understanding, can have "as cause a great knowledge of mechanical science or a great subtlety of mind, which has enabled someone to invent it without any previous knowledge,"[88] it is evident that here the cause, whether it is formal or eminent, has no resemblance with its effect. Consequently, the link that necessarily unites the formal reality of the cause with the objective reality of the effect has no relation with the link that unites the model with its copy. The principle of the correspondence of the idea with what is ideated appears therefore to have been completely suppressed by the principle of causality. Although the cause of the objective reality of ideas must always finally be sought outside it, it does not follow that the formal reality outside it is necessarily the *object* of this idea, nor does it follow that the formal reality, the cause of the idea, is the model whose idea is its reflection. Moreover, since this cause can be eminent, it is evident that it cannot resemble its effect. Is that not precisely the case with God? Is not God the eminent cause of his idea in me? How could he not be the eminent cause, since this idea is, by definition, in its objective reality, a manner of being that is less perfect than the manner of being suitable for formal reality, being like "falling short" of perfection?[89] How could God not be the eminent cause since he is posited as an absolutely free and all-powerful will, and since consequently he could not be a slave to the necessities of the idea that I perceive in my understanding? And how could he not be the eminent cause since he must have instituted it freely, remaining above it, revealing to me by means of it everything that is incomprehensible, everything that lifts him incomprehensibly above my self? By following this direction to its end, could we not say after all that, in the proof by effects, the idea of God allows us to know that God exists, but does not allow us to know what he is? Is not his will an unfathomable abyss for us? Are not his ends impenetrable? Are not the eternal truths truths only for us? In this way we would recover the observation that the critique against common sense had brought up: it is not sufficient to know that a thing is the cause of my idea in order to be ipso facto legitimately certain that my idea conforms to this thing. A true agnosticism would be introduced by this subterfuge.

In any case, even if one refuses to go that far, would it not be at least evident that the God to which the Cartesian proof leads is not at all an immutable being, an eternal model of his ideas in us, but an infinite omnipotence, a freely creative will that has no other bounds to its omnipotence than the concept of this omnipotence itself (it cannot tend toward nothingness)? Would not this God which is defined solely by efficient cause and which is established beyond the realm of ideas, be incompatible with the notion of an impassive archetype, barren of life, purely and simply reflected in his idea in us as in a picture? And is this not what makes the polemic between Arnauld and Malebranche so interesting, this collision between the conception of a transcendental omnipotent divinity, whose aims are impenetrable, in whose "counsels" we are not admitted, which dispenses to us the light of our intelligence from above without allowing us to participate in its light, and the conception of a wholly intelligent divinity whose will is subordinated to wisdom—meaning to idea—who cannot, any more than we can, rid himself of the rational relations I perceive in him by means of his own light in which I participate, and not by means of a light distinct from his light, illuminated in me by his arbitrary decree?

10. The Principle of Causality as Instrument of Proof

Certainly the God of Arnauld is closer to the God of Descartes than is the God of Malebranche. Is that to say that we ought to ascribe to the whole interpretation? We shall see that we do not need to. We can, at first, credit that incontestably the principle of causality plays a basic role in the proof, that it even constitutes its essential strength, and that the positing of God as efficient cause agrees remarkably well with the image that we find in ourselves of a God whose absolute infinity entails a freedom without limit. Moreover, the name that Cartesians have accepted for the proof, *proof by effects,* is by itself sufficiently edifying.

This primacy of the principle of causality seems to be explained by four different reasons, which, in order of increasing depth, are as follows:

The first reason is Descartes' wish to have a proof by effects: he would have thus transposed the traditional argument within the frame of his idealism. This explanation, which has often been proposed, is perhaps partially correct; but it does not account sufficiently for the internal necessities of the doctrine.

The second reason would be that the Cartesian notion of the incomprehensible God, free Creator of all things, including the eternal truths, led naturally to a conception of efficient causality that, putting God's omnipotence above the content of his own idea in us, allowed us to establish the objective reality of this idea and of other ideas without confining God himself in the necessity of any one of our ideas. This reason is already less superficial. In fact, as we shall soon see, it is the idea of the perfect, meaning of the infinite containing unlimited omnipotence, which governs latently, from the start, the process that allows one to conclude by positing its necessary existence. By giving this reason one assumes that the concept of God's incomprehensibility inspires the original process of the Cartesian proof, instead of resulting from it.

The third reason is drawn from the order of the meditation so far. As we can recall, the Cogito is posited only by abstraction of the representative contents of consciousness and by the knowledge that it later derives from itself. The thinking self can immediately attribute to itself thoughts as modes, but it cannot attribute their contents to itself, which, although falling within its realm, remain unexplained with respect to their origin. Knowledge of the self by itself can therefore only be achieved by an inquiry into this origin, which, in order not to be the first aim that is pursued, is linked to the inquiry of objective validity. And this inquiry into the origin is possible only by the application of the principle of causality to the contents, considered in themselves.[90]

We note that, with respect to this, the dissociation of objective reality, relative to the form of my thoughts, as well as relative to external things, and its attachment to God as the cause of the objective reality of my idea of the infinite, with respect to which the objective realities of finite ideas can only be limitations, tends to be a doctrine of total innateness in which the content of ideas in me, as parts of the content of the idea of infinity, ought to be completely explained by the infinity of the objective reality of the idea that is imposed on me by God. It would be sufficient to modify a few details of the theory in order to go from this innateness doctrine to the Malebranchian conception of the vision in God—which is wholly different.

The fourth reason is drawn from the nature of the notions put into play. It is the most solid and decisive reason. Once stripped of its applicability by the provisional suppression of every external thing real or possible, by means of the hypothesis of the evil genius, the principle of correspondence of the idea with what is ideated cannot recover its legitimate usage by itself—meaning, it cannot be immanent to the givens of our consciousness. Such a legitimate usage is, in fact, conceivable only from the intrinsic character of the objective realities present in us. But no intrinsic character of this kind allows this principle to be applied in such a way that one can conclude, in all certainty, the existence outside of us of something external to which my idea would conform. The principle of the conformity of the idea with what is ideated only affirms a resemblance between two terms; the principle of causality affirms an equation—*ad minimum*—between two terms. The quantitative evaluation of the perfection contained in one of the two terms (the one present in me) cannot therefore serve in the case of resemblance to determine correlatively the quantity of perfection in the other—which is unknown or stricken out in itself—and therefore can never give the means of positing its external reality (by disproportion with the quantity of perfection proper to internal reality). In fact, resemblance is never the property of a single term. It is impossible to measure the degree of resemblance (the perfection in the resemblance) of a term taken apart. One must also possess preliminarily or simultaneously the term which it resembles and with respect to which this resemblance can be evaluated. And the term in question is precisely the unknown that we are seeking. Since all perception of resemblance, and a fortiori, all evaluation of the degree of resemblance, is impossible as long as the two terms are not given, the intrinsic consideration of the resembling term—taken in isolation—will never allow one to pass on to positing the unknown and problematic term that it would resemble. The quantity of perfection contained in an idea cannot be evaluated by its resemblance to the thing, since this resemblance is unknown a priori, and must, on the contrary, be established.

11. The Principle of Causality and the Principle of the Conformity of the Idea with What Is Ideated

That said, it suffices to remind oneself of the order of reasons and the aim pursued by Descartes from the beginning of *Meditation III* in order to perceive with full clarity the error of an interpretation that would consider that Descartes merely attempted to prove, against the Scholastics, the existence of a living, free God who is irrational to a certain degree, and that Descartes has dismissed the principle of the correspondence of the idea with what is ideated in order to do so.

At what does Descartes aim? Doubtless it is to demonstrate that God exists; but this end, which is the most spectacular, is in no way the most important. We know that he aims to resolve the problem of the objective validity of ideas and that consequently he wishes to seek if there are ideas in us such that I am assured to know objects outside of me in this way: to know them, meaning to be certain that they are in themselves such that my ideas represent them to me, and not simply to be certain that there are things outside of us that are their cause, for in this way I could know that these things exist without expressly "knowing" them, the nature of these causes possibly remaining hidden to me. Is this not precisely the case for the objects of my sensible knowledge? Descartes' philosophy demonstrates that the ideas of these objects effectively have their cause in external things and that I can know in this way that these things exist, but also that these things do not remain any less *unknown* in these ideas, because these things do not "conform" to them.

Let us suppose, as it has been previously stated, that the proof by effects revealed only the existence of a mysterious, omnipotent God, without getting us *to know what he is* in any other way: how would the knowledge we would have of him differ from the knowledge that sensible ideas give us of bodies? The objective content of his idea, which would allow us simply to posit his existence, would leave us without any knowledge of his nature, in this case as well as in the other case. And the objective validity of the idea of God, which is incapable of guaranteeing for us the conformity of this idea with the thing, would not surpass the objective validity of sensible images. Why then would we criticize the thesis of common sense on this point and assert that it is not sufficient for me to know that an idea has its cause in an external thing to which it refers in order to be assured of its resemblance with this thing? How can one then affirm, given that the objective validity of the idea of God is not established, that God effectively possesses in himself the properties that we represent to ourselves, by means of his idea, clearly and distinctly as having to be in him—namely, his attributes, beginning with veracity? Therefore the proof, if it succeeds, must not end up proving that God exists, but establishing that we really know this existing God, that our idea is the exact tracing of his essence, that it is the exact copy of his nature. That is the condition under which Descartes' design can be realized: that the evil genius can be refuted and that the truth of science can be established as the truth of things. It is, consequently, impossible that consideration of the conformity of the idea with what is ideated be eliminated from the proof.

The new way is therefore not defined by the substitution of the principle of causality for the principle of the conformity of the idea with what is ideated. It is defined above all by its opposition with the way of common sense. And the way of common sense, as we have seen, is the way of *judgment* applying freely the two principles. The new way consists in setting aside all judgment preliminarily in order to determine the foundation of the legitimate applicability of one and the other principle. It sets aside the *judgment of causality* as well as the *judgment of the conformity with what is ideated.* As for the principles themselves, although Descartes tells us that the principle of causality, such as he formulates it at the beginning of his inquiry, is revealed to us by natural light, he also declares, a few pages later, that the principle of correspondence of the idea with what is ideated is no less so.[91] What then characterizes the new way is the determination of the means that allow one to establish this dual legitimate applicability: the distinction between the objective reality and the formal reality of the idea, the recourse to the evaluation of the degrees of objective reality, and the possibility of applying immanently, therefore legitimately, the equation of causality (equality *ad minimum* with the effect) with respect to various qualities of objective reality.

The principle of causality and the principle of the conformity of the idea with what is ideated reciprocally condition their respective applicability. On the one hand, the possibility to put into play the principle of causality is conditioned by the appeal to the subjective necessity of the correspondence of the idea with what is ideated; on the other hand, the discovery, by means of the legitimate application of the principle of causality to ideas, of a thing existing as necessary cause of the objective reality of an idea allows the discovery of a privileged case in which the application of the principle of the correspondence of an idea with what is ideated becomes legitimate. The two principles collaborate closely; and this collaboration does not imply a paralogism, as we shall see.

With respect to the first point, it is evident that the principle of causality, conceived by itself, does not authorize a relation of cause and effect between the formal reality of the thing represented and the objective reality of the representing idea. It only authorizes the establishment of a relation between the objective reality of my idea and *its cause.* But is this cause precisely the formal reality of the thing? To affirm this, one must invoke the constitution of the idea[92] and posit in principle that the cause of its objective reality cannot be found elsewhere than in the formal reality of the thing. If one abstracts away this principle, this axiom of causality allows me to posit only, either that an objective reality must have as cause another objective reality of at least the same quantity as its effect, or that a formal reality must have its cause in another formal reality, in the same way, or even that each of these realities must have a cause that remains indeterminate in this respect. It therefore only allows me to conclude with the two parallel series of Spinoza's philosophy. In order for the two series to interfere with each other, one must expressly posit that the objective reality of the idea necessarily proceeds from the formal reality of the thing in itself that it represents as outside it; one must have the intervention of the postulate of the correspondence of the idea with what is ideated, which defines image as the *reflection* of an archetype.

Since Descartes admits that certain derived ideas can find their cause in the objective reality of more primitive ideas, he tells us that one must arrive finally at a first idea that cannot draw its cause from another idea and that, consequently, would draw its cause from a *formal reality outside it* which would be its "model." The definition of the nature of the idea necessarily entails a definition of the nature of the *cause of the idea*, because it belongs to the nature of the idea to be representative, meaning to contain an objective reality, it belongs to the nature of its cause to be a formal reality: "Just as this manner of being objectively belongs to ideas by their own nature, so also the manner or fashion of being formally belongs to the causes of these ideas by their own nature."[93] This way of characterizing the necesssary nature of idea and correlatively the necessary nature of its eventual cause, is in some measure "phenomenological."

The definition of the idea as the copy of an archetype is therefore what establishes the application of the principle of causality in such a way that it establishes a link of cause and effect not only between two formal realities, or between two objective realities, but between an objective reality and a formal reality, between the idea and the thing it represents. That is why Descartes specifies that "the first or principal cause" of ideas, or what comes to the same thing, the cause of the first idea, must also be the "model" or "archetype" in which "all the reality or perfection that is found only objectively or by representation in ideas, is contained formally or in actuality."[94] From this results paradoxically that the necessity my understanding conceives of an effective conformity of the idea with what is ideated, in the case in which this idea must have objective validity, is finally concentrated, to the detriment of the other ideas, only in the first idea, meaning in the idea of God, which, since it cannot derive from another idea, cannot draw its cause elsewhere than in a formal archetypal reality of which it would be the picture—on the supposition that one can legitimately prove that such a cause really exists. Thus, begun by the affirmation of the necessary play of the principle of causality, "which is manifest by natural light,"[95] the exposition of the new method is achieved by the affirmation of the principle of the correspondence of the idea with what is ideated, which "natural light allows me to know clearly."[96]

But does not the introduction of this latter principle prejudge the solution of the problem? If our first idea, meaning God, by its nature of idea and by its property of being first, necessarily has its cause in a formal reality outside itself, is not the question decided in advance and does not the definition of the idea by itself entail finally, automatically, the recognition of its objective validity? No. The principle of correspondence that natural light reveals to us, indicates to us only where we should try to discover the real cause of the content of the idea, *if our ideas effectively possess objective validity*—of which I am unaware. It prescribes for us to seek this cause in the formal reality of the thing represented, but it does not itself allow us to discover it and does not allow us to posit its existence. Certainly I am constrained by the internal necessities of my understanding to conceive that the cause of the objective reality of the idea—at least of the first idea—cannot be posited elsewhere than in the formal reality of the thing represented. But that is a completely subjective necessity: nothing proves to me that this truth for my understanding entails the truth of the thing. I do not yet know whether such formal reality could be effectively posited outside of me. And the necessity of my understanding would be established as objective only under that condition. The sole aim of the proof is precisely to seek to demonstrate that I can legitimately attribute to the idea the *objective validity* whose certainty could not result from the fact that its *objective reality* is necessarily announced in me as the copy of an archetype. It is only by means of causality, after having evaluated the quantity of objective reality present in the idea and after having realized the impossibility to discover in me a sufficient formal reality in order to account for it, that this subjective necessity would have been transformed into objective necessity in a privileged case (God).

It therefore seems impossible to subscribe to the opinion of Liard, who sees in the introduction of the principle of the correspondence of the idea with what is ideated a logical fault,[97] as if positing such a principle ought inevitably to entail the objectively valid certainty that the idea effectively has its cause in the formal reality that it reflects. Hamelin does not seem better to us when, wishing to set aside Liard's interpretation, he sees in the intervention of the principle of the correspondence of the idea with what is ideated traces of an unfortunate realism contrasting with the method of causality.[98] The definition of the principle of the correspondence of the idea with what is ideated is none other than a kind of phenomenological description of the idea and does not imply any certain conclusion with respect to the effective existence of what is ideated. However, without this principle, the proof cannot be accomplished. The proof consists entirely in discovering a case in which it is legitimate to apply the principle concurrently with the principle of causality. Moreover, taken in themselves, these two principles cannot be touched by the evil genius. It is a fact that the idea is announced in me as the copy of an object; the evil genius could not make this fact be null when I contemplate it. It is a fact that the principle of causality presents itself to me such as natural light makes me perceive it. But the evil genius strikes at their applicability, their claim to be objectively valid, which goes beyond the sphere inscribed by the subjective certainty of the Cogito, which alone is invulnerable to hyperbolic doubt. Descartes, to his credit, perceived the essence or signification of representability, such that he saw it as a consubstantial or innate property of consciousness, entailing that some thoughts are represented—rightly or wrongly—as images that are received from their objects. This first property cannot be acquired by experience; it is a first condition of my knowledge, of my perception, and even of my sensible perception.[99] But the presence of this principle in us, the phenomenological description of the idea as picture of an archetype, does not coincide with the *affirmation* that ideas are *effectively* images of things, nor of course with the other affirmation, that *sensible* ideas are effectively images of things, and even less with the presumption of defining idea by means of *sensible* image and thereby reducing it to sensation.[100] The term *picture* is taken here in its largest sense—that of representation. The ideas of the understanding are in fact the only ones to be *effectively* representational, the only ones to possess an objective reality that is the *thing* itself, present in us in the manner in which it can be present in the understanding, meaning objectively.[101] Moreover, objective reality, meaning the content of ideas having a representational character, in no way entails its necessary *objective validity*. However, it is impossible to establish this objective validity without starting from its representational character, meaning the objective reality that distinguishes ideas from all the other kinds of thoughts.

The necessary intervention of the principle of the correspondence of the idea with what is ideated (without which the proof would not even have any meaning, since the aim that defines it is to discover an idea that is effectively the same as its presentation, meaning in conformity with the thing it claims to represent) therefore excludes the possibility that the objective reality of the idea can ever be conceived, even occasionally, completely outside all reference to this principle of resemblance. Certainly the formal reality of my self can be hypothetically conceived as the eminent cause of the objective reality of my idea of extension, but this hypothesis would simply have as consequence to deprive this idea of its objective validity, not of its objective reality, the latter not always defined merely as the image of an extension. Moreover, this hypothesis does not necessarily signify that the formal reality of my self can be conceived as the eminent possible cause of the objective reality of the idea of extension, but (with greater likelihood) that the formal reality of my self can be conceived as the eminent possible cause of the formal reality of extension (as essence), of which my idea would contain the objective reality. With respect to the artifice of a machine,[102] we are concerned, in this instance, with a formally valid artifice, meaning an artifice realizable in a formal reality, and the objective reality of my invention is definable with respect to this real possibility: the knowledge of mechanical science or the intelligence of my mind is the cause of the objective reality of this machine only insofar as it entails in itself an objective reality, which is the reflection in my mind of geometric and mechanical combinations that are enclosed as formally possible within the essence of extension and movement taken themselves as formal realities. But assuming that there can be objective realities having no resemblance to the formal realities that would be their cause,[103] it remains that the proof cannot be accomplished unless we prove that, in the case in question, the idea conforms with what is ideated, which it purports to represent. The fundamental problem is to know whether there exists outside me "things of which I have ideas,"[104] not simply things that I do not know.

With respect to the second point—the use of the principle of causality in order to render legitimate the use of the principle of the conformity of the idea with what is ideated—the discovery of the existence of God as certain cause in me of the idea of God conditions effectively this legitimate application, for in order to be certain that my idea resembles the object to which it refers, I must be certain first, at the very least, that this object exists. And only the principle of causality can allow me, in this instance, to acquire this certainty. Moreover, I must be certain that there is no radical disproportion between the thing that causes my idea and the representation that this idea gives me of it. The principle of causality also brings me a useful certainty with respect to this point. In fact, even though the formal reality necessarily required in the cause in order to account for the objective reality of the effect is only *at the minimum* equal to this objective reality and even though it can in principle be more than it, it happens that since the objective reality of the idea of the perfect is an absolute *maximum* (absolute infinity), it requires as *minimum* the absolute *maximum* of formal reality in its cause, for there can be nothing more ample by hypothesis than absolute *maximum*. There is therefore necessarily an equality between the representative content of my idea and the being that is its cause; there is nothing more in the formal reality of the cause than in the objective reality of the effect. This *equality* is the first condition of perfect *equivalence*[105] that allows my idea of God to have an objective validity, meaning to be the faithful picture of the archetype.

There is therefore a close collaboration between the two principles. And this collaboration does not stop there. To prove that there is nothing more in the represented existing thing than in the representing idea is, no doubt, to prepare the proof of the conformity of the idea with what is ideated, but not to assure it rigorously. The principle of the correspondence of the idea with what is ideated, the very definition of idea, must be the final foundation of this rigorous and certain conformity; and the idea of God presents the privileged case in which such a conformity could not, in fact, be so small a representation that it does not conform with the object it represents, for through this imperfection itself, it would stop representing perfection, and consequently it would stop being the idea of perfection. To represent the idea of perfection to oneself is to have perfection itself in one's understanding, in the manner in which things commonly are in the understanding, meaning objectively.[106] Therefore, on the one hand, the principle of causality gives me, in all certainty, the existence of the perfect thing whose idea I have in myself, by adding the certainty that this thing contains no more reality or perfection than the objective reality of my idea; on the other hand, I am certain, in virtue of the definition of idea, that this objective reality necessarily gives me an image in perfect conformity with its object. Thus I know, in all certainty, not only that God exists, but that I have the most faithful idea of his nature possible. This does not mean that I have a complete knowledge of him in this way (no more than the clear and distinct idea of the triangle, in conformity with its essence, gives me ipso facto complete knowledge of all its properties), but it does mean that his idea gives me an image of him in perfect "conformity."

If the principle of causality nevertheless governs the whole process, that is because it is the only principle that allows me to go outside myself. The principle of the correspondence of the idea with what is ideated can intervene only if the existence of a formal reality that is the cause of my idea has been demonstrated. No doubt it is a condition of the application of the principle of causality as an inquiry into such a formal reality; however, it leaves us within the purely subjective sphere. It is only by means of the force of the principle of causality that the leap to the objective sphere is accomplished and that the objective validity of the conclusions drawn from the principle of the correspondence of the idea with what is ideated, in this instance relative to the conformity of our idea with the thing, is established. In brief, if the proof by effects can neither begin nor end without this principle of correspondence, neither can it be essentially accomplished without the principle of causality.

In spite of its dominant role, the principle of causality is therefore not the single instrument of the proof. The proof is accomplished only through the interweaving of the principle of causality with the principle of correspondence, one and the other being indubitable in itself and finding in the idea of God the criterion of its legitimate application. And *this criterion* is perfection, or the absolute maximum. Because of it, I am certain that my idea is necessarily produced by the thing it represents and also that it resembles it effectively. That is why this idea that "God placed in me while creating me . . . like the trademark of the worker on his work, . . . is not necessarily something different from the work itself"; and "it is extremely believable . . . that I conceive this resemblance, in which the idea of God is contained, by the same faculty by which I conceive myself."[107] A production by something external to me and a resemblance with this thing, two properties that common sense would attribute without reason to sensible representation, are finally attached—in all certainty—to the idea of God alone, which is thus the first and best known of all things. This idea is the only idea that not only authorizes, but imposes on itself, the simultaneous application of the principles of causality and of correspondence of the idea with what is ideated. This idea is therefore the only idea that necessarily possesses full and complete objective validity.

12. Reconciliation between the Concept of God as Cause and the Concept of God as Archetype

Thus we perceive the originality of the Cartesian proof. As many interpreters have felt, it emphasizes the living and active character of the Author of our origin by posing God as efficient cause. Because of it, we see how an idea can require me to attribute properties to God without having divine omnipotence be subordinated to the necessities of our finite understanding. There is therefore a remarkable agreement between the results of this proof and the conception of a God so free and omnipotent that he is exempt from the necessities inscribed within the eternal truths—which is something that Duns Scotus did not dare to affirm. But even though this result agrees with the idea of God's absolute freedom, that does not mean that the proof itself gives rise to it as its single aim. What this proof tends toward is above all to establish that the idea of God in me is the conforming reflection of a formal reality, an archetype existing outside of me. The enterprise to prove God's existence appears for the first time directed toward the solution of a problem concerning the critique of knowledge, a problem that until now remained foreign to the theologian. It aims to establish the objective validity of the ideas of our understanding.

Descartes' originality thus consists in resolving this seeming impossibility—by reconciling Saint Anselm and Duns Scotus—consisting in establishing the objectivity of science by means of an omnipotent God, radically foreign in himself to the implications of this science; it consists in proving by means of my idea that God is the eternal archetype of this idea and that, however, he is an infinite will that cannot be enclosed within the necessity of any one of my ideas.

Therefore a kind of equilibrium is established between the living God and the rational God: a limitation, through the rationality of the idea of perfection, of what the infinity of divine reality can allow with respect to omnipotence, of absolutely free will escaping the grasp of our reason—an equilibrium that we will rediscover by means of another perspective in *Meditation IV*. Certainly I do not know everything about God; his aims are impenetrable, his truth is above the truths of my understanding, and the finite cannot "embrace" the infinite.[108] But, on the other hand, I am certain *to know his nature faithfully, if not exactly and totally*.[109] It is not because we have proven God's existence by means of efficient causality that God appears as completely different from an inert archetype without life and freedom; for his life, his freedom and incomprehensibility are already inscribed in the idea or image that is his reflection in me. It is because I *represent* God as incomprehensible to myself and having a freedom that exceeds my understanding, that I can affirm, once I am assured of the objective validity of this idea, that God possesses all these characteristics. If not, what would allow me to attribute them to him? Thus I do not know that God is free because I demonstrate that he is the efficient cause of my idea, but I know that, from the moment that I have proven that he is its cause, he must cause it freely, since my idea teaches me that the infinity of God necessarily entails absolute freedom. Similarly, I do not prove that God is incomprehensible by proving that God is the cause of my idea of infinity, since, on the contrary, it is the incomprehensible content of that idea that allows me to posit the existence of God outside of me. The free creation of the idea of God in us signifies *the arbitrariness of the positing of this content in us,* not *the arbitrariness of the content of that idea.* Belonging to the content itself, divine freedom is founded in perfection, to the extent that, insofar as our idea of God is the idea of perfection, we can say that God is tied to the internal necessity of that idea and, at the same time, that this idea does not posit anything other than God's freedom within the frame of his perfection. As we see him, God's incomprehensibility has a dual source: on the one hand, in our finitude, which places outside of our grasp every infinity, whatever it may be and, on the other hand, in the absolute freedom of divine infinity such as the idea of perfection reveals it. Thus, whatever freedom and incomprehensibility is recognized with respect to God, the correspondence between the idea of God and what is ideated is never broken. On the contrary, because we are certain of this correspondence (because of the first proof by effects), we are in this way assured that this freedom and incomprehensibility that prevent enclosing God within "the limits of our understanding" is found in what is ideated—meaning in God. Incomprehensibility is in us *the expression of what is beyond the finite,* not *the expression of what is beyond intelligence.* It is beyond the finite, given clearly and distinctly as unable to be grasped by my intelligence by means of a *reason,* to the extent that it is capable of allowing me to know, not simply that God exists, but what he is, he who exists. Because of it, I *know* that he is infinite, that I cannot embrace or "comprehend" *(comprehendere)* him, but that I can "conceive" *(intelligere)* him,[110] since I know many of his properties clearly and distinctly. Therefore, far from rendering God unknowable to me, incomprehensibility, although entailing a certain necessary limitation of my knowledge (I could never exhaust the infinite, or have an "adequate" or complete knowledge of it), is at the same time like the *ratio formalis* of infinity, that which allows me to know it as such. In brief, incomprehensibility is the effect in us of absolute perfection, and this perfection brings the double guarantee that the idea I have of it is *caused* by the perfection itself and that it is entirely *in conformity* with it. The German language expresses this nuance most neatly: God is irrational in the mathematical sense of *irrational,* and not in the mystical sense of *unvernünftig.*

Consequently, whatever is the importance of the aspect of the proof that allows positing God as efficient cause, we see, by considering the order of reasons, that its principal aim is to show, by establishing that we have certain knowledge of God, of his existence as well as of his nature, that there are ideas in us (clear and distinct ideas) that have objective validity, and that our science is possible and legitimate. However, Descartes' demonstrations, as we have already said, are polyvalent. Beyond their principal result, they most often entail many other results that it is advisable to rank according to their importance, situating them according to the general perspectives that the order of reasons opens up for us. That is why, failing to keep their eyes fixed on these perspectives and on this order, the novelty of God as efficient cause has hidden from many interpreters the novelty of God as *instar archetypi*, conceived as the foundation of the only one of my ideas that attests by itself a necessary objective validity.

13. The Role of the Notion of Perfection

The reconciliation of God as efficient cause and God as archetype arises, as we have seen, from the interweaving of the principle of causality and the principle of the conformity of the idea with what is ideated through the intermediary of the notion of perfection. Since this notion is the notion of an absolute *maximum*,[111] it allows one to posit the conformity of the idea to the thing in two different ways: by means of causality, God as formal reality, the cause of the objective reality of his idea, which is not able to have more reality than this effect since the latter is itself an absolute *maximum* and there is nothing greater than this absolute *maximum;* by means of the principle of the conformity of the idea with what is ideated, since the idea is incapable of being the imperfect image of the perfect, without which it would not be truly its image, and hence it would not be the idea of the perfect—which contradicts the hypothesis.

This coincidence of equating the cause and the effect with the conformity of the idea and its standard through the intermediary of perfection, a coincidence that assures the coincidence of God as efficient cause and God as archetype as its consequence, imparts a particular meaning to God's transcendence with respect to his idea.

On the one hand, God can be called the eminent cause of this idea. In fact, this idea is only an effect that *can* always, in principle, have less reality than its cause; moreover, since it is an idea, it ought always be inferior to the real thing of which it is a reflection (because it is a copy) because this manner of being by which a thing is objectively or by representation in the understanding, is "imperfect" and denotes "a fall" with respect to the perfection of represented things.[112] But, on the other hand, God can be called the formal and not the eminent cause of his idea, for there can be nothing in the objective reality of his idea, an idea of the perfect, that can be so small that it is less perfect (as an effect or as a copy) than something in the formal reality of God's being itself.[113] Thus the difference between God as formal cause and God as eminent cause of his idea tends to become unassignable, while it seems that it is maintained as a rule: on the one hand, the perfection of the effect excludes all differences of reality and of perfection between it and its cause, and on the other hand, the definition of the idea as incomplete with respect to its object reintroduces this difference.

We end up with the same result if we consider the question from another perspective. The perfect agreement of the idea with what is ideated does not prevent the idea from being conceived as having been freely impressed in us by God's causality; this implies, on the one hand, that God is not constrained by the internal necessity of this idea to create this idea in us and, on the other hand, that this necessity of the idea does not emanate from ourselves, but from God. If the idea we have of God can also be based on the necessity of the thing itself and if I can escape in this way the purely subjective necessity of my understanding and definitively receive its objective validity, it is precisely to the extent that we know that God has freely created the idea. The condition of the objective necessity of our knowledge therefore appears to require its establishment in God's freedom itself; and God's intelligibility therefore appears as being able to supplant his incomprehensibility. However—by a remarkable compensatory correction—incomprehensibility does not reside in the separation that we would be tempted to establish between the idea of God manifest in us with its own necessities and God's freedom, which would have given rise to it. For the internal necessities of this idea could not be foreign to God's being itself, since the perfection that establishes the incomprehensibility of this being, entailing the negation of nothingness, entails that God cannot do other than exist and hence posits his being.[114] In this way the difference by which one would attempt to oppose in God himself his freedom and his necessity to exist would become unassignable. And once again, according to this perspective, the agreement of the idea (of its representative content) with what is ideated, should be realized rigorously. If God is *incommensurable with myself,* that is not because he is *incommensurable with the idea* I have of him in myself, but because the objective reality of this idea itself in me (meaning the picture of God I have in me) is incommensurable with the formal being of my self.[115] On the contrary, there is a perfect common measure between God and my idea of God, and it is because of this common measure that I can know that there is no measure between myself and God. The gap is not located between God and the idea I have of him, between the cause and the effect, but between the content of this intelligible idea and my mind, which can conceive but not comprehend this content. Thus one sees still another way in which God is intelligible without being comprehensible, incomprehensible without being unknowable, *irrational* without being *unvernünftig.* One also sees that the dissociation in my idea of its form and content as objective reality allows the principle of the correspondence of the idea with what is ideated to assume its function without depriving God of his character of efficient cause, without reducing the exemplary cause to the format of our understanding representing it, meaning without reducing God's infinity to the finiteness of my idea as modification of my finite consciousness. The faithful copy of the archetype is not the modification itself. It is a content of an idea that my consciousness perceives directly in itself as incommensurable with itself. It would suffice to install in God himself this objective reality that Descartes situates in my idea as its content, in order to strip the form of the idea in me of all its representative character, to reduce it to a purely affective modification of my soul, to remove from it even its title of idea, reserving this name for the representative content sublimated in the Verb as divine archetype. We would derive an entirely different perspective in this way—Malebranche's perspective, in which the possibility of a Cartesian proof by effect would vanish.

14. The Perfection of Objective Reality as "Fall" from the Perfection of Formal Reality

The preceding considerations certify that: 1) the success of the demonstration of God's existence, insofar as it ends up positing the objective validity of the idea of God, meaning insofar as it proves that an object outside of me corresponds with God and that this object resembles my idea, supposes the convergence of the principle of causality and the principle of the correspondence of the idea with what is ideated; and 2) this convergence is only assured insofar as the two principles equally appeal to the notion of perfection. It is the notion of perfection that, from the point of view of the cause, guarantees that there is not, and cannot be, in this case, neither more nor less (objective) reality in the effect than in the (formal) reality of the cause, while the principle of causality by itself simply guarantees that there cannot be less. It is the notion of perfection that, from the point of view of the correspondence of the idea with what is ideated, guarantees that nothing should be missing, in this case, from my representation of the object and that it resembles me fully; otherwise we would be constructing, in contrast to the hypothesis, a representation whose objective reality would be imperfect.

But in this way arises one of the most difficult problems. In fact, what differentiates the objective reality of the idea of God and the formal reality of God is the *existence* of the thing that is present in the latter and absent in the former. Thus we ought to conclude that, with respect to objective reality, the lack of existence of the thing represented, as simply represented, does not reduce in any way the intrinsic perfection of the content of the idea. This amounts to saying that existence in itself is not a perfection, but something posited sui generis, without relation to the perfection or imperfection of the thing. Then we would understand that an idea can be differentiated from the thing and yet represent it congruently in its perfection, since this difference, which consists in being a concept without existence, does not remove anything from it belonging to the perfection of the thing. That will be one of Kant's arguments in his critique of the ontological argument: if existence is a perfection, meaning a predicate of a thing, the concept could never be adequate to the thing since one of the constitutive predicates of the thing will always be missing from the definition of the concept.[116] There will then be a logical difference between the thing and the concept: this difference will set off the latter with respect to its object, which is contrary to the possibility of the concept. The concept will cease being the concept of the thing. Existence therefore cannot be a perfection.

But the doctrine that consists in denying that existence is a perfection is Gassendi's doctrine, and Descartes rejects it. As a result, the fact that the image of the object is deprived of the existence belonging to the object entails a defect of perfection that implies an imperfection in the content of the idea itself, with respect to the thing it reflects. This consequence is precisely affirmed in *Meditation III:* "Ideas are in me like painting or pictures, which can truly easily *fall short of the perfection from which they are drawn."*[117] In addition, one can affirm that "as *imperfect* as" the objective reality of an idea is compared to the formal reality of its object, "it is not a pure nothingness."[118] Finally, the formulation of *Replies I* is categorical: "The manner of being by which a thing is objectively or by representation in the understanding by its idea, is imperfect."[119] If that were so, the proof would seem to collapse from all sides at once. Since the objective reality of the idea is so imperfect, how can we draw the existence of the perfect being in the name of a principle of causality that only allows one to posit *in all certainty* a formal reality that is *at least equal,* but not greater in perfection to the reality of the effect? The perfect being contains, from the moment it exists, a greater perfection than the representative content of his idea. The existence of this being, meaning this supplement of perfection, is therefore only *possible* inasmuch as the cause of an effect *can* always contain more perfection than this effect, meaning, in this case, more than the objective reality enclosed within the idea; but it is not necessary, for nothing *requires* us to affirm that the cause actually contains such a supplement. It is therefore impossible to prove that God exists. The perfection of the objective reality, which is only the perfection of a representative being deprived of the perfection of existing, *requires* me to posit as its cause only a formal reality of *equal perfection.* And God's formal reality, containing all the perfection of objective reality as well as the perfection of existing, which objective reality lacks, constitutes a superior total of perfection than the perfection of objective reality, and the relation of cause and effect—which is only *ad minimum*—does not require me to posit it. Therefore I cannot affirm it legitimately. Consequently, God's existence remains merely possible.

The proof can result only if we assume that there is no more perfection in formal reality than in objective reality, in the existing thing than in the represented thing. But Descartes starts from the inverse principle. He affirms that this objective reality is less perfect—that it constitutes a kind of "fall." He confirms this thesis in *Meditation V* when he makes existence a perfection. The difficulty appears insoluble.

This dual play between objective perfection and formal perfection appears entailed, to some degree, by the ambiguity of the principle of the correspondence of the idea with what is ideated. On the one hand, natural light certifies that, in the relation between the archetype and the copy, what is the copy or reflection has less being than the fully fleshed thing itself—meaning what defines the image insofar as it is differentiated from the thing[120]—the copy as copy does not have the being of the archetype, otherwise it would not be a copy.[121] But, on the other hand, as a copy or image, it must contain (objectively) all the perfections of the thing; otherwise it would not be an authentic copy and it would no longer represent it—that is what defines the image according to its resemblance with the thing.[122]

It is evident that this is the final consideration that allows Descartes to accomplish his proof. It is according to the perspective of the relation between the idea and what is ideated that the principle of causality, as we have seen, enters into play in order to link the formal reality as cause and the objective reality as effect; and it is the notion of picture or image together with the notion of model or archetype that lead to the affirmation that one ought not consider, under the pretext that the reality considered in my idea "is merely objective," that "it is not necessary that the same reality be formally or actually in the cause of this idea." These are the notions that allow the assertion that this cause "is an archetype in which is contained formally or in actuality all the reality or perfection that is found only objectively or by representation in my idea."[123]

That said, it seems that Descartes' justification can only be the following: since natural light immediately gives me, in the idea, the thing represented as "the thing itself" in all its perfection, distinguished from this "manner of being objectively," which holds to the form of the idea, meaning to myself, it relates the imperfection of this manner of being to myself, and not to the thing represented. Consequently, when we are attempting to discover what is the formal reality that causes the objective reality of my idea, this objective reality must be considered in itself, abstracting away the imperfection that arises from me and is explained by me. The intrinsic perfection of the thing surpasses the perfection of my representing self, and this perfection (in the case of the idea of God) is infinite; the fact of its being represented is extrinsic to it and could not constitute an intrinsic imperfection for it. The cause of the content of my representation, having abstracted away the imperfection that is inherent to representation, must therefore necessarily be a formal being that is just as infinite. In brief, the imperfection of the representative form would not be able to introduce any imperfection in the representative content insofar as it delivers the object itself to us, and it is this content whose cause must be sought for in a sufficient formal reality.

These considerations can be drawn from the *Preface to the Meditations*[124] and the *Reply* that Descartes gives to Caterus' objections.[125] But do they effectively resolve the difficulty? That is another problem. The fact that the thing represented is objectively the *thing itself,* meaning "in the manner in which objects commonly are in the understanding," does not entail that this thing is not thus deprived of the perfection of existing formally. And if I abstract away the imperfection that results for a thing from the fact that it is represented by myself, I do not obtain in this way the formal existence that is lacking from the content of the idea and that is in itself a positive perfection. The difficulty therefore remains in its entirety.

15. Ambiguity of the Cartesian Concept of Idea; Idea-Image (Psychologism) and Essence (Mathematism)

The role played by the principle of the correspondence of the idea with what is ideated and the definition of idea as the picture of an archetype emphasize the more or less apparent ambiguity of the concept of idea in Cartesian philosophy. The latter presents two aspects: one psychological and the other mathematical.

According to its psychological aspect, it is defined as a representation, "a picture" of an external thing. Of course, as we have stated many times, and as Descartes has specified so often, by *picture* or *image* Descartes does not understand the sensible image of the object.[126] In fact, if this were not so, only sensible ideas would warrant the title of idea; and we know that, on the contrary, they are the only ones not giving a faithful copy of the object, a privilege reserved for the ideas of the understanding. The picture then can be sensible—in which case it is deceptive—just as easily as it can be intellectual—in which case it is veridical. In brief, we are concerned with the correspondence of the idea in general with the object in general.

According to its mathematical aspect, idea is defined by its internal necessity, the clearness and distinctness of its constitutive elements, independently from any reference to any external thing represented, and without having to care about "whether an existence corresponds to it in nature."

At first, these two aspects appear incompatible. In the first case, the truth of the idea is under the jurisdiction of the reality of the thing it represents: it has validity insofar as a thing exists effectively outside it, of which it is the faithful copy, having been impressed on me by the thing. From this results the radical passivity of all ideas, whether rational or sensible, and as a consequence of my whole understanding.[127] Ideas arise from the thing; they are its reflection, and even its degraded reflection. This point of view is anti-Copernican, as Kant will say: the subject revolves around the object.

In the second case, on the contrary, the existence of the thing is under the jurisdiction of idea, and idea, to the extent that it is innate, appears to emanate from my own nature. This doctrine of innateness therefore seems to require a certain spontaneity of the understanding, drawing from itself, by its own force, series of items of knowledge extending to infinity. From this arises the conception of the "seeds of truth," which need only germinate and propagate in us by themselves, if we do not smother them.[128] Moreover, Spinoza, as the protagonist of mental spontaneity, needs only to push to its natural conclusion this doctrine of "the native virtues of the understanding," in the *De Intellectus Emendatione*. From this point of view, the certainty of the existence of the object depends on the preliminary certainty of the idea, which is alone capable of guaranteeing it and positing it. The idea appears to be at a higher level than the object it determines. The object revolves around the idea—the point of view is Copernican, as Kant will say. By going as far as we can in this direction, we arrive at Malebranche's conceptions, in which the perception of the thing is stripped of all representative validity and in which a perception is no longer an idea, but a sensation, while idea as archetype is not the copy of the thing, but the model of which the thing is the copy. Since it involves the efficacious substance of God under some aspect, it is the cause of passion and is no longer passion itself.

Common sense psychologism when it is linked with a realism about the object, therefore appears to enter into conflict with mathematism when it is linked to an idealism that hangs the possibility and reality of the object on the intrinsic truth of the idea, or as the adherents of transcendental philosophy would say, on the "reality" *(Realität)* of the concept.

Finally, the question appears to be more complicated because of the fact that mathematical ideas themselves seem to be conceived in two different ways, according to whether one is situated before or after *Meditation III* according to the order of reasons. Before *Meditation III* they are ideas in us, necessary for us, that are conditions of possibility of our representations of objects (wax, for example), but that have only a doubtful objective validity, for I do not know whether objects effectively correspond to my representations; and consequently I do not know whether these ideas, which condition the said representations, are at the same time in themselves conditions of real things outside of me that would be the objects of these representations. In brief, I do not know whether they refer to essences that would have been instituted outside of me by God as conditions of possibility of things themselves. These essences, at this level, are distinguished from my ideas, and are posited as true things—*"Res arithmeticas, vel geometricas"*[129]—independent of me, that my ideas express in me. No doubt, in conformity with mathematism, the objective validity of these essences consists in their capacity to render possible the existing object. But the validity of the ideas of my understanding is founded on the certainty that these ideas are confused with these essences, which are rational things, and that they are related to them as realities of which my thought receives the impression. Mathematism therefore appears to be subordinated to psychologism in the end.

This dual aspect perhaps verifies the fact that Descartes has not completely or always been able to rid himself of the habits of common sense, of the current conception of the idea as reflection of the thing. But one can also think that the subordination of mathematism to psychologism is also, in this case, less evident than it appears at first. The question is not decided merely by the definition of idea as the image of an archetype, or of truth as conformity of the representation with the thing. Even Kant adopts this nominal definition. What decides is the method by which this objective validity is finally attributed. And this attribution is always established in Descartes' philosophy as a function of the intrinsic properties of the idea. The internal characteristics of the idea of God, necessarily entailing his existence, testify at the same time to the character of essence of that idea and later to the character of essence of mathematical ideas. The discovery in these ideas of a sufficient quantity of objective reality accounts for the natural certainty of the understanding in this respect. The rule of attribution of objective validity therefore remains finally in conformity with the requirements of mathematism, since it is founded entirely on the internal rationality of the notion. And it happens that the only ideas having true objective validity, meaning being the faithful pictures of an archetype, are precisely mathematical ideas or, more generally, the clear and distinct ideas that are not defined by themselves as reflections of objects existing in nature.[130] In this way one understands also that these ideas have a double objective validity: first by themselves, as terms, insofar as they reveal rational realities (essences) that have as such an independent being from the existing things that render them possible; and then relative to these existing things, insofar as they allow us to know a priori the real properties, since the essences they reveal render these things possible, much as ideas themselves render possible the representation of these things in us.[131]

16. Sensation and Representative Character; Objective Reality of Sensation; Minimum and Maximum Objective Reality; Correlative Variation of Objective Validity

Since the obscure and confused ideas—the sensations—are not the copy of something external, they do not have an ideated thing, properly speaking. Ought not one then refuse them the character of representation and consequently, if this character defines idea, ought one not refuse to think them ideas? Ought not this label be suitable only for the clear and distinct ideas that alone have an objective validity? That will be Malebranche's conclusion against Arnauld.[132] But surely that is not Descartes' conclusion, even though Malebranche, in this case, is following Descartes. In fact, what constitutes idea is not the objective validity that it can really possess—its effective correspondence with what is ideated—it is the character it possesses that an internal observation reveals, to be manifest to our consciousness as the picture of something external, even if, in fact, nothing of this kind corresponds to it. All thought that is discovered, during an inspection of the mind, as possessing this character must therefore be considered as an idea. Such is the case for sensations, even though nothing in the thing conforms to the qualities they reveal to us. Therefore sensations are ideas. That is why there are ideas having a certain material falsity that comes from what, by themselves, "they represent of things that do not exist,"[133] meaning that they represent "what is nothing as if it were something."[134]

But then, how can one reconcile the attribution of the representative character to sensation and the definition of the objective reality of the idea as being "the thing itself such as it is objectively in the understanding?" Since the thing itself is not in the mind, it seems that we would have to conclude that sensation has no representative content, therefore no objective reality, and therefore no representative character. We ought to conceive that it would borrow this representative character, of which it would be stripped intrinsically, by usurping it from "the thing itself that is in the understanding," meaning *from the clear and distinct idea of the thing* that in sensible perception is cloaked in sensible qualities in themselves entirely deprived of objective validity. Such will be Malebranche's conception. Sensation will then be reduced to a pure affection of my soul, and all objective reality reduced to clear and distinct ideas alone. Is not this consequence clearly implied in this reservation by Descartes: "And when he asserts that the idea of cold is cold itself such as it is objectively in the understanding, I think that one must use a distinction. For in the case of obscure and confused ideas, among which the ideas of cold and heat must be placed, it often happens that they are referred to other things of which they are truly the ideas. Thus, if cold is only a privation, the idea of cold is not cold itself insofar as it is objectively in the understanding, but something else that is falsely taken for this privation, namely, a certain sensation that has no existence outside the understanding."[135]

Descartes should rightly draw this conclusion, since he maintains that obscure and confused ideas have a representative character. But the refusal of this consequence is not a logical error. It stems from Descartes' conception of the nature of the soul and ideas. If Malebranche can draw his conclusion, that is because he considers that sensation, being an original property of my soul, is radically subjective and consequently does not require anything foreign to myself for its explanation. On the contrary, for Descartes, sensation, even though subjective in the sense that it is never the real quality of any body, is foreign to the essence of the soul alone. By itself the soul cannot account for it. It is subjective because it is a state of my consciousness; it is objective because it encompasses something other than my mind alone and it is not reducible to it. In brief, it is the result of the substantial union of my soul and my body; it is *subjective-objective.* As an expression of that union, it is presented consequently to myself as giving me information on the states of my body, and through their intermediary, on the existence of external things with relation to my body insofar as they are relevant to its subsistence or destruction. In this way it preserves a residue of objective reality—the weakest residue it is possible to conceive—since this representative reality is never a copy of external things. Certainly sensation is entirely alien to the nature of external things, but it is caused by them in me, and it varies according to their geometric variations, which remain unknown to it and whose discovery belongs to the understanding alone.[136] Even though it does not represent things to me, it does refer me to them.

It is therefore natural to grant some objective reality to sensation. Moreover, is it not impossible to conceive an idea completely stripped of objective validity? In fact, it is the difference in objective reality that distinguishes ideas among themselves and consequently renders them perceptible.[137] We perceive and distinguish the idea of heat and the idea of cold.[138] These ideas must therefore contain some objective reality: however little is the (objective) reality contained in "the idea of heat or the idea of a stone [. . .] we cannot say that this way or manner of being is nothing at all."[139]

However, this objective reality is, in this case, only a *minimum.* In fact, it is so small that one can barely distinguish it from nothingness; and one risks mistaking nothingness for being. We are therefore dealing with real *differentials* of objective reality here, even though Descartes himself did not define such a notion. They are the limit or difference between being and nothingness, and consequently, they are just as easily the one or the other. From this results the impossibility for my understanding to express itself about them and the doubt with which my understanding must strike them naturally. If, in fact, their objective reality is so small that I cannot know whether it is or it is not, I cannot know whether they are true, since only what is real is true, and since God is the author of the real and is not the author of nothingness. On the other hand, since clear and distinct ideas have a finite quantity (not an infinitely small quantity) and in a privileged case an infinity of objective reality, it is impossible for my understanding to confuse them with nothingness; it is impossible that my understanding does not immediately recognize them as true—meaning, having God as their author. In brief, it is impossible to doubt them naturally: "Every clear and distinct conception is without doubt *(procul dubio) something,* and thus it cannot draw its origin from nothingness, but must have God as its author."[140] Sensible ideas having an objective reality as close to zero as possible are therefore in me only insofar as I participate in nothingness maximally: "Natural light lets me know that they proceed from nothingness, meaning that they are in me only because something is lacking in my nature."[141]

Sensation derives its ambiguity from this character of limit proper to its objective reality, in which being and nothingness are confused. For it is in turn and simultaneously, both being and nonbeing. In the perspective of nonbeing, sensible idea *represents* nothingness as something. It then manifests itself as "materially false," as proceeding from nothingness, being in me insofar as I am imperfect. In the perspective of being, it is materially an infinitely small objective reality, as close as possible to zero, but not reducible to it, and conserving something positive. "One must not ask what is the cause of this positive objective being which, according to me, makes this idea materially false. This is more so since I do not say that its material falsity proceeds from some positive being, but from its *obscurity alone,* which to be sure has something positive as its subject and foundation, namely, sensation itself. And in truth, this positive being is in me insofar as I am a true thing; but obscurity, which alone gives me the occasion to judge that the idea of this sensation represents something outside of me that we call cold, has no real cause, but arises only from the fact that my nature is not entirely perfect."[142]

The representation of cold as a real property of bodies outside of me is the representation of nothing as something, since this property is nothing with respect to a body. It arises from the limitation of my knowledge, from my nothingness. But, on the other hand, it is nothing only with respect to the external body, to which representation as copy of what is ideated refers it; but it is not nothing in its content, which has some reality in sensation, under an obscure and confused form, something that certifies that a property of a body unknown in itself (for sensation) acts on mine. Nevertheless, this objective reality is also as small as possible, since the true property of the body to which it refers is for me a void of knowledge.

One can see the importance of these views for the remainder of the deduction. Although sensible ideas are rejected as false by the understanding because they are obscure for the understanding, meaning because it is impossible to discern them in the objective reality that can belong to them, it is not possible that this condemnation remains without being appealed. No doubt the objective reality of sensible ideas is itself only a *minimum;* and no doubt, as a result, it is obscure and thus even doubtful for my intelligence; but, as a result, it is no less certain that it is not nothing and that its *minimum* of reality must correspond correlatively to a *minimum* of truth. In virtue of its own principles, the understanding will therefore be required to reendow sensible ideas that were first absolutely condemned, restoring to them some *minima* objective validity, proportionally to this *minimum.*

The problem of the objective validity of ideas therefore appears in its fullest extent, such as it will be developed until the end of *Meditation VI.* It will lead to the unfolding of all the objective realities, from the highest, meaning from the *maximum* absolute, in which it is infinite (God), to the *minimum,* in which it is at the limit of being and nothingness, a differential (sensible idea), passing through the intermediary that contains a finite quantity of this objective reality, namely, clear and distinct ideas of finite essences.[143] It is the solution of the problem for the absolute *maximum* (the idea of God) that, since it furnishes the principle of everything that is— however little that is—the real is necessarily true (the principle that is at the foundation of divine universal veracity), it will impart the key to the solution of all the other quantities of objective reality, including the *minimum* (sensation).

17. The Order of Reasons from the Cogito to God.
The Problem of Evaluative Judgments Relative to the
Quantity of Perfection of Objective Realities

We are now concerned with specifying the nature of the relation that unites the *Cogito* and *God,* according to the order of reasons.

If Descartes was able to follow an order of reasons, in *Meditation III,* that led him from one to the other, that is because, "in order to pass by degrees from notions discovered first to those that can be discovered afterwards,"[144] he has cleared the ground by eliminating everything that was not an idea properly speaking, that is, representations[145] and everything that was alien in them to the consideration of their content, that is, of "their objective reality." Thus he was able to determine the degrees of perfection or of reality of these contents and survey those degrees, from the lowest (the objective reality of sensible ideas) to the highest (the objective reality of the idea of God), by passing through the intermediaries (the objective reality of the ideas of animals, men, and angels), or by raising himself from modes to finite substances, and then to God.[146]

We note here that the degrees of the order of reasons are governed by the degrees of perfection of the contents and no longer by the relation of subordination of the different internal conditions of my knowledge. Correlatively, the term with which we end up is no longer the thinking self, but the perfect being. The self-sufficiency of God substitutes for the self-sufficiency of my self. Is it necessary to emphasize further that the order of reasons seems to have changed nature and principle, and that it thus presents a notable contrast with the order that has prevailed until the end of *Meditation II?*

Until then the principle of the progression of reasons was the Cogito, pure intellect, conceived as the ultimate term positing itself as the ultimate condition of all representation (whatever the content) and, having abstracted away the content, without itself being conditioned by any. It was therefore situated in the form. Now the directive principle concerning the representative contents appears to us as residing in the content of a certain idea, which, by its perfection, alone conditions the lower degrees of perfection of the other contents, arranged in a hierarchy according to an order that is the order of reasons. In addition, this directive principle posits itself independently from the Cogito, not in virtue of the Cogito, but in virtue of the perfect being of which it is the perfect expression—which, for it, amounts to being posited by itself, the idea of the perfect implying by itself the perfect being that gives rise to it by itself. The principle of order is therefore situated in matter and outside the Cogito. Thus the dissociation of the representative contents (the objective reality of ideas) and the condition of representation (meaning ideas in their formal reality), which was already announced in the process by which the Cogito was constituted epistemologically as substance by abstraction of all contents, appears here as having consequences that are infinitely more serious than one had previously thought: it seems to cause within the system something like a schism between two orders of reasons, each having its own principle and point of application.

No doubt, in the proof of God's existence, what qualifies the perfect representative content as supreme reason, as the term for the inquiry of the final foundation of certainty, is not that it establishes and contains in itself imperfect contents. Here Descartes does not seek to account for various representative contents themselves, according to the synthetic order (which would be what relates to an explanation of things). He only bothers to determine to what extent these contents can or cannot find their reason *in the self*, in order to determine, in this way, to what extent the self has or does not have objective knowledge. It is always my knowledge that is in question: we are concerned with an explanation of myself to my self, and not with an explanation of the reality of contents according to a synthetic order. The investigation has not changed its goals: we are concerned with establishing science and certainty; but its principle and its domain seem to have changed. What until now made possible my knowledge and at the same time established its certainty, was that it appeared immediately and indubitably to the subject that I am as a necessary condition of my knowledge in general, meaning of my thought as intelligence, with all that it implies. That is why it alone escaped the evil genius. Now, what establishes the possibility of my knowledge (of my knowledge relative to God) are judgments of validity brought upon the content of my knowledge. And the Cogito does not entail the validity of these kinds of judgments; it is merely implied necessarily in all judgments, valid or not. What then is the foundation of these judgments? Cannot the evil genius trick me with respect to them? Since he can deceive me when I judge that $2 + 2 = 4$, why can he not deceive me when I judge that an idea contains in itself more "perfection," more objective reality than another idea? In order to be certain of the truth of these judgments, we have to establish that they are included as a rule in the judgment that posits the

Cogito as that without which no knowledge, whether true or false, is possible. Thus only the principle of their possibility appears unable to be dissociated from the subject insofar as the subject in general renders possible all knowledge. At the same time, their certainty appears identical to the certainty of the Cogito.

And that is what seems impracticable at first. These judgments are judgments of validity (or more exactly judgments of evaluation)[147] brought to bear upon the content of my knowledge. The Cogito posits necessarily and indubitably only the condition without which no knowledge is given to me, meaning the existence of the consciousness as immediate testimony of an appearance to myself. Its evidence can only concern appearances to myself, either of myself, or of the contents in myself, that it renders possible *for myself.* It is evident that it cannot render possible judgments about the perfection or degree of reality of the contents in this way. The Cogito abstracts away the validity of the contents (quantity of reality), the contents themselves, and the differences in contents, in order to be able to express itself simply concerning the fact that it thinks them in general and in order to draw from the meditation of this certain fact the knowledge of intellectual nature in general, whether finite or infinite.[148] With respect to the knowledge of my existence, it does not bother with knowing whether I am perfect or imperfect, but simply that I think and that I exist. The only principle it requires is that "in order to think one must exist." Enclosed within this limit, it could not furnish by itself the standard that allows the measurement of the quantity of perfection or of reality. Would we assert that it is sufficient for consciousness to observe clearly and distinctly the appearance of more or less reality in the ideas present in it? But can consciousness, the principle of this observation, be at the same time the principle of the evaluation of this greater or lesser quantity? From what does it draw the power to interpret these differences of contents into differences of degrees of perfection? From what does it draw the power to build a hierarchy in which the thinking self itself is inserted? Would we assert that the degrees of clearness and distinctness of the various ideas immediately allow the Cogito to evaluate the degrees of perfection? But that assumes that the degrees of clearness are identified with the degrees of reality and of perfection, and that is precisely what one has to prove and what will be established only by the existence of the veracious God. Moreover, we perceive that it is the evaluation of the quantity of objective reality of the idea that specifies its clearness and distinctness rather than the contrary: it is because the ideas of cold and hot contain infinitely little reality and are in me because of my imperfection, that they have a certain confusion that implies their material falsity; it is the fact that the idea of God encompasses an infinite objective reality excluding everything negative and contradictory that entails and verifies the fact that this idea is the clearest and most distinct of all ideas.[149]

The foundation of possibility of these judgments and the foundation of their certainty could not therefore reside in the Cogito; they reside in a completely different principle, namely, the idea of the perfect as condition of the evaluation of the degrees of objective reality of ideas, a condition that determines their clearness and distinctness, and that is consequently a condition of their certainty. Once the mind passes from the Cogito to the investigation of the contents, a directive principle provided by the content (through the reality of a certain idea) is substituted for the directive principle given by consciousness, the foundation of the formal reality of ideas. The ultimate reason, which is a principle of the order of reasons, is no longer given by the ultimate subjective condition of our possible knowledge, but by the content of a certain ultimate item of knowledge that immediately places in evidence the cause of this content. The source of the clearness and distinctness, and consequently the necessary condition of certainty, is transferred from the Cogito to the nature of the contents. Thus, once the proof for the existence of God begins, the Cogito, as defined in *Meditation II*, is practically dispossessed of the prerogatives that it had enjoyed, and the idea of the perfect is established as the directive thread of the whole inquiry.[150]

This radical change can be clearly perceived in the *Discourse* when Descartes, going from the Cogito to the problem of God's existence, substitutes a judgment of evaluation for the judgment of existence, substitutes for the principle "in order to think one must exist" as condition of necessity for the judgment of existence in the Cogito, the idea of the perfect as condition of a judgment of validity and as new principle: "Having noted that there was nothing in 'I think therefore I am' to assure me that I was saying the truth, unless it was that I see very clearly that to think one must exist, I judged [. . .] After that I reflected upon the fact that I doubted and that, consequently, my being was not at all perfect, for I saw clearly that it was a greater perfection to know than to doubt. I decided to ascertain from what source I had learned to think of something more perfect than me and knew clearly that it must have been from some nature that was in fact more perfect."[151] The idea of the perfect, as principle of evaluation of the quantity of perfection, is substituted as point of support for the Cogito. We then seem to be confronted with two foundations of certainty, two principles of order. Whether we interpret this fact as the conflict of an Augustinian current and a modern mathematical idealist current, or the consequence of the dissociation between form and content, we still have the following problem: are these two principles able to be reconciled? Because the Cogito founded possibility, it founded certainty ipso facto; can the idea of the perfect that renders possible certain judgments also establish their certainty at the same time? Is there a conceivable link between the certainty that the idea of the perfect can establish and the certainty of the Cogito?

18. Substitution of the Idea of the Perfect for the Cogito as the Directive Principle. The Original Intuition

It appears impossible to discover such a link if we do not refer to the actual linkage of reasons and if we do not conceive that the Cogito, instead of being the absolute simple nature, can only be thought clearly and distinctly by the intermediary of the perfect as the only absolute reason. Otherwise, we will fail, persisting in attempting to discover in the Cogito what it is by nature incapable of furnishing. If the perfect being is the absolute reason to which the Cogito is subordinated as a relative reason, then we will seek in vain in this relative reason for something that can account for the absolute reason. Similarly, mathematical ideas account for the possibility of sensible representations, and the Cogito accounts for mathematical ideas, and not vice versa, even though we do not succeed in grasping the higher reason in its own independence except by going from the subordinate reasons that the higher reason links to itself by the unity that governs along the whole chain. The problem of the legitimacy of judgments about the perfection of objective realities based on the idea of the perfect therefore cannot be resolved except by inverting the direction of the inquiry, meaning, by asking not whether the condition of their possibility resides in the Cogito, but on the contrary, whether the *ultimate condition of possibility of the Cogito itself* ought not be discovered in the principle that establishes them and renders them legitimate.

That is precisely Descartes' solution. *In fact, I cannot think of myself without the idea of the perfect,* for originally I have no consciousness of myself except as an imperfect being; and this consciousness is impossible without the prior knowledge of the idea of the perfect: "My notion of the infinite is in some way prior in me to my notion of the finite."[152] The idea of the perfect is a condition of the Cogito, and the perfect being is the absolute reason of my thinking self, a relative nature. If it is thus, if the thinking self can no more be separated from the perfect being than the abstract can be separated from the concrete, or the relative reason from the absolute reason, or a mode from its substance, it is clear that the idea of the perfect, originally present at the core of my self, must also be originally present at the core of the inquiry, once the Cogito "considers what is within itself" in order to know itself, to extend its knowledge, and to discover the proof that God exists together with the ultimate foundation of the objective validity of ideas. We understand that the idea of the perfect has, because of its nature, the legitimate power to constrain the Cogito to recognize that it is powerless to account for it and that this idea must find in itself, and not elsewhere, the reason for its manifestation in me; we understand that it can establish, within the Cogito, judgments of evaluation that, while arising from it alone, must be imposed on the Cogito. In *Meditation II,* second-order substantiality, the substantiality of the thinking self, was announced from the start as the latent condition for the progressive passage going from composite sensible representations to their composing elements, and then from the composing elements to mathematical ideas, in order to end up with the form of representation in general as ultimate indubitable condition of all knowledge; similarly, in *Meditation III,* the first substantiality of the perfect being is announced from the start of the methodical investigation when it renders possible latently the progressive passage from the objective reality of sensible representations to richer objective realities, in order to end up with God's objective reality that entails the independent positing of the perfect being.

But is the positing of the idea of the perfect as condition of possibility of the Cogito itself legitimate? I do not preoccupy myself with knowing, in the knowledge of my existence by means of the Cogito, whether I am perfect or imperfect, infinite or finite, but simply that I think and consequently that I exist. Since the idea of the perfect is the condition of knowledge for my thinking being as finite and imperfect, not as merely existent, is it not illegitimate to make it a condition of possibility of the Cogito, which requires no principle other than "in order to think one must exist?"

This objection would be justified only if "I think, therefore I am" exhausted all the certain reality of my thinking self and if the whole being of my thinking self consisted only in the form of representativity obtained by abstraction from the contents. But if the indubitable existence of my self as first truth can only be posited by considering my thought as condition of all knowledge and if, in this way, I am assured that my being consists only of my mind and that the mind is essentially an intellect, it does not follow that this thought is reducible to the simple empty power to know and to know oneself. The actual intuition that allowed me to know that I am, soon made ne know with no less necessity what I am, meaning not simply a thinking self in general, but a finite thinking self in general, not simply a thought having consciousness of its own existence, but a thought also having consciousness of the imperfection of its being; consequently having conjointly consciousness of its self, of perfection, and of the incommensurability between the perfect and itself; and finally a thought having consciousness not simply of its various faculties and various ideas, but of the various contents that fill these ideas, in particular, of the content that fills the idea of the perfect, a consciousness by which the degree of perfection of the other contents is evaluated. Self-consciousness and consciousness of the perfect are therefore united from the start in a first indivisible intuition;[153] the self and the perfect are known by *one and the same faculty:* "I conceive this resemblance [with God—M. G.] in which the idea of God is contained, by the same faculty *by which I conceive myself,* in other words, when I reflect upon myself, not only do I know that I am an imperfect thing, incomplete and dependent on others, that strives and aspires constantly toward something better and greater than what I now am, but also at the same time

I know that the thing upon which I depend possesses in itself all these great things to which I aspire and whose ideas I find in myself."[154]

My nature is not simply to be a thinking being, thinking itself as thought, but a being thinking itself as finite and consequently thinking of the infinite: "I recognize that it would not be possible for *my nature* to be what it is, meaning that I have in me the idea of God, unless God truly existed."[155] The separate knowledge of the Cogito as simple consciousness of self is therefore an incomplete knowledge, meaning it is conceived apart by means of an abstraction of the mind that renders the thing confused, because it cannot think itself distinctly except with respect to the simple absolute nature that is its condition.[156] The method of division of the difficulty that prescribes the separate study of what is in me, for example, to consider provisionally substance apart from its modes (ideas, inclinations, will), was able to distinguish the Cogito as consciousness of self from the Cogito as consciousness of finitude, but this division is a provisional artifice that could not legitimate a definitive separation, a disjunction between relative reason (Cogito) and absolute reason (God).

19. Substitution of God for the Cogito as First Principle

The result of this positing of the infinite and perfect as an ultimate principle of my knowledge (Cogito) and of my finite being (the thinking self having the idea of God) is to confer on the Cogito of *Meditation III* a different character from the one presented in *Meditation II:* an unfinished character that is insufficient by itself, for it cannot conceive itself nor subsist detached from the infinite—the only concrete or complete thing, or substance, capable of conceiving itself and explaining itself completely by itself. Since the finite self can only be detached by an abstraction that renders my idea confused, the Cogito can be clearly and distinctly known only by completing itself by means of the intuition of the perfect. In this way two orders of substantiality are sketched: the one absolute and positive, the other relative and negative.

My thought manifests its substantiality in the Cogito only negatively, insofar as we can conceive it clearly and distinctly by abstracting away all the modes it conditions; but this manner of being, which is in some way residual and negative, does not by itself furnish my thought any proper and positive foundation of subsistence by itself. That is why this pretendedly substantial existence can become obscure to my eyes once I stop having an actual intuition of it *in fact*. On the contrary, God's substantiality, which imposes itself on me by the efficacious action of an infinite power on me, entails an internal positive foundation that not only establishes its independence with respect to my own thought, but also the dependence of my own thought with respect to it. The independent principle of self is therefore perceived as in itself foreign to the vicissitudes of my intuition.

When this intuition stops being actual, I am not less convinced that it remains what it is. I am therefore freed from the precariousness due to the impossible maintenance of my actual intuition and from subjection with respect to temporality. The infinity of the objective reality of the idea of the perfect requires a necessity that extracts evidence from the contingency of temporal findings. However, even though the existence of these two substances is assured, the distinction between the two orders of substantiality is established here only from the epistemological point of view. The Cogito appears in this case as a second substantiality because it is an incomplete knowledge; the simple and absolute nature of God is manifested as authentic and primary substantiality because it is complete knowledge by itself and it renders complete the knowledge of the Cogito, without needing the Cogito for its own clearness and distinctness. The second proof by effects will have to advance this distinction on the ontological plane and establish deductively the metaphysical thesis exhibited in article 51 of the *Principles.*

I have attained absolute certainty by means of this complete and self-sufficient knowledge since the knowledge remains unshakable, given that nothing can put it into question once again; I have also attained the foundation of all certainties, since the destruction of the evil genius subtracts the Cogito itself from the perpetual oscillation that this hypothesis imparted to it, and establishes the truth of all clear and distinct ideas. The necessarily objective validity of the idea of God transfers the foundation of certainty, which was up to now located in the subject (Cogito), to a higher principle that transcends it. The Cogito imparted only a subjective foundation to my certainty. The knowledge of my self that it rendered possible led to the discovery in me of a reality and a necessity that, while imposing itself from inside me, does not, however, come from me. The idea of God therefore gives an objective foundation to my certainty. These contents of my ideas that the Cogito, when it was reduced to itself, cut off from any relation with an object outside of me can be supported by the idea of God. This idea carries me outside of me and destroys all the reasons for doubt that enclosed me tightly inside me and even inside the punctual moment of the intuition of my self. Although the certainty of the Cogito was suppressed in the recollection of its evidence, the certainty of God subsists unshakably in the recollection I keep of it, because I know that, as a rule, no evidence could be doubtful.

Thus the evidence of the Cogito no longer needs to be actualized constantly in order to preserve its certainty: the presence of its intuition is no longer indispensable in order to extract from myself a doubt, which has stopped being valid as a rule. God's certainty therefore constitutes the definitive certainty of the truth of the Cogito.

20. Priority of Knowledge of God over Knowledge of Soul; Parallel with the Priority of Knowledge of Soul over Knowledge of Body

Several consequences result from the above:

1) Since the Cogito can never succeed, because of the nature of our mind, to assure in an unshakable fashion (meaning in a certain fashion) the certainty of the certainty which it obtains only in a precarious way in some fleeting instants, the knowledge of God, which eternally encompasses this certainty of certainty and can confer it to the Cogito for eternity, is more certain than the Cogito itself. There is the same relation between the third-power certainty of the knowledge of God and the second-power certainty of the Cogito, as between the second-power certainty of the Cogito and the first-power certainty of mathematical truths. Although mathematical truths are certain of their object, they can never find in their object the certainty of the certainty that the Cogito immediately finds in its own during the time that it actualizes itself.

2) As something abstract posited outside of God, meaning separated from the concrete to which it is necessarily bound, the Cogito considered separately still implies a certain confusion in its knowledge; it is itself less clear and distinct than the knowledge of the true God. It is therefore less evident. This conclusion confirms the fact that the Cogito has less reality than God, the Sovereign Being; for, as we have seen,[157] clearness and distinctness are functions of the quantity of reality of the idea, and are at the maximum in God. This conclusion confirms the place of the Cogito as a lower reason. In fact, being the first reason, God is strictly speaking known before the Cogito.[158] An item of knowledge, properly speaking, is a completely clear, distinct, and definitive science. And if, in the course of the analysis, we encountered the Cogito before God, as we encountered mathematical ideas before the Cogito, that was because we still had imperfect and precarious knowledge that only the knowledge of God can transform into perfect and stable knowledge: "I recognize very clearly that the certainty and truth of all science depends only on the knowledge of the true God, and that before I knew him, I could not know any other thing."[159] In fact, a thing known before another is more evident than the other thing, since according to the order, it is a condition of it; thus it is more certain than that which depends on it, since it participates in the evidence of the first principle through a smaller number of interposed natures: "A thing is proved more manifest and better known than another when those who have sufficient knowledge of both recognize that the one is known first, with more evidence and more certainty than the other (cognitio prior evidentior et certior)."[160]

3) God is better known than the thinking self. In fact, the more attributes we know of a thing, the more distinctly we know the thing;[161] and

we know many more attributes of God than attributes of our mind: "I have so carefully noticed that there are precious few things we know with certainty about corporeal things that we know more about the human mind, even more about God himself."[162]

4) For all these reasons, God is easier to know than the mind, and consequently, of all things he is the easiest to know: "And as for God, certainly, if my mind were not prejudiced and if my thought were not distracted by the continuous presence of the images of sensible things, there would be nothing that I would recognize sooner and more easily than him."[163] God's incomprehensibility therefore is in no way his unknowability, since not only is God known, but of all things he is the most known. Cartesianism is therefore the refutation of agnosticism.[164]

Consequently, knowledge of God is more certain, more clear and distinct, more evident, more rich, more immediate, and easier than knowledge of my soul. Knowledge of God has the same advantage over knowledge of soul as knowledge of soul has over knowledge of body, and its primacy with respect to knowledge of soul is established by means of the same general arguments that established the primacy of soul with respect to body: "And certainly the idea I have of the human mind insofar as it is a thing that thinks, not extended in length, width, or depth, that participates in nothing belonging to the body, is incomparably more distinct than the idea of anything corporeal. And when I consider that I doubt, meaning that I am something incomplete and dependent, the idea of a complete and independent being, meaning God, presents itself to my mind very distinctly and clearly. And from the fact that such an idea occurs in me, or that I, who possess this idea, exist, I so evidently conclude that God exists and that my existence depends entirely upon him every moment of my life that I do not think that the human mind can conceive anything with greater evidence and certainty."[165] To these general arguments is added the particular reason that I know God before myself (in the scientific meaning of the term *know*) because he is a complete substance with respect to myself, who is an incomplete substance—meaning epistemologically, a relative reason, and ontologically, as we shall soon see, a created substance, subsisting only with God's cooperation. However, the particular reasons that assured me that I knew the soul before the body were of another order: 1) the soul is given to me by itself, while the body is known to me only through the intermediary of the soul; 2) my existence as mind is given to me by pure intelligence, while existence as body is given to me only by imagination, a mode of intelligence that is repugnant to the intrinsic nature of body.

21. The Dissociation of Consciousness; Form and Content; Cogito, the Principle of Form; God, the Principle of Content. The Problem of the Reconciliation between the Two Principles. *Nexus rationum*

Once one establishes the existence of *another* constraining me to "go beyond myself," necessarily posited as an absolute reality, as the author of the objective realities that constitute the content of my ideas, these objective realities receive a foundation rendered definitive for science and their reality, insofar as it is distinct from the simple reality of the consciousness that thinks them, and their change with respect to the thinking consciousness. Even though it is present in me, and perceived within me, this objective reality is sublimated expressly in philosophical science as an essential and intelligible reality that God himself has introduced in me and that does not proceed from me. Thus we have *established metaphysically* what until now has been *established* only *psychologically* in the Cogito, by the reflection of my mind on itself *(mens in se conversa)*, namely, the division of consciousness into pure and simple consciousness, or the form of knowledge from which ideas as modes of thought that are equal among themselves proceed, and the content of that form, or the objective reality of those ideas, which makes them "varied" and "unequal" (in degrees or in quantity of perfection or of reality)—an objective reality that my psychological reflection had, from the start, refused to admit as truly arising from me.[166] This division is completed and confirmed by the attribution of a distinct principle to each of these elements: the *Cogito,* principle of the form of knowledge in general and of consciousness as form of ideas, having abstracted away the unequal contents; *God,* principle of these contents and of the objective reality that is present in various degrees in all ideas.

We understand that, under these conditions, philosophical science can and even *must* reclaim these two primary principles without contradicting itself. Not only will one *or* the other appear to be first according to one's point of view, but one *and* the other will be first, for it is necessary to place oneself in two points of view at the same time.

If we situate ourselves according to the point of view of pure consciousness, of the subjective certainty and the necessity of *my* understanding, the first principle can only be the Cogito. The Cogito is the first truth, and God is only the fourth truth since the first is my existence, the second is my nature, and the third is the priority of the knowledge of soul over knowledge of body. In fact, only consciousness renders possible the methodical unfolding of philosophical science; only the necessities of *my* understanding tie the various links of the chain together, according to the order, beginning with the Cogito as the first indubitable truth. There is no other possible first foundation for the truth of my affirmations other than the impossibility that I ascertain of denying myself without rejecting myself.

But the necessity of this chain, however absolute it is, is only subjective. It deals with me, with the necessities of my understanding. I cannot even affirm that my own nature such as I am constrained to represent it to myself is in itself such as I represent it to myself. A fortiori, my understanding, reduced to itself and its own necessities, can only speak about the objective validity of the objective realities constituting the contents of its ideas and referring, by the constitution of these ideas themselves, to objects outside of me, which remain absolutely unknown on the plane of the Cogito alone.

If we situate ourselves not according to the point of view of the necessities for my consciousness, but according to the point of view of these necessities insofar as they are valid for things themselves, the first principle can only necessarily be God, since it alone can confer objective certainty to my ideas.

Thus the Cogito appears as the first principle of all *possible* human science, since science can be constructed as a system of reasons tied together by a rigorous necessity only through it and by reflection on it. And there can be no science without this necessity. But God appears as the first principle of all *valid* human science, for it alone establishes the truths imposed on myself by my own understanding as truths imposed by things themselves; it alone transforms the *veritas rationum* into *veritas rei*. And there can be no science if the truth of my reasons remains foreign to the truth of things. Thus the Cogito establishes for philosophy its factual possibility as necessary science, while God establishes for it its legitimacy, as a rule, as science that is valid for things. But there can be no science properly speaking without the union of a rigorous necessity and an assured objective validity; the *Cogito,* as condition of the former, and *God,* as condition of the latter, must both be affirmed as first principles. But if we situate ourselves according to the point of view of the *ratio cognoscendi,* the Cogito is the only first principle, while if we situate ourselves according to the point of view of the *ratio essendi,* God alone is the first principle, since being the author of all things, he is both the principle of the Cogito as simple consciousness and of the objective realities that constitute the content of the modes of this consciousness. Finally, for us who construct science, the Cogito is the simplest of reasons, and God depends on it; while in himself, from the point of view of the objects of science, God is the simplest of natures, and the thinking self depends on it. If science considers itself as a system of linked items of knowledge, it perceives itself as depending completely on the Cogito; if, on the other hand, it considers itself relative to the object it discovers and from which it draws its objective truth and its knowledge of the foundation of that truth, it perceives itself as depending entirely on God.

The problem of the two first principles would therefore be resolved most satisfactorily if the examination of the analytic order of reasons had not let something of a break appear in the line that was followed. At the moment my mind decides, in its reflection on itself, to transfer its reflection from the thinking subject to the contents of which the subject is thinking, the analysis seems to abandon the leading thread it derives from the Cogito—namely, the thread of the conditions that render possible my knowledge in general—in order to adopt another that derives from the idea of the perfect that is originally present in us. From that moment on, meaning once we begin the basic investigation of *Meditation III* about the problem of the objective validity of ideas, the foundation of the possibility of judgments of evidence from which results the construction of my science, and consequently even the merely subjective certainty of its linkage, is no longer the Cogito, but the idea of God; this is true to the extent that God, through the intermediary of the idea of the perfect, no longer appears only as condition of the objective validity of my subjectively necessary science, but also as direct condition of this subjective necessity. He is no longer merely *ratio essendi* but also *ratio cognoscendi,* for he enables me to *recognize* the inequalities of perfection of the contents of my various ideas, the imperfection of my self, and the imperfection of the philosophical knowledge of the Cogito, when it is posited separately, independently from the knowledge of the perfect that is alone capable of lifting the Cogito to a perfectly clear and distinct knowledge. Finally the knowledge of God modifies the character of my subjective certainty itself, by stabilizing the certainty of the Cogito by means of a third-power certainty. Surely, this encroachment of the idea of God, as *ratio essendi* and foundation of the objective validity of an already subjectively certain science, over the Cogito as *ratio cognoscendi* and foundation of this subjective certainty of science, can be justified, as we have seen, by the indissoluble and original union, of our first consciousness of the idea of ourselves as finite and imperfect, and the idea of God as infinite and perfect, a union that is implied, basically, in the original union of my consciousness and its contents; if, in fact, in order to raise myself to the consciousness of the Cogito, I had to abstract away these contents, it is because they referred to something other than the consciousness enclosing them, but not in themselves—meaning *insofar as they are in consciousness (abstraction,* let us recall, is not *exclusion).* Nevertheless, it still seems that a break in the "unilinear" linkage of reasons is produced.

It remains for us to discover whether this linkage must be rigorously unilinear. Descartes not only spoke about a *series,* but a *nexus rationum.* Mathematical analysis, when applied to the realities of extension, because of the diversity and complexity of these realities, must give rise to a plurality of long chains that are sometimes entangled, while remaining single and unified; similarly, philosophical analysis is not a purely abstract and empty deduction, but a methodical application of an essentially mathematical reason to the set of realities offered to our intelligence by the scope of our consciousness. And these realities are no less diverse and complex than those of extension. It is therefore natural that philosophical analysis, while remaining single and unified, excludes the elementary simplicity of a purely unilinear linkage and is resolved into a *nexus rationum*.

22. *Nexus rationum* or Vicious Circle? Different Hypotheses Concerning the Solution of the "Circle"

We are now concerned with knowing in what this *nexus rationum* consists. Is it the legitimate crisscrossing of independent series? Or is it, on the contrary, the mutual dependence of first terms that could not be first unless they specifically escaped all dependence? That is the classical problem of the Cartesian circle.[167] If the Cogito is used to prove God and God is used to prove the Cogito, we are no longer confronted with a *nexus rationum*, but with a paralogism, a characteristic violation of the basic principle of the order "which consists only in that the things that are proposed first must be known without the help of those following, and that those following must then be disposed in such a way that they are demonstrated by only the things that precede them."[168]

There are two means for resolving the problem: either reduce the two series into a single one (either to the one governing the absoluteness of the Cogito or to the one governing the absoluteness of God) or reestablish the complete independence of the two series such as to make them just intersect.

Under the first type of solution is referred the thesis that consists in interpreting the relation of the Cogito and divine veracity according to the analogy of the relation between a fact given in physics and its explicative principle: God gives the explanation of the certain fact that is the Cogito, and the Cogito establishes the truth and certainty of the principle that allows it to be explained.[169] We then have dealings with a single series whose first term, an independent principle sufficient for the certainty of all the others, is the Cogito.

This interpretation must be rejected because it reduces God's existence to a likely hypothesis, lacking absolute certainty. The physical fact does not become more certain by having been explained; and the principle that explains it, instead of possessing its own certainty, a greater certainty than the certainty possessed by the fact, is only a *hypothesis* which, on the contrary, borrows its certainty from it. That is why this principle can always be replaced by another, more convenient principle, in virtue of the *aequipollentia hypothesium*. In opposition with the physical fact, the Cogito is rendered more certain once it is founded in God, for it then escapes the doubt that strikes at it without fail once it stops being the object of an actual intuition; in addition God not only possesses his own certainty, but an absolute certainty that is the condition of all others, including the certainty of the Cogito, which it renders unshakable. In fact, the idea of God is the clearest and most distinct idea of all, and adherence of will is firmer than the affirmed idea is clearer and more distinct.[170] On the contrary, when a truth of physics is founded solely on its capacity to explain a given fact, it remains in a state of simple *supposition*[171] and gives rise only to a moral certainty, in the same way that a decoding hypothesis draws its certainty solely from its ability to give meaning to a given cryptogram.[172] Consequently, God and divine veracity would remain suppositions and would have only moral certainty, if their truth were founded only on their ability to explain a fact: the fact of the Cogito. They would be deprived of this absolute certainty that they derive, as do truly demonstrated physical truths, only because they are founded on internal independent reasons possessing an intrinsic evidence. The intrinsic evidence of God, which is the greatest evidence of all, imposes the greatest absolute certainty and serves as ultimate foundation for the certainty of the Cogito.[173]

We could not then object that evidence is always evidence and nothing can increase it or diminish it.[174] That, of course, is an indubitable psychological assertion. But although it is true that all evidence is evidence, evidence is valid only *within some limits*. An evidence can be limited and partial, or precarious and easy to obscure or to suspend. Thus mathematical evidence is incontestable within its own limits, meaning within the assertion of some relations between notions or properties of notions that are necessary for my understanding; but it is not incontestable beyond these limits, when we are concerned with knowing whether these necessities are also valid in themselves, outside my understanding; for beyond these limits there is no mathematical knowledge and no mathematical evidence—there is no mathematics. Similarly, the Cogito has an incontestable evidence within the limits of its actual intuition; but it has no such thing beyond these limits, when it is maintained by memory alone, outside the intuition. That is why an atheist, in spite of the evidence he may possess of mathematical truths and of the Cogito, has only "prejudices" and must remain uncertain of everything, if he does not accede to the ultimate evidence, the evidence of God that alone procures an unshakable certainty.

We would then broach the other variant of the first type of solution. We would attempt to reduce the two series to a single series, governed by God, considered as a single absolute term. Is not the circle avoided, in fact, if the evidence of the point of departure, however partial and precarious it is, is only employed within some strict limits in which it is truly evidence and truly indubitable? And such is the case, since the passage to God is accomplished within the actual intuition of the Cogito, subtracted in fact, from the grasp of the evil genius. Instead of the Cogito and God being situated on two separate planes each serving as support for each other, they are originally given on the same plane, indissolubly tied in the same fashion as the incomplete is tied to the complete. The passage to God is only the accomplishment of the clear and distinct knowledge of the Cogito, which, opening itself to the full intuition of God, an intuition that it implicitly encloses and that sustains it, rids itself of what burdened it with confusion while it remained separate from him, meaning ignorant of him. There is therefore one and the same intuition that becomes real, one and the same development of the light (in which, according to Lessing's expression, when commenting on Spinoza: the light illuminates itself and becomes total). The intuition of the absolute nature, which alone is complete, imparts total evidence and total certainty; the limited and temporal evidence of the Cogito, serving as a springboard on which the evidence of God first seems to depend, on the contrary, appears then as dependent on the absolute *ratio* that sustains it and uprooted from temporal precariousness by the self-sufficiency of that reason. The ontological translation of this relation will then be given by the second proof from effects, in which is established the continuous dependence of my finite self having the idea of God with respect to God as its cause maintaining my existence in time at each instant, by his continuous creation. There is a circle only for someone, lacking the evidence of the infinite, who believes that there are two distinct criteria where there is only the development of one and the same intuition.

However, the problem cannot be entirely resolved except by responding to the difficulty posed by the question of the validity of judgments of perfection concerning the objective realities contained by the various ideas and the formal reality of my self. If one attributes an evidence of objective validity to these judgments, how can one legitimately establish the knowledge of the existence of God through them, given that the certainty of that existence validates the evidences of that nature? If, on the other hand, we agree to attribute only an evidence of purely subjective validity to them, how can I be assured that these judgments express what is the truth of things? And this alternative is the circle itself, from which I thought I had escaped.

By means of a new reflection we could achieve the reduction of the two series into one—on the side of the Cogito—but this time without reducing the existence of the veracious God to an explicative hypothesis having only moral certainty. It would be sufficient to perceive that the subjective necessity of judgments of perfection immediately attest to their own objective validity, from the fact that we could not refuse them without contradicting this subjective necessity that is known immediately. In brief we would note that we could not deny them without denying ourselves, which would be impossible, because in order to deny myself, I must exist. First the hypothesis of the evil genius would not be able to reach the judgment of imperfection concerning my being, since this hypothesis flows from this judgment and arises from this occasion. The verification of my state of doubt and imperfection, which renders indubitable the certainty of my imperfect existence, is intimately linked to the two conditions that are as indubitable as this certainty because they render it possible. These two conditions are "in order to think one must exist," and then that, in order to judge myself fallible and imperfect, I must have the idea of the perfect, to which by definition objective reality, which is incommensurable with the formal reality of my self, is irreducible. The objectivity of the perfect being would therefore be contained immediately in the subjective-objective necessity of judgments concerning my existence. If I doubt that I exist, I must exist, since I doubt and consequently I think. Because I doubt, I am an imperfect being. Moreover, I have the idea of the perfect, since I conceive the imperfect. I know that the perfect is not reducible to the imperfect, since I can conceive one only through the negation of the other. I know that the perfect does not stem from me, etc. In brief, all these ideas appear to belong to the category of "those that are true as soon as I think of them, because their mere thought excludes the possibility of doubting them; and consequently, they are true as soon as I doubt them, for in order to doubt them I must think them."

But still the difficulty is not yet exorcised except in appearance. Certainly, it is impossible for me to doubt that I exist the moment I doubt, but it is not subjectively impossible to doubt that I am imperfect the moment I doubt, if I am aware that I can be deceived on the valuation of good and bad. Moreover, even if it were subjectively impossible for me to doubt the imperfection constituting my doubt, would my judgment be objectively valid? In other words, if judgments of perfection claim to objective validity only in virtue of a necessity that is proper to my thought and that is subjective, how can it be certain that this claim is in itself objectively established?

We are then left no other choice than to have recourse to the second type of solution: the reciprocal independence of the series of the Cogito and the series of God, and their crisscrossing at a given point. We encounter a nature that reveals itself to our intuition as a foundation finding a point of support in itself, and not in us, imposing itself on me, *in spite of myself*,[175] irresistibly testifying about its objective validity by getting me to touch the Other directly within myself. If God is the ultimate condition of certainty, it must be that at a given moment this certainty manifests itself in me as unconditioned and appears in consequence as no longer depending on conditions emanating from the subject. The subject must be erased before it. No doubt this solution is not specified in the *Meditations* in these exact words, but it arises indisputably from an internally felt constraint that led Descartes to state that "my thought does not impose any necessity to things, but on the contrary, the necessity that is in the thing itself, meaning God's existence, determines me to have this thought."[176]

This solution can be viewed from another slant. In mathematics I know only the intrinsic necessity of certain properties or certain notions, not the objective validity of this necessity, which is arbitrarily added to the knowledge I have. With respect to the Cogito, the necessity that I exist is known only in the moment I think of it; it is affirmed arbitrarily once, but having become memory, it escapes the circle of the intuition that allows me to know it. As for the necessity that characterizes the knowledge of my nature, which is drawn from the consciousness of my existence as thinking self, it is directly perceived in me; but as long as I do not know whether God exists I cannot know whether my nature is in itself such as I represent it to myself—the objective validity of my knowledge is therefore the object of no knowledge here and can only be affirmed gratuitously. On the other hand, with respect to God, the objective validity of my conclusion constitutes the content of my knowledge itself. Its objectivity reveals itself within me. Its affirmation is therefore entirely founded. The necessity to unite the idea of the perfect being to the perfect being itself as its cause effectively falls within the circle of the actual intuition. It thus imposes itself validly on us in all certainty. It is the only case in which the relation to something outside of me is not purely and simply assumed, but *known*. What is grasped directly by my intuition is no longer simply the necessary relation of two concepts (whose objective validity I do not know), it is the necessary relation of the concept to the thing itself. The objective validity of this necessity could not therefore be contested, since my knowledge bears precisely, in this case, on the necessity of this objective validity.

This solution is certainly the closest solution without yet being rigorous. This objective necessity and this change are not yet so, for me to whom they appear, and we would be able to wonder again what is the validity of this phenomenon, whether it truly expresses the other, or whether I *think* that I touch this other, I *think* that I am constained by it.

23. A Fundamental Reason for the Difficulty of the Circle

The impossibility of arriving at a rigorous solution must allow the true nature of the problem of the vicious circle to be specified. This problem at first only appears to express the difficulty that would result from the opposition between the Cogito, in a strict sense, and the Cogito, in a broader sense. The latter unites two different points of departure: 1) the form of the representation that includes the affirmation of my own existence—Cogito in the strict sense that is posited without having recourse to God; and 2) the judgment of perfection that includes the affirmation of God. This duality of points of departure reflects the classical duality of idealism and realism.

But that is still a superficial view. For the Cogito in the strict sense depends on the principle "in order to think one must exist," by which I can posit that I exist *necessarily* if I think. And this principle is a variant of the principle "nothingness has no property," which itself flows immediately from the notion of the Infinite Being.[177] The Cogito in the strict sense is therefore also dependent on the idea of the perfect, and the problem finally bears on the legitimacy of the validity that is attributed before it and independently of it, in spite of the evil genius, on all these principles that natural light reveals to us—which are, in addition to the axiom, "in order to think one must exist," the principle of causality, the principle of the correspondence of the idea with what is ideated, and the principle of the judgments of perfection on the contents of ideas.

The solution of this problem can only be the following: in order to advance certainty, Descartes is compelled, at the start of his investigation, to place himself at the level of common consciousness, meaning obscure and confused consciousness. The hypothesis of the evil genius, which he employs in order to obtain an absolutely rigorous certainty, leads him, in fact, to take as starting point a consciousness that does not know itself, but also a consciousness that denatures itself by rejecting from its certainty everything that is not *consciousness of consciousness* pure and simple. The hypothesis of the evil genius is reflected in the Cogito itself, since it constrains it to think itself at first only as consciousness separate from God's consciousness. And *there is no consciousness in reality that is not at the same time consciousness of God* (meaning a consciousness of one's own imperfection, etc.): the true Cogito is the Cogito bound to God. The preliminary negation of God, which leaves me no way to escape universal skepticism, except by affirming myself as doubting, can only lead to an inauthentic Cogito, meaning a Cogito rendered obscure because it is thought by means of an abstraction of our mind separating it from what it is necessarily united to and known clearly and distinctly.[178] But since, in order to satisfy a scientific requirement, we had to situate ourselves at the level of common sense, where the veil of sensible ideas hides the rational truth of God's existence, since we had to demonstrate this truth that is self-evident *against it,* we had to start from an evidence capable of imposing itself immediately on this atheist consciousness, by provisionally agreeing with it about atheism, by means of the hypothesis of the evil genius. And the Cogito, as a consciousness of self separated from consciousness of God, was alone able to impose itself at that level as first evidence, since it is alone able to be revealed as necessarily entailed in all judgments of common consciousness whether true or false.

However, the Cogito in the strict sense is only the denatured image of myself. Moreover, it is evident that the true cannot arise from the false. If, beginning with the Cogito, we can rise to the level of God, upon which the Cogito is in fact founded, that is possible only with the help of true light: the light that illuminates itself can only be the true light. From this stems the absolute necessity, after having already used for the Cogito itself the principle "in order to think one must exist," to appeal to the principle of causality, the principle of the correspondence of the idea with what is ideated, and the principle of judgments of perfection on contents, all principles that emanate directly from the true light of God. The demonstration of the true God must necessarily rest on principles actually established in him, but whose validity cannot be established before the conclusion (before the positing of God), although their validity is recognizable before that. That is why Malebranche will give absolute primacy to the proof of God by simple view, economizing on the hypothesis of the evil genius. Everything becomes convenient if one departs from the self, seeing God, or if one restores the Cogito in its authenticity as union of finite and infinite.

Therefore, if one takes the point of view of the *ratio essendi*, or truth of the thing, the difficulty disappears. It even disappears similarly from the point of view of the *ratio cognoscendi*, or truth of science, if one posits expressly from the start at the same time as the first truth, relative to the form of consciousness (the existence of my thought), this other truth that arises from the content of that consciousness: the existence of the infinitely perfect God.

But the demonstration requires us to pretend to deny it. This results in an oscillation between the denatured image of myself, installed at the same time as the hypothesis of the evil genius, and the true image of myself as the union of the finite and the infinite, of the imperfect and the perfect. The intricacy arises from the need to reduce to nothing the hypothesis of the evil genius (the absolute form of atheism) by a demonstration that, implying the true light coming from God, claims not to presuppose it—by a demonstration that, departing from a light that does not know itself (the Cogito in the strict sense), cannot bring itself to the full light except by having recourse to the true light, the light that is not denatured by its separation with itself, meaning with God.

On the other hand, because these difficulties stem from an effort to convince the common man and the atheist by situating themselves on their level at first, these difficulties are in a certain sense external. The authentic Cogito, which seems to dispel them, does not compromise the idealism that characterizes the proceedings of the new philosophy. The union with God, which the authentic Cogito reveals to me originally, does not entail any realistic postulate, for it does not suppose any mystical union or participation with a reality other than mine. God's presence in me is not the intuition of God in flesh and bone, as it is in Malebranche's proof by simple view. It is my illumination by the *idea* of the infinite: God is posited as *cause* of my idea beginning from my idea; therefore it is the light of my understanding that illuminates itself. Thus the inspiration does not cease being idealistic and does not, in this case, clash against a relic of ancient ontology.

If the Cogito has given us the absolute nature that subjectively constitutes the first link of the chain of reasons as the principle of a subjectively necessary and valid science, God has allowed us to attain the absolute nature that objectively constitutes this first link, that is, the principle of the objectively necessary and valid science. The idea of God has received the rigorous proof of its objective validity. At once, all its properties, meaning all the perfections included for us in this idea, can and must rightly be objectively affirmed of God himself.[179]

However, the second proof by effect and the ontological proof each will establish directly two of these properties, the two considered most fundamental: the first, *causa sui,* and the second, *eternity,* by the existential necessity to exist.[180]

The first proof by effect, which is completely based on the incommensurability of my finite self with the infinite, emphasizes God's incomprehensibility, established as the first and sufficient reason of the positing of its being for us. This character remains dominant, and the subsequent attribution of the two other characters to God *(causa sui* and the existential necessity to exist), does not make this disappear and does not even attenuate it. No doubt, in opposition to this first proof (and to the Thomist proof), which only enables us to know that God exists and not in what way he exists, the proof by *causa sui* and the ontological proof reveal to us *how he exists.* To that extent, we can affirm that these two proofs force an intimacy with God, "they open up, if we dare say it, the divine essence, in order to show why and how existence is implied in it."[181] But the heart of divine nature is not revealed to us in this fashion, for in order that these two properties be the object of clear and distinct knowledge, they must have an incomprehensible root.[182] Incomprehensibility saves rational theology since because of it alone I can go out from myself, I can know and affirm God. Without it the first proof would flounder, and consequently so would these other two proofs which, as we shall see, derive their sole foundation from it.

CHAPTER VI

The Second Proof of
God's Existence by Effects

I. Analysis and Discussion of the Proof

In opposition with the ontological proof that brings forth a higher and even the highest *truth of the thing,* the second proof by effects, situated *as a truth of science* on a lower plane, subordinate to the proof by effects that conditions its validity, is, *as a truth of science*, at the same level as the first proof by effects, and as Descartes tells us, simply gives us an easier version of it.[1] That is why it is treated in the same *Meditation.*

But Descartes states that it allows us to explain the first proof by effects "more absolutely (*absolutius*)."[2] We must therefore consider that it adds something to it and that it is not merely another exposition, with Scholastic terminology.[3] In fact, the first proof posits God relative only to ourselves, characterizing him only as an efficient cause of the idea of the perfect in us; the second posits God absolutely in himself, considering his causality not only relative to ourselves, but also relative to himself, meaning as *his own cause.*[4] Correlatively, God is no longer simply posited as cause of an idea in us, but as cause of us, who have this idea. Thus, God is certified as the *Creator* of my substance.

1. The Functions of the Different Proofs. The Order and the Second Proof by Effects

Descartes introduces this second proof through psychological considerations.

The reasons that lead to positing that the cause of the idea I have of a perfect being can only be the perfect being and cannot be myself require much attention and are fought against by the images of sensible things (which induce me to think that everything represented in me is caused by corporeal things). Surely my attention would be more easily kept if I focused it simply upon myself, an imperfect being possessing the idea of the perfect. Consequently, I wish to consider whether I, having this idea of God, could exist if there were no God. From where would I derive my existence? Would I derive it from myself, from my parents, or from some other cause less perfect than God?[5]

If I were the author of my own being, I would have given myself all the perfectious lacking to me, whose ideas I have in me, since I have the idea of the perfect. In fact I am conscious that these perfections, being only accidents, are less than substance and consequently easier to create than it. If I gave myself this *extra amount*, I would not have refused myself this lesser amount. If I could not do this because the perfections would constitute an *extra amount* that exceeds my creative forces, I would actually, in fact, be conscious that they are an *extra amount*, for I would experience that my power had limits with respect to this.

Would I then say that I was always as I am now? No, for I can only persist for some time as long as I am created anew at each instant. There is only a distinction of reason between preservation and creation. The present time does not depend on the preceding time. That is why, in order that a substance be preserved for all the moments it lasts, it needs the same necessary action to create it anew, as if it were still not in existence. And I do not have such power. If I had it, I would know it, for, being a thinking thing, there is nothing in me that remains unretrievably unknown to me. Therefore, I am not the author of my being.[6]

Does my being then derive from my parents or from some other cause less perfect than God? In any case, this cause must think and have the idea of God, for I have the idea of the perfect, and there must be at least as much reality in the cause as in the effect. Does this cause itself derive from itself or from another? If it derives from itself, it must be God, for it cannot refuse itself the perfections of which it has the idea. If it derives from another, this other will have to derive from itself or from another; and if this other derives from another, the other will have to derive, etc., until we reach a cause that is self-caused—that is necessarily God. There can be no infinite regress here, because we are concerned with a cause that preserves me presently, not one that produced me at another time.[7]

But could I not be the product of several causes, that, having given me the idea of a single cause containing all the perfections I attribute to God, is not collected into a single God? No, for I have the idea of the unity, simplicity, and inseparability of God's perfections. And the idea of the unity of a plurality is inseparable from the plurality and could not have been placed in me by a cause that would not have included it in itself. As for my parents, although they might have produced me, they do not preserve me. Moreover, they did not produce me as a thinking thing, they merely introduced some dispositions into the matter in which I judge that my (thinking) self is enclosed.

It remains only for me to examine in what way I acquired the idea of a being that possesses all perfections. I did not receive it from the senses, for it never presents itself against my will, as the ideas of sensible things do. I did not form it by myself, for I cannot subtract or add anything from it. Consequently, this idea was produced with me, along with my idea of my self, at the time I was created: it is the mark of God on his work. Therefore there is a God, and this God cannot be a deceiver, since he is perfect.[8]

2. The Second Proof by Effects

The second proof by effects has two parts.
1) A proof that I cannot exist by myself.
2) A proof that I cannot exist by an external cause other than God.
That is the schema that is followed constantly with respect to the a posteriori demonstration of the existence of things outside of me: something in my self or belonging to it is demonstrated as not being caused by me, but by something other than me; then an elimination is run between the possible external causes, leaving only one remaining. Such was the schema of the first proof by effects, and such will be the schema of the proof of the existence of bodies.

The first part of the proof considers two hypotheses corresponding with two conceptions of existing by oneself: i) a positive conception: existing by oneself is being one's own cause—I am my own cause; ii) a negative conception: existing by oneself is being without cause, never needing to be created—I am without cause.

3. The First Part of the Proof: First Hypothesis

The refutation of the first hypothesis rests on a conception of will that Descartes, as we have said,[9] defines as the Scholastics do, as a necessary appetite for the good.[10] In fact, the good is identified with being;[11] and willing can only be willing for being, for willing for nothingness is necessarily a nothingness of will. The necessity for God to exist, the impossibility for him to deceive, etc., will be founded on this axiom.[12] Moreover, my will is infinite in me as it is in God.[13] Therefore, if I could not have given myself the perfections of which I have the idea, it is because this infinite will has only a finite power in me. As a result, I could not have created myself, for the distance between nothingness and even finite being is infinite, and consequently the passage from one to the other presupposes an infinite power. All creation *ex nihilo* entails omnipotence. That is what is at the basis of Descartes' expression that to create substance is something greater than to create its accidents and that since I am incapable of giving myself the lesser thing, I could not have given myself the greater thing. That accidents are something less than substance is an item of evidence that intervened in the preceding proof and is certified by natural light.[14]

Nevertheless, here all accidents are *perfections;* that these perfections I am lacking are qualified as accidents of my finite self, although they are infinite (for we are concerned with "perfections contained in the idea I conceive of God"),[15] and that the founding of infinite things is something less than the founding of a finite being, are surprising assertions.[16] Descartes is here constrained to adjust his language for an absurd hypothesis—the hypothesis of infinite power in man, a finite being. On this plane, the act of giving oneself the perfections one is lacking is conceived as a progressive increase to infinity of properties that the finite being already possesses finitely—for example, knowledge, power, etc. That is why, even though the attributes are one with substance, to produce a substance is more difficult than to produce attributes, since they are produced "individually, one at a time, and even the totality in this way." And "the attributes, taken all together, are the same thing as substance, but not when they are taken one at a time, distributively."[17] Thus by being situated in the perspective of a progress of a finite being, or in the fragmentary acquisition of the attributes of the infinite, the act of creating or preserving an existing being appears to entail "something more" with respect to the act of developing to infinity the already existing perfections, or acquiring separately the infinite properties that all together make up a unity in the indivisibility of the infinitely infinite substance.

It remains no less true that the correct expression of the metaphysical truth implied in this absurd hypothesis consists in declaring that the creation *ex nihilo,* of any being whatever entailing infinite omnipotence, implies *ipso facto* all the perfections whose privation is incompatible with this power. This thesis can be derived clearly from the *Replies to Objections IV,*[18] which specifies that the actual meaning of this proof is only a manner of speaking due to the fiction that it takes as point of departure, namely, the supposition "if I were the author of my being."

The preceding argument, which leads from the infinite power necessary to create a finite and imperfect being to the necessity for this power to give itself all the perfections of which this being has the idea, does not give to the idea of the perfect as decisive a role as the one given to it by the first proof by effect, in which this idea in me directly establishes outside of me the infinite power necessary to implant it in my soul; it also does not give it the role that will be given to it by the a priori proof that derives the necessity of existence from the essence of perfection and consequently the necessity of having infinite power. No doubt this idea continues to play an indispensable role. The point of departure is not simply the finite self, but the self insofar as it has the idea of the perfect. It is through the presence of the idea of the perfect that I can know a) *what is* God, whose existence I am seeking, b) that I am defective and cannot exist by myself, and c) that the cause of my self is necessarily perfect and must be God.[19] It does not matter that the axiom, "to create a finite substance is greater than to create the perfections that this being lacks," makes the perfection of the being the *consequence* of the infinity of the power necessary to create the being, while, in the other two proofs, it is the perfection, either of the idea in me, or of divine essence in itself, that constitutes the *ratio* of infinite power. Doubtless, one ought not exaggerate the importance of what here is only a nuance. Power, being, perfection, and good are, as we have seen, and we shall see again, reciprocal notions that have only a difference of reason between them. This nuance is, however, the sign of an alteration due either to the absurd hypothesis that serves as point of departure, or to the function this proof assumes of placing more particularly into evidence the infinity of power by which the being causes itself, not the perfection of the being that causes me.

One of Arnauld's objections specifically attacks the important point for the proof that to preserve me is greater than to give me the perfections (like omnipotence and omniscience) that would make me be God himself.[20] The objection leads Descartes to limit the argument, almost changing the whole tenor of the argument; it also leads him to justify in as curious a fashion the application in this case of the axiom, "whatever can do the greater can do the lesser." "The axiom 'whatever can do the greater can do the lesser,' seems to be self-evident, with respect to first causes that are not limited; but in the case of a cause determined to a particular effect, we commonly say that it is a greater thing for this cause to produce some effect other than the one to which it is determined by its nature. In that sense it is a greater thing for a man to move the earth from its place than to understand and to conceive. It is also a greater thing to preserve oneself and to give oneself *some* of the perfections we perceive ourselves lacking; and that suffices in order to validate the argument, although it may be a lesser thing to give oneself omnipotence and *all the other divine perfections.*"[21]

Certainly, by limiting his argument, by excluding omnipotence and the other divine perfections from the perfections I would be able to give myself if I were preserving myself, Descartes renders it more plausible. It would amount to saying: I, who am incapable of escaping doubt, inconsistency, sadness, and other similar things,[22] am certainly incapable of producing myself and preserving myself. It is no longer a matter of stating that it would be easier to create my finite substance than to give myself *all the infinite attributes* (God). Actually, Descartes abandons the argument of the *Meditations,* which he later defends against Burman, in order to substitute a weaker argument for it. However, the real argument is the argument of the *Meditations,* such as Descartes produces it in the *Principles,* but no longer dependent on the axiom *whatever can do the greater, can do the lesser:* "whoever knows something more perfect than himself is not the author of his own being, because then he would have given himself, by the same means, all the perfections that he has known."[23] This amounts to saying that whoever has the power to create being also has infinite omnipotence, which can give itself necessarily all the perfections of which it has the idea, for its infinity necessarily excludes limitation—meaning the imperfect. In brief, the *maximum* cannot not be the *maximum,* and under this form the difficulties arising from the assertion—that to create infinite perfections (the accidents of a substance) is easier than to create a finite substance—disappear. The reply that Descartes gives to Arnauld in order to defend the latter principle therefore lets escape what is essential; it leads Descartes to assert that to preserve oneself is easier than to confer omnipotence on oneself—something that is difficult to ascribe to since he has declared many times, specifically in axiom 9 of the *Geometrical Summary of Replies II*,[24] that it is not more difficult to create than to preserve. Moreover, the power to create *ex nihilo* seems hardly distinguishable from omnipotence. As for the reasons attempting to justify the applicability of the axiom, *whatever can do the greater can do the lesser,* for the case given here, they appear, if one excepts the two first lines of the text, to destroy radically the whole basis for the argument: we would deduce "whatever cannot do the lesser cannot do the greater" from "whatever can do the greater can do the lesser." Consequently, what cannot acquire perfections (the lesser) cannot preserve itself (the greater). *Lesser* and *greater* are applied here to one and the same power, in the same way that one says of a man incapable of lifting a weight of ten pounds, that a fortiori he is incapable of lifting a weight of twenty pounds. But if *greater* does not refer to the magnitude of the one and same power, if it refers to a number of entirely different powers that a man can or cannot have, then there is not even the shadow of an argument. Surely, if a man can add to his faculty of conceiving, the faculty of being able to move the earth, there would be something greater, for there would be two powers instead of one; but we would never be able to conclude the necessary absence of one of these powers (to move the earth) from the weakness of another (understanding) since they are not related. We could therefore not conclude from the fact that I am incapable of producing in me the perfections of which I have the idea (the lesser), to the necessary incapacity to preserve myself (the greater), for these two orders of productive activity are two different orders, according to the reply.

However, once we recognize that the axiom is valid only "with respect to first causes that are not limited," we indicate the real manner by which we can give the argument its full strength. It suffices that we perceive that the latter concerns, in reality, only a first unlimited cause, meaning a cause not specified by nature for the production of particular kinds of effects to the exclusion of others; for since such a cause is one and the same infinite power that causes everything indistinctly, with respect to any kind of effect that one can conceive, it alone creates the being and perfections of this being. Then if to create the perfections of a being is, within this power, what is the lesser, and to create the being is what is the greater, the absence of the lesser necessarily entails the absence of the greater, meaning the absence of the whole power itself. Consequently, if through the fiction of an absurd hypothesis we conceive this unlimited power at the level of limited human existence, it will be evident that the incapacity to produce the lesser (namely, the perfection of which I have the idea) will entail the incapacity to produce the greater (to create myself or to preserve myself), which will amount to the verification that such an unlimited power does not exist in me. The necessity to deal with the same kind of power (or with an identical *ratio operandi)* in order to establish the axiom on which the argument depends, was expressly recognized elsewhere by Descartes: "The axiom 'whatever can do the greater can do the lesser' applies only in the same order of operations *(in eadem ratione operandi),* or in things requiring a single power. For among men, who doubts that a person who could not make a lantern may be able to make a good speech?"[25]

Descartes ends this first argument by an implicit appeal to the definition of self by consciousness. If I had the power in me to create myself actually, limited by the impossibility of giving me the perfections of which I have the idea that such a power would experience, I would necessarily be conscious of this limit and of this power in this way, for nothing can escape my consciousness. I would therefore be conscious that it is more difficult to give oneself perfections than to give oneself being. And not only is this consciousness lacking in me, but natural light expressly teaches me the contrary.

4. The First Part of the Proof: Second Hypothesis

The refutation of the second hypothesis, that I am a being existing by myself, without cause, having existed from all time, rests on two basic conceptions that are closely linked to one another: the discontinuity of time and continuous creation. No instant of a thing depends on the preceding instant; the existence of material or spiritual things can stop at the next instant. Like every other thing, I must therefore be preserved at each instant by a positive instauration in existence—meaning I must be created anew, as in the first creation. As we shall see, the theses of the discontinuity of time and of continuous creation conceived as the direct intervention of the Creator at each instant in the duration of things (in opposition to the Scholastics' continuous creation)[26] arose, in Descartes, from a double requirement: a metaphysical and physical requirement.[27]

Since I cannot exist by myself except by recreating myself at each instant of time, I must have the power to preserve myself, a power identical to the power to create myself—that is, I must be *causa sui.* We therefore return to the first hypothesis, which has already been refuted. However, the first hypothesis expressly concerned only the power that I might have had to create myself. Here we are concerned with the actual power to recreate myself in this present instant. The definition of my being as consciousness is therefore expressly invoked in order to prove that, once I am not conscious of this actual power, I do not have it.[28] Here the use of this definition concerns the positive: actual creative power. In the preceding hypothesis, it concerned the negative, namely, the so-called limits my alleged creative power encountered, through its incapacity to give me actually the perfections lacking to me. Since I was not conscious of such limits with respect to such a power, I concluded that this incapacity does not limit any such power of this kind in me and that, consequently, this power does not exist.

5. The Second Part of the Proof, the Problem of the *progressus in infinitum*

The second part of the proof determines what is my external cause, I who possess the idea of the perfect.

The principle of causality, such as it was formulated in the first proof, allows one to indicate a first fundamental prerequisite: this cause must have in itself at least as much formal reality as there is objective and formal reality in the effect—meaning in myself. It must therefore think, and have the idea of God and all the perfections I attribute to him.

If this cause is self-caused, it is evident, in virtue of the first part of the proof, that it will have to cause itself with all the perfections whose idea I have—meaning it will have to be God. If this cause is caused by another, this other will have to be caused by another or by itself, etc. But we must definitively arrive at a self-caused cause—meaning God—we cannot accept a *progressus ad infinitum* here, because we are concerned with the cause that preserves me actually,[29] not with the cause that produced me once—with causes *in esse,* not with causes *in fieri.* The effect can clearly subsist without the cause that once produced it (the house can subsist without the mason or the architect, and children can subsist without their parents), but the effect cannot subsist without the cause of its subsistence or continuation (for example, light cannot subsist without the sun from which it proceeds).[30]

The reason might have appeared insufficient. Certainly, since we are concerned with the cause preserving me at an instant, the progress to infinity *in time* is thus excluded, without having to exclude in principle the notion of *progressum ad infinitum,* under the pretext that it would be inconceivable in itself. In fact, we do not have the right to deny such progress generally for the reason that we cannot understand it, since the character of infinity by definition surpasses the capacities of my finite understanding.[31] But is this progress to infinity legitimately eliminated by the fact that we are situated at an instant, meaning in a present "where there is no past and future"?[32] No, since, as has already been noted,[33] Descartes, in virtue of his conception of the instantaneous propagation of movement in the plenum, is required to divide matter to infinity and to admit an infinite progress in the actual series of material causes in the instant. Thus he declares to Mesland, with respect to this second proof, that he does not accept the principle that *non datur progressus in infinitum,* referring specifically to the infinite division of matter occurring in the instant. "I do not admit [that principle—M. G.]; on the contrary, I think that there really is such a progression in the division of parts of matter *(datur revera talis progressus in divisione partium materiae),* as we shall see in my treatise on philosophy that is almost printed."[34] Since such a progress to infinity takes place in the instant, the fact that it is situated in an instant does not exclude its possibility. There would therefore be a kind of inconsistency when, in *Meditation III,* Descartes invokes causality in an instant as an exception with respect to the progression of causes to infinity.[35] And this inconsistency is confirmed by his reply to Caterus.

But there is no real inconsistency unless we omit considering the kind of cause in question—namely, the metaphysical cause that *creates* or *preserves existence,* whether we are concerned with myself or with movement. In fact, for physics, the infinite series of material causes in the instant of movement does not have any relation with the cause that begins (or preserves) the movement at that instant; it is an infinite series of terms that, at the same instant, transmute their places in order that the *created* movement propagates itself at that instant through all matter. We are not even concerned with a series of causes, but in a rigorously metaphysical fashion, with a series of effects, or rather with the fragmentation to infinity in the present instant of a single and same effect (instantaneous movement) whose cause or creation *(actio instantanea, sive creatio)* is itself outside this fragmentation. This cause is the founding act of movement, at the same time, at once, in all the parts of matter divided to infinity. The idea of a series in which movement *is propagated successively* in the *instant* is only an abstract and fictive representation of our finite understanding. The radical independence of each instant of movement created with respect to other instants of movement verifies that the creative act from which it emanates *directly* does not depend on anything other than itself and consequently is external to any finite or infinite series, being itself external to time and extension—in brief, to anything that is divisible to infinity.[36] Thus the concept of continuous creation that accounts for what *is preserved in existence* (meaning what is recreated anew at each instant) and is tied to the theory of the discontinuity of time, is sufficient to exclude all progression, not only infinite, but finite,[37] when we are concerned with enacting the *metaphysical cause* that at each moment preserves, meaning *creates,* either movement or the universe. There is therefore no inconsistency between this thesis and physics requiring, at an instant, the progression to infinity in the division of the parts of matter. By recalling this particularity of his physics to Mesland, Descartes only emphasizes the illegitimacy of any argument that would be based on a so-called a priori impossibility of all *progressus ad infinitum.* Whether we are concerned with material causes *in esse* or *in fieri,* it is not sufficient, in order to deny this progress, to invoke its inconceivability for our finite understanding; we must, in addition, lay out a positive, specific, and sufficient reason, derived independently from this inconceivability.

But we are not concerned with physics here, for we do not yet know whether bodies and movement exist and whether God himself, to whom we attribute the creation of movement at each instant, exists. We are concerned with myself, who knows that I exist in all certainty. And, insofar as I conceive myself as thinking, existing as long as I think, because I think, able to stop existing at the next instant, if ever I stopped thinking, I would appear to myself as depending on no series of causes;[38] I would discover myself as substance, *primo per se,* meaning the reason for all my thoughts without depending on any one of them. Therefore, if in this sense I exist by myself, it is natural that I ask whether I preserve myself or create myself at each instant myself, or if by chance I exist by another.

Actually, the self about which I ask this question is not the simple Cogito, the pure "I think therefore I am." In fact, I perceive myself in the Cogito as establishing myself from the fact that I think and existing only insofar as I think. Therefore nothing can make me know this as long as I cannot be the cause of myself. Am I not free to think or not to think? Actually, I am simply free to reflect and to concentrate my thought, meaning to accomplish this or that act of thinking. Therefore although nothing allows me to deny that I can be the author of my being on this plane, nothing allows me to affirm it either, for "the mind can be itself the cause of such or such acts of thinking," without being "the cause of its being a thing that thinks." Similarly "it depends on a flame, as an efficient cause, whether it turns to this side or that, but not that it is an extended thing."[39] Therefore it is the second Cogito, the consciousness of the self as imperfect that imposes both the problem and its solution. Conceiving myself as imperfect, because of the idea of the perfect present in my mind, I perceive myself immediately as not being the author of my own being, since if I were the author of my own being, I would have created myself perfect. Moreover, knowing that the author of my being cannot exist by itself without being created perfect, I cannot refuse positing this self-caused being by arguing for an infinite series of causes by others, since this real perfect cause must definitively be there in order to preserve me actually as I am, meaning as a thinking being that has the idea of God. And the argument is legitimate, since in this case we are concerned with the relation between a true actual effect and its true cause, and not, as with the so-called material causes (in the propagation of a movement, for example), with the modality of an effect (namely, the instantaneous fragmentation, in the infinite parts of matter, of the movement caused in this instant), given that we have set aside the relation between this effect and the cause that establishes it all together at this punctual instant.

The result of this argument is to promote on the ontological plane the difference between the two orders of substantiality that the first proof by effect could only establish on the epistemological plane. That is how the demonstration of the thesis specified in article 51 of *Principles I* is brought forth. In the first proof the clear and distinct character of the knowledge of God rendered this absolute nature into the first substance without which the relative nature of the Cogito could be known only confusedly. At that time the Cogito was reduced to a secondary substantiality from the point of view of knowledge. Here we are not concerned with knowledge, but with being—not with what is conceived by itself, but with what is created by itself. The difference between the two orders of substantiality now expresses the two possible ways of existing by oneself, "of needing only oneself." Either a being exists by itself because, without being able to create itself, it does not need the cooperation of other created things in order to exist (such is the case for my thinking substance and such is the case, as we shall see, for extended substance) or else the being exists by itself because it is self-caused. The latter is the only time the expression "needing only oneself" is given its full meaning; and "properly speaking, only God needs nothing else." Thus the name *substance* is not used univocally with respect to both God and his creatures.[40]

We can consider that, to some extent, the second proof by effects is a proof by absurdity: it establishes that the infinite being is the only one having the power to create itself by demonstrating the absurdity of the hypothesis according to which a finite substance, I, would be self-caused. It is true that, in this initial hypothesis, we are not concerned with any finite substance whatever, but with a thinking substance having the idea of infinity. However, assuming what science does not yet know, that there is in the universe another finite substance deprived of such an idea (the substance of bodies, for example), it is evident that since it is less noble than the thinking substance, it would not have a greater power and be able to create itself if the thinking substance is unable to create itself.

Two subsidiary considerations terminate the proof.

1) The impossibility that the ideas of various perfections I conceive in God each have separate causes, results from my idea of the infinitely perfect that represents it to me as indivisible. It is impossible for me to conceive the indivisibility of perfections as separate from the perfections themselves. This impossibility and the idea in me that the simple totality of these perfections is less than their indivisibility in an infinitely infinite perfection[41] cannot come from me, since it is closely united with the idea of perfection itself, whose necessary author is the perfect being.

This unity of perfections in God has already conditioned several parts of the proof. It has contributed toward the demonstration that to acquire the various perfections a little at a time or separately is a lesser thing than to give oneself the substance in which all the attributes are undivided.[42] It has allowed the application of the axiom "whatever can do the greater can do the lesser" and its correlative "whatever cannot do the lesser cannot do the greater" to the case in consideration, since this application requires the absolute unity of the infinite creative power of different perfections.[43]

Finally, this doctrine will prove, if it were still necessary, that the infinite will in me cannot furnish the idea of God, since this will is a relative separated infinity, which is disproportionate with the infinitely infinite, with the unity of all the perfections that the idea of the perfect represents to me. On the contrary, it is the presence of this idea that allows me to know what there is of infinity in my will, of what order is this infinity, and in what way I resemble God and differ from him.

2) The demonstration of the impossibility that I am caused by my parents is given entirely for the use of common sense. In fact, my parents are the cause of my body, that is, of the dispositions required in a certain portion of matter for my soul to be inserted in it.[44] In the proof we are concerned with knowing from where my soul as *thinking substance* derives its existence; and there is absolute heterogeneity between the soul and body, which is only a mode of extension subject to mechanical laws. The cause that has put these laws into play, in this case the laws of the formation of the fetus, is not related to the cause of a spiritual substance. Moreover, at this point on the chain of reasons, bodies, my body, and the material causes of my body (my parents) are rejected as outside science and are consequently unknown. Therefore we would not be able to demonstrate anything with respect to them, since scientifically we do not know them, and it is their existence, on the contrary, that needs to be demonstrated.

6. Consequences of the Proof: 1) Definitive Proof of the Innateness of the Idea of God; 2) Applicability of the Axiom, the Effect Resembles the Cause

Since God is promoted to creative substantiality, with respect to himself as well as with respect to myself in this proof, there are two consequences that follow for me: 1) The problem of the origin of the idea of the perfect is resolved not only implicitly, but explicitly: the creation of my being and the positing of the idea of God in me appear as incapable of being dissociated. The idea of God is therefore innate: "Like the idea of myself, it is created and present in me, from the moment I was created."[45]

2) The common axiom, "the effect is similar to the cause," which was unusable in the first proof in which God was simply posited as "a cause that merely applies active things to passive things,"[46] is used fully here. All created things (stones, animals, man) must resemble their Creator, from the fact that they must be substances like him and must resemble him in proportion to their degree of being. Since I am among all creatures the one that has most being, I must resemble God maximally:[47] *"From the fact alone that God has created me* [our emphasis—M. G.], it is very believable that he has produced me in his image and likeness in some way."[48] Therefore the principle of causality suffices to establish completely the resemblance between myself and God, which it was incapable of doing in the first proof.

Moreover, this resemblance differs from the perfect resemblance that was established by another means, in the first proof, between the objective reality of the idea and the formal reality of its cause, for this objective reality was itself infinite and perfect. Here we are concerned with the resemblance between myself, who is finite and imperfect, and my creative cause, who is infinite and perfect. The word *maximum* therefore has, in this case, the sense of a superlative comparative. I have the maximum resemblance with God that it is possible for a created being to have, which does not mean at all that this resemblance is perfect. On the contrary, since the maximum of objective reality of my idea of God is an absolute superlative, there is a necessary equality between the quantity of formal reality of the cause and the objective reality of its effect; moreover, the perfect thing cannot be more perfect than the thing whose idea I have, for otherwise I would have merely the idea of an imperfect thing, and not the idea of a perfect thing. Finally, what makes me, of all created beings, be the one possessing the maximum of reality and consequently the highest degree of resemblance with God, is that I am, as a man, the only one among them that has the idea of God—meaning because I have the infinite in my understanding, I have perfection itself under the form of objective reality. Because of this idea, I can in fact recognize that I am different from God, but similar to him at the same time: I discover in myself the presence of an objective reality equal to the formal reality of God; in brief, if I have the faculty of conceiving myself as finite, it is because I possess the idea of an actual infinity that I can contrast to myself.[49] It is therefore the absolute resemblance of my idea of God to God that establishes the distant resemblance of my whole being to God himself.

In this way it becomes possible to establish God as the eminent cause of my being, insofar as he is the infinite Creator of the finite. The first proof could only succeed in positing him as a formal cause of the infinite content of my idea of God, given that there is an equality of perfection between the effect (perfection of the objective reality of the idea of infinity) and the cause (perfection of the formal being of infinity). In order to reintroduce God as eminent cause of his idea in me, we had to argue from the imperfect character of the idea, which as an image, does not have the perfection of existence of the thing that is its author. But we have seen that this consideration involved a host of difficulties.[50]

Since this second proof is more absolute than the first and it can do without the principle of the correspondence of the idea with what is ideated, can it be considered as independent from the preceding one? No. It is conditioned by it, not because it assumes together with it that there must be at least as much formal reality in the cause as objective reality in my idea of the perfect, but because one of its most fundamental principles is that no faculty can be in me without my being able to have knowledge of it.[51] This principle implies that I cannot be in myself other than what I know myself to be and that the inference from knowledge to being is valid. And this proposition is valid only if I know that God exists and cannot deceive me—which is what the first proof demonstrates.

7. The a priori Elements of the Proof

The most important problem posed by the second a posteriori proof is the determination of the number, role, and nature of the a priori elements that condition it. This problem is linked to the problem of the structure of the proof and its relation with the order of reasons.

On the one hand, this proof seems to fault the a posteriori character of the first proof insofar as it tends to appear as the Cartesian substitute for the proof *a contingentia*. Instead of starting from the objective reality of ideas, whose nature as an effect is not immediately perceivable to non-Cartesians, it starts from an unimpeachable given, which at first glance is an effect for anyone, namely, my existence as finite self having the idea of the perfect. Moreover, since it substitutes as effect the thinking self whose existence is indubitable for anyone, Cartesians or non-Cartesians, for the sensible world that Cartesians hurl into nothingness (the absolute nothingness of science) because of hyperbolic doubt, it gives the proof a starting point that can only be the object of a unanimous certainty.[52]

On the other hand, the passage of this evident effect to its cause assumes a number of a priori axioms that are subtracted from metaphysical doubt and that are not derived from the effect we wish to account for—meaning the idea of the perfect imprinted on my mind. Since these a priori elements are more numerous and more important in this proof than in the first, one ought to wonder whether this proof, in spite of appearances, is not really less a posteriori than the former.

First, the axiom imposing the necessity of an actual cause for the effect that it preserves actually is an a priori notion independent from the idea of the perfect. And it is a basic element of the proof, for without it, it would be impossible to exorcise the progress of causes to infinity. However, the first proof was also constrained, in order to block the path of progress to infinity, to depend on an axiom and on an a priori notion external to the idea of the perfect. This progress assumed at that moment the form of a series of objective realities deriving one from another and never attaining a formal reality as final cause. And the axiom[53] was derived in this case from the *"nature of idea"* that constrained me to admit, finally, at least for the first of all ideas, that the cause of its objective reality must *by its nature* be a formal reality. The definition of idea as signifying necessarily a relation with what is ideated therefore plays in the first proof with respect to the *progressus ad infinitum* the same role that the principle of causality assumes in the second proof under the form: *"Sublata causa, tollitur effectus."*

Moreover, the two proofs intersect at this point, for although it is impossible to progress to infinity in causes external to me (who has the idea of the perfect) without ever reaching the self-caused cause, meaning the perfect being itself, we also could never attain the formal reality of the perfect that must be discovered as the cause in myself of the objective reality of the idea of the perfect. In this sense, the two proofs come to the same thing: "For the sake of those whose natural light is so weak that they do not see the first notion, all perfection that is *objectively* in an idea must be *actually* in one of its causes, I have demonstrated it in a manner easier to conceive, by showing that the mind that has this idea cannot exist by itself."[54]

But in the second proof we must also conceive a priori the possibility of a self-caused cause in order to be able to dispose of the progress to infinity: "If I thought that nothing can be related in some way to itself as the efficient cause is related to its effect, I would never arrive at a first cause when seeking the causes of things."[55] Self-caused cause and first cause are synonymous. Consequently, since my soul is finite, I cannot know that the order of causes is not finite, unless I have the idea of a first cause in me.[56] Besides, a first cause thus defined as self-caused cause cannot be understood except as an essence whose nature is such that it necessarily gives itself existence.[57] The notion of *causa sui,* which is indispensable for the proof, is related, in this case, not to the *idea* of the perfect as an *effect* of which I am seeking the cause, but to the *essence* of the perfect being, considered in itself a priori, being one of the necessary properties that I know as such a priori. The a priori proof will do no more than establish the necessity of existing by oneself, by basing itself on the simple inspection of this essence. Thus, with respect to its fundamental principle, this a posteriori proof seems finally to be supported by the a priori proof.

Correlatively, the primary notion that governs the whole proof concurrently with the idea of the perfect is the notion of existence by oneself. The two conceptions of existing by oneself *causa sui* or *existing without cause* are each challenged with respect to the hypothesis of my existence by myself. With respect to the former notion, it is demonstrated that it cannot apply to my self, and with respect to the latter, it is demonstrated that it cannot apply to anything whatever. The former therefore remains the only one useful in characterizing that other that I myself am constrained to recognize as the author of my being, that is God.

That is why, although the first proof had a single point of support, the effect (the idea of the perfect in me) with respect to which and because of which its cause can be posited and defined, the second has a dual point of support: 1) the effect and what its nature implies necessarily for the nature of its cause, and 2) the cause and what its nature entails for itself as self-caused cause. First, since the effect involves the idea of the perfect, the self-caused cause, on which the effect depends, must itself be a perfect being. Second, since the self-caused cause is both an efficient cause and its own effect, in the efficient cause, the cause must neither be different than its effect, nor precede it in time; it must participate both in the formal cause and the efficient cause, in an intermediary concept that is between *"the efficient cause"* properly speaking, and *"no cause,"* namely, "the positive essence of the thing."[58]

Thus this second proof, detaching us from the a posteriori point of support external to the cause, allows us, in some way, to penetrate within this cause that, while producing us, produces the idea of the perfect in us. On the other hand, the first proof lets us remain outside it. The cause was posited only with respect to its external effect—the idea that it impressed in us—while it is now considered, in addition, with respect to its internal effect—the production of self by itself.

This penetration into the intimacy of the first cause allows Descartes to reveal the active character of divinity. The refutation of the conception of existence by oneself as being without cause (which has general scope), in fact, ends up positing God as a being causing himself, and not as a being without cause, in opposition to the Scholastic thesis.[59] Efficient causality manifested by the impression of the idea of the perfect in me and by the creation of myself having this idea, is not only affirmed outside, but inside the divine sphere. And, even though God cannot be the efficient cause of himself in a positive sense, but in a negative sense, since he would not be able to distinguish himself from his effect nor precede it in time,[60] nevertheless he exists by himself in a positive and not negative fashion, in virtue of "his real and true immensity of power,"[61] having done in some way the same thing with respect to himself as the efficient cause does with respect to its effect.[62] Since the infinite clearly does not need any efficient cause outside itself in order to exist, it must necessarily enclose this efficiency in itself.[63] That is why it exists necessarily in virtue of its essence.[64] "The concept of efficient cause can be extended [to this positive essence] in the same way that in geometry we commonly extend the concept of a circular line that is as long as possible, to the concept of a straight line, or the concept of a rectilinear polygon with an indefinite number of sides to the concept of a circle."[65] Thus, from the fact that essence cannot be distinguished from existence in God, formal cause is "quasi-efficient" in him.[66]

God's rationality and his free creative self-causality are therefore closely linked here. Hence, we are witness for the first time to the *intimate* union in God of a *ratio* analogous to geometric reason and an urgency stemming from the character of a creative will that is absolutely omnipotent and free. Although the necessity for an infinite essence to develop its existence is referred to the internal necessity of a geometrical reason, it also coincides with a necessity of an entirely different order that arises from the nature of an omnipotent, infinite, and free will. Being deprived of giving oneself existence contradicts such an omnipotence, for a will that can lean toward nothingness, that would not or could not create its own existence, would be powerless, limited, and consequently not free. Thus God could not not give himself existence and could not not want to give it to himself, because of his omnipotent and infinitely free will.[67]

But this coincidence of formal and efficient cause is at the same time the internal union of two characteristics that the first proof by effects could unite only externally. With respect to the idea of the perfect as idea and as effect, God, who is its author, appears on the one hand as a standard or archetype, *"instar archetypi,"* meaning a quasi-immobile *form,* a model of which my idea is the copy, and on the other hand as the efficient free cause of the passion experienced by our understanding that receives the idea of God.[68] These two characteristics of form and action are here established within the *causa sui* that unites "the *formal cause,* and the *efficient cause,* the *efficient cause* and *no cause, what is by itself* and *what is by another"* in the concept of a positive essence.[69] And while causal power tends to rejoin the necessity of a reason, form tends to lose its rigid immobility in order to become a principle of an internal means from which effects emanate.

8. The a posteriori Character of the Proof. Conformity with the Order of Reasons

If the proof depends above all on a priori notions, if it is based on the concept of *causa sui,* and if this concept is itself based on God's essence, which, in the ontological proof, reveals to me its necessary property to cause itself by its own power, ought we not conclude that this proof by effects is a posteriori only in name, that in fact it is absorbed into the a priori proof?

Such a conclusion would misjudge the analytic order of reasons, which was scrupulously followed by Descartes. Certainly, the notion of *causa sui* depends *a parte rei* on the nature proper to the essence of God. It finds in this essence the internal reason that is revealed by the a priori proof. Certainly, Descartes, in the *Replies to Objections,* in order to elucidate this concept, places into evidence these necessary links. However, in the proof considered in itself, the necessary link between the essence of the perfect and self-caused causality never intervenes as an element of the demonstration. The a priori notion of *causa sui* is used apart from its foundation in God's essence, taken in itself, detached from this essence, accepted as first evidence subtracted from doubt, with the same status as the other axioms: *In order to think one must exist, nothingness has no properties, an accident has less being than a substance, the cause contains at least as much reality as its effect, everything has a cause.* As an axiom, the concept of *causa sui* is only an aspect of the principle *everything has a cause,*[70] which, after having suggested the idea of an infinite progress in causes, ends this progress of the effects that the causes *in esse* preserve, in virtue of this other evident aspect of the principle of cause: *sublata causa, tollitur effectus*—the preserving cause must exist as long as the effect exists.

The first cause or self-caused cause is itself posited as a perfect being, or

God, not in virtue of the fact that I perceive a priori that it is necessarily implied in the essence of God, but in virtue of the idea of the perfect present in us as an effect to be explained, the cause needing to have at least as much perfection in its formal reality as its effect.[71] Hence in spite of the multitude of its a priori elements and its link *a parte rei* with the a priori proof, the proof is maintained on the a posteriori plane.

But we see at the same time to what respect it can be called *absolutius,* since it lifts us higher than the first proof in the truth of things, allowing us to go from the point of view of the relation of cause and effect, which is external to the cause itself, to the point of view of the positing of the cause by itself, which is internal to it. We can glimpse here the essential relation that the a priori proof will develop, and thus we can discover that the *causa sui* depends on the infinity of the essence. But this relation that is a relation of the truth of things is not yet the relation that actually illuminates the truth of science. Neither does it itself establish this truth of science. The synthetic order is distinct from the analytic order; the *veritas rei* is distinct from the *veritas rationum.* Science does not yet have the right to base the truth of the *causa sui* on the necessary property of the essence of God, since it has not yet expressly derived from the already acquired truths the conclusion that everything that I perceive clearly and distinctly in my idea as the necessary property of a thing is effectively the necessary property of that thing. Moreover, although *a parte rei* the notion of *causa sui* is based on the infinite essence of God, I do not need to know this in order that its evidence be manifest, no more than I needed to know that in reality the propositions *in order to think one must exist, nothingness has no properties, everything has a cause, there is at least as much reality in the cause as in the effect,* etc., are based on God's infinite being, in order to be certain of their evidence, or in order that they be invulnerable to the evil genius, since no existence is affirmed by them. The problem of the legitimacy of the use of a priori axioms in the second proof is the same problem as in the first proof, or as in positing the Cogito. If the light of these axioms proceeds from the light of God in reality, the former is visible for common consciousness, while the latter is hidden to it at first glance. We must therefore make use of the former in order to unveil the latter, even though the former proceeds from the latter. Thus the light illuminates itself. But the philosopher is constrained to place himself at the level of those he wishes to convince and persuade, meaning at the lowest level, and he is required to take absurd hypotheses as points of departure—atheism, evil genius, inauthentic Cogito separated from the thought of God, and here the hypothesis of a finite self thinking the infinite, a finite self that might be the author of its own being. All these difficulties are but one. They express under various forms the seemingly impossible aim of the analytic order of reasons: enable the truth to rise with all its strength out of absurd positions.

II. The Discontinuity of Time

9. Continuous Creation and Temporal Discontinuity. Critique of the Classical Thesis by Laporte

Since he demonstrated that God is necessarily the author of myself, in virtue of continuous creation, and since he proved the continuous creation by the absolute independence of the various parts of time of my life, Descartes often appears to hold the thesis of the discontinuity of time.

This traditional interpretation has been rejected by Laporte. For Laporte, there is only separability of the parts of time, which just denotes their independence and contingency. Since contingency only establishes the need that a finite being has for continuous creation, it is contrary to language and good sense to derive the discontinuity of time from it. Since time is a quantity like force, movement, and speed, like extension, it is divisible to infinity.[72] And since this infinite divisibility is the object of clear and distinct knowledge, it is true. Certainly, it is incomprehensible for our finite thought, but everything that is infinite is perceived clearly and distinctly as incomprehensible.[73] The negation of material atomism entails ipso facto the negation of temporal atomism.[74] Moreover, an instant is never defined as a nothingness of duration, but as *"brevissimum tempus."*[75] It has a length, since Descartes speaks of conservation "across a moment of time *(per momentum temporis)."*[76] It is, as in Bergson, the shortest segment of duration that can be grasped *totum simul et unico intuitu.*[77]

However, it seems difficult to understand the *distinguo* established here between contingency, separation, and reciprocal independence of parts, on the one hand, and discontinuity on the other, given that discontinuity is defined by these three characteristics. Moreover, if the instant were a segment of time, and not something indiminishable, not something rigorously indivisible, light, which is transmitted in an instant, would go some distance, and would have a temporal movement and a real speed. And that is specifically denied by Descartes.[78] That light takes some very short time to be transmitted is the discovery that Cassini and Huygens will make, a discovery that Descartes expressly rejected in advance as radically destructive of all his physics. In fact, by substituting dynamics for statics at the core of created things, it would render impossible the reduction of physics to pure geometry. The instant of light, being neither distance nor movement in time, is a *state* in which all becoming is banished. In this instant, taken rigorously, time is entirely abolished, and the instant is opposed to duration as rest to movement and nothingness to existence.[79]

The difficulty for Cartesianism consists in deriving duration from an instant that denies it, movement from a *state* (meaning rest), dynamics from statics, existence that is identical to duration from nothingness that is identical to the instant. There will result an ambiguity from this enterprise, for although Descartes posits the instant as an outer-bound concept, being both being and nothingness, time and nontime, rest and movement, he does not succeed in detaching fully the concept of a differential, and the instant is then defined in a different way according to the aspect under which it is considered, meaning according to whether it is considered as the negation of all time, or as an extremely short time. But, as we will show, this latter definition that could lead to the infinitesimal as a vanishing minimum, does not actually lead to it and is only an imperfect manner of speaking—the instant is essentially a radical negation of all duration.

From this one sees that the problem of the discontinuity or continuity of time cannot be resolved by appeal to dispersed quotations, but by reference to the whole Cartesian conception of movement.

10. Metaphysical and Temporal Discontinuity.
The Point of View of Creative Action
and the Point of View of the Created Thing

It is clear that if Descartes had conceived an instant as a differential, a vanishing quantity of duration, temporal continuity could have been affirmed. It is no less clear, on the other hand, that such a concept is opposed to the theory of the instant of light as absolute intemporality, state and not movement, and that it is inconsistent with the reduction of movement to a succession of different *states*, separated from each other in themselves, each lacking motion. Bergson has rightly characterized this latter concept as "cinematographic" and, contrary to Laporte, contrasted it expressly to his own conception, affirming that the Cartesian instant is not a segment, but a nothingness of duration.[80]

How then can this conception be reconciled with the assertion that duration is existence and movement? If an instant is a limit, a nothingness, how can duration and existence stem from the summation of instants? The difficulty is resolved in Descartes' philosophy by the concept of divine creation. The act of creating is the act of positing in duration and in existence. It is therefore in itself neither duration nor existence. It is a nothingness *of duration and existence,* but not pure nothingness since it is, on the contrary, God acting. This act is the means by which something promoted to duration and existence arises from nothingness in an instant that is not a fragment of the enduring created thing, but a moment of the free and indivisible decision that establishes the thing in its duration. The creative moment of each thing with duration is thus subtracted from dependence with respect to what previously could have existed or endured. It is enclosed within itself, radically separated from all others.[81] In this indivisible act is located the principle of the radical and essential indivisibility of temporal instants—of their discontinuity—that is identical to their contingency and is founded on it.

There are therefore two points of view from which to consider time (and movement). There is first the concrete and real point of view, which is that of the creation of existence, or of the cause.[82] From this point of view we are concerned with a repetition of indivisible discontinuous creative instants, and no longer with duration as a *given*. There is also the abstract and imperfect point of view of created existence, which is that of the effect, in which duration is proposed as something infinitely divisible and continuous. Then the instants no longer appear as rigorously indivisible, nothingnesses of duration, but as fragments of durations of existence, of movement, that are as small as possible, *brevissima tempora*, but not differentials, however, for they are infinitely small actual things.[83] But the internal essence of time is not within created things, it is in the creative act that makes something endure or exist. This act is the fundamental element of duration. Thus, as we can see, the specific element of duration, creative becoming—dynamics, properly speaking—is sheltered within divine creative freedom. Bergson has also rightly perceived this point when he described the Cartesian conception of divine freedom as constituting a kind of substitute for pure duration.[84]

We can understand how time can, like extension, be conceived as indefinitely divisible without this property implying necessarily for it the continuity that extension implies. In fact, time is not homogeneous with extension since it is not a created *reality* like it, but the property or the very fact of existing (existing and enduring are synonymous),[85] which accrues to everything created, whether it is thought, which is in itself indivisible, or extension, which is in itself divisible.[86] Thus the argument that destroys spatial atomism is not valid with respect to time. The negation of the atom is not implied completely in the clear and distinct knowledge of infinite divisibility,[87] since we can affirm only an indefinite divisibility.[88] Even if we consider that "an atom . . . can never be conceived distinctly because the only meaning of the word implies a contradiction, namely, being a body and being indivisible,"[89] we still cannot affirm for that reason alone that the atom is impossible in itself, for God can create what we cannot conceive. Moreover, if the notion is contradictory with the notion of body with respect to our understanding, it is not contradictory with the notion of duration, since a duration is not a body. In truth, the negation of atomism is based, above all, on God's omnipotence, which would be limited if it had to be deprived of the ability to divide a portion of extension even though it was able to do so.[90] This reasoning is clearly not valid for duration, since duration is not a reality, a substance distinct from creative omnipotence, but is this same omnipotence insofar as it has created existence—in brief, it is the act of creating grasped at its origin, in the indivisibility that characterizes its absolute freedom. The indivisibility of the creative instant that is opposed to the divisibility of the created instant therefore has nothing in common with the indivisibility of the atom of extension, which would be that of a reality *resistant* to creative omnipotence and limiting it. It is, on the contrary, the indivisibility of creative freedom itself.

11. Physics and Temporal Discontinuity. Abstract Point of View (Continuity) and Concrete Point of View (Discontinuity). The Union of the Two Points of View. Two Contrary Aspects of Elementary Movement: Null Speed and Infinite Speed. Preeminence of the Concrete Point of View

This metaphysical view is closely linked to views in physics. Completely opposed to Aristotelian physics and rejecting all virtuality, all dynamism, Descartes refuses to conceive movement as a flux in which the present filled with past will also be filled with future. The negation of this dynamic continuity leads him to enclose strictly each moment of movement in the present instant, to consider it as self-sufficient, owing nothing to the past, entailing nothing for the future. This absolute discontinuity of moments destroys the existence of movement in each moment. All movement is accomplished in time, not in an instant,[91] and since the different moments of movement are instantaneous, they are not movements;[92] each of them is a set of geometric relations defining statically at each instant the different situations that bodies occupy with respect to one another.[93] The radical instantaneousness of change at each moment is merely the *creation* at each time of a new *state* of things or of a new universe in which the geometric relations of distance between bodies *are* different. Since there are only different geometric *states* at each instant, the instantaneous movement defined by this *state* (compared with the preceding state) is in reality a nothingness of movement. But on the other hand, this instant of movement is also an instantaneous creation of this *state* of the universe by God. The action *(conatus)* that is not a movement, but a tendency toward movement,[94] is this *creation* that *instaurates* this state: *"Activitas instantanea [significat—M. G.] creationem."*[95] That is why one can consider the instant of movement either as absolute rest (state), or as actual movement (creation, instauration). But this instant is not, as in Leibniz, a true differential—meaning a *transition* from one state to another, in which the state is to some extent action and action, to some extent a state, a vanishing movement that is confused with rest as an infinitely slow movement, being virtual movement, and not a portion of actual movement.[96] In any case, whether one considers the series of instants as a series of different states or as a repetition of free creations, the discontinuity is never resolved into a true continuity.

As a result, even though the movement considered is always the movement of a body transported from one place to another in a particular time,[97] the idea of transfer, transport, and route is only a view relative to the weakness of our finite understanding. Since movement is constituted by an infinity of absolute instants in which, by hypothesis, there is no movement, the temporal movement of translation described by a moving body is resolved into a repetition of creations of the universe in which the reciprocal situation of bodies *is* different each time, each of these instantaneous creations in no way depending on the previous one and *entailing nothing for the succeeding one.* There is no transport of bodies, but something is created here, and then it is created there. The reality of movement is completely and uniquely located in instantaneous action, and its most perfect image is the movement of the scales of a balance at equilibrium—meaning nonmovement[98]—or the action impressed upon a stick by two blind men that immobilize it by pulling it or pushing it, each on his side.[99] The transmission of light is nothing other than its simultaneous presence at the point of emission and at the point that it illuminates, in the same way that the movement of the end of a stick is felt immediately at the other end.[100]

However, one can foretell the future of the movement of a body by its present instant. Does not Cartesian physics translate the repetition of discontinuous creations into a continuous series in which the position of the body at the next instant *depends* mathematically, according to factors of volume and speed, on the one it had at the previous instant? Does not this necessary dependence of the next instant on the previous instant contradict the discontinuity and independence of moments that constitutes the deep reason for movement and time? There is no contradiction as long as the dependence is based on laws of regularity that are real in the world, since God gave rise to them, having voluntarily prescribed them by his will in the creation of things, in virtue of the generality of means,[101] and holding to them inflexibly in virtue of his immutability.[102] Because of these laws, creations that are in themselves independent repeat themselves in such a way that the differences between the states of the universe or between the slices of the universe at each created instant are infinitely small and that the successive differences (meaning the changes) of the geometrical relations between bodies in the series of instant of creation are arranged in such a way that at each instant the present relation appears to proceed and derive mathematically from the preceding relation, according to a rule. Thus our mind, in conformity with the law that imposes regularity, as if from the outside, on the intrinsically independent acts of creation, translates the continuous repetition of the free and discontinuous creation of independent and self-sufficient states, into the continuity of one and the same movement, which is proposed to our eyes as accomplishing a path, developing and engendering itself in time. But this mode of genesis and this regularity do not belong to the intrinsic dynamic reality of the being in movement; they express the rules that the free will imposes externally on the free action that manifests it. However, and even because of this, this translation is not simply a point of view of our mind that is purely relative to itself, since it is based on laws that God has created along with things and that are laws of things.

As a consequence, when emphasizing these extrinsic laws that are external to things, and not the intrinsic and discontinuous acts of this continuous or repeated creation that constitutes the basis of the duration of things, this translation represents an abstract point of view. Under this aspect, duration (as well as force, movement, speed, and impact) appears to be a quantity divisible to infinity—like a measurable length,[103] the instant is defined as an extremely short time,[104] and the series of movements is conceived as necessary.[105] Within this sphere, in contrast with duration, time is founded as the number of movement, as a method allowing one to submit the duration of things to a single measure by the comparison of this duration with the duration of other regular movements that make up days and years.[106] And this time is nothing in itself outside the real duration of things; it is only a manner of thinking.[107] As for duration, it is itself considered here from the aspect of the enduring created things, and not from the aspect of the created act that allows it to endure—meaning the creative act that posits it in existence. Duration appears in consequence as infinitely divisible. When we locate ourselves on this plane, we refer it to God's eternity itself, and we are led to consider this eternity also as continuous and infinitely divisible, even though it is absolutely indivisible in reality.[108]

However, physics is not completely enclosed within this abstract point of view, since it could not constitute itself without being referred to a concrete point of view, meaning to the absolute indivisibility of the instant, to the instantaneousness of light, to the radical discontinuity of the instants of time, and the instants of movement that are themselves reduced to states that are self-sufficient with respect to their own geometric characteristic.

From the union of these two points of view rises the original traits of Cartesian physics. From their union is also explained the presence of the two kinds of texts, the ones that seem favorable to continuity, and the others, to discontinuity.

From the abstract and created point of view, we would say that the first creation is absolutely different from the others in that it is first, thereby causing the being of this world to rise from the nothingness of the world, while the other creations only preserve the existence of the world.[109] In other words, they recreate it *beginning from* a certain state, which has not been abolished before the other is created, such that there is no null interval, and no null solution of continuity.[110] From the concrete point of view of creation we would say, on the contrary, that the other creations are identical to the first and differ from it only by a distinction of reason;[111] for even though the creation of the novel state of the universe beginning from the *preceding* state assumes the reality of the law that, allowing its *derivation*, establishes a bond of *dependence* between the two—the creative act, from which this state derives, renders this bond into something external to the state itself. This dependence does not imply any real transition, nor any internal passage from the one to the other. The second state is, as was the first, the expression of a free creation of something new (a new geometric relation) that the antecedent does not contain. And certainly, the various creations are a unity, since the creative act of God is in itself one and since it would be inconceivable for them to be separated by intervals of time. In fact, since existence is what constitutes duration, intervals without existence would be intervals without duration; thus, there cannot be intervals of empty duration.[112] However, the various creations are discontinuous, since none of them is intrinsically tied to the preceding one, since there is no passage, but an instauration,[113] a repetition of free creations, somehow infinitely close to one another, but that are all amenable only to the present instant in which God has created them: "God preserves movement in matter by an extremely simple operation; for he does not preserve it as it could once have been, but as it is precisely at the same instant in which he preserves it."[114]

From the abstract, created point of view, we would say that all thought occupies time,[115] in the same way that all movement does.[116] From the concrete point of view of creation, we would say, on the contrary, that all temporal movement arises from the repetition of instants of movements that, since they are instantaneous, cannot be movements but indivisible and discontinuous actions or creations. We would say that all temporal thought arises from indivisible instants that are referred to the acts of creation by which our thought is placed into existence again and again continuously. Like light, thought is instantaneous: *"Lumen cognitionem [significat—M. G.], activitas instantanea creationem."*[117]

The necessary union of the concrete point of view of the cause and of creation, with the abstract point of view of the effect and what is created, is equal to the principle of the physical explanation of the change of the universe at each instant. Since the universe must be considered as recreated *beginning from* what it was, the new universe (or the new state of the universe) is conceived as rising from an instantaneous *displacement* of its parts in the whole plenum according to the rings of matter, each part needing to occupy the place of the other at the instant in which the other left it. This instantaneous movement is conceived as an actual infinitely small elementary movement.[118] It cannot be diminished since the instant cannot be: "I do not consider the movement of light, but the action or tendency to move, which is instantaneous and hence cannot be diminished."[119] While Galileo justified the infinite diminution of speed by the infinite divisibility of time, which implies the infinite divisibility of the instant, Descartes, considering that the instant cannot be diminished and is rigorously indivisible, concludes that elementary speed is also absolutely indivisible and that real movement (temporal) is derived from the repetition of these indivisibles. He therefore espouses an atomism of movement based on the indivisibility of the instant. Moreover, this absolute indivisibility of the instant requires the infinite divisibility of matter; this indivisibility requires circularity of movement for the instantaneousness of the displacement of parts. And since the rings of matter have irregularities (meaning constrictions), in order for the same quantity of matter to pass, in the same instant, in tight places as well as in loose places, it must be the case that matter passes faster in the tighter places than in the looser places. "The speed of movement must compensate for the tightness of the place." From this it results that matter must be infinitely divisible in order to be able to fill congruently these places that are innumerable and different from one another. And from this we see that the absolute indivisibility of the instant entails the infinite divisibility of extension, instead of the divisibility of extension entailing the divisibility of time.[120]

Finally, the union of the creative point of view, of the instauration of the instant, with the point of view of created instant in which the thing *is* another, the union of (dynamic) action with (static) state leads to an equivocal conception of the instant, given the lack of an explicit notion of a differential. On the one hand, the instant must radically exclude movement and speed, and on the other, it seems in some respect to require them as *elementary* movement and speed. And if we are situated from the point of view of the instantaneous *states*, what we call elementary speed (which cannot be diminished) is null, since there is no movement in the instant, but only rest, a state that, compared to the preceding state, *is* another, but does not *become* it. When the other appears, it would have disappeared; it does not itself change. Here speed cannot be diminished because it is equal to zero. If, on the other hand, we are situated from the point of view of instantaneous *action,* meaning of the *creation* of the state, elementary speed (which cannot be diminished) must be considered as infinite, or as great as possible, in virtue of its radical instantaneousness, which causes that the change with respect to the state in the preceding instant (the "displacement") be operated suddenly *without time.* We cannot conceive that the operation can occur in a *shorter time,* since there is no shorter time. We must therefore conceive that it is impossible for it to happen with a greater speed. Here speed is conceived as not capable of diminution because, since the instant cannot be diminished, it is impossible that speed is not infinite. Moreover, since there exists a multitude of movements of differing speeds, the elementary infinite speeds of which they are composed must be different. In brief, the reciprocal relation of position, at each instant, of bodies in movement, must differ according to their speeds. The infinitely small difference between these relations at each instant does not have the same value. In other words, the *impetus,* or length of space that is said to be "run through" in an instant and that measures the quantity of action or of *conatus,* may be different. For example, it is necessarily different at each instant in a uniformly accelerated movement.[121] However, at each instant, in spite of the inequalities of the lengths of the *impetus,* which increase or reduce the space "run through" in an instant, and consequently speed itself greater or lesser, the speeds can always be said to be null. In fact, the new relation of position between bodies (expressed by length of *impetus*) is a state that succeeds instantaneously, meaning without transition from the preceding state. At each instant we face a *changed state*, not a *changing* of state—meaning that there is no movement. But, from the other point of view, all these different elementary speeds can always be said to be equal infinities (or the greatest possible), since for each instant, and *regardless of the length of the impetus*, the instauration of the new position that is accomplished in the indivisible instant cannot be accomplished any faster, since the instant cannot be diminished. The elementary speeds can therefore be greater or lesser, even though they are infinite. In fact, nothing prevents us from conceiving infinites of differing magnitudes.[122]

Thus, in an instant, whatever is the "magnitude" of the elementary speed (the number measuring the quantity of *conatus*), the absence of speed, meaning the absence of movement, and infinite speed, meaning the greatest possible speed such that no time could measure it, can always be simultaneously affirmed and identified with one another. Finally, we see that there is never any "running through" since there is never any transition and since the different successive states never flow into one another. There is only a succession of creations that are in themselves independent isolated instants *(sejuncti)* that touch without melding into one another and that are ordered to one another externally by a law.

These analyses confirm the correctness of Bergson's interpretation, which characterizes as "cinematographic" the Cartesian conception of attempting to account for dynamic and continuous movement by reducing it to a series of instantaneous, immobile, and discontinuous [frames]. By becoming aware of the real notion of differential, Leibniz escapes, to a certain degree, the Bergsonian critique, since Leibniz fashions real movement out of vanishing elements, out of virtual movements that are themselves things becoming.[123] The Cartesian analysis, which prepares the ground for the Leibnizian analysis, is in opposition to the latter precisely because, at the basis of things, it holds a radical discontinuity in agreement with the freedom of divine creation at each absolute instant. This creative divine freedom metaphysically compensates for the predominance of statics over dynamics in physics. And to the extent to which Leibniz removes it for the necessities of laws, he commits, according to Bergson, the most serious mistake leading him to stray farther than Descartes from the paths that lead one to the truth about time.

12. The Real Discontinuity of Cartesian Time

Clearly, one can conclude that it is not contrary to language and good sense to deny the continuity of time, by affirming continuous creation. If all existence or duration required the continuation of divine action, it would still not be true that the created thing must have the same character as the creative power, for the properties of the creature are not necessarily the same as the properties of the Creator.[124] On the contrary, in this case, the defect of the creature constrains us to conceive it as requiring a Creator that possesses this self-subsistence that it is lacking and that can sustain its existence. Finally, continuation is not synonymous with continuity,[125] for it can be accomplished with a repetition of the discontinuous. The sole act of creation, together with its indivisible freedom, is present at each instant of creation as the continual renewal of existence outside nothingness (of existence) *arising from divine power,* and not *arising from the created existence that had been previously there.* Thus this freedom, by establishing the absolute contingency of the moments of the creation or of duration, establishes their intrinsic self-sufficiency, their absolute reciprocal independence that constitutes their discontinuity. Instead of resting on "false reading," the conception of discontinuous time, as was defended by Vigier[126] and Wahl,[127] is a fundamental condition of all correct thinking about Cartesian physics and its relation with metaphysics.

Of the True and of the False

1. The Place of the Problem of Error in the Order

Meditation III marks a decisive stage in the progress with respect to the order of reasons. It attains the absolutely absolute simple nature; it touches that clay, that rock upon which the certainty of a science that really knows the *truth of things* can later be established.

From the perspective of the *ratio essendi,* it arrives at the supreme reality from which all others are derived, the principle of deduction that, following the order of synthesis, climbs back down the ladder of beings beginning with their cause and with respect to their relations of mutual dependency.

From the perspective of the *ratio cognoscendi,* which is the perspective of the *Meditations,* the fundamental problem, the problem of the foundation of science as valid objective knowledge, seems completely resolved. God, the fourth truth in the analytic order of reasons, is given to us in all certainty as the first objective truth of science, the principal truth and the warrant for all the others. Since evidence is thus definitively invested in its objective validity, deduction, following its course according to the analytic order, will be able to irradiate the certainty relative to the truth of the thing in the most backward domains of knowledge, by rising from the simplest idea (God) to the more and more complex ideas: clear and distinct ideas of various essences, and obscure and confused ideas of material existences.

It must now be asked why and how the analytic order of reasons necessarily requires posing the problem of error after the proof of God's existence by effects.

2. The Priority of the Problem of the Intrinsic Truth of Ideas (Understanding) over That of Formal Error (Will); the Problems of the Foundation of Truth and the Limits of Intelligence

We must first consider that *Meditation III* resolved fundamentally only one aspect of the problem of truth. The demonstration of divine veracity, destroying the hypothesis of the evil genius at its root, definitively renders to clear and distinct ideas the objective validity that only this hypothesis had removed (since only metaphysical doubt, and not hyperbolic doubts of natural origin, could have truly overtaken them). Thus mathematical certainty is rendered unshakable, and the point of view of the *Rules* is established metaphysically. In contrast, hyperbolic doubts of natural origin that had struck at sensible knowledge appear confirmed and justified. In fact, on the one hand, the critique of the judgments of common sense that had set them up as objectively valid has revealed that they cannot possess any resemblance to the things they purport to represent. On the other hand, the analysis of their objective reality, without stripping them entirely of all conceivable reference to an external thing, which in any case they would not resemble, has established within *their own nature* the impossibility for our judgment to conclude with certainty about their objectivity. In fact, they have so little reality that it is impossible to know whether they have any, or in the case in which they have some, to distinguish it from nothingness; consequently, they are by nature such that one always risks affirming in them nothingness for being and vice versa—which is the definition of the false itself.[1] These ideas are therefore definitively rejected as outside science, not for the external and natural reasons for doubt that *Meditation I* had expressed, but in virtue of their own essence.

Thus the question has been settled with respect to the intrinsic nature of true and false ideas, that is, with respect to the understanding, the seat of ideas in general. One now knows that truth in actuality is possible: 1) because we have, in fact, in our thought, ideas that are objectively valid; and 2) because we have at our command in order to recognize them, a completely established criterion—that of clearness and distinctness-and consequently we have a norm that judgments must obey in order to affirm the true—they must assent only to clear and distinct ideas.

But although the problem is resolved for what concerns the subject of the true (the idea), that is, the understanding, there remains for one to examine what concerns the form, that is, the will, which as judgment is the source of "true or formal falsity."[2] And if one refers it to the relation between modes and substance epistemically defined, which teaches us that for man the intellect can be without will, ideas without judgment, but not inversely, one sees that the investigation of will and judgment must necessarily follow the investigation of ideas and the understanding. The problem will no longer be to seek if and how truth is possible, but how error is possible, that is, how and why the will that judges allows us to pass from material falsity to *true and formal falsity*. It is only after having discovered the reasons and conditions of error that man, knowing what he must do or avoid in order to obtain knowledge of the truth,[3] will be able to advance with certainty on the road of science and to express himself about knowledge of external things *(Meditations V* and *VI)*. Thus, initially, the order imposes, after the solution of the problem of the objective validity or the problem of the material truth of ideas, the investigation of the problem of error, that is, the conditions of formal truth and falsity.

From there the problem of the *limits to our understanding* will succeed the problem of the *foundation of truth*. The program of the *Rules,* to base truth on intelligence and then to define the limits of intelligence *(limites ingenii definire),*[4] is coming true point by point, in accordance with the rigor of the order. Even the way in which God has been necessarily instituted as the foundation of all truth ipso facto involves the limits of our understanding, for God could only have been posited because he infinitely surpasses the possibility of our self, and he is, in the strictest sense of the word, *incomprehensible.* Incomprehensibility, "the formal reason of infinity,"[5] is, in my understanding, the reason that constrains me to posit God outside of me; and the positing of God outside of me, almost thrusting all ideas on me, starting with his own, implies that, if my understanding is subject to God, he need not, in return, subject himself to it. The richness of the idea of God testifies to the ineptitude of my consciousness—as the source of the form of ideas—to account for this idea by itself and establishes implicitly (but also unquestionably) the limited nature of our intelligence. Thus the problem of the limits of intelligence is posed, inevitably, by the very solution of the problem of the foundation of truth.

In any case, the path by which one must seek the solution has already been foreseen. Until now, we have set aside judgment, or will, which has been characterized as the power from which emanates "true and formal falsity." It is easy to foresee that the explanation of the possibility of error will have to be sought in the capacity to act outside the limits of the understanding that this power possesses, which supposes the ability to exceed them. Moreover, specifying the problem of error as a problem of the confrontation between will and a limited understanding should orient the solution toward the determination of the limits within which will might be certain to proceed to affirmations that escape error. To resolve the problem of error is to discover how and why an affirming will can transgress the limits of legitimate affirmations and how it can avoid transgressing it. The investigation relative to the foundation of truth, that is, to the certain objective validity of different ideas, has already sketched, in *Meditation III,* the outlines of that limit. By prescribing that one must affirm as true, by virtue of divine veracity, only clear and distinct ideas, which alone possess in all certainty an objective validity, a first limit is assigned to my power of affirming, if it wishes to exercise itself legitimately; it is the limit circumscribing the domain of these ideas. But beyond these ideas, is all legitimate affirmation radically excluded and is it not possible to trace limits of another kind? While justifying, by considering their nature, the ultimate exclusion of sensible ideas as outside science, *Meditation III* does not radically exclude them from knowledge in a larger sense, and it does not seem to prohibit eventual legitimate affirmations on their account. In fact, it is not stated that these ideas are entirely devoid of reality. On the contrary, it does not seem that they are a pure nothingness. As little reality as they possess—being in some way at the limit of the real—they possess some *minimum* of it, and since the true is reciprocal with being, it seems they must have some *minimum* of truth.[6]

Consequently the path toward the determination of this *minimum* or this limit remains open. In brief, what remains open is an investigation that would attempt to specify how and by how much our judgment can rightly affirm these ideas; in other words, how it can limit its affirmation to the *minimum* of truth (or reality) that they can allow. This limit is from now on virtually traced: supposing that we have just discovered that these ideas in some way concern external things; here and now we know, in all certainty, that they cannot impart their image. Thus judgment seems applicable legitimately beyond the limit that separates clear and distinct ideas from obscure and confused sensible ideas, as long as when affirming the latter, *it limits its affirmation* to the infinitely small amount of reality they enclose, as long as it affirms it with restrictions. Here then occurs another limit that *Meditation IV* will determine and that will concern the legitimate mode of affirmation of sensible ideas.[7]

The problem of the limits of intelligence turns out to be a more complex problem than that of the foundation of truth, since the finiteness of our understanding entails several kinds of limits for the former. First there is a limit with respect to God. This limit is discovered by recognizing the incomprehensibility of divine nature that escapes the necessities proper to our limited understanding. One of the consequences of this limitation, which is not mentioned in the *Meditations,* is the theory of eternal truths, which purifies physics and theology at the same time, by eliminating finality from the former and all that compromises God's infinity from the latter. Second, there is a lower limit, the limit that separates the knowledge of the essence of bodies from the knowledge of their existence, our clear and distict ideas from obscure and confused ideas, our understanding from imagination. Finally, in the region of obscure and confused ideas one ought to conceive a certain limit: the limit between reality and nothingness where the quantity of reality is so small that one confuses it with nothingness. The misappreciation of these limits ruins science fundamentally. Is it necessary to remark that, according to Descartes, Scholasticism had confused all these limits by its physics of substantial forms, on the one hand, by granting to obscure and confused knowledge the objective validity that can only accrue to clear and distinct (mathematical) ideas of the understanding, and on the other hand, by uniting physics and theology, the truths of our finite intellect with the ideas of the divine understanding, irrevocably compromising one and the other, the former by introducing divine finality into it and the latter by introducing into God the finiteness of our understanding?

3. The Conflict between the Principle of Universal Veracity and the Exception in Fact Constituted by Error: The Recognition of the Fact of Error as a Necessary Condition for the Possibility of a Human Science

But considerations of a different kind necessarily insert the examination of the problem of error at the exact place in which it is located, between *Meditations III* and *V*.

We have seen that in *Meditation III* the epistemic and psychological investigation relative to the objective validity of ideas intersected the metaphysical investigation relative to the proof for the existence of God. The solution, at first a partial solution of the former problem, entailed the entire solution of the latter, and the entire solution of the latter immediately completed the solution of the former by universalizing it totally. But this total universalization requires an excess, which provokes a conflict with the more moderate solution that allowed a glimpse of the methodical examination of the objective reality of various ideas. In fact, we have seen that this examination, while leading to establish the objective validity of clear and distinct ideas, far from justifying all ideas, seemed to legitimate substantially the condemnation of obscure and confused ideas and to foreshadow in certain ways the partial solution of the problem of limits. The demonstration of the absolutely perfect and veracious God is opposed as a rule to these conclusions, and this opposition engenders the need for a reconciliation that is possible only through the solution of the problem of error. In other words, the metaphysical path determines the place of the problem of error in the analysis with as much rigor as the epistemic-psychological path determines it, for its part.

In fact, the demonstration of the veracious God, implying the refutation of the evil genius hypothesis, determines in our attitude with respect to truth and certainty a radical reversal from pro to con. To the evil genius, the block of universal falsity, succeeds the absolute veracity of God, which gives rise to the block of universal truth. From there a symmetry of contrary positions results. The evil genius would extend his radical doubt not only to the items of knowledge that natural doubt reaches, but also to the clear and distinct ideas that are "by the nature of our mind" immediately and legitimately indubitable; inversely, God's veracity extends a priori the basis of its warrant not only to the clear and distinct ideas that are affected only by metaphysical doubt, but to the totality of our knowledge, that is, to these obscure and confused ideas that natural doubt legitimately stamps as worthy of suspicion. While the evil genius would attack as a rule the natural reasons that justify our confidence in clear and distinct ideas, divine veracity attacks as a rule the natural reasons that justify our distrust of obscure and confused ideas. The evil genius would make all truth impossible and doom all affirmation as error; divine veracity renders impossible all falsity and devotes, in principle, all affirmation to the true. We have oscillated to the other extreme.

And this extreme is no better than the other.

First, in fact, error exists. So that, after having labored to prove that God does not deceive me, I suddenly find myself confronted with the inverse problem: how is it possible that I am sometimes deceived? The fact of error plays, with respect to the thesis of divine veracity, a role symmetric to that which the fact of the Cogito plays with respect to the hypothesis of the evil genius. With respect to the hypothesis of the evil genius, which imposes universal deception, the Cogito was in its existence the *exception in fact* that, without being able to destroy the rule, required its revision. With respect to the thesis of universal veracity, *error* is in its existence the *exception in fact* that puts the charter of divine veracity into question. It tends to cripple the consequence derived from God's perfection. If in fact error exists incontestably in creation, it is impossible to admit that this perfection necessarily entails absolute universal veracity. In that way the demonstration of the objective validity of clear and distinct ideas, which rested on the certainty of this absolute veracity, and at the same time the possibility of a valid science are again put to the test.

But on the other hand, if one posits as intangible the principle of a universal veracity that excludes all possibility of error, one perceives that science is just as impossible as in the inverse case, in which the principle of universal fraudulence would exclude all possibility of truth. For certainly, if all is false, nothing is true; but if everything is true, nothing is false: here as there, truth and falsity no longer have meaning, and neither does science. Thus the order of reasons imposes necessarily for Descartes, exactly on this point, the problem that the sophistry of Antisthenes imposed on Plato: to establish the distinction between the true and the false, the possibility of the one and of the other, in order to establish the possibility of science.

4. The Intersection of the Psychological Problem of the Possibility of Error in the Human Soul and of the Problem of a Theodicy Relative to the Presence of Human Error in the Work of God

Even though they appear more independent than ever, the epistemic-psychological inquiry and the metaphysical-theological inquiry combine more closely than ever, since each imposes for itself exactly, at the same time, the necessity to examine the problem of error.

For the order of reasons, which imposes to the problem of error its place, will at the same time impose on the inquiry the rule that it will have to obey from now on; the substitution of divine veracity for the evil genius alters the working hypothesis adopted until now and substitutes another for it, one that is totally opposite. During *Meditations I, II,* and *III,* especially during *Meditation II,* the investigation with its segregative aspect derived its strength from the necessity to admit nothing that does not agree with the hypothesis of the evil genius.[8] Now it is necessary to admit nothing that does not agree with the principle of divine veracity. Whereas until now the most natural and most legitimate certainties (concerning the Cogito and mathematical ideas) were arraigned before the uncompromising tribunal of the evil genius, from now on, the most natural and most legitimate doubts (concerning obscure and confused ideas of the senses) will be arraigned before the uncompromising tribunal of divine veracity. This double ordeal, while submitting our knowledge to two contradictory treatments, does not allow it any contradiction; our knowledge will emerge, on the contrary, with a doubly assured certainty, within the precise limits circumscribed for it.

The consequences that result from this reversal may be evaluated as follows: the inquiry into the truth of ideas must extend itself automatically to confused and obscure ideas, and in seeking the extent to which these ideas can offer grounds for a legitimate affirmation, one will have as a goal not only to prove the existence of the bodies attested to by these ideas, but at the same time to justify divine veracity and to prove that God has not deceived us by putting imagination and the senses in us. In this way one sees how debatable is the objection currently directed against Descartes by the most distinguished historians of Cartesianism, according to which he would have sinned against his method by invoking the principle of divine veracity as a deus ex machina in order to justify the existential validity and the role of biological information of sensations, as well as our natural inclination to believe that our bodies are the cause of our sensations. For these historians, divine veracity would qualify in principle only in order to justify clear and distinct ideas.[9] We see that one could rightly state almost the contrary: in fact, the principle of divine veracity, far from being able to intervene as a device in the solution of the problem of the validity of sensible knowledge, *demands,* in order to be legitimated itself, that sensible knowledge be, in its turn, entirely justified, within the limits in which it possesses a *certain reality* (namely, the extent to which it does not allow us to know things in themselves, but their existence and how they can help or harm our bodies).

At the same time, one conceives that such a problem could not have been taken up and that the basis for its solution was missing—at least explicitly, if not implicitly—in the works in which the hypothesis of the evil genius and the principle of universal falsity were not mentioned, and in which the principle of universal veracity was consequently not invoked in return. This is the case of the *Discourse on Method,* in which, since the thesis of the evil genius is absent, the thesis of universal veracity is also absent; this has as a consequence that the treatise says nothing about the proof of the existence of bodies by means of the justification of my sensible knowledge, a justification that expressly requires divine veracity. One finds only, toward the end of the fourth part,[10] a passing reference to the reason that dictates that all our ideas or notions must have some foundation in truth, having been put within me by a truthful and perfect God, an argument that refers directly to a previously formulated principle of the *Discourse* itself,[11] that falsity is but nothingness and that everything real is consequently ipso facto true. The fourth part of the *Discourse* interrupts the chain of truths exactly where *Meditation VI* begins to demonstrate the existence of material things, after the ontological argument.

The necessity that thrusts itself, in the *Meditations,* to justify divine veracity, gives a dual aspect to it; if in fact, under one aspect, it is an instrument of proof (in particular, for the existence of bodies), it is, under another aspect, the final goal of a great proof that the last three *Meditations* unfold, for it is not definitively established until everything in the created universe that seemed to belie it is eliminated. It is not as if the theological preoccupation to vindicate God carries it toward proving the existence of bodies and justifying the senses in their biological function. On the contrary, the preoccupation to establish science still remains the principal objective. But in the *Meditations,* with respect to this problem as well as others, metaphysical-theological preoccupations and epistemic-psychological preoccupations are closely associated, and the close implication of their dual lines of demonstration strengthen the proof greatly.

The agreement between these two inquiries not only manifests itself externally, by the necessity that requires them to treat fully, at the same time, the problem of the possibility of error and the legitimacy of hyperbolic doubts based on natural reasons, it testifies for itself internally by the way that the one prepares the elements of an eventual solution for the other. In fact, since the hyperbolic doubt that weighs legitimately on sensible knowledge, because of natural reasons to doubt, necessarily has to confront divine veracity, it will either have to disappear, or to adjust to it. According to this last hypothesis, it will have to reabsorb itself in order to make room for a *minimal* affirmation relative to the capacity that our sensations would have of signifying to us the existence of material things and concerning the validity of the simple biological utility presented by their data. For does not the investigation of the contents that, in principle, justified the hyperbolic doubt based on natural doubts, reveal in sensible ideas a *minimal objective reality* that leaves open the way for a completely true and founded *minimal affirmation?* What this investigation allowed to be glimpsed merely as possible, the investigation brought forth in the name of divine veracity will render completely necessary. One rediscovers here the fortunate intersection of the two inquiries that already, from the time the elaboration of the proof for the existence of God in *Meditation III* had allowed one of them to render necessary, for the totality of clear and distinct ideas, the objective validity that the other had left merely as possible for ideas in general, except for an idea (God) whose validity was necessarily recognized.

However, if the investigation is going to succeed in demonstrating the partial illegitimacy of the doubt that strikes at items of sensible knowledge to the extent that it reveals that they can give ground to restrained affirmation—but nevertheless a true one within the limits of this restriction—it would not be able to abolish the fact of error itself, and the correlative necessity to doubt before arriving at truth. Therefore, the problem of error will have to be posed, not only on the psychological-epistemic plane (on the plane of the theory of knowledge), by asking how error is in fact possible for man, but also on the metaphysical plane, by asking, since error is actual for man, how is it directly compatible with the veracious God.

Here a double preoccupation and a double inquiry also intersect; the problem will not only be to show *how error is possible,* but *how God is not responsible for it.* And as in *Meditation III,* this double inquiry will arrive, by means of a remarkable convergence, at a single and only solution for the two problems, a solution brought forth by human freedom, a psychological and at the same time metaphysical faculty, a first "notion" that the natural light reveals to me.[12] By this faculty, error is conceived as possible for man, and God is conceived as not being responsible for it. The responsibility is borne by man. At the same time, divine veracity appears not only as the tribunal before which the hyperbolic doubt based on natural doubts must be tried, but as what is itself compelled to be arraigned before the tribunal of my reason, which must absolve it from the error to which man seems given.[13]

On this metaphysical plane, the conception of the limits of our intelligence, to which the inquiry on the epistemic-psychological plane was introduced, will unfold in all its scope. First, the tribunal of man is constituted by its understanding that we know ourselves to be limited by the fact of God's incomprehensibility. For the finite would not be able to be used as a means to judge the infinite. By introducing the trial of the veracious God, man will therefore have, above all, to bring before his mind the limitation of his intelligence, meaning the incomprehensibility of the being he claims to judge, the impenetrability of his ends.[14] Consequently, the consciousness of this limitation must be for him, in his effort to comprehend the metaphysical possibility of error, the norm to which he must strictly adhere in order to avoid any illegitimate judgment about God. Second, divine veracity a priori disputing the validity of doubts striking at sensible knowledge leads us to limit these doubts by restoring to these items of knowledge a limited objective validity (limited to material existences and biological information) conceded in accordance with the extreme limitation of their objective reality.[15] Thus the knowledge of a perfect God itself, on the one hand, requires me, when arraigning before the tribunal of divine veracity the hyperbolic doubts that strike at sensible knowledge for natural reasons, to limit these doubts when justifying this knowledge by the intrinsic function (existential and biological) that a truthful God has given them; on the other hand, it requires me, because of my consciousness of the limits of my understanding, to limit judgments relative to God and about the relationship between God and his creatures (to put aside on this topic all thoughts of finality in physical things),[16] in virtue of the consciousness I have of God's incomprehensibility.

5. General Metaphysical Solution. Conflict between This Solution and Human Psychological Realities

As we have just seen, the problem of the possibility of error for man and the problem of the incompatibility in principle between this error and divine veracity or perfection necessarily intersect; for the solution of the first problem is governed by the solution of the second. In other words, the *metaphysical problem governs the epistemic-psychological problem in this case.*

This primacy is inevitable, since the general solution of the problem of objective validity has been obtained in *Meditation III* only by the demonstration of divine veracity. To allow the fact of error to put it again into question would be to shake up the foundation of truth that was so painstakingly acquired. Moreover, we have seen that the confrontation between error and divine veracity necessarily introduced limits to the problem. We ought not be surprised, then, if Descartes, perceiving the key to the whole problem of error in the general solution of the theological problem contained in it, discovers this general solution in the principle that resolves the problem of limits in general, namely, in the metaphysical principle of all possible limits as the *union of being and nothingness in man, conceived as intermediary between the two.*[17] The veracious God and the evil genius, truth and falsity, are opposed as being and nothingness: the presence of error in man on the side of truth is explained by the limitation of the one by the other in man. I participate in being because of truth; I participate in nothingness because of falsity. The problem is in principle effectively resolved, for God would not be responsible for error since he cannot metaphysically be its cause. In fact, he is the Supreme Being, and nothingness cannot proceed from being. The cause of error is therefore outside God. It is in man to the extent that he involves nothingness because of his finiteness. And this cause does not derive from something positive, since *the cause of nothing is not something.* There is in man only a limited reality, the true, for which God is the cause. Above this limit where there is not something and where no cause has posited anything real, extends the domain of error, meaning the domain of metaphysical void.[18]

Meditation IV will do no more than explain this solution of principle by progressively resolving the theological and psychological difficulties contained in it. This result will be obtained by rejoining the epistemic-psychological plane at the level at which the conception of limits receives a new determination in the guise of a theory of man's faculties within which the limited understanding and the unlimited will are opposed.[19] The metaphysical opposition between being and nothingness is manifested then as a psychological opposition between a finite faculty and an infinite faculty. Man's character, as intermediary between being and nothingness, is then specified not only as finite (the "mean" between zero and infinity) but also as the union of the infinite and the finite.

For it is the latter specification that will permit the resolution of the theological and psychological difficulties implied by the solution of principle discovered on the metaphysical plane. While in *Meditation III* the investigation on the epistemic-psychological plane introduced the solution of the metaphysical inquiry (which in return provided the general solution that the former was not able to furnish), in *Meditation IV* it is the investigation on the metaphysical plane that reintroduced the inquiry on the psychological plane (which in turn discovers the solution of the difficulties entailed by the principle of the general solution expressed on the metaphysical plane). Moreover, although this general metaphysical solution resolves the principle underlying the problem of God's nonresponsibility for error, it assigns to the latter only a general reason: nothingness. It therefore allows, with respect to God, only its simple metaphysical possibility to be conceived. It does not at all, in this fashion, resolve the problem of its possibility for man, that is, the problem of its psychological possibility, which implies, not the discovery of a general cause or metaphysical reason (nothingness), but the discovery of a proximate psychological cause: human free will. Better yet, it seems to exclude the positing of the problem itself, for if error is a void where no cause can intervene, since there is nothing to cause, it does not require any cause, strictly speaking. Therefore what seems excluded is that one could find a psychological cause to account for this nothingness, that is, an agent that would be something real and positive. For on the one hand, nothingness is the metaphysical principle of error; on the other hand, freedom will be its psychological principle. If Descartes were to resolve the difficulty by identifying freedom and nothingness, he would be upholding, in this case, the philosophical conceptions of the later Fichte, who defined freedom as nonbeing, and those of contemporary existentialists. But he does not quite consider this assimilation. On the contrary, freedom is for man what is most real, an infinity that is the closest image of God's infinity itself. And from this results the difficulty of the Cartesian solution.

The metaphysical solution contained, in fact, a double difficulty, metaphysical and psychological. Since nothingness is not a positive principle—except for an absurd Manichaeism that would confer on the negative a positive efficacy and would make of it something positive, turn it inside out—it is a simple absence of being. Consequently, error is also only a simple limitation of being. But it appears immediately as more, that is, as the lack of a perfection my nature ought to possess, that is, as a *privation*.[20] Natural light represents error and sin (the latter's representation being strengthened by supernatural light) as a fault, and not as a simple absence.[21] Limitation involves only ignorance; error adds to ignorance its affirmation as science—it adds to nothingness its affirmation as being. That is the positive thing that constitutes its essence and that *ought not be*. If it is thus, error cannot be merely negative. It does not correspond to the least quantity of reality or perfection, to the limitation of a positive quantity, but it is an intrinsic and "positive imperfection,"[22] a negative quantity that destroys the positive quantity. Neither is it a limitation or absence of being, but a corruption of being, the positing of something contrary to what *ought to be*. For insofar as some positive element is introduced in error—however contrary that may seem—it is impossible to account for it by nothingness.[23] A positive cause is required to establish this positive imperfection, and God, the being in which everything resides, and the positive and efficient cause, must necessarily appear again as the agent responsible for error—which contradicts his perfection and his veracity.

6. An Attempt at a Metaphysical Solution; God's Incomprehensibility and Perfection; Different Kinds of Possible Solutions; the Insufficiency of the Metaphysical Solution

We had to recognize that the opposition of the essence of error (that is, "true and formal falsity" that psychological analysis reveals to us) to the general principle of the metaphysical solution that reduced it to mere nothingness, seems to put the principle itself into question and to lead to an impass.

In order to resolve the difficulty, Descartes again finds himself before two paths, a metaphysical path and a psychological path. The first leads him to set aside the exact formulation of the problem, to set aside the question of whether error is privation or negation, positive imperfection or nothingness, in order to attempt to reconcile it in principle with God's perfection. The second leads him, on the contrary, to consider as strictly as possible the conditions of the problem of error in order to ask whether the privative character of error on the psychological plane actually involves a privation on the metaphysical plane.

The inquiry will proceed, in turn, upon each of the two paths.

Since the problem is motivated by a metaphysical concern and since the posited general principle seems to exclude at first the possibility of discovering a true and efficient cause of error on the psychological plane, it is natural that Descartes first proceeds on the metaphysical path.

It leads one to conceive of two hypotheses. The first relates to God's incomprehensibility; it is tied to the limits of our understanding. It tends to limit a priori the legitimacy of judgments about the perfection of God's works and, consequently, the legitimacy of judgments about God's culpability that we might have been tempted to bring forth because of the alleged imperfection that we believe to have noticed in his works. The metaphysical problem of the possibility of error with respect to God will thus be excluded from the philosophical investigation in the name of the mystery of God: his aims are impenetrable.[24]

The second hypothesis refers to God's perfection, which seems to include a creation free from all defects. The existence of error is therefore an enigma.

These two hypotheses, which are entirely different from one another (it is impossible to affirm that the creation is perfect; it is necessary to affirm that it is perfect, or that it is as perfect as possible), are based on the two characteristics of divine nature, incomprehensibility and perfection, which are in some respects identical (for God is incomprehensible only because he is perfect), and in other respects, that is, according to their consequences, opposite (for if God is incomprehensible, I cannot utter a verdict on the meaning and the greater or lesser intrinsic perfection of his creation; and if he is perfect, this perfection seems necessarily to entail in some way or another the perfection of the things he wished to create).

Although confronted by certain objections and wishing to avoid theological controversies, Descartes goes very far with the first hypothesis. He allows that God could have created an imperfect work and that the existence of error does not pose any problem,[25] given that the finiteness of our mind does not allow us to affirm the necessity of the contrary. If he considers the other hypothesis, it is only to exhaust all the possibilities of the question. For, of the two, only one is true: either the creation is imperfect and the presence of human error in it poses no problems, or it is perfect and one has to establish how human error is compatible with such perfection: "I have not determined that God always does what he knows to be most perfect, and it does not seem to me that a finite mind can judge of this. But I have attempted to cast some light on the proposed difficulty dealing with the cause of error by assuming that God created the world most perfect, because if I assumed the contrary, this difficulty would completely disappear."[26]

But it is evident that the chain of reasons renders necessary only the conception of the hypothesis of a perfect creation. This hypothesis, in fact, is included in the conception of divine veracity that renders unavoidable the problem of the compatibility of human error with the perfection of a creation that excludes all deception. Despite the limits of my understanding, I cannot conceive contingencies other than a world as perfect as possible, since its Creator is perfect[27] and since God's omnipotence, along with his perfection, makes it impossible for God to incline toward the imperfect, that is, toward nothingness, which is contradictory to the infinite existence of his omnipotence.[28]

We must therefore reduce by a degree the provisional conclusions that the notion of God's incomprehensibility offers to us, being required to judge that the omnipotent God could not do otherwise than make his work as perfect as possible. It however remains that, because of the finiteness of our understanding, we are incapable of judging of what this perfection consists. Thus to the first hypothesis, *error is an imperfection, but God's creation may be imperfect, for God's aims are radically impenetrable,* must succeed another, which in some respects is the reverse of the first, *God's creation is perfect, or as perfect as possible, but error may not be an imperfection.*

This second hypothesis leads to two different types of solutions.

Our understanding is too limited to be able to decide what would constitute the perfection of the work in general or the perfection or imperfection proper to its parts. Consequently, either error is good in itself (since God wanted it and God is perfect), or on the contrary, it is effectively, considered in itself, an imperfection—in which case we would say that considered as such, it is no doubt required for the perfection of the whole. Consequently, we will have to conceive that it plays a necessary role in the creation, one that escapes us. By that we rejoin the traditional arguments of Stoic origin that Saint Augustine had employed against the Manichaeans.[29]

These two kinds of solutions impose themselves alternatively according to whether the consideration of incomprehensibility leads to that of perfection, or vice versa, the consideration of perfection leads to that of incomprehensibility. But there is a third possibility; incomprehensibility can lead us to consider the problem as insoluble. This latter hypothesis then becomes almost as negative as the former hypothesis that denied the problem.

This reference to incomprehensibility seems initially imposed by the Cartesian doctrine of the limits of our intelligence. If we are required to confront error (because of the fact that it exists) with divine veracity and to pose the problem of knowing how it is metaphysically possible to establish the distinction between the true and the false in man, if we have to arraign God himself before the tribunal of our reason to accomplish this end, this audacious summons to compare is only legitimate insofar as we have previously taken into account our awareness of the limits of our intelligence. For the obligation to remind ourselves of these limits is only the obligation to maintain God's incomprehensibility before our mind. To mistake these human limits or this divine incomprehensibility is to doom in advance the tribunal of our reason to render a judgment as unjust as it is absurd.

But if God is incomprehensible, is it not fruitless to even attempt to institute the proceeding that has as its precise goal *to understand* how God, while being veracious, has created a being capable of being deceived? God's incomprehensibility would then not merely trace the limits within which the proceeding would be argued, but it would suppress radically every possibility of a legitimate suit. It would then remain for us to accept with resignation these two contradictory truths, contradictory only for us, that

God is absolutely veracious, but that he has, however, created us capable of being deceived. In brief, limiting the consequences of divine veracity for man would not lead to limiting this veracity itself, since that would be to limit God. God would then be veracious even though he has created man fallible, and if he has created us thus, it is for reasons that are beyond us and that would be fruitless for us to seek.[30]

This renunciation would result in upholding that it is impossible for man to discover the metaphysical principle of the possibility of error and to arrive at the final foundation of the distinction between the true and the false by clear and distinct knowledge. Doubtless the certainty that God is veracious would suffice in order for us to affirm fully the truth of clear and distinct ideas, but we would not know *why* these clear and distinct ideas are true while the obscure and confused ideas are false. Correlatively, there will remain an antagonism between divine veracity and hyperbolic doubts based on natural doubts directed against obscure and confused ideas; it would not be possible to trace the limits that would allow for a reconciliation between divine veracity and doubts, and to determine to what extent sensible ideas, being outside the true, are nevertheless capable of legitimate affirmation. In brief, this recourse to the mystery of divine nature *(O altitudo!)* will abort the enterprise of establishing science almost at its end. Descartes will therefore not be able to uphold it.

That is why this consideration is associated with an appreciably different view. The latter consists in deriving from God's incomprehensibility, not the impossibility to resolve the problem, but a certain kind of solution: it would suffice to postulate as necessary, in the name of God's perfection, the effective reconciliation, however incomprehensible, of error with perfection, by denying that error has an evil nature.

This other conception of God's incomprehensibility is not simply an illegitimate move in the system; though God is incomprehensible, he is neither irrational nor unknowable, since he has given us the clear and distinct idea of his perfection for which incomprehensibility is only the formal reason.[31] The limitation of our intelligence has for Descartes neither the foundation nor the same import as it has for Kant. For Kant it is the immediate result of the function of our understanding as the formal condition for knowledge, and from it flows the impossibility of knowing the essence of the infinite. For Descartes, on the contrary, it is the immediate result of our knowledge of the essence of the infinite, a condition for our knowledge of our finiteness, an intuition of a being whose magnitude is such that my intelligence perceives it while grasping that it cannot encompass it.[32]

Thus the limitation of our intelligence and God's incomprehensibility, far from prohibiting knowledge of God, on the contrary, imply and presuppose it.[33] It is precisely from this knowledge of God as perfect that we have derived his incontestable veracity. Although the limitation of our intelligence prohibits us forever from knowing the whole reality of God, it does not at all prevent us from knowing that everything in him is determined according to the reason of the perfect. The mysterious reasons that have driven God to create man as fallible must then agree with his perfection and consequently must aim for the best. "It is certain . . . that he [God—M. G.] always wishes for what is best";[34] and without knowing the basis of things, nor the aims of God, nor the final nature of error, I can be certain that the existence of error is better than its nonexistence. Thus, God's perfection introduces the principle of the best, and this principle combines with the principle of God's incomprehensibility to propose to us a general solution of faith that, it is true, we would have to accept with our eyes closed.

But the principle of the best, on the one hand, and divine incomprehensibility, on the other, are capable of a different interpretation, depending upon whether, in this scheme, it is the best (perfection) that determines incomprehensibility or incomprehensibility that determines the best.

In the first case the perfect (or the best), determining incomprehensibility and consequently limiting it, seems to limit God's omnipotence. God necessarily acts in conformity with what is best, which is itself determinable by rational criteria, universally valid for him as for me. Thus his omnipotent will seems to be subject to an order. What I perceive as an imperfection (error, sin, etc.) is, relative to this order, either the consequence of the perfection of the means, on the whole constituted by the paths and the work (Malebranche), or a perfection relative to only the perfection of the work that is a *maximum* realized by a *minimum* (Leibniz). The limitation of my understanding has as consequence not to deprive me of a universally valid concept of perfection itself, not to prohibit me from knowing the intrinsic good or evil of each thing considered separately, but to prevent me from encompassing in my knowledge the whole of God's work, hence to relate clearly and distinctly the parts to the whole and, consequently, to be able to judge of the perfection of the parts relative to the perfection of the whole. "*O altitudo!*" is not the expression of the mystery of God's will, but the expression of his science, in accordance with the letter of the Pauline exclamation: "*O altitudo divitiarum scientiae et sapientiae Dei!*"[35]

In the second case, the perfect is defined, on the contrary, as that which emanates from omnipotence: the proof that something is best is that it was created by an omnipotent God. In brief, God did not create it because it was best, but it is best because God created it. Any judgment about the alleged defects of God's creation is reckless. In truth, we have no norm by which we can judge the imperfection of things. That is the thesis that will agree very well with Jansenism; it will be the thesis of Arnauld, Dirois, etc., and the one to which Malebranche will not fail to object that, with it, it will be no less impossible to judge of perfection or imperfection, whether it be the perfection of God or of his work. "*O altitudo!*" is then the expression of the unfathomable depths of God's will.[36]

It is evident that the Cartesian arguments unite these two opposite tendencies.[37] First, the conception that determines the best by omnipotence and incomprehensibility agrees with the conception of God as the Free Creator of eternal truths, alien to our considerations of finality, instituting the good without being determined by it.[38] This tendency dominates the first reason invoked, according to which the existence of error is better than its absence, since God has permitted it. Before attempting to confront a possibly insoluble problem in its precise formulation, it would be natural, being faced with something incomprehensible, to have recourse first to God's incomprehensibility.[39]

However, this recourse would flatly interrupt the attempt to establish science. And above all, it would threaten directly what it was supposed to save.

If in fact incomprehensibility determines what is best and if, consequently, my not wishing to be deceived is not necessarily better than my wishing it, how can one affirm, by virtue of the best and God's goodness, that God must necessarily be veracious? If he freely decides about what is good, can he not decree that universal deception is good and that lies are better than truth? Can he not allow lies to prevail, and these would be good from the fact that they prevail? If God's omnipotence and incomprehensibility are such that the notions of good and evil valid for me have no sense for him,[40] how could one affirm, by virtue of the goodness we ascribe to God, that he is necessarily veracious and that his goodness limits his omnipotence? Thus the proof for the existence of God, insofar as it posits an incomprehensible and omnipotent God, would not be able to refute hypothesis of the great deceiver, and by attempting to justify error by recourse to God's incomprehensibility, one risks to compromise irrevocably the certainty of his veracity.

This remark further confirms that the refutation of the hypothesis of the evil genius would not be obtained efficaciously by an appeal to God's perfection, conceived as goodness limiting his power, but rather by an appeal to the perfection of his being, conceived as his immensity that, identifying, on the one hand, power with being, truth and goodness, and on the other hand, powerlessness with nothingness, falsity, and evil, excludes deception and evil from God as contrary to his omnipotence itself. Here the necessity for our understanding cannot be different from the necessity for God, since God cannot not be God, that is, a Supreme Being excluding all nothingness.

The second kind of solution,[41] which will be the only one to reappear at the end of the psychological investigation,[42] tends, on the contrary, to determine incomprehensibility from perfection. It immediately reintroduces the notion of finality by conceiving that God, in conformity with his own perfection, has *organized* the universe with a view toward the perfection of the whole and has thus determined the parts in keeping with the perfection of the whole. Thus we cannot penetrate the aims of God, but we can, in virtue of the idea of his perfection, affirm that he has acted for the best, according to an order, and that, although we do not know his aims, we can be sure that they are good.

This consideration cannot be added to the previous one unless it limits and corrects it to some extent. And it cannot be reconciled with it unless one admits that, although understanding does not precede will in God, will does not precede understanding either; they are both simultaneous in him.[43]

Moreover, this consideration is far less dangerous than the preceding ones. It does not preclude the possibility of the process; it merely traces the limits within which it will have to be argued, if it is to be argued. It does not lead to the eventual consideration of deception as an intrinsic good. However, it furnishes no component for a positive solution. It merely affirms that error is able to be reconciled with God's perfection, that it must have its use in the creation; but it does not tell us in what way, and it does not at all allow us to know how it is possible. And it is this knowledge alone that will permit man to know how he can avoid error and arrive at the truth. Metaphysics therefore furnishes only an insufficient solution. It must make way for psychology.

7. Inquiry on the Psychological Plane; Simultaneous Solution of the Metaphysical (Theodicy) and the Psychological Problems

The problem is then to be specified in the following way: since error can no longer be considered as an intrinsic imperfection incompatible with God's perfection, it must, in spite of the positive nature of privation that it wears on the human plane, amount to the purely negative nature that it is recognized to be on the divine plane. Thus metaphysics appeals to psychology to resolve a problem that is essentially metaphysical. The problem is psychological because it can only be resolved by psychological elements; but it is neither psychological in its intention, nor in its formulation, which is, after all, as follows: *To discover how the psychological positive can be inscribed within the metaphysical negative;* it is a formulation rather like the formulation of the following geometrical problem: *Discover how a triangular or square figure can be inscribed in a circle.*

Thus we see that here psychology is subservient to metaphysics and that the psychological problem of error appears more and more closely governed by the metaphysical problem of the compatibility of error with God's perfection. Certainly we are concerned with giving a *psychological* explanation of a psychological phenomenon as it was originally understood. But, above all, psychology is required to find an explanation such that it satisfies the requirements of metaphysics. It will have to develop its inquiry within the framework that metaphysics had traced for it. It is required beforehand to show that, in spite of his perfection and veracity, God does not radically exclude the possibility of error as a privation in us; that, even though he does not exclude it and it exists, his perfection and veracity remain intact;[44] and that he appears as having had absolutely nothing to do with it. That is Descartes' true aim. No doubt, for Descartes, it does not appear urgent to exculpate God, a subject about which he truly did not need to reassure himself; but it appears urgent to exculpate God if that is what is needed to safeguard his fundamental veracity, for upon that veracity is established the objective validity of clear and distinct ideas and, consequently, the possibility of a science that is certain. And to discover the foundation of a certain science is the fundamental design that governs the whole enterprise of the *Meditations*.

Moreover, it is evident that these are the subjective conditions of error, meaning the factors upon which depend the attitude of the subject confronted with the representative content or the objective reality of ideas that are at the root of the problem. They are the ones that condition the passage from the material falsity of ideas to the "true and formal falsity" of judgments. What is positive in error—privation—in opposition to simple negation, arises only with respect to judgment. Taken in themselves, ideas include nothing of the false, they have objective realities that always include being in variable quantities, ranging from the infinite (God) to the infinitely small (sensations). Material falsity of ideas is therefore nothing more than the extreme limitation of being. The explanation of falsity by means of nothingness and of truth by being is therefore perfectly adequate and satisfactory, as long as we are concerned with this material falsity. It is no longer adequate and satisfactory once one goes on to formal falsity, that is, to the act of judgment that affirms what is nothingness as being. Here we encounter what is positive in error, the intrinsic imperfection that seems not reducible to an explanation by simple limitation of being. The point of insertion of the difficulty is therefore located where *judgment is applied to the objective reality of ideas* and where there seems to be a disproportion between the area of this reality and the area described by the affirmation. From this we see that the key to the problem must be sought for in the relations between understanding and will.

From the point of view of psychology, we can therefore now give a new formulation to the bond that links *Meditations II, III,* and *IV—II* and *III* being devoted to the understanding and *IV* to will. *Meditation II* gives a *theory of the understanding in general (mens, sive intellectus),* "intellectual nature in general," considered in *its form,* as necessary ultimate condition of all knowledge, having abstracted away the contents. *Meditation III* treats the problem of the objective validity of ideas, meaning their material truth or falsity, and completes *this theory of the understanding in general* by a *theory of the faculty of knowledge of external things,* by examining the *representative contents,* meaning the objective reality of ideas, which the Cogito abstracted away, as the principle of their forms only, by which they are all "equal among themselves." It ends up with the general principle of a metaphysical solution of the problem of the true and of the false, by means of the reduction of true to being and false to nothingness. *Meditation IV* treats the problem of error, meaning of formal truth and falsity of judgments, and gives *a theory of the will* as a faculty that affirms the representative contents or objective realities of ideas. This theory ends up with a psychological solution to the problem of error that is intended to account for the positiveness of error on the human plane without compromising the general metaphysical solution, inspired by *Meditation III,* that excludes the positiveness of error on the divine plane.

In opposition to the metaphysical investigation, the psychological investigation tackles the problem directly. Its aim is to explain error as a *privation* by a combination of psychological factors such that its positive imperfection, which is undeniable in the human soul, does not entail any positive imperfection from the metaphysical point of view. In fact, pursuing the epistemological-metaphysical path that was followed with much success during *Meditation III,* I continue the examination of my soul according to the method already used at that time, meaning I evaluate the degree of reality of what is discovered in me by means of the idea of the perfect taken as the principle of this possible evaluation, but I apply it this time, not to the objective reality of our ideas (to their representative contents), but to the faculties I find in myself relating to knowledge, meaning the understanding, the place of ideas, and will, the principle of judgments.[45] I then perceive by this comparison with the infinitely perfect that my understanding is finite and that my will is infinite; that is what allows me to know that my will is in me that by which I resemble God.[46] I then discover from where error arises: "From the fact that will is much more ample and far-reaching than understanding, I do not restrain it within the same limits, but extend it even to those things that I do not understand; since it is itself indifferent to such matters, it easily strays and chooses false for true and evil for good. And thus it happens that I err and sin."[47]

In that way the privative character of error is recognized and justified psychologically; and at the same time, the problem of the nonculpability of God is resolved, in conformity with the general principle of the metaphysical solution announced at the start. This twofold result is attained because the privative character recognized with respect to error on the psychological plane is explained psychologically in such a way that it has only a negative character on the metaphysical plane (that is, with respect to God). In fact, psychologically speaking, error is not just negative, it does not just reside in a simple limitation of my knowledge tied to the limitation of my faculty of knowledge, but it is, in some way, something positive inside out; it assumes a transgression of the limit of my intelligence by my will, which allows nonknowledge to be positively affirmed as knowledge. Thus to the limitative elements constituted by the limits of my understanding is added a privative element instituted by the infinity of my will, which transgressing these limits, transforms the nothingness located beyond these limits into being, and creates true and formal falsity. Thus error is confirmed in its character of irrationality in actuality (nothingness posited as being), which renders it into something it ought not be: a deterioration of rationality (an absurdity) that, with respect to my rational nature, constitutes a privation, a "positive imperfection."[48]

Nevertheless, God is not responsible. No doubt, he has created in me the faculties whose operation engenders error, but he has placed nothing positively imperfect in them, nor anything that renders error irrevocable. Finally, he is not the author of the operation: "It is not an imperfection in God that he has given me the freedom to judge or not to judge about certain things of which he has not placed clear and distinct knowledge in my understanding; no doubt it is an imperfection in myself not to make proper use of this freedom and to pass judgment rashly on things I conceive only obscurely and confusedly."[49]

Of course my understanding is limited; but this fact does not entail any positive imperfection or privation. In itself it is a perfection, a reality whose magnitude alone is limited.[50] It is the same with respect to my will, except that its perfection is not limited in magnitude, being infinite in me as in God—it cannot therefore entail any privation since it does not even suffer limitation.[51] And God is my cause only insofar as I have these realities in me. As for the ill use of my free will, "in which we find the privation that constitutes the form of error,"[52] it is no doubt an intrinsic imperfection, but not of my will itself, since the very nature of this perfection or reality that constitutes my will includes freedom, meaning precisely the possibility for my will to make whatever use of itself it wishes to make, whether good or bad. Thus, the very acts by which I err, insofar as they express directly the nature of will as a free faculty, are, taken in themselves, absolutely good, since they are the immediate and authentic expression of a reality, of a perfection: "Privation is found in the operation insofar as it proceeds from me, but it is not found in the faculty that I have received from God, nor even in the operation, insofar as it depends on him."[53] Therefore "I must not complain that God concurs with me in forming the acts of this will, that is, the judgments in which I am mistaken, because these acts are entirely true and absolutely good insofar as they depend on God; and there is somehow more perfection in my nature because I can perform them than there would be if I could not."[54]

As for the operation of the faculties from which error results, God has nothing to do with it either: the whole operation is accomplished without his willing it. It has its cause in the faculty, the freedom, whose character is precisely to render me into a cause independent from God, at least with respect to its point of application. Finally, the phenomenon that results from the operation—error itself—insofar as it is engendered by the arbitrary operation of two realities, the one finite and the other infinite, is only a mirage projected on nothingness and, consequently, has no reality in itself.[55] Below this mirage, one discovers nothing more in me than the limit of one of my perfections, merely an absence of being. Since it is pure nothingness, error could not therefore be caused by God, who can cause only being: "As for privation, in which alone consists the formal reason of error and sin, it has no need for any involvement on the part of God, since it is not a thing or a being, and since, if it is referred to God as its cause, it should not be called a privation, but only a negation, according to the meaning given to these words in the schools."[56] Thus, since it entails no positive imperfection of my nature or of my faculties—given that it is not a reality at all—the psychological phenomenon of error, in spite of the privative character it presents, does not entail any privative character on the metaphysical plane. Because of this fact, it requires no cause, in the metaphysical sense of the word. And yet its psychological explanation is not thus excluded, for in this case, the psychological explanation concerns not error, but a real operation in my consciousness, namely, the operation of my faculties, of which error is only epiphenomenal.

By allowing the establishment of the nonpositive character from the metaphysical point of view of privation or positive imperfection that characterizes error on the psychological plane, the psychological path leads to the solution of a problem essential to metaphysics, in conformity with the requirements of the latter: to safeguard completely divine veracity with respect to the doubt that can be raised against it from the fact that error exists, by locating the cause of error everywhere else but not in God. God creates only realities and perfections in me. Whether they are limited or unlimited, that changes nothing with respect to their intrinsic character of perfection and reality. Error arises in me from the fact that one of the perfections of my being (the understanding) is limited in its amplitude; therefore error arises from the nothingness in me. No doubt it is a privation for me, since it is a positive imperfection with respect to what could and ought to be my judgment, if my judgment were not precipitous, but since it is nothing more in its fabric than an illusionary reflection that hides nothingness—since in itself it is neither a being nor an intrinsic alteration of my being or of the being of one of my faculties—it is not in itself a positive imperfection, and it has no substratum other than nothingness. God cannot be the cause of this nothingness, for Being can only produce being and not nothingness. Moreover, that is why nothingness is without cause, for a cause is required only in order to explain the presence of a being. Of course, the reality of the cause must be as ample as the reality of the effect, which entails that the former must have more reality than the latter, but where the effect is null, meaning where nothingness reigns, we can no longer speak of any reality of *the cause,* since there is not the least causality. Thus, nothing real in me can give rise to error, since error is linked with nothingness.

In this way it becomes possible to link directly the truth of clear and distinct ideas to their reality. If in fact nothing real can give rise to error, it is sufficient that I capture some real thing in order that I capture something of which God is the cause and which is necessarily true. Therefore, what is indisputably something in me is caused by God and is necessarily true. And clear and distinct ideas are always something, indisputably. In fact, *Meditation III* has taught us that the quantity of their objective reality is of sufficient magnitude that it is impossible to mistake nothingness for being with respect to them. Therefore we cannot doubt that they are real; we cannot have doubts about what is real in them either, since there is nothing that is not real in them. Consequently, clear and distinct ideas, which necessarily must be recognized as real, are according to the evidence caused by God and thus materially true. Therefore all judgments brought upon them are formally true, and by affirming only clear and distinct ideas, it is impossible that I am ever mistaken. But clear and distinct ideas are the only ideas included within the limits of pure understanding. Consequently, if I limit my will to the limits of that understanding, I would escape error. This series of deductions is summarized by the following pithy formulation: "Whenever I restrict my will within the bounds of my knowledge, such that it makes no judgment except upon things clearly and distinctly represented by the understanding, it cannot happen that I am mistaken; since *every clear and distinct conception is without doubt (procul dubio) something, and thus it cannot derive its origin from nothingness, but necessarily has God as its author*—God, I say, who is supremely perfect and *cannot be the cause of any error*—and consequently we must conclude that such a *conception* or such a *judgment* is true."[57] This conclusion implies a method: to trace rigorously and precisely the limit between pure understanding and everything else, that is, "to separate" carefully clear and distinct ideas from obscure and confused ideas.[58] This demonstration has as consequences the avoidance of the doubt that the fact of error placed on divine veracity, and the intrinsic explanation of this veracity from the notions of being and nothingness. Divine veracity is thus not only affirmed externally, in virtue of a certain attribute of God—goodness—but also internally, because of the impossibility of being to be untrue, to cause something other than being, and consequently to engender error or the nontrue that is nonbeing. Thus, from the fact that God is the Supreme Being, he is supremely *true* and ipso facto necessarily veracious, true designating intrinsic reality and consequently the necessary truth of what he has created, and also designating God himself insofar as one refers to him the truth of which he is the author.

That is why, where Descartes has not put into play divine veracity, when he did not need it in order to destroy the hypothesis of the evil genius, the hypothesis not having been mentioned (that is, in the *Discourse),* he simply guarantees the truth of clear and distinct ideas by referring to the identification of the true and the real, based on the identification of the real and the perfect, itself entailed in the necessary demonstration of the infinitely perfect God. It suffices then that the clearness and distinctness of ideas teach me about their reality in order that I be sure that the all-perfect God, the cause of the real, has placed them in me and that, consequently, they are true, since error and falsity, being imperfections, are a part of nothingness and cannot proceed from God: "The very principle that I took as a rule to start with, namely, that all those things that we conceived very clearly and distinctly are true, is assured only because God is or exists, he is a perfect being, and everything in us comes from him. From this it follows that our ideas and notions, being real things that come from God *insofar as they are clear and distinct,* to that extent cannot fail to be true. Consequently, though we often have ideas that contain falsity, they can only be those ideas that contain some confusion and obscurity because they participate in nothingness, meaning that they are as confused in us as we are not wholly perfect. It is evident that it is no less repugnant to assume that falsity or imperfection as such is derived from God than that truth or perfection is derived from nothingness. But if we did not know that all reality and truth came from a perfect and infinite being, however clear and distinct our ideas may be, we would have no reason to be assured that they were endowed with the perfection of being true."[59]

Meditation III, whose entire investigation rests on the appreciation of degrees of objective reality of ideas by means of the idea of the perfect, and which establishes the degree of clearness and distinctness of ideas upon their degree of objective reality, is sustained by this intuition.

Finally, this intrinsic justification of divine veracity through the identification of being and truth, and the necessary exclusion of all falsity outside God, in virtue of the necessary exclusion of nothingness from the Supreme Being, confirms that the true foundation of divine veracity is not goodness, but the very being itself or omnipotence of God: goodness does not have to limit omnipotence in this respect, since by definition, omnipotence excludes deception. God *cannot create* anything other than the true; he *can never* deceive. The recourse to God's goodness as the foundation of his veracity therefore belongs to the order of extrinsic reasons. The metaphysical reasons of a theodicy based on the relations between incomprehensibility and divine perfection had already led us to the same conclusion.

The psychological investigation has fulfilled the goals that had given birth to it—the psychological and metaphysical possibility of error is completely explained and God's responsibility is completely set aside. I cannot reproach God for having given me a finite understanding, since I am a finite being, and I cannot reproach him for having given me an infinite will, since, in this case, nothing more perfect could have been given to me. I must thank him for having given me the small amount of perfection that is mine and the means to avoid error, by suspending my judgment when I do not have clear and distinct knowledge.[60] Divine veracity is completely safeguarded. The duel between the universal principle (divine veracity) and the exception in fact (error) concludes with the complete victory of the universal principle, in opposition to what happened during the duel between the principle of universal deception (the evil genius) and the exception in fact constituted by the Cogito, in which the universal principle was completely destroyed.

8. New Final Recourse to the Theodicy

But although God is neither the direct positive cause nor the indirect positive cause of error, and although he had not wished that I be deceived, error, which is indisputably something evil, does exist, nevertheless. And since God has the supreme power to do everything, could he not have created me such that I never fail, either by giving my understanding a clear and distinct intelligence of all the things about which I could ever deliberate, "or by always maintaining before my mind the resolution never to judge about anything without being able to know it clearly and distinctly?"[61] Since nothing can contradict his omnipotence, if error exists, it is because he has allowed it. And is one not responsible for the evil one has allowed, if one has the power not to allow it?[62]

This final question requires psychology to yield the stage again to metaphysics. And metaphysics does not furnish any other answer than the one it has already furnished,[63] when advancing the principles of sufficient reason and of the best, together with considerations about the whole of the universe. There is no more sufficient reason for God to have accumulated all possible perfections in me alone than there is for the human body to be covered with eyes, under the guise that there is no portion of the body more handsome than the eye. There is, on the contrary, a sufficient reason drawn from the principle of the best for "certain parts of the universe, and man in particular, not to have all the perfections,[64] for the good of the universe, because the universe is undeniably more perfect for having a greater diversity in its totality, through the defect of some of its parts"[65]—an argument that Leibniz will repeat ad infinitum. Thus the solution can only be achieved by an explicit appeal to the subordination of God's action on account of his being and his creation, meaning his perfection, which, establishing his incomprehensibility, includes it in its notion and thus limits its scope. Thus the doctrine of the impenetrable aims of God seems to be specified, not as a total negation of all aims for God, but as the impossibility for us to "examine" them. In fact, if we must admit that in virtue of his perfection, God refers the imperfection of the parts of his work to the perfection of the whole, we must also admit that we cannot know whether he acts according to his ends, and even whether these ends are for the best. The negation with respect to these divine ends begins only with respect to our asking ourselves what are these best ends and how does God realize them; error, on the other hand, begins only when one supposedly discovers in God's work, meaning in physical and natural things, a finality that is accessible only for an infinite understanding.[66]

9. Results of the Intersecting Solutions

The general problem of error has been resolved, as we have just seen, by going back and forth between metaphysics and psychology, stopping only when the double solution to a double problem is discovered at once. We should not be surprised if this solution entailed a multitude of complex results.

Above and beyond the metaphysical result, which is to confirm divine veracity while making room for error, it entails consequences on epistemic, psychological, methodological, and moral planes.

On the epistemic plane, the explanation of the possibility of error allows the distinction between the true and the false to be established solidly, a distinction without which no human science is either possible or conceivable.

On the psychological plane, the mechanism of the phenomenon is revealed.

On the methodological plane, the knowledge of this mechanism allows one to discover the subjective conditions of the knowledge of the true, about which *Meditation III* had established objective conditions: Never pass judgment on something without conceiving it clearly and distinctly; as long as such a conception is not attained, engrave that rule on my mind; concentrate my attention on what I conceive perfectly in order to separate it from what I conceive only obscurely and confusedly.[67]

Meditation III, by discovering the principle of truth in being, guaranteed certainty and established the objective possibility of science. *Meditation IV*, by discovering the principle of error in nothingness, reveals to man the conditions of access to certainty and establishes the subjective possibility of science. It establishes the method metaphysically by basing itself on the nature of God and the nature of the human mind at the same time. Thus, these two truths (God and the soul) doubly appear as the foundation of all the other truths; on the one hand, they furnish the principle of true objects, and on the other hand, they furnish the principle of true judgments, that is, of rules by which the subject can grasp only true objects. The progress in this chain of reasons beginning with God, with an eye toward bringing the reality of objects and science (essence and existence of bodies) into the domain of knowledge, was not possible as long as the philosopher, assured by *Meditation III* that there is only truth in the world, did not have the technique that allowed him to attain it "by ridding himself *of all doubts*"[68]—doubts having no root other than the principle of error itself, the nothingness symbolized by the evil genius, the principle of radical doubt.

On the moral plane, "the discovery of the cause of falsity and errors" gives me the possibility to acquire the habit of not failing and confers on me "the greatest and principal perfection of human beings,"[69] a perfection that is such by itself and because of its consequences on moral action, since "it suffices to judge well in order to act well."[70]

However, despite this important result for practical morality, there is a plane upon which the theory of error has no consequence: the plane of ethico-religious metaphysics. As suggestive as the theory of freedom can be in its depth, as important as is the role that it imparts, in fact, to free will in the edification of human knowledge, the theory is considered only within some strict limits with respect to the psychological phenomenon, also considered only with respect to the solution of the problem of a theodicy posed by the existence of this phenomenon. The problem of man's fallibility in his use of free will, which engenders the often debated question of *divine permission* for error, fault, and sin (which also gives rise to extremely vast and varied theories and controversies for Arnauld, Malebranche, and Leibniz), is resolved in a few sentences by an appeal to the perfection of the whole of the universe. There is not even the least reference to the situation resulting from this for man, to a possible function of fallibility in the acquisition of a higher spiritual or moral value by means of effort and fight; nor is there even a reference to the eventual superior merit of a morality that is gained and of a science that is acquired, over the merit of simple innocence, and a science that is completely given. This deliberate abstention (Descartes explains it on three separate occasions)[71] with respect to an implicit problem that is so manifestly posed, given that the word *sin* comes several times from Descartes' pen at the same time as the word *error*,[72] cannot be explained simply by a prudential worry about questions concerning theology. Care with respect to this topic will not stop either Arnauld or Malebranche; and when the question is dear to him, for example, when he is dealing with questions of physics, Descartes does not hesitate to assume great risks. The abstention derives from the fact that Descartes does not consider the ethico-religious problem one of his primary preoccupations, and the fact that his interest in morality is limited to the extent that it depends on science and could be ultimately reduced to medicine (or at least that is his hope), or in any case, could be reduced to the technique of passions. Descartes has no care other than to establish the possibility and certainty of a universal system of science, which to him is the only measure of wisdom. That is why *Meditation IV* draws from the examination of error and freedom nothing more than conclusions of method. As Descartes has told us, the *Meditations* concern only the "main points"[73] of his philosophy. If he devotes only two pages to our infinite will, without saying anything about the ethico-religious problems posed by freedom, nor about the elements that the former can furnish in order to resolve the difficulties of theodicy raised by the existence of error, it is because the ethico-religious problem does not figure among the "main points" of his philosophy. These main points can be reduced to three: the existence of the soul, the existence of God, and the existence of bodies; they constitute all the phases of the only problem that Descartes considered as fundamental in his philosophy, the problem of knowledge: first certainty and first criterion of truth, foundation of the objective validity of ideas, objective validity of clear and distinct ideas relative to the essence of material things, objective validity of obscure and confused ideas relative to their existence.

The order of reasons and the proportions between the parts of the whole work add to Descartes' assertions in order to dissuade us from treating, against his wish, his philosophy according to the order of topics and not according to the order of reasons, to inflect his philosophy in a direction that, although it is the direction of some contemporary philosophical preoccupations, is certainly not Descartes' direction.

10. The Order Constrains *Meditation IV* to Treat Only a Portion of the Problem of Error

Although the problem of error is resolved essentially in *Meditation IV*, it is not, however, resolved in its entirety. The order requires that it is treated at two different places on the chain of reasons, in *Meditation IV* and in *Meditation VI*, in the same way that the order requires the problem of God to be treated twice, separately, in *Meditation III* and *Meditation V*.

It was both possible and necessary to pose and resolve in principle the problem of error, once a first notion of what is intrinsic truth was acquired by *Meditation III*. That is why, as soon as truth was defined in its foundation as certain objective reality of the clear and distinct idea proper to the understanding, we had to ask ourselves in what could formal falsity consist and how formal falsity is possible, both in fact, psychologically in man, and as a rule, metaphysically, from the point of view of an absolutely veracious God.

But it was impossible to go farther, since for the understanding, the point of view from which I am uniquely situated, only clear and distinct ideas can be guaranteed by God and be reputed true. In fact, I am only sure with respect to them alone that they have objective reality and that consequently God is their author—God being necessarily the author of what is real and of only what is real. Thus, from the fact that I now understand the reason why my understanding *naturally* considers only clear and distinct ideas as true, I understand why it must exclude sensible ideas from truth: it is because it must, at this point on the chain of reasons, deprive them of God's guarantee, since they are lacking sufficient objective reality in order that this guarantee be given to them. Since sensible ideas are thus stripped of any truth, it seems that there cannot be any error in us consisting of mistaking their truth. There is no other conceivable error, at this point on the chain, except an error committed against the truth of the ideas of the understanding, either by an usurpation of them by sensible ideas being taken as them, or by a contamination of the clearness and distinctness of the ideas of the understanding, due to their mixing with sensible ideas.

And even if the truth recognized with respect to clear and distinct ideas remained theirs exclusively, for they alone reveal to us the true nature of things, the investigation would not stop there, since it must exhaust the entire content of consciousness. If, with respect to the truth concerning the nature of things, and from the point of view of the understanding, error appeared legitimately as a confusion of being and nothingness, is that to say, once the source of this confusion is recognized in the confusion of clear and distinct ideas with sensible ideas, that sensible ideas must be assimilated to absolute nothingness? Of course, they are pure nothingness and pure falsity with respect to the truth concerning the nature of things, meaning *with respect* to the truth of the ideas of my understanding; but my understanding does not go so far as to affirm that they are—as objective reality—an *absolute* nothingness; it simply notices that *it does not know whether they are something or nothing.* And if it happened that they were something— however little—they would necessarily have God as their author; they would necessarily have some truth to which God's guarantee would extend. Then the problem of error would be posed with respect to this guarantee, for the truth of sensation could be mistaken just as much as the truth of the understanding, and it could happen that the understanding appears as the falsifier of this truth, in the same way that sensation appeared as the falsifier of the truth of clear and distinct ideas in the realm of the understanding. Finally, it could happen that the understanding, considering itself as the only positive thing, rejects as a pure negative the truth of sensation that is foreign to it (in the same way that sensation rejected it as negative with respect to its own teachings, by considering itself as positive), and that thus, in order to attain the truth of sensation, we must take the same precautions against the understanding that we took against the senses in order to attain the truth of the understanding. If, in order to reach the truth of the understanding, we had to close ourselves to the senses—"shut our eyes, plug up our ears, etc."—in order to reach the truth of sensation, must we not shut ourselves from the understanding in order to deliver ourselves to only pure living, which is only authentic when it is dissociated from everything that is not itself?[74] But it is clear that this aspect of error relative to the senses cannot manifest itself as long as the linkage of reasons has not led us to the point at which it would be possible and necessary to determine if and to what extent sensible ideas have some reality and truth, in the same way that the problem of error in the realm of the understanding *(Meditation IV)* could not be posited as long as we had not established that clear and distinct ideas are realities having God as their author, and consequently are truths guaranteed by his veracity *(Meditation III).* In brief, in the same way that the problem of error could not be posed in the region of the understanding as long as the existence of God had not been demonstrated (the foundation of the objective validity of clear and distinct ideas), the problem of error cannot be posed with respect to the region of the senses as long as the existence of bodies has not been demonstrated (the foundation of this substitute for objective validity, which is completely different from the objective validity of intellectual ideas), and as long as the specific truth of living that will be attributed to the sensible ideas has not been demonstrated. Thus, the error defined and treated from the point of view of the understanding in *Meditation IV* will have to await *Meditation VI* in order to be defined and treated from the point of view of sensation.

11. Remarks on the Infinity of Human Will

The infinity of human will is a complex concept in Descartes' philosophy.

This infinity assumes three forms:

1) Infinity in extension as the capacity to apply oneself actually to all possible objects: "Will can seem infinite in some way, because we do not perceive anything that can be the object of some other will, even of the immensity of will that is in God, to which our will cannot extend."[75] This ability of will to be extended to infinity contrasts with the finiteness of our understanding; there is nothing that the will cannot deny or affirm.

2) Infinity in extension as infinite aspiration toward something else that man does not have: "Each person's desire to have all the perfections that he can conceive and consequently all the perfections that we can see in God arises from the fact that God has given us a will that has no limit. And it is principally because of this *infinite will in us that one can say that he has created us in his own image.*"[76]

3) Infinity as absoluteness: the absolute decisive power of *yes* or of *no,* which is an indivisible[77] "freedom of free will . . . which consists only in that we can do a given thing or not do it, that is, in that we can affirm or deny it. . . ."[78] Descartes reserves resemblance with God for this kind of infinity in the *Meditations:* "There is only will alone, or the freedom of free will alone, that I experience to be so great in myself that I cannot conceive the idea of any other more ample and more extended, so that this is what principally allows me to know that I am made in the image and likeness of God."[79] On the other hand, the infinite aspiration is not here conceived as that by which I resemble God, as it was in the *Letter to Mersenne* previously cited, but as

that by which I differ from him: "When I reflect upon myself, not only do I know that I am an imperfect thing, incomplete and dependent on some other being, *a being that strives and aspires constantly to become better and greater than I now am,* but also at the same time I know that the being upon which I depend has in itself all these great things to which I aspire and whose ideas I find in myself, and has these qualities, not indefinitely and potentially, but has them actually and in fact, and thus that he is God."[80] It is true that in the *Letter to Mersenne,* Descartes did not identify aspiration with our limitless will; consequently, he did not make of the latter the principle of aspiration. In fact if this limitless will was manifested only under the form of an aspiration, it is because it is limited in its power and cannot give itself all the perfections that the subject conceives—as God can. In any case, since aspiration is only something indefinite, it cannot be an adequate image of a true infinity, but only its degraded reflection. From all the evidence, what conditions the judgment that I bring on the infinity of my will and the knowledge of the various aspects of this infinity (indefiniteness of extension and of aspiration, absolute infinity of the decisive power), as well as the knowledge of the differences that separate this infinity from the infinitely infinite infinity of God, is the innate *idea* of the infinitely infinite, the unity of all perfections and infinities, whose definition is given in *Meditation III.*[81] Hence this idea cannot be drawn from the infinity of my will, not only because my will is only an infinity of a certain kind *(in suo genere perfecta),*[82] but also because my will could not be known as infinite in me as in God, unless I first possessed in me the representation of divine infinity with respect to which I can evaluate my own will and judge that it resembles God's.

We must now remark that the contrast between will as infinite and the finite understanding is not with respect to infinity characterized "formally and precisely in itself," meaning the indivisible absoluteness of the act of denying or affirming, but with respect to its infinity in extension, meaning the power it has to extend itself to an infinity of things to which understanding does not extend,[83] in keeping with the phrasing of article 35 of part I of the *Principles.* And it is not through its capacity of indefinite extension that will can be said to resemble God, but only through its absolute faculty of deciding. In fact, the extension of God's will is indefinitely greater than the extension of my will: "Even though it [the will— M. G.] is incomparably greater in God than in myself, either because of the knowledge and the power joined to it, . . . or because of its object, since *it applies and extends to infinitely many things,* nevertheless it does not seem any greater when I consider it formally and precisely in itself."[84] One sees in this way that the absolute infinity of will, taken formally and precisely, does not constitute the principal explicative factor of the psychological possibility of error with respect to the understanding. It is the disproportion between the respective *extensions* of the two faculties that is the key to the problem.

On the other hand, the absolute decisiveness constitutes the principal factor allowing one to safeguard, in this case, God's lack of responsibility and his veracity. The fundamental indifference or absolute decisiveness of free will intervenes in the psychological explanation of error only to establish the act of judgment itself and to account for the extreme ease by which will errs before what it does not understand. In fact, indifference is then carried to a maximum: "I extend it [the will—M. G.] also to things I do not understand; since it is in itself indifferent to such things, it is easily led astray and chooses the false for the true."[85] From this results the link with true judgment and the *minimum* of indifference, from which freedom is carried to the *maximum,* etc.

This inverse proportion between indifference and freedom seems to entail a conception of freedom as a spontaneity capable of degrees, which constrasts with the conception of freedom as free will constituting an indivisible by its absolute indifference. This engenders the accusation that Descartes upheld contradictory doctrines or that his thought evolved with respect to this matter. In truth, he does not contradict himself, and his thoughts have not evolved either. He has distinguished two kinds of indifference, one due to the weakness of our understanding and the other due to the positive power that essentially constitutes my freedom.[86] The indifference constituting the absoluteness by which human will is truly infinite and resembles God's will (which nothing determines) must subsist in the most enlightened choice, meaning in the most indifferent one, otherwise my will would stop being the image of divine will. That is why there always remains the metaphysical possibility of denying what we know clearly and distinctly as true.[87] The fact that in man will is always something like a receptive form with respect to a content (the truths constituted by God) does not eliminate the reality of that form. And the subsistence of that faculty in all cases in no way implies indifference with respect to reasons for choosing. A faculty goes through exercises that must be determined by clear and distinct ideas, without being abolished by them, because it tends to be determined in the most internal fashion, and the choice that depends on clear and distinct ideas is the most internal choice, meaning it is the most consonant with its own nature. We thus understand how the definition of absolute freedom seemingly leads to that of pure spontaneity and why, however, even when one can only adhere to what the understanding shows us clearly and distinctly, freedom keeps its specificity, meaning the essential indifference that is not suppressed by the determination that it contracts, but is manifested most deeply within itself by its agreement with clear and distinct reasons, the reasons that are most consonant with it. Although in Spinoza's philosophy the element of indetermination (which in itself is purely apparent, in any case) vanishes when clear and distinct ideas are present, it always remains in Descartes' philosophy. The Cartesian conception of freedom, with its dual aspect of indifference and spontaneity, is therefore completely coherent. And we can observe no evolution of thoughts about this matter from the *Meditations* to the *Letter to Mesland.*

12. A Remark on the Finiteness of Human Understanding

The concept of the finiteness of human understanding is no less complex than the concept of the infinity of human will. Are we concerned with finiteness strictly speaking, or with indefiniteness? Descartes' texts are not always in agreement on this point. In *Meditation IV* we are concerned with a finiteness, strictly speaking: "If I consider the faculty of conceiving that is in me, I find that it is of very small extent and greatly limited."[88] But elsewhere he speaks a different language; only the imagination has narrow limits, while the understanding is conceived as quasi-unlimited: "Whatever we conceive without an image is an idea of the pure mind, and whatever we conceive with an image is an idea of the imagination. And since the imagination is tightly and narrowly limited, *while our mind has hardly any limits,*[89] there are very few things, even material things, which we can imagine, even though we are capable of conceiving them."[90]

First we have to note that it is not necessary to render the understanding into a radically and tightly finite faculty in order to oppose it to will; it is sufficient that will has a greater amplitude than it.[91] Then the understanding would not need to be finite in the sense in which we say that the imagination is finite, for the capacity to imagine is enclosed in somewhat material limits from which the understanding is completely exempted. In fact, the imagination is conditioned by the need we have to etch with the tip of our mind the details of the representations we imagine on the pineal gland. This operation, which is possible as long as the details of these representations are not numerous, quickly exceeds our capacity when the details are numerous. Thus it is easy for the soul to etch a three-sided figure on the gland; but it is more difficult to etch an eight- or twelve-sided polygon. The operation becomes radically impracticable with respect to a chiliagon. When, on the other hand, the understanding considers these figures, it considers them easily, whatever is the multiplicity of their sides (and even an indefinite multiplicity) because it knows them by the *single reason* that defines them.[92] Thus the capacity to conceive ideas is not finite in this respect; geometric proportions, properties of numbers, mathematical truths, and series of ratios are infinite, and are offered without limit to our understanding, which has before it some perspectives of an infinite series. That is the idea of the infinite fecundity of intelligence that appears at each instant in the *Rules.* However, even in this respect, the understanding is not truly infinite, but indefinite. It can always push its knowledge farther, but it can never possess actually the infinite plenitude of knowledge. Moreover, it never happens to know *in fact* what it can know in principle. Finally, there are things that it can never know *as a rule,* unless it were God, whose infinity in actuality entails incomprehensibility. In this respect, the understanding appears encumbered by a formal finiteness. Finally, we must distinguish between the infinity of ideas in the understanding and the understanding's capacity to grasp them, which is extremely limited. The understanding can have only a small number of intuitions at the same time; it cannot give itself instantaneously to the chain of reasons; and this chain is often too long for the understanding to perceive it at once or completely. From this arises the necessity for the understanding to develop itself over time and to have recourse to memory. From these finite aspects, which are disabilities, the understanding derives the inability to remain fixed on a single thing, and never to know more than a small number of clear and distinct things at the same time, save only one, in conformity with the principle of the conservation of the same quantity of thought.[93] It is clear that, in all these respects, will appears as without limit, for it can instantaneously act on all the ideas of objects that the understanding knows, has known and no longer knows, does not yet know, cannot yet know, and will never know, and actually put forth a verdict of yes or no.

CHAPTER VIII

Essences (of Material Things and of God)

1. The Place of the Problem of Essences in the Order

Having in his possession the criterion of truth and the techniques indispensable in order to avoid error, Descartes can now methodically go from the first truth that is objectively valid to secondary truths and, following the analytic order of reasons, establish the two degrees of science: mathematics and universal physics (and subsidiarily, medicine, psychology of passions, and morality). These two degrees correspond with the two possible objects of our knowledge of external things: essences of material things or mathematical ideas, and existences of material things brought to us by sensible ideas.

Before we had established divine veracity, there corresponded two kinds of doubts for each of these two kinds of objects: a hyperbolic doubt based on the nature of things, ranging over sensible realities; a hyperbolic doubt rising out of the fiction of the evil genius, alone capable of striking at mathematical objects; and a metaphysical doubt extending also to the sphere of sensible knowledge, adding itself upon and reinforcing the hyperbolic doubts arising from the doubts that sensible knowledge aroused naturally. The refutation of the hypothesis of the evil genius, and the substitution of the thesis of divine veracity for this hypothesis, radically abolishes the doubt that struck at mathematical ideas. As for sensible ideas, they are also delivered from the hypothesis that metaphysical doubt had weighing on them. But they remain under other hyperbolic doubts, those rising from natural reasons, which justify the obscurity and confusion explained and established by the nothingness contained by these ideas for our understanding. Under these conditions, the universality of divine veracity enters into a necessary conflict with these doubts and puts their legitimacy into question. Moreover, since the presence of obscure and confused ideas in us is possible only because they are not pure nothingness, it seems that something true must correspond with the little reality that they imply.

Meditation V and *Meditation VI* will be devoted in turn to these two kinds of ideas, to these two sciences that correspond to the essence of material things, on the one hand, and to their existence, on the other. These two Meditations will therefore be entirely devoted to the foundation of knowledge relative to material things. In this respect, in contrast to what occurred in *Meditation IV,* the epistemic preoccupation takes over the stage and suppresses metaphysical-theological preoccupations. Setting aside the ontological proof, for which we will soon see why it is placed in a *Meditation* reserved for mathematical essences, we are concerned with completing the founding of science by means of divine veracity.

Nevertheless, the metaphysical preoccupation cannot disappear completely, since divine veracity itself cannot be fully confirmed until the doubts based on natural reasons, doubts that are antagonistic to divine veracity and that strike at sensible knowledge or obscure and confused ideas, are effectively reduced. In fact, God is veracious; it is impossible that he deceives me by putting these ideas in me, ideas that in addition can be in me only because they have some reality. It is therefore necessary to destroy all doubts that strike at them. From this arises the intent stated by Descartes at the beginning of *Meditation V:* "My principal task is to attempt to escape and relieve myself *from all the doubts* into which I have fallen in these last few days, and to see whether we can know anything for certain about material objects."[1] *All the doubts,* meaning not only those that struck at mathematical ideas, but also those that struck at sensible ideas. The necessity to banish *all doubts* is twofold: it is imposed first with respect to God, for, if sensible knowledge must finally be recognized as completely false, or irreparably doubtful, we could no longer affirm God's veracity or the perfection of his work within the frame in which his own perfection determines it necessarily; it is also imposed with respect to science, for, if material things cannot be affirmed as real, physics would become purely illusory, while the existence of sensible experience itself would become radically and definitively unintelligible.

The program of *Meditations V* and *VI* is therefore completely determined by the task of eliminating all doubts, that is, by giving divine veracity its full value. But this task has different degrees of difficulty depending upon whether we are concerned with doubts about mathematical ideas or doubts about sensible ideas. In the first case, the difficulty is of small magnitude: by its presence divine veracity can abolish metaphysical doubt and restore ipso facto the objective validity that the understanding naturally accorded to mathematical ideas by confirming this validity. In the second case, the difficulty is particularly difficult and delicate, since the presence of divine veracity is not sufficient in itself to destroy the hyperbolic doubts that the nature of the object raises, and since the analysis of these obscure and confused ideas has established these doubts philosophically on their infinitely small degree of objective reality. Thus, the proof of their existence requires a lengthy development while the proof of the essence of material things is drawn up in a few words. Moreover, although it is true that *Meditation V,* by establishing the foundation of mathematics, also establishes the basis of physics, to the extent that the reality of physical objects is reduced to the intelligible reality of geometrical objects, physics cannot be established, however, if we do not succeed in granting a *minimum* of truth to sensible knowledge, by reserving for it the privilege of furnishing us with the knowledge of the existence of material things—if we do not legitimate, within some precise limits, sensible experience as an indispensable instrument for the construction of the science of existing material things. Already these limits have been glimpsed: this experience could not allow us to attribute a sensible property to things, nor could it explain them by sensible combinations; it serves only to put us before the physical universe that God has decided to create freely under the form that it takes—a universe that we cannot know intelligibly by analysis except as the result of a certain number of geometrical and mechanical combinations.

2. Proof of the Objective Validity of the Truths Derived from Mathematical Essences

Meditation V scientifically restores the truth of mathematical essences; by establishing this truth, it raises us to the plane of the *Rules,* that is, to the plane of geometry and arithmetic, considered as indubitable sciences to which all others will have to be referred in some way in order for them to accede to certainty. It suffices that divine veracity has destroyed metaphysical doubt in order for mathematical ideas to recover automatically the *natural* certainty that the *Rules* recognized of mathematical ideas, that every man attributes spontaneously to them, and that no natural doubt can shake up since, even before I had demonstrated God's [existence], "The nature of my mind is such that I cannot prevent myself from thinking them true while I am conceiving them clearly and distinctly."[2] Henceforth I know that I was right to grant objective validity to mathematical ideas. Not only do I see now that they are true, but I also understand why they are true without having to know whether something exists corresponding to them in nature. In fact, I know, in all certainty, that since they are clear and distinct, they are entirely real; and everything real is true, as is God in which the real participates. We are concerned here with an intrinsic truth based on authentic intelligible reality. The objective validity of an idea is completely independent from the existence of something in nature, because it is based on the unquestionable presence of an objective reality in it, on the internal reason of its being that is in itself independent of this existence. Instead of being based on existence, existence is based on it. Thus clear and distinct ideas are innate, since they depend only on my understanding—which certifies the fact that many mathematical notions or figures are such that they could never fall under my senses.[3] Moreover, in the same way that divine veracity allows me to affirm their objective validity in all certainty now, it allows me to affirm in all certainty that all the properties I perceive clearly and distinctly as belonging to their nature are true, that is, belong effectively to them. Arithmetic and geometry are therefore completely established.[4]

3. Proof of the Objective Validity of the Truths Derived from God's Essence: Validation of the a priori Proof of God's Existence (Ontological Proof)

At the same time, the a priori proof (the ontological proof) is completely established. I discover the idea of God among all the clear and distinct ideas I perceive in me. What is valid for all the other clear and distinct ideas (the idea of a figure or a number, for example) is also valid for the idea of God. I can therefore attribute existence necessarily to the nature of God—since this property is clearly and distinctly perceived as belonging necessarily to his notion—with as much certainty as I attribute a property that I perceive clearly and distinctly as belonging to a figure or a number. Thus God exists.[5]

The ontological proof is therefore as certain as a mathematical proof, for from the point of view of the analytic order of reasons, it is exactly of the same order. Consequently, it cannot be invoked validly as long as mathematical truths have not been established, meaning as long as the objective validity of clear and distinct ideas has not been established. But that is precisely what has been accomplished, for, as Descartes tells us, "I have *already amply demonstrated* above that everything I know clearly and distinctly is true."[6] Also, he adds, *"now"*[7] the ontological proof is possible. Without this preliminary demonstration, mathematics, and generally the truth of clear and distinct ideas, would be affected by metaphysical doubt. The evil genius would prevent us from attributing to them the least objective validity. The ontological proof would therefore be doubtful, as would mathematical truths and their demonstrations. It would be struck by the same metaphysical doubt that cannot be abolished unless I already possessed the certainty of a veracious God. And we can add that the proof would not convince an atheist, for since the atheist doubts God, he cannot be assured of the objective validity of the clear and distinct ideas that this proof presumes acquired.

Nevertheless, without this preliminary demonstration and lacking absolute metaphysical certainty, the ontological proof would preserve the natural certainty that attaches spontaneously to truths of arithmetic and geometry, that is, the certainty that cannot be reached by any natural doubt inspired by the thing itself and arising "from the nature of our mind": I also "would not be able to keep myself from thinking it true while I conceive it clearly and distinctly."[8] That is why "even if everything I concluded in the preceding *Meditations*[9] were not true, the existence of God should pass in my mind *as at least as certain as I have hitherto considered all the truths of mathematics, which only deal with numbers and figures.*"[10] In brief, if we had not already established the objective validity of clear and distinct ideas by means of the proof by effects, the ontological proof would have neither more nor less validity than mathematical truths.

It would not *be more certain* than they, since it would no more escape metaphysical doubt than they do.[11] It would not *be less certain* than they, since like them, it would escape the doubt based on natural reasons. The fact that it is less manifestly known than any of the properties of mathematical notions would not diminish its certainty, no more than the great difficulty one has in establishing the property of the square of the hypotenuse of a right triangle would render this property less certain than the more easily known property of the necessary opposition of the largest side of this triangle with its largest angle. Once the demonstration has been accomplished and the property recognized, "we are as convinced of the truth of the one as of the other."[12] In addition, even from this point of view, when considering the natural order of notions, we would have to recognize that this property that God has of existing would be more manifestly known than any property of any mathematical notion whatever. Since the idea of God is "the first and principal"[13] of my clear and distinct ideas, and since it is intrinsically the clearest, given that it is the most real, it is in itself more manifestly known and more easily known,[14] since it comes before all other ideas that depend on it and participate in it. In fact, if it does not seem to be thus, it is in virtue of a contingent circumstance with respect to it, namely, the unfortunate presence of images of sensible things in us. Even though these images, instead of bothering the mathematician, offer some sort of support for him, materializing extension for him, in some way, and even though they agree with geometrical notions, they disturb the intuition of the idea of God, for they do not entirely agree with metaphysical notions.[15] But once this idea is recognized, it appears to me as evident and as certain as geometrical truths, which are in fact more accessible for most men. One could then affirm that, *in the sphere of knowledge based on essences,* it is the most certain truth of all, since, once I grasp it, I perceive that the certainty of mathematical truths and, generally, that the certainty of all truths, depends absolutely on it and is rendered possible by it.[16]

4. The Place of the a prior Proof in the Order; the Simultaneous Validation of Mathematical Demonstrations and the Ontological Proof

In brief, even if, after it has been accomplished, it allows us to attain a higher certainty than geometric truths, the ontological proof remains no less situated *within the same sphere,* insofar as it is subject to the same preliminary conditions as these truths, that is, it is subject to the demonstration of the objective validity of clear and distinct ideas. And this demonstration has been supplied by the proof of God by effects. This latter proof did not need to have recourse to the objective validity of any essence whatsoever in order to be accomplished. By simply relying on the objective reality immediately perceived in the considered idea, it came to attribute necessarily to the principle of this reality the veracious God who abolished the hypothesis of the evil genius as well as the metaphysical doubt striking at the objective validity of mathematical knowledge and, generally, the knowledge of all essences.

Under these conditions, we understand that the ontological proof must come after the proof by effects in the order and that it must not be developed in the same *Meditation* as the latter. Each *Meditation* constitutes a link in the chain of reasons.[17] *Meditation III* belongs to the first link of the chain of objectively valid certainties. It exhibits the absolute reason, which, while instaurating absolute certainty, establishes the objective validity of essences. The ontological proof, which relies on the consideration of an essence, belongs to the secondary reasons. It comes under the jurisdiction of the reason that establishes the truth with respect to the knowledge of essences. It therefore must be inscribed necessarily in the *Meditation* that takes as task to extend to all of our clear and distinct ideas, whatever they may be, the benefit of absolute certainty possessed by the first reason, in order expressly to uproot metaphysical doubt in this way. Once this doubt is destroyed, the task imposed, in fact, was to examine the consequences resulting from the instauration of a universal veracity for the various degrees of knowledge (essences, sensible ideas). First, clear and distinct ideas regain the objective validity that they had lost. And the consequences of this recovery must extend to all essences, as much to essences of material things as to God's essence, which is the "first" essence.

Thus placing the ontological proof within a *Meditation* devoted expressly and primarily to *the essence of material things* (which is disconcerting at first) appears, once we are aware of the order of reasons, as natural and necessary: *Meditation V* is devoted to essences; it must therefore consider the essence of God as well as the essence of material things. It must use what they have in common: an assured objective validity, and subsidiarily, it must specify what they have that is different: the finiteness of the latter entailing only possible existence in all certainty and the infinity of the former entailing necessary existence in all certainty.

We cannot therefore ascribe to the opinion of those who, like Hamelin,[18] explain the place of the ontological proof as "an unexpected encounter" and attribute it to the happenstance of a biographical event recounted by the *Meditations*. Despite its personal affect, the biographic itinerary of the *Meditations* is not the pragmatic history of contingent discoveries, but the necessary chronology of intellectual proceedings that, in opposition with sensible obstacles, progress toward truth. The "order of invention" or the "order of discovery" is not a disconcerting *succession* of fortuitous discoveries, but an *order,* meaning, as in mathematics, the necessary and rigorous production of reasons one by the other. It is, as

Descartes states, the order according to which the thing has been "invented *methodically*," and he adds, *"tamquam a priori."*[19] Only the dissimilarity between sensible and metaphysical notions imparts to the philosophical process, in order for it to succeed, the appearance of an intellectual exercise, the specific and personal accent of a *Meditation* that is alien to treatises on geometry.[20]

5. The Priority of the Proof by Effects, the One and Only Proof for the Existence of God

Since the validity of the ontological proof is conditioned by the proof from effects, as is the validity of mathematics, and since the latter belongs to the primary reason and the former belongs to the secondary reason, according to the order, as a result, the ontological proof, being derived from the proof by effects, cannot subsist without it,[21] while the proof from effects can subsist without the ontological proof. Consequently, the proof by effects must be considered as the principal and even sole proof of the existence of God. This conclusion is expressly emphasized by Descartes: "I think that it is manifest to everyone that consideration of the efficient cause is the first and principal means, if not to say the only means, that we have to prove the existence of God."[22] The proof considering the efficient cause is the only proof, in fact, that is capable of demonstrating the objective validity of clear and distinct ideas, the only one capable of being established without having recourse to the objective validity of clear and distinct ideas. It escapes the vicious circle, and, by establishing the ontological proof, it allows it to escape the circle also.

6. Discussion of the Eventual Self-sufficiency of the a priori Proof

But, in a different perspective than the one we have just assumed, can we not think that God's essence is of such nature and so different from other essences that it is sufficient for us to have a clear and distinct intuition of it in order for us to perceive immediately that it possesses objective validity in itself? Under these conditions, the conclusions that we could draw from it relative to its necessary properties would be unquestionably valid for the thing itself, without having it necessarily referred, in this case, to the proof by effects conceived as the preliminary condition of any affirmation of the objective validity of our ideas. In other words, the simple view of the essence of God would be sufficient to abolish all possibility of metaphysical doubt.[23] The intuition of the essence of God constrains me, in fact, to attribute necessarily to the perfect being all the perfections, that is, not only existence, but also veracity. Consequently it brings me at the same time the objective validity of the idea and the absolute guarantee of that validity. In this way it differs from the intuition of mathematical essence, which no more implies the necessity of the existence of its object than it entails a guarantee against universal deception—therefore leaving me with metaphysical doubt as soon as its intuition is substituted for by the memory of its intuition. In brief, if the natural certainty attached to clear and distinct ideas allows me to discover in one of these ideas a truth such that no metaphysical doubt can threaten, would not the natural certainty of this truth be ipso facto protected from metaphysical doubt? Having thus abolished this doubt, could one not, at the same time, absolve the other clearly and distinctly perceived truths and thus render metaphysically certain the science of essences?

And does not the above conclusion seem expressly developed by Descartes toward the end of *Meditation V?* In fact, he first notes that the memory of evidence is struck by metaphysical doubt with respect to mathematical truths, but escapes it necessarily with respect to the clear and distinct knowledge of the necessary existence of the perfect God. He then adds that once this knowledge is acquired doubt can no longer remain with respect to mathematical truths.[24]

God's essence would thus be in the same situation as the Cogito with respect to mathematical notions: the content of the Cogito is such that it guarantees me the certainty of my certainty. When I say "I think therefore I am," I am both certain of this truth and certain that it is impossible that I am deceived in this case; when, on the other hand, I say "the sum of the angles of a triangle is equal to two right angles," I am certain of this truth, but I cannot derive from the triangle itself anything that guarantees me that my incontestable certainty is not in itself deceptive, in this case. And, when I say "God's essence necessarily entails existence," I am certain of this truth, and I am also certain that I am not deceived in this certainty, for the object—God—being veracious, immediately guarantees that such a deception is impossible. Moreover, since the necessity of this idea belongs to the idea itself, whether I think it or not, I am certain of this certainty, not only when I have the actual intuition of the idea, during the time when I "think" it (as is the case with the Cogito), but even when I merely remember it, without actually realizing the rational intuition of the necessities it implies. The necessity for God to exist does not derive from the fact that at such an instant my thought has an intuition of it, but from the fact that I see positively in his nature that he cannot not be posited eternally by himself. Thus I pass from fact to rule, and from time to eternity. Instead of saying, "I think, therefore I am , as long as I think; and perhaps, if I stopped thinking I would stop existing," I should say "God exists necessarily, therefore eternally, and not merely when I think of him, for in himself, he cannot not cause himself eternally; even if, in fact, I actually stopped thinking his idea, his idea would always still imply in itself the necessity for him to exist." This consideration is the one that allows Descartes to begin with the ontological proof and to refute by means of it the metaphysical doubt that strikes at mathematical ideas in the writings in which he follows the synthetic order

(Principles,[25] *Geometrical Summary of Objections II).* Under these conditions, it is evident that the proof by effects does not need to be conceived as necessarily conditioning the validity of the ontological proof: the ontological proof can immediately guarantee its own validity to itself.

However, Descartes stated the contrary at the start of *Meditation V.* He repeats this in another form when he states to Arnauld that the proof by effects is not only the principal but the one and only proof. And, in fact, if with respect to God the object of the idea is such that it guarantees that we cannot be deceived in the certainty that we have of the necessities that the object implies, that is, on the condition that we are certain that the certainty of the notion results from the necessity proper to the object it represents—in brief, on the condition that we are certain that it has an objective validity. And it cannot have such objective validity unless we already know that God exists.

We can conceive of two hypotheses in order to resolve this difficulty.

First, it is perhaps not certain that the final pages of *Meditation V* have as a goal to derive from the ontological proof *alone* the objective validity of clear and distinct ideas, given that the beginning of that *Meditation,* on the contrary, assumes this validity as previously established and as a condition of that proof. Descartes does assert, in his conclusion,[26] that if I do not know that there is a God, I can doubt that validity and that once I recognize that there is a God and he is not a deceiver, I can no longer doubt it. But are we concerned there to develop the consequences of the ontological proof or only to recall the consequences that result, in general, from the certain knowledge of the existence of God such that it has been demonstrated by the proof from effects and subsidiarily confirmed by the ontological proof? Nothing prevents us from seeing in this, on the occasion of the ontological proof, a general recall of the consequences that result without fail from the certainty that God exists, in whatever way that certainty has been acquired. If we relate the texts of p. 65, l. 4,[27] p. 68, l. 21,[28] and p. 69, l. 26,[29] we would lean toward this interpretation.

However, if we considered the text of p. 69, l. 10,[30] we would lean to the other side, but then the solidity of the proof would be compromised in a vicious circle.

With respect to this second hypothesis, it would be useful, in order to illuminate the case according to the spirit of Cartesianism, to relate the end of *Meditation V* with the text of the *Principles* and the *Geometrical Summary of Objections II,* in which the ontological proof seems to be used in order to establish the validity of clear and distinct ideas. We would then be distinguishing two possible attitudes corresponding with two degrees of proof, according to whether we are more or less exacting about the conditions of validity. If we are dealing just with a mathematician who is impervious to atheism and who does not doubt God's veracity, the ontological proof suffices. If we are dealing with an obstinate atheist or a scrupulous and "shrewd" philosopher, the ontological proof no longer suffices, and the proof by effects appears as its necessary condition. Nothing can bring about logically that a proof subject to a doubtful condition can bring forth anything but a doubtful result; and this doubtful result could never transform the doubtful condition into a certain condition. Since the necessity that requires me to link the idea of God and his eternal existence has no objective validity except in virtue of the clearness and distinctness of that idea, the legitimacy of the conclusion requires that the objective validity of what is clear and distinct be established as certain and indubitable. But if this conclusion itself served to establish this validity, the circularity would be patent. Even admitting that the ontological proof is intrinsically more certain than any mathematical demonstration, the obstinate atheist or the scrupulous philosopher would still be hindered at first by the preliminary metaphysical doubt concerning the objective validity of clear and distinct ideas; and in order to conquer this doubt, it would have to be assumed that we are certain of divine veracity. It would therefore have to be assumed that we are not or that we have stopped being atheists ourselves and that, on the contrary, the nothingness of atheism has been proven. There is therefore no way to lead an atheist—or someone who feigns atheism—to the certainty of God except by having him experience it, without appealing to the objective validity of clear and distinct ideas, that is, by means of the proof by effects, that the idea of the perfect he has in his soul could not have been introduced there except by the action of God himself and that, consequently, God exists, and his idea in me thus has an objective validity, and his veracity then guarantees me the very truth of ideas present in my understanding.

In addition, if we examined the thing closer, we can come to realize that the ontological argument, as it has been developed in *Meditation V,* does not merely refer generally to the preliminary demonstration of the truth of clear and distinct ideas. It includes a specific reference to the proof by efficient cause. In fact, in order to forestall any objection with respect to the objective validity of clear and distinct ideas, Descartes argues for the immutability, the indeformability, and indivisibility of this idea, which, because of its resistance to the efforts of our subjective thought—which can neither add nor subtract anything to it—certifies to its objective nature.[31] In this way I can say that if I conceive God as necessarily existing, it is not because "my thought can bring about this result or that it imposes any necessity on things," but because, on the contrary, the existence of God itself determines me to have this thought.[32] And the immutability and indeformability of the "true immutable nature"—its resistance to my subjective thought—certify the truth of this nature only because they attest to its reality, since they are the incontestable signs that it has been placed in me in spite of myself and, consequently, caused in me by God. And this immutability, this indeformability of the idea with respect to my conscious and voluntary thought, cannot be considered as the sign of its objectivity unless we could evoke, with respect to this, the hypothesis that is so often alleged, of a faculty present deep in me, capable of producing unconsciously what appears as complete and as resistant to my conscious will. From this it follows that the criteria about immutable nature cannot be valid except in virtue of the proof by effects that establishes that the objective reality of the idea of the perfect must necessarily be produced by an existing God, and not by me. That is how we can conclude that everything real in ideas is placed there by God insofar as God is Being, that what is real is consequently innate in us and not invented by us, and that the truth of clear and distinct ideas is based, by means of the intermediary of their reality, in the perfection of God who is their principle.[33]

7. Proof of the Necessarily Subordinate Character of the a priori Proof by Means of the Order

If this interpretation is justified by the satisfactory explanation that it imparts to the position occupied by the ontological proof in the *Meditations,* the position also brings to it a somewhat lofty confirmation— which seems unusual at first.

Descartes has insisted too often on the importance of the order not to have chosen this position by design. Surely he deliberately intended not to exhibit this third proof with the others in *Meditation III,* which is completely devoted to the problem of God; similarly he intended to treat the problem of the true and of the false before it, and to introduce it in *Meditation V,* which is devoted to mathematical essences: "It seemed to me quite reasonable," he wrote, "that the things requiring specific care, which must be considered separately rather than with others, must be placed in separate *Meditations.*"[34] It is therefore evident that the ontological proof and the proof by effects are considered by Descartes as separate questions, while the question of mathematical truth and the question of the ontological proof are a unity for him.

Thus, at first look, the sequence of the *Meditations* testifies to the fact that the ontological proof does not belong to the positing of the first principle of the objectively valid science, but to its consequences. And the position it occupies appears as the most striking illustration of this opposition, on which Descartes insists, between the order of topics and the order of reasons.

And if Descartes prefers the order of reasons, that is because, according to him, the order of topics is incapable of giving proper proofs: "It should be noted that, in all my writings, I do not follow the order of topics, but the order of reasons, that is to say, I do not say in a single place everything that could be said about a topic, for in that way I would not be able to give proper proofs, there being reasons that must be drawn from farther off than others. But in reasoning by the order, *a facilioribus ad difficiliora,* I make what deductions I can, first on one topic, then on another. This is in my opinion the true way to find the truth."[35] Therefore if the ontological proof is not treated in the same *Meditation* as the others, it is because the order prevents it from being sufficiently established at that point. In fact, it cannot be sufficiently established until the validity of all mathematical demonstrations is established, that is, generally, the validity of all the necessary relations included in clear and distinct ideas.

We can therefore conclude that the position occupied in the order by the ontological proof is sufficient to demonstrate that it is not a primary truth, but a secondary truth; that it depends on the proof by effects as a higher reason; that it is not valid if it is isolated from it;[36] that it assumes reasons that are not assumed by the proof by effects; that the proof by effects is the fundamental proof of the existence of God and truly the only proof; that the ontological proof is located in *Meditation V,* and not elsewhere, in virtue of a rational necessity; that its case is the same as the case of mathematical truths and its certainty is at the same level, except that, among the clear and distinct ideas, it is the "first and principal" and "clearest and most distinct of all ideas."

8. Reduction to a Unity of the Aspects Called Analytic and Synthetic in the a priori Proof

The discussions with respect to what some authors have called the synthetic aspect or the analytic aspect of the proof consequently have become uninteresting.

One might have thought that Descartes presented the a priori proof in two different ways. In the *Discourse,* the *Meditations,* and the *Principles* it appears—according to various nuances—as immediately grasped by intuition. In *Replies I* and *II,* it appears as a syllogistic reasoning in the form: *major premise:* what we conceive clearly and distinctly as belonging to nature or to essence, or to the immutable and true form of something, can be affirmed or stated truly about that thing; *minor premise:* we conceive clearly and distinctly that existence belongs necessarily to God's nature; *conclusion:* God exists.[37]

These two processes have been thought by Brunschwicg[38] as governed by two different attitudes of the human mind, namely, by "two incompatible structures of intelligence," the one "based on a logical necessity across the various propositions of a reasoning, the other being a necessity of an immediate implication, in which is founded the two terms of a single judgment in the intuition of an act."

But if we examine these two aspects, we can see that in the end their difference does not amount to much.

In fact, in the writings called analytic, the immediate intuition of the necessary implication of existence in the essence of the infinitely perfect is always preceded by a reference to the case of mathematical ideas, with a view toward establishing that the case of the idea of God is the same as theirs. Thus, in the *Discourse,* after having considered the objects of geometers and their demonstrations, and after having noted that the certainty one attributes to them *"is based on their being conceived evidently,"* Descartes goes on to the idea of the perfect being and discovers "that existence is included in it in the same fashion that it is included in the idea of a triangle that its three angles are equal to two right angles, or in the idea of a sphere that all its parts are equidistant from the center. Perhaps the existence of the Perfect Being is even more evident [because, as we shall see, it concerns an even simpler relation—M. G.]; consequently, it is at least as certain that God, who is this Perfect Being, is or exists, as any theorem of geometry could possibly be."[39] Descartes also refers to the example of the equality between the angles of a triangle and two right angles in the *Principles.*[40] Clearly, it is this identification with mathematics that renders the argument valid for Descartes. And *Replies I* and *II* do no more, with their syllogisms, than stipulate expressly that the argument would not be valid if the case of the idea of God were not identical with the case of the other clear and distinct ideas, under the relation of objective validity that must be granted to the necessity of its internal implications.[41] No doubt this stipulation is accomplished, in this case, by the subsumption of the particular case of the idea of God under the general case of all clear and distinct ideas by means of a syllogism, and not by a simple reference to the case of mathematical ideas. One can allow that this is a concession to the Scholastic reader's habits of reasoning. But this concession modifies only the preliminaries of the argument, and not the argument itself. We are still concerned with recalling the condition without which the argument would not be valid. Whether this recall is accomplished in one way or another does not change the proof that follows.

9. Consistency of the Proof: Is It a Reasoning or an Axiom?

Thus the question is soon raised with respect to where the proof resides. Does it reside in the syllogism that refers the particular case of God to the general case of clear and distinct ideas? Under this hypothesis the whole proof would consist only in opening the eyes of the blind to the identity of the case of mathematical truths (or clear and distinct ideas) with the case of the idea of God. After having been led to recognize that the essence of God is a clear and distinct idea, as are mathematical essences, the atheist (or the Scholastic), who has never refused to accept the necessities of mathematical truths, would be constrained to accept the necessity of God's essence. He will be led to grant the objective validity that he recognizes naturally for geometrical essences to the essence of God, by the force of a reasoning framed in traditional syllogistic form, requiring him to notice in the idea of

God the same objective validity that he had always noticed effortlessly in geometrical ideas. And if an effort had been necessary in one case but not in the other case, that is because sensible images, which are suitable for mathematical notions, have never diverted the mind from the necessities they possess, while they have prevented it from having a direct intuition of the notion of God, since they are not suitable for it.

If it is thus—since a syllogism is useless in order to demonstrate to lucid minds who perceive immediately that the clear and distinct idea of God could not be deprived of the objective validity that belongs as a rule to all clear and distinct ideas (and in particular to mathematics)—we could then say with Descartes that the conclusion of this syllogism ("Therefore it is true to say that necessary existence belongs to the essence of God and that he exists") can "be known without proof by those who are free from all prejudices."[42]

But it remains to know whether the proof of the ontological argument, in the case in which the argument would require a proof, would ever reside in the syllogism. For to demonstrate or to state the condition that renders a demonstration valid is not to effectuate the demonstration itself. Let us take a necessary mathematical demonstration as an example: the sum of the three angles of a triangle is equal to two right angles; in order that the demonstration of this theorem be valid, I can say that I have to be certain that everything clear and distinct is true. In order to get a weak mind to notice this condition, I could introduce the statement of this theorem in the following syllogism: "Everything clear and distinct is true; I perceive clearly that the notion of the triangle necessarily entails that the sum of its angles is equal to two right angles (for example, by accomplishing the classical construction, either by means of parallel lines, or by inscribing a triangle in a circle): therefore it is true that the triangle itself has angles such that their sum is necessarily equal to two right angles." It is evident that this syllogism is perfectly useless for a normal mind; but it is no less evident that it is false that, in the absence of this syllogism, the theorem is known without proof. In fact, the proof resides elsewhere, namely, in the demonstration of the theorem itself; and this demonstration is accomplished by means of auxiliary constructions. It is the same for the ontological argument. It is completely useless to have recourse to a supposed demonstration that attempts to establish that it is founded only after we have attributed the objective validity proper to clear and distinct ideas to the idea of God—this fact can be perceived by itself. But to establish this uselessness is not to prove that the minor premise of the syllogism that constitutes the statement of the argument in this case, namely, that "the Supremely Perfect Being necessarily implies the perfection of existence," can itself be known without proof. It is only to establish that there is no need of proof in order to place into evidence that this minor premise (whether it is known without demonstration by the immediate intuition of a necessary relation or deductively by means of a more or less syllogistic reasoning) cannot establish an objectively valid affirmation unless we recognize the objective validity of clear and distinct ideas in it.

Thus all the interesting consequences that were thought to be derivable (concerning the various structures of the human mind) from the analytic or synthetic form taken by the indispensable preliminary assumption of the objective validity of clear and distinct ideas, are devoid of meaning, since the ontological argument, whether it is demonstrable or indemonstrable in itself, resides elsewhere than in the preliminary recall of the condition that gives it its validity and since in itself it could not be interested in the various forms that this recall can take.

In order to affirm truly that the necessary existence of God is perceived without proof from its essence, the minor premise itself, meaning the statement of the argument, must appear as immediately self-evident—in brief, as an *axiom*. And the argument seems to require, on the contrary, a proper demonstration that would constitute the body of the proof and that would take the form of the following syllogism: *major premise*: by definition God has necessarily all perfections; *minor premise*: existence is a perfection; *conclusion*: God necessarily has the perfection of existence. But this syllogism can be found in *Meditation V*,[43] a text that, according to Brunschwicg, perhaps manifests more than the others the tendencies of the modern mind. The major premise of this syllogism is constituted by an immediate intuition (the intuition of the nature of God), and the minor premise is constituted by a postulate ("existence is a perfection"), a postulate that is rejected by empiricists like Gassendi and that will be rejected by critical philosophers like Kant.

But in other texts, especially in the *Geometrical Summary of the Replies to Objections II*,[44] which Brunschwicg considers as particularly imbued with the reactionary spirit of Scholasticism, this new syllogism is, in turn, considered as useless. Descartes substitutes for it the immediate intuition of the possible, as a requirement for existence, which necessarily leads to existence when this possible is not limited—which is the case for infinite essence. Everything is therefore reduced to a single proposition that constitutes an *axiom*. And one can legitimately assert that henceforth the necessary existence of God is known without proof. The minor premise of the first syllogism (of the "synthetic" texts) and all of the second (the syllogism of the *Meditations)* are reduced to *axiom 10,* according to which "Existence is contained in the idea or concept of everything, because we cannot conceive anything except under the form of something existing, with this difference, that possible or contingent existence is only contained in the concept of a limited thing, and perfect and necessary existence is contained in the concept of a Supremely Perfect Being."[45]

Under the above form, the argument can no longer, from all evidence, discover something corresponding to it in truths with respect to the properties of triangles, rhombuses, etc., for these truths are not axioms and thus require a demonstration. But it still remains comparable to a mathematical demonstration, as long as we choose as term of comparison an undemonstrable immediately evident mathematical truth. That is precisely what Descartes specifies during the *Geometrical Summary,* in the *Fifth Postulate*: "In the case of the idea of God, existence is not merely possible, but wholly necessary; for, from this alone, and without any reasoning whatever, they will know that God exists, and it will be no less evident to them than the fact that two is an even number, and three is an odd number, and so on. For there are certain truths evident to some, without proof, that can be made intelligible to others only by lengthy discourse and reasoning."[46]

Thus, the knowledge of the necessity of God's existence, although it is, as an axiom, known without proof and different from mathematical truths that are amenable to demonstration (like the square of the hypotenuse, the equality of the sum of the angles of a triangle and two right angles, the ability of a rhombus to be or not to be inscribed in a circle, etc.), does not cease to be of the same nature as the knowledge of mathematical truths in general, as long as we relate it to those that are incapable of demonstration and perceived as an immediate intuition. We cannot therefore state that when Descartes, in *Meditation V,* uses the necessary union between the concepts of mountain and valley along with numerous mathematical examples, he intends to detach his proceedings from mathematical knowledge, in order to render it less logical and more intuitive, "more immediate and less discursive."[47] In fact, where could we find anything less "discursive" than the immediate intuition of what renders a number even or odd? And, moreover, where could we find something more "logical" than the example of the mountain and valley, since it constitutes for Descartes the most typical and most familiar expression of the *principle of identity and noncontradiction?* The impossibility of thinking of the mountain without the valley is disclosed by a necessary relation between two terms that have only a distinction of reason between them—which are "two names for the one and same thing"—such that we can think of them separately only by an abstraction of the mind that renders their knowledge incomplete and consequently obscure and confused: "We cannot have any knowledge of things except by the ideas we conceive of them; and consequently, we must not judge of them except in accordance with these ideas, and we must even think that *whatever conflicts with these ideas is absolutely impossible and implies a contradiction.* Thus we have no reason to affirm that there is no mountain without a valley, unless we see that these ideas cannot be complete when we consider one without the other; though, of course, by abstraction we can obtain the idea of a mountain, or of an upward slope, without considering that the same slope can be traveled downward."[48] The example of the mountain and the valley is therefore of a nature as logical as any mathematical example whatsoever, and Descartes relates it expressly to the impossibility for our understanding to conceive that one and two do not add up to three[49]—in the same way that he relates it expressly to the absurdity of atoms that have to be both extended, meaning divisible, and indivisible, meaning unextended, "which implies a contradiction."[50] The only thing we can assert is that the necessity that links the ideas of mountain and valley together is more accessible to the common man than the necessity that links mathematical notions, because it is less applicable and more familiar, and because it has support in the imagination of particular things. There is no passing from the discursive to the intuitive in the passage from the geometric comparison to the comparison with the mountain and the valley, but a passing from a pure concept of the understanding able to be realized under the highest form of the imagination, to a concept of particular thing that the senses exemplify under the basest form, but at the same time, under the most expressive form of this imagination.[51] It is therefore most expedient in order to convince common men, meaning minds that are not "free of all prejudices" since they are extremely taken with the senses.

Descartes' final thought is therefore, no doubt, that the ontological argument does not require any proof and that it resides wholly in the direct perception of a necessary relation included in an essence that is grasped immediately by intuition, but that it remains no less comparable to mathematical truths, at least with those that are incapable of demonstration.

The fact that this argument has even more certainty than mathematical truths because it concerns the simplest, the clearest, the most distinct of all ideas, as well as the "first and principal idea," does not entail that the knowledge we have of it is of another kind and belongs to another sphere. It remains under the same condition, that is, under the preliminary condition of the objective validity of the idea.

Thus, with respect to this, we could not affirm anything valid in itself outside our conception, if we did not know that God, who is capable of creating truths other than those our understanding conceives, is incapable, because of his veracity, of creating something other than what he allows us to conceive clearly and distinctly. Of course, God's existence is inseparable from his essence, as certainly as the mountain is inseparable from the valley for me, but *could God not make a mountain without a valley?* And does the impossibility for my conception correspond with an impossibility for things in themselves? I could never discard this doubt unless I knew that God could not deceive me in what he teaches me clearly and distinctly: "I do not think that we should ever say of anything that it is impossible for God, for since everything true and good depends on omnipotence, I would *not even dare to say that God cannot make a mountain without a valley, or that one and two should not be three.* I merely say that he has given me a mind of such nature that I cannot conceive a mountain without a valley, or an aggregate of one and two that is not three, etc. *And I merely say that such things imply a contradiction in my conception.*"[52] As long as I do not know whether God exists and that his very omnipotence excludes that he placed clear and distinct ideas in me that are capable of deceiving me, that is, not corresponding to the truth of things that he could have made otherwise, I must be satisfied with the conclusion that "the nature of my mind is such that I cannot conceive a mountain without a valley, and God without existence," and that consequently, "I cannot dare say" that this "contradiction in my conception" necessarily entails an impossibility for the thing outside my understanding; likewise, "I cannot dare say" that God exists necessarily in himself, in the way my understanding conceives him. In order "to dare say this," it must be that I know that my conception has an objective validity—which could not have been accomplished except by *Meditation III.*

10. The Extreme Ease or Extreme Difficulty of Knowledge of God

We thus understand that I can affirm at the same time both that the necessary existence of God is known without proof by merely inspecting his essence, this truth being an axiom grasped by intuition, and that it is thus, in virtue of the high degree of clarity proper to its essence, the best known and most easily known thing, and that nevertheless I cannot succeed in positing this existence except by means of a lengthy and laborious demonstration.

First, I do not have an intuition of *God himself* as I have an intuition of my own self. I only have an intuition of his idea, which supposedly reflects his being, in the same way that I have an intuition of the idea of a triangle. Consequently, not only is a first effort necessary to set aside the sensible veils in order to discover his idea, in the same way that I have to set aside the senses in order to grasp my own self, but I must, in addition, assume a second effort in order to ascend again from the idea to the thing, to prove that the idea represents the thing and that the thing exists, and thus to prove that the idea has objective validity and, in addition, that the certain existence of that thing—the good and veracious God—guarantees this validity, not only for that idea, but for all others. In brief, after having well perceived the idea, I have to establish that it is not deceitful.

Thus, God appears as the object of some knowledge that is, on the one hand, more evident, more certain, and easier than that of our soul and, on the other hand, as requiring more than twice the effort as the latter; similarly, the knowledge of my soul, which is easier than that of body, appears, from another point of view, to require more effort than the knowledge of body that is perceived and affirmed before the soul by the common man. We rediscover here the dual meaning of the words *easy* and *difficult.* What is the easiest for science is what is most difficult for those who are outside science and who must conquer with difficulty the obstacle of the senses in order to be raised to the height of the first principle, from which develops the true linkage *a facilioribus ad difficiliora.*

We therefore see the reconciliation of statements that seem contradictory at first. Descartes affirms, to the authors of *Objections II,* that "God can be known without proof,"[53] by considering his essence. To the Marquis of Newcastle, he affirms that knowledge of God is "a troubled and doubtful perception that requires much work from us."[54] It is evident that, on the one hand, we can know the necessary existence of God directly by an intuition of his essence and that, on the other hand, since we do not have the intuition of God himself, but only the intuition of his idea, since he *himself* is not present in us, we can only posit him "by the force of argument," in opposition to what happens for the existence of my self, which is itself present in the Cogito.[55] It would be impossible for me, in fact, to derive anything certain from the intuition of the idea of God, unless I had demonstrated, by a long and laborious process (that of *Meditation III),* the objective validity of this idea grasped by my intuition. And by affirming, from the start, that the ontological argument is valid only under the condition that we have already proven the objective validity of clear and distinct ideas, *Meditation V* confirms that the "principal and, so to say, single" proof of the existence of God is the proof furnished by *Meditation III.*

11. Three Aspects of the a priori Proof for Three Kinds of Minds

If we return to the various texts that have been opposed as analytic and synthetic, we would notice that they all agree, for all of them require the same preliminary condition for the ontological proof. Only they do not all require it in the same way. In this respect, we can classify them into three groups.

1) The texts called "synthetic"[56] *(Replies to Objections I* and *II)* attempt, by means of a syllogism, to constrain dull minds to consider as similar God's essence and mathematical essences, and to grant to God's essence, in virtue of its clearness and distinctness, that which they grant spontaneously to mathematical essences, namely, the truth of the properties that the essences necessarily entail. The argument is then put into syllogistic form and takes the form of a demonstration, which, in reality, is purely fictive, a simple teaching device intended to allow the penetration of an elementary truth into *weak minds,* by using their habits of reasoning; it is a device of the same order as the use of the sensible example of the mountain and the valley, which is intended to facilitate, for minds clouded by imagination, the intuition of a truth of the understanding.

2) The texts called "analytic" *(Discourse, Principles)* are addressed to

lucid minds. They include only a brief recall of the objective validity naturally attributed to clear and distinct ideas. This brevity is sufficient for quick intelligences, who immediately perceive the necessity to recognize, for God's essence, the privilege they grant *naturally* to mathematical essences.

3) The text of *Meditation V* occupies another place. Referring to *Meditation III*, it is addressed to philosophical minds. It does not merely recall that, since the notion of God is a clear and distinct idea like mathematical notions, the argument is not established unless the objective validity of all these ideas is accepted as a condition. In addition, it specifies that this condition itself must be demonstrated and that it has been demonstrated amply *(fuse)*. This demonstration was necessary for philosophical minds, for without it, they would not have been able to take, with respect to essences in general, including mathematical essences, the attitude of spontaneous conviction that they had naturally, but that the hypothesis of the evil genius, through the intermediary of metaphysical doubt, had artificially lifted from them. This demonstration, that of *Meditation III*, is not merely verbal and futile, like the syllogistic argument of the "synthetic" texts, but profound and metaphysical. That is why, while responding specifically to the preoccupations of philosophical minds, it is also useful for the other types of minds. No mind, whether philosophical or not, naturally doubts the objective validity of mathematical ideas; moreover, philosophical minds believe that the idea of God is clear and distinct like mathematical ideas, but required by *metaphysical doubt* to put into question the objective validity of all ideas, they also had to doubt the objective validity of the idea of God. As for the minds obscured by prejudices and the images of senses, who are not at the level of philosophy, they believe naturally in the objective validity of mathematical ideas; they have never thought to doubt them. On the other hand, they naturally doubt the objective validity of the idea of God, because they do not see that it is a true essence, in the category of mathematical notions. Like the philosophical minds, they doubt God, but in another way and for other causes. They doubt him involuntarily, through intellectual shortsightedness, and not voluntarily and metaphysically, because of a scientific requirement.

The proof by effects satisfies both needs at the same time. For, by establishing that the idea of God has an objective reality that is so rich that only God can be its cause, it abolishes the metaphysical doubt that led philosophical minds to reject the objective validity of all ideas; and at the same time, since as a result of it the idea of God has still more objective reality than any mathematical idea whatever, and since consequently it is more clearly and distinctly known than any of them,[57] it contrains the shortsighted mind of the atheist to recognize that what he naturally grants mathematical essences, namely, objective validity, he must also grant, with even more reason, to the essence of God. Thus the doubt with respect to God, whether it is metaphysical and arises from a reflection of the foundation of certainty, or natural, meaning it arises from the obscuring action of imagination, is destroyed in any case.

12. The Different Places of the a priori Proof According to Analytic Order and Synthetic Order: The a priori Proof as Truth of Science *(veritas rationum)* and as Truth of Things *(veritas rei)*

If the ontological proof necessarily comes after the proof from effects in the order of reasons, since it is conditioned by the proof from effects, then why is it placed before it on two occasions, in the *Geometrical Summary of Replies II* and in the *Principles?* Descartes himself has explained this. These two latter works follow the synthetic order of reasons, while the *Meditations* (like the *Discourse)* follows the analytic order.[58] Moreover, Descartes has specified that the analytic order is the true order.[59] And Descartes, in the *Meditations* and *Discourse,* and every time he alludes to the proof by effects, does not fail to present it as the principal proof and as self-sufficient. On the contrary, in *Replies II* and in the *Principles,* he does not fail to add to the statement of the a priori proof a remark concerning the initial difficulties of this proof and to indicate, either implicitly (in the *Principles*),[60] or explicitly (in the *Geometrical Summary of Replies II*),[61] that it is urgent to refer the proof to another proof capable of resolving these difficulties. Briefly, here as there the proof by effects remains the ultimate condition of the validity of the ontological proof, except that this condition is indicated sometimes before the proof and sometimes after. The true order indicates it before; it rises from conditions that render valid the affirmation of the thing to the positing of the thing itself.

Although it is completely derived and subordinate as a *truth of science,* the ontological proof is, on the other hand, independent and primary as a *truth of things.* That is why the synthetic order of reasons that expresses the real order of the dependence of things must place it before the proof by effects. Through the a priori proof we situate ourselves in the intimate essence of God and we do not merely know that he exists, but how and why; we grasp his existence with respect to himself, not with respect to ourselves. Not only does the infinity of his essence reveal the necessity and consequently the eternity of his existence, but it also gives the reason of this *causa sui* that the second proof by effects did not succeed in positing except by means of our incapacity of creating ourselves. Moreover, the reflection on divine will reveals to us that divine will cannot be infinitely free or infinitely powerful if it limited itself to nothingness and refused to impart being to itself.[62] Thus, this necessity to exist that derives from the definition of an essence, like a geometrical truth, is merely the other aspect of freedom that *cannot* refuse being to itself, in virtue of its own omnipotence and infinity.

This primacy of the a priori proof in the order of *the truths of things* does not, however, suppress its complete subordination in the order of the *truths of science.* If the object of philosophy is to promote an unshakable certainty and to discover the foundations of that certainty, then the first truth must be located in the highest truth of science, meaning in the truth that, satisfying all the conditions of such a certainty, definitively establishes the former for itself and for all the other truths. That is the case for the truth brought forth by the first proof by effects. And in this way this proof must appear as "the primary and even single" proof. Without it, not only would the a priori proof, but the validity of all of science, fall into uncertainty. On the other hand, without the a priori proof, our knowledge of God would be less complete than it could and should have been, of course, but it would remain as indubitable as before while, on the whole, the edifice of science would remain unshaken.

Moreover, we can go against Descartes' explicit warning and make the a priori proof the principal proof only by misunderstanding the fundamental distinction between the truth of science and the truth of things, and by forgetting that, for Descartes, what is most important does not reside in the principle of things, which are the objects of our knowledge, but in the principles that render this knowledge certain and make a *science* of it, in the strict and rigorous sense of the word.

13. Consequences of the Subordination of the Ontological Proof to the Proof by Effects: Reconciliation between the Necessity of the a priori Proof with Divine Freedom, Which Transcends the Necessities of Our Understanding

The explicit subordination of the ontological proof to the proof by effects has important consequences. It renders void many classical objections.

First, it ruins the objection that Kant will insist upon, as we have seen, which consists in denying to it any objective validity.[63] It refutes the critique of Kant and Vico, who denounced its vain pretension of attempting to enclose God's nature inside the necessities of our understanding.

Considered in itself and detached from the proof by effects, the ontological proof appears to justify this latter objection. In the *Letter to Mersenne,* in which he argues for the free creation of the eternal truths, Descartes in fact had neatly opposed mathematical truths and the truth of the existence of God. He had placed them on two radically different planes. It appears then that whoever holds to the level of the necessity of essences is incapable of rejoining the true God and must inevitably *lower* him, by bringing him to the lower plane of the necessities of our understanding. Whoever proceeds in this way is led to make the incomprehensible power of God disappear completely, to abolish his freedom, to subject him, like Jupiter and Saturn, to the Styx and the fates. Thus, the recourse to the necessity of essences leads to atheism. The true way, therefore, is to start by setting aside this essential necessity and to place into evidence the incomprehensible power of God. We would then perceive that this power governs these necessities because it is their cause. We would realize that it is thus absolved of them. If it is possible to understand the necessity of essences by beginning with God's incomprehensibility, which has given rise to them, it is, on the contrary, impossible ever to conceive this divine incomprehensibility by beginning from this necessity, which is internal only to our faculty of understanding: "And because they perfectly understand mathematical truths and not the existence of God, it is no wonder that they [the atheists—M. G.] do not believe that the former depend on the latter. But, on the contrary, they should judge, that since God is a cause whose power surpasses the bounds of human understanding and since the necessity of these truths does not exceed our knowledge, they *are something less than,* and subject to, this incomprehensible power."[64] And is not the ontological proof based on the necessity of a reason discovered in my understanding? Is not this idea explicitly assimilated to mathematical essences (except for the infinity of its content)? Is it not based, exactly as they are, on the objective validity attributed to the necessities that I perceive clearly and distinctly in my intelligence? Ought we not end up with the feared consequence, that is, the annihilation of God's incomprensible freedom? For what can remain of such freedom and such incomprehensibility where there is no more than an absolute necessity to exist, completely included in the mathematical definition of a clear and distinct essence?

These difficulties disappear if, on the contrary, we perceive clearly that the ontological proof, considered separately and as self-sufficient, is not valid, and that the whole force of its demonstration comes from the fact that it is based on the incomprehensible power of God, as are mathematical truths. If mathematical truths are "something less than this incomprehensible power," something "subject to it," then a truth concerning God that arises from his essence in the same way that a truth arises from a mathematical essence, or a proof supported by the objective validity attributed to some essence because we attribute this same validity to mathematical essences, can only be "something less" with respect to this incomprehensible power and "subject to it," as all mathematical truths and demonstrations are. And in this way, even the ontological proof (just like mathematical demonstrations) must also appear as something less with respect to the proof by effects that raises us to this higher power from which stems this lesser thing—the idea of God, which constitutes a "defect" with respect to what it represents. Separated from the power that establishes it, the necessity of divine essence no longer impels me; we can no longer know whether this necessity arises from myself or from God himself. Instead of basing our understanding in God, we come to base God in our understanding: we suppress his freedom in order to enslave him to the necessities of our thought. However, as soon as we base the objective validity of the necessity of the essence in the incomprehensible power of God, by means of the proof by effects, the constraint that this necessity exercises on me appears to me as exercised by God himself. I can "dare to say" that what is necessary for my conception is also necessary for things. To bow to this necessity is to bow to the necessity that God allows to govern in me, not to bend him to the necessity of my mind. The necessity of the essence is only the effect in me of God's freedom, which has instituted in us the idea of this essence in order to reveal to us, through its intermediary, that he exists necessarily: "My thought does not impose any necessity on things."[65]

14. Distinction between Essences and Ideas of Essences: Between the Created (Mathematical Essences, Ideas of These Essences, Idea of God's Essence), and the Uncreated (God's Essence); the Equality of Level between Mathematical Ideas and the Idea of God, and between Mathematical Truths and the Truth of the a priori Proof, as Truths of Science; the Difference of Level between Mathematical Essences and God's Essence, and between Mathematical Truths and the Truth of the a priori Proof, as Truths of Things

However, these considerations are not immune to criticism. We seem to suppose that if the proof by effects is capable of providing what the ontological argument cannot provide, namely, knowledge of divine freedom and incomprehensibility, that is because it transcends the plane of essences. But does not the essence of God itself involve the notions of freedom, absolute omnipotence, and incomprehensibility that are immediately encompassed in the idea of its infinity? We cannot see how we would legitimately posit this power and freedom, unless they were necessarily included in the idea of infinity. And if the proof by effects can allow me to attribute them effectively to God's being itself, it is in virtue of the certainty it procures for me that this being is similar to the idea I have of him and that it encompasses in him everything I perceive clearly and distinctly in the idea. The gap separating the finite from the infinite, the comprehensible from the incomprehensible, is, as we have shown it, situated, not between my idea of God and God himself, but between the formal reality of my self and the objective reality of my idea of God itself.

The argument that renders the mathematical truths into something *less* than the incomprehensible power that gives rise to them would therefore not be valid for divine essence, since this essence encompasses the notion of the power impressing its idea in us, while nothing in mathematical ideas is able to reveal to us that they are impressed in us by God.

Moreover, to create freely the idea of an essence in me is not to create freely the essence itself. Of course, if God freely impresses the ideas of mathematical essences in me, he also freely creates those essences; but if God freely impresses the idea of his essence in me, we would not be able to conclude that he freely creates this essence itself, for this essence is necessary and eternal, and consequently is uncreated. To affirm the contrary would be to deny the truth of his essence, of the ontological proof established by it, and to admit that God could have been, existed, and acted, before having been and existed.

Consequently, we must limit ourselves to asserting that, detached from the proof by effects, the ontological proof would remain enclosed in the sphere of subjective necessities. Allowing me to posit God's freedom and incomprehensiblity only in virtue of a subjective necessity, it would not authorize me to affirm that they are the true properties of God in himself. The proof by effects alone would allow me to establish the objective validity of my conclusions, in the same way that it establishes that of mathematics. On the other hand, the fact that it establishes God as the cause of his idea in me does not render it indispensable for proving that God is an absolutely free power, for everything that characterizes this cause is by hypothesis already represented in the effect itself—namely, in its idea—and certain for me once the idea is certain. It is therefore sufficient that I consult the essence of God in order to perceive the freedom of the Creator in it. Moreover, we would not be able to conclude, from the fact that God freely creates the idea I have of him, that he creates the very essence that this idea represents to me and that he is free of the necessities it entails. He cannot, in fact, transcend his essence without contradicting the definition of his essence, and even the Cartesian definition of all essence. Finally, even though he creates in me the idea of this essence, he does not even transcend the very idea, since he does not contain formally anything more than what is objectively contained in this idea.

These objections emphasize two important truths that are linked to each other:

1) Although the ontological proof is situated at the same level as mathematical truths in the analytic order of reasons, being justifiable like them by a preliminary demonstration of the objective validity of clear and distinct ideas on which it is based, God's essence is not itself, *a parte rei,* at the level of mathematical essences, for the latter are created, while the former is not.

2) There is a difference between clear and distinct ideas and the essence that we perceive by these ideas. Attributing to God the power to cause in me the idea that we have of him does not necessarily entail the independence of God himself with respect to the necessity that this idea reveals to us. It merely entails its independence with respect to the necessities of our understanding. God is not above his own essence as he is above

mathematical essences, but he impresses his idea in us in the same way that he impresses their idea in us. And this distinction between the necessities proper to our understanding, or at least proper to the finite, and the necessities proper to the infinite and God, is fundamental, for while the necessities perceived by finite understanding express a passion contrary to freedom in the person who perceives them, the necessities proper to the infinite express, on the contrary, an action that involves freedom in the infinite being encompassing them, for they are not necessities except in virtue of the very concept of God's omnipotence, which would be limited if we denied them.[66] Moreover, once I know that the finite essences imposed upon me emanate from a free decree of divine omnipotence, I see that they also cannot threaten divine freedom. But if I reduce the necessity implied by the essence of the infinite (necessity that involves the freedom and omnipotence of the being in which it resides) to the necessity impressed in my finite understanding, which involves the negation of freedom and omnipotence of what is subject to it, I reduce God to "something lesser"; I subject him "to the Styx and to the fates."

On the other hand, these objections could not establish that the ontological proof can instruct us on these fundamental differences without the aid of the proof by effects. In fact, only the a posteriori proof can allow us to know effective omnipotence, in which the idea of the created necessity of mathematical essences and the uncreated necessity proper to God's essence derive their principle. The ontological proof, on the contrary, depends explicitly on the assimilation it is advisable to accomplish in some respect (from the point of view of objective validity) between the necessities of the properties of mathematical essences and the necessities of the properties of God's essence. Of course, the gap between the finite and the infinite is opened up between the content of my idea of infinity and myself, who has this idea, and not between my idea of infinity and God himself. However, the free activity of God, who causes this idea in me, is not only outside myself, but also outside the idea of infinity that I have in myself. If there is no gap between this idea and God, as between the content of this idea and the formal reality of my self, there is, nevertheless, a separation between the plane of the objective reality of my idea of infinity, which is the plane of the effect, and God's plane, which is that of its cause. Moreover, it is the disproportion between the finiteness of my self and the infinity of the content of my idea of God in myself that establishes outside of me this real separation between the free cause that impresses the idea in me and the idea itself thus impressed. Finally, God acquires, by means of this separation that places the infinite existing cause higher than the idea that is its effect in me, a certain transcendence with respect to this idea, a transcendence by which he can appear to some extent as an eminent cause; on the other hand, if we are referred to the perfect conformity of his idea in myself with what he is in himself, and to the infinite amplitude of the content of that idea, which is an absolute maximum, he tends to appear as a formal cause, since there is nothing more perfect than the perfection of the content of the idea, nor nothing more in his reality as cause than in his effect. The first proof by effects, while establishing the perfect necessary conformity of the idea of God with what is ideated, and the equality of perfection between the infinite reality of the effect and the infinite reality of the cause, leads, in spite of everything, to a certain transcendence of this cause with respect to the idea of God itself, because of the positing of the cause outside the idea.[67] And this separation between God's active being and the idea, the passive being that he impresses in me, establishes the independence of God with respect to the necessities I perceive within me. As long as God's being is not effectively posited outside of me and outside my idea of him in me, I can perhaps *conceive* by means of this idea that he has a freedom exempting him from the necessities perceived in my understanding, but I am incapable of *proving it adequately.* Of course, I can perceive, by considering the notion I have of God, that his infinity entails his absolute freedom, but by just holding on to this notion, without going outside it, I can only succeed in demonstrating some *necessities* that seem immanent to my own understanding—the necessity to exist, the necessity to be free, and generally the necessity in God for all the properties that I conceive clearly and distinctly as belonging to him.

That is why the Descartes text cited above[68] affirms that, if I remained on the plane of the only necessity immediately perceived by my understanding, the plane of mathematics, it would become impossible for me to conceive the infinite freedom of God who would appear as subject to the Styx and to the fates. If, in fact, nothing informs me that the necessities of my understanding have God as their cause, cause to which I am subject, how could I conceive that, on the contrary, God himself is not subject to them? And in the ontological proof, we are concerned only, as in mathematics, with considering the intrinsic properties of notions and not with seeking their cause (that is, we are concerned with asking ourselves about the origin of the necessary content of these notions). As in mathematics, I can therefore only attribute to the thing itself, that is, in this case, to God, the necessities I perceive in the notion that my mind has of them, without rising to the consideration of the cause by which I would place God definitively above them taken as his effects. Even though I *knew* him as free, God would therefore, in fact, be captured by the necessities of my understanding. Thus detached from the proof by effects, the ontological proof would not only be deprived of objective validity, but also would appear to enter into conflict with the idea of an absolutely free God, freed from the necessities that weigh down my mind. It would not seem to lead one to affirm the free God except in virtue of a necessity that would be of the same nature in me as in God. Instead of emphasizing what is fundamentally different in the necessity of mathematical essences and in God's essence, it reaches its conclusion only by relying on what they have that is similar in some respects and on the impossibility to refuse for the latter what one grants the former.

Once the subordination of the ontological proof to the proof by effects is perceived, we see God's intelligibility, implied by the proof drawn from his essence, reconciled with his incomprehensibility, implied by the infinity of his reality and his infinitely powerful and free will. If we are brought to *comprehend* that God exists necessarily by means of the knowledge of his essence, that is because we have understood that God is incomprehensible, since it is this incomprehensibility that, in the final analysis, establishes the objective validity of what we understand as necessary by considering his essence. In fact, the necessities inscribed in his essence possess this objective validity in themselves, because God has instituted in us the idea of this essence as true. And we know that it is thus because we have demonstrated that God, being necessarily the cause of the content of his idea in me, exists as a veracious being and an incomprehensible power. The necessity that springs out of the ontological argument is reconciled in the same way with God's freedom as creator of ideas since it is because he has freely implanted the idea of this essence in me that I see that he exists necessarily; and because I know that he is the author of this idea in me, having imprinted it on me like a trademark, I know that the necessity inscribed in essence is objectively valid. This proof that God exists necessarily in virtue of his essence appears as the result of a free revelation accomplished by God for my reason. But because it appears finally as based on a free and incomprehensible revelation, it does not allow me to understand God, nor to understand how his freedom can be reconciled with his own necessity to exist even though I understand that this reconciliation must take place.[69] To understand that God exists necessarily, therefore, is not to understand God. On the other hand, incomprehensibility, the formal reason of infinity, is what allows me to understand and to affirm in all certainty that everything I understand in clear and distinct ideas possesses an objective validity.

In this way we see even better the distance that separates the notions that Descartes and Kant have about the limits of our knowledge. To posit that the necessity of essence—mathematical or other essences—"does not exceed our knowledge," is not for Descartes to stamp the former with relativity, but to allow God to establish and confer an objective validity to our knowledge of him—not only a merely relative, but absolute objective validity—by releasing God himself from the necessities of our understanding. The necessity of my knowledge therefore becomes the intellectual experience, which is absolutely valid in itself, of an effect of the will of a rational God. Consequently, everything I perceive clearly and distinctly, whether in the essences of created things or in the essence of the infinite, is absolutely valid for these things and for this infinite. God's incomprehensibility is the warrant of this necessity; it is at the same time the principle that, on the one hand, limits its domain—with respect to finite essences—and, on the other, sublimates it—with respect to infinite essences—by reconciling it thus in the two cases, but in a different way, with divine freedom.

15. The Elimination of the Final Classical Objection; the Idea of God and the Perfection of Existence; the Essence of God and the Perfection of Existence. The a posteriori Proof as the Foundation of the Passage of the Idea of God outside the Existence of God to the Essence of God Including His Existence

What becomes of the other objection traditionally proposed since Gassendi[70] to the a priori proof: existence is not a perfection, it is a form or act without which there can be none (we do not say that something lacks perfection when it does not exist, but simply that it is null)?

Descartes' reply, as we know, is derived from his mathematical idealism. What kind of thing would we think existence to be "if it could not be said to be a property like omnipotence, taking the term *property* as any kind of attribute? [. . .—M. G.] Necessary existence," he adds, "is in God truly a property taken in the least extended sense, because it is suitable for him alone and only in him is it part of essence."[71] If in fact existence is an intelligible reality, it is homogeneous with essence; and if we are dealing with infinity, it is impossible by definition that it is lacking in him—it accrues to him internally.

No doubt, notes Hegel, the fact of representing something to myself does not imply its being; that is a banal observation, for in everything finite, existence and being are removed from the concept. But God, because he is infinite, cannot be thought of except as existing, for it is this unity of the concept with being that constitutes the very notion of God.[72] Moreover, Descartes was right in saying that necessary existence is in God a property in the least extended sense of the word, in that it is applicable to him alone. The objection truly involves, as Hegel felt it, the sensationalist reduction of all existence to a kind of sensible existence, accrued from the outside to finite things. That is why, according to Hegel's expression, the Kantian example of the hundred thalers is "barbarous," since it assumes that the existence we are attributing to God is this kind of sensible existence that accrues to thalers. And we are concerned with the intelligible existence that is alone applicable to the infinite.

For Descartes, it is the reality of sensibles that needs to be guaranteed by thought, not the reality or object of thought that must be guaranteed by sensible experience. It is always thought that is the judge of existence, and it would be inadmissible to make an exception for the case of God alone, since this case constitutes, on the contrary, the only case in which the affirmation of existence is imposed on us as necessary. And if existence derives from thought, it cannot be posited as irreducible to thought. What would be a limit for it is something unknown and obscure like the substance of some Scholastics. Truth touches being and makes up a unity with it; its positing implies being. Since idealism entails an intelligible realism, nothing is more alien to it than to reduce truth to the human mind. Truth is, on the contrary, based on being, with respect to what it has that is eminently intelligible and rational.

Therefore the objection can be lifted on this plane. But there is another, namely, the plane of the definition of idea as copy of an archetype, of the truth as conformity of the idea to a model *existing* outside it, of the idea necessarily entailing, in its nature of idea, a radical imperfection with respect to the thing it represents, which possesses the perfection of existence formally as a thing—which is what is necessarily lacking to the idea. From this arises the conception of the idea as a "defect" with respect to the thing itself. These definitions, as we recall, constitute the indispensable premises of the proof by effect. But although they are necessary for it, as we have seen, they also constitute a stumbling block. In fact, since the objective reality of the idea of the perfect has, from the fact that it does not possess the existence proper to the thing represented, *necessarily less perfection* than the perfect existent thing, it is impossible to posit *necessarily* more perfection in the cause of this idea than in the idea and, consequently, to posit the perfection of existence, for the only principle that would allow me to conclude this, is *only* that there must *necessarily be at least as much* perfection in the cause as in the effect. The perfection of existence exceeds this *necessary* minimum required in the cause in order to explain the whole perfection of the effect. In this case, this extra perfection *can* be discovered there, but it is not there *necessarily.* Existence therefore remains merely possible. And we were concerned with proving that existence is necessary. The demonstration therefore appears to be insufficient.

The same definition of idea now threatens the a priori proof.

If, in fact, what defines every idea, including the idea of the infinite, is its property, as representational, of being necessarily deprived of the existence that accrues to the thing that it represents alone, as an exclusive property, it seems impossible to perceive existence as a property internal to idea, even with respect to the idea of the infinite.

However, the objection fails here. The property of existence necessarily belongs to the essence of the thing itself, to its intelligible reality or its formal reality whose conformable representation is in me, and not to the idea as representative of the thing, not to its objective reality. And the proof by effects, by revealing this perfect conformity between my idea and the thing, allows me to be certain that I am grasping its essence by means of the idea and that all the properties I perceive as necessary are the necessary properties of the thing itself. That is what Descartes specifies in *Meditation V,* when he notes that the idea of God with which the *Meditation* is concerned is a true and immutable nature.

I do not depart from this nature in the proof by effects, I end up with it. I go from the content of my idea without even asking myself whether this idea is innate, artificial, or adventitious. I can even allow that it is a chimera[73] (therefore artificial); this does not matter once I discover in its content (in its objective reality) an amplitude such that I am constrained to recognize that God alone could have placed it in me and that the necessities of the properties I perceive in it come from God and not from myself. Then I recognize both that God exists outside me and that his idea in me expresses a true and immutable nature. Thus I obtain at the same time God as essence and God as existence.

That is because in this case essence and existence are one. God's existence is, in fact, nothing more than his intelligible reality, and his intelligible reality is nothing more than his essence.[74] Thus, once it is established that God, or his intelligible reality, exists outside me and that the idea I have of him reflects him faithfully in me, I can, by considering this reality, perceive that because of his nature he cannot not be or exist— meaning that as infinite and perfect, God is or exists necessarily and necessarily has (intelligible) reality.

But, pursuing this further, if, in order to demonstrate that God exists necessarily, we must already know that he exists (what we have just agreed upon), is not the ontological proof a useless and arbitrary tautology? Is that not Kant's objection? Kant asserts: "For if all positing (no matter what it may be that is posited) is entitled reality, the thing with all its predicates is already posited in the concept of the subject and is assumed as actual; and in the predicate this is merely repeated." But if we admit the contrary, meaning that the existing thing is outside the idea I have of it and would not be able to be extracted from it, "how can we profess to maintain that the predicate of existence cannot be rejected without contradiction?"[75]

And the former case is, as we have seen, the case of the a priori proof.

The latter case is, as we have seen, the case of the a posteriori proof. In fact, I consider, in this proof, that my idea is outside the existing thing and could not contain it, since it is merely the picture that, by definition, lacks the existence of the model it represents. Thus, as a result, we would not be able to derive analytically from this the existence of the idea, and the a priori proof now seems impossible. Since the idea is deprived of the existence of the thing, it seems less perfect than the existing thing, and the perfect cannot be extracted from the imperfect. In other words, the perfection of the existing thing is greater than the perfection of its idea; it *adds* existence to it, a perfection that is lacking to the idea. That is what Kant expresses by saying that existence can be referred to the idea only *synthetically*. Consequently, not only is it not contradictory to deny of the idea the existence that accrues to the thing, but it would be contradictory to attribute it to the thing.

Thus existence is added synthetically to the idea in the a posteriori proof and it is derived analytically from the essence in the a priori proof. If these two proofs are different, it is because of the double conception of idea, conceived as picture in the one and as essence in the other—and also in virtue of the different place they necessarily occupy in the order of reasons. It is sufficient to render to the proof by effects its conditioning function with respect to the a priori proof in order to see the difficulty vanish, in this case.

First, it is true that we ought to know already that God exists in order to prove that his essence necessarily entails his existence, since it is in proving the existence of God that we have been able to establish that the idea we have of him faithfully reveals his essence. Without the proof by effects, we would have in ourselves only a purely representative idea, not an essence. The result, like the object of this proof, was precisely to raise us from the idea as picture of the thing to the idea as the expression of an essence, that is, as having objective validity coinciding with the nature or the intelligible and formal reality of the thing. There are therefore truly two conceptions of idea: idea as picture and idea as essence; but instead of being in conflict, one of these conceptions introduces the other. Descartes' effort consists in *demonstrating* the existence of *essences* beginning with the *representative content of my ideas,* a content present *in me. That is how the psychological evidence of the Cogito manifests its capacity of principle with respect to mathematical evidence.* For the evil genius can deny the existence of ideas having objective validity, meaning mathematical or other essences, but it would not be able to make me doubt the objective reality of ideas as it is present in me, immediately within me, accessible to the first glance of my mind, as the picture of models outside me, models that perhaps do not exist. It is therefore upon this first evidence—concerning objective realities—that we should rely in order to save mathematical beings and God's Being from doubt, by constructing the proof that there are ideas in us—clear and distinct ideas—that have an objective reality reflecting or expressing *effectively* some intelligible realities imposed on us by our Author, and whose necessity is the necessity of things—in brief, ideas that have objective validity. The ontological proof that is located on the plane of *essences,* which the evil genius renders problematic, necessarily had to presuppose the proof by effects that was located on the plane of the indubitable evidence of *psychologically perceived ideas.*

Second, it is true that, since it is necessary to know already that God exists in order to prove that he exists necessarily from his essence, the ontological proof appears as a useless tautology, if we think we want to establish the existence of God by it. In any case, Descartes has told us that the first proof by effects suffices fully for this task. Moreover, deprived of its support, the ontological proof, as we have seen, is without force. But basically its role is completely different; it consists in establishing that God exists *necessarily* and that, consequently, God is eternal. The first proof by effects established directly that God exists *indubitably*. The ontological proof thus brings forth a new specification, in the same way that the second a posteriori proof brought forth its own specification by establishing God, not only as cause of his idea in us, but as cause of himself. Each of the derived proofs brings its complement of characteristic knowledge. however, even in this respect, they are not absolutely indispensable, since once we knew by the first a posteriori proof that our idea of God has an objective validity, we could, without any further demonstration, attribute to him with certainty all the properties we clearly and distinctly perceive in the idea we have of him—namely, *causa sui*, necessary existence or eternity, etc. However, this attribution is not completely understood until we discover the specific reasons and, above all, until it appears necessary in virtue of God's essence.

In conclusion, since the proof by effects had as result and as goal to raise us from an idea of God excluding from its content, in virtue of the definition of idea, the perfection of existence proper to the *thing itself,* to the thing such as it exists in its intelligible reality, we cannot deny to this very thing the property of *necessarily* including its existence (if truly our idea allows us to know this property in that thing), under the pretext that idea as objective reality in my consciousness is defined as deprived of the existence that belongs to the thing.

Thus the two classical objections directed against the ontological proof—the arbitrary attribution of an objective validity to ideas of my understanding and the arbitrary assimilation of existence with a perfection or a property of the idea—completely disappear, once, in conformity with the order of reasons, we reestablish the close subordination of the ontological proof with respect to the first a posteriori proof. In addition, the refutations of one and the other objections are confused at the limit, for if the demonstration of God's existence as a cause and model of my idea allows me to attribute to my idea a complete and assured objective validity, it is because it has succeeded in revealing to us that the objective reality of the idea is the very imprint of existence, or being, or intelligible reality, or of the actual essence of the thing outside me. And in this imprint, I grasp the essence of the very thing through the objective reality of my representation, such that, when I speak of the properties of the idea, I consider—and I can legitimately consider—not the properties of its objective reality as such (meaning of its objective reality as distinct from the thing represented), but those of the very *thing* that this reality reflects.

However, the difficulties of the proof by effect remain without solution, for the perfection of the existing thing, which the idea lacks, cannot be necessarily posited in the perfection of the cause, since what is necessary is only that there is not *less* perfection in the cause than in the effect.

16. The Identity in Itself of All Essence with Its Existence; Essences as Ideas and Essences as Existences Outside of Me

The preceding considerations allow me to perceive distinctly that God's necessary existence is nothing other than the necessary positing by itself of his intelligible reality, meaning of his essence. God exists necessarily; in other words, his essence cannot not be—it is uncreated, eternal. From this we see that if essence is identical to existence in God, it is insofar as his existence is only the very being of his essence outside of me.

This discovery illuminates with one stroke the whole theory of essences. This identity of essence and existence *outside of me* is not, in fact, a characteristic of God alone, but it is a characteristic of all things, finite or infinite. In brief, there does not exist anything in itself in the world other than essences, whether in me or outside of me. The existence of my self itself is reduced in itself to what the Cogito attests to me, meaning to the actuality of my essence, since it is certain that I am and, because of divine veracity, that I am such as I represent myself to myself—meaning as an intelligible essence. I then grasp myself as substantially united with another actual essence, pure extension, from which arises the actuality of my composite nature. The existence in itself of all things outside of me is reduced to the actual being in itself of their essence outside of me. For example, matter existing outside me is only the actual being, outside me, of its essence: geometrical extension. When we say that in God alone is existence part of essence, we do not mean by that that the essence itself of God has the privilege to add necessarily some existence to itself, but that his being, or essence, is the only one to be such that it cannot not be. From this it results that my understanding, which has this essence objectively in it, such that it is formally outside of us, sees in it that it is necessarily present outside of it.

As a result, there is no world of essences distinct from the world of existences prior to God, outside our thought *(extra cogitationem nostram)* —whether in God's thought or outside God—there is only a single world, the world of things that exist, meaning of formal essences outside me. God has created essences outside him that *are* the existing things, and these existing things are nothing more than the created being of these essences. Moreover, God has created in me the ideas of these things, and these ideas that I call essences, when I see in them the authentic expression of beings outside me, are then distinguished from existences as ideas are distinct from the things they represent. The true nature of existing things (which involve in themselves no more than this nature) is what *I* call their essence. Thus the dissociation between essence and existence takes place only in my thought and for my thought: "We are right to separate the two in our thought, for we can conceive [of essence—M .G.] without actual existence, as in the case of a rose in winter; however, we cannot really separate the two, in accordance to the customary distinction. For there was no essence before existence, since existence is merely existing essence, and consequently, one is not prior to the other, nor are they separate or distinct."[76] If I consider essence as "the thing such as it is objectively in my understanding," meaning as an idea, there is a real distinction between it and its existence outside me, since the former is a mode of thinking substance and the latter is a mode of extended substance. If I consider the idea of essence within my consciousness as that of the *representation* of the thing and the idea of existence as that of the *thing* outside me, represented in me, there is only a modal difference between the two ideas, since they are each a different representative content (meaning an objective reality). Finally, if I place myself outside my thought, with the things, there can be not the least difference between essence and existence, neither a modal nor a real distinction: "It seems to me that the only thing that causes difficulty in this matter is the fact that we do not distinguish sufficiently between things existing outside our thought *(extra cogitationem nostram)* and the ideas that are in our thought. Thus when I think of the essence of a triangle and of the existence of the same triangle, these two thoughts, as thoughts, even taken objectively, differ modally in the strict sense of the term *mode*; but the case is not the same with the triangle existing outside thought, in which it seems manifest that essence and existence cannot be distinguished. The same is the case with all universals. Thus when I say Peter is a man, the thought by which I think of *Peter* certainly differs modally from the thought by which I think of *man,* but in Peter himself, being a man and being Peter are one and the same thing [. . . .] Again, if by *essence* we mean the thing as it is objectively in the understanding and by *existence* the same thing as it is outside the understanding, it is manifest that the two things are really distinct.[77] Thus, almost all controversies of philosophy arise only from misunderstandings between one another."[78]

One sees in this way that the essence of extension is nothing more than its existence; the essence of space nothing more than extension;[79] geometric extension nothing more than matter; the *corpus mathematicum* nothing more than the *corpus physicum*.[80] That is why there are no magnitudes outside of things with magnitudes, no numbers outside of things numbered, no duration outside of things that continue to be, no order outside of things ordered, no shapes outside of things shaped, no movement outside of things moved.[81] Magnitude, number, order, duration, shape, and movement considered apart as notions of our mind are only universals, "which arise from the use we make of an idea in order to think of several particular things that have a certain relation between them and from the fact that we understand them under the same name."[82]

However, are not essences eternal truths, while existences of things are merely temporal, fleeting, subject to the vicissitudes of generation and corruption?

No doubt; but that is because God has freely decided that, when things exist, they *always* exist with the constitutive nature, the necessary properties that are theirs—that they would have between them some determined relations that would never change. For example, the destruction of a body is the destruction of its essence, meaning of the geometrical essential structure that assures it, necessarily, the properties that belong to it, for the benefit of the appearance of another structure from which other properties flow. But it is no less true that such a body could not reappear in existence without the geometrical structure that assures it the properties that make up such a body, without the properties that depend necessarily on that structure and without maintaining with other bodies relations that are settled immutably, in such a way that we see eternal truths there. These necessities are *actually* present in the formal essence of extension. Finally we have in us the indubitable knowledge of this eternity and this necessity. Thus, the essence of a body, as conceived by us, is an eternal *truth* without being an eternal body outside us, for outside us this essence can stop being actual, meaning stop existing, while the necessity of being incapable of existing other than by its essential structure remains eternally, for all bodies of that kind, and the knowledge of that necessity remains for my thought.

If the essences of things are in us like universals and rendered possible by an abstraction of our mind,[83] does it not follow that they are empirical generalities stripped of truth, or deriving their truth from particular sensible things from which they would be abstracted?[84] No, for we ought not confuse universals as conceived by dialecticians with those conceived by the true philosophy.[85] In fact it is impossible to derive *essence,* by abstraction, from what is properly sensible, given that it is never there.[86] Even though the nature of things outside of us is constructed out of perfect geometrical figures, they are so small that they make no impression on our senses. What the senses present to us is, with respect to geometrical figures, so imperfect that we could not see the geometrical figure if our mind did not receive its idea from elsewhere.[87] The abstraction from which geometrical ideas arise is rendered possible only by pure understanding. The latter contains in itself innately the ideas of structures and necessary relations that constitute things outside of me. This abstraction exhibits a dual character: on the one hand, it consists in stripping clear and distinct ideas from the sensible qualities that conceal them; on the other hand, it consists in pushing the analysis up to the simple by dissociating the rational elements that are *a parte rei* mixed and often indissolubly tied together in complex beings, which are opposed to simple natures as the concrete (in its composite sense) is to the abstract.[88] This last analysis and abstraction bears only on purely intellectual notions.[89] We conceive the extreme complication of existing things, the object of physics, in which essences are inextricably mixed. That is why science is impossible without the processes of simplification, abstraction, and division,[90] which aim "to detach a thing that depends on so many things mixed together so skillfully that no step requires a greater capacity of the mind than is needed for making the simplest inference."[91] The simpler are the beings with which we are concerned, the more universal they are, for the composites in which they are found and for which they account are more numerous then.[92] This universality involves singularity, for all simple nature is singular.[93] Thus we see that the truths of mathematics and geometry, which put into play "the simplest and most general" natures, have inescapably an abstract character, but that this abstraction, instead of compromising their reality and validity, on the contrary, is their fundamental condition.[94] In fact, our understanding deals with essences that, since they are the simplest (shapes, extension, movement, unities), are discovered in all things, because all things are composed of them.[95] The algebraist who abstracts from figures and numbers by increasing the abstraction further[96] can perceive with the greatest distinction "the nature of the difficulties,"[97] the universal mathematics that is detached from mathematics by abstraction from its *integumentum*,[98] carrying the abstraction to the maximum, and allowing one to grasp in its purety *the system that renders all combinations of essences possible*.[99] These disciplines, in spite of their extreme generality, by assuring to the understanding its complete possession, instead of weakening the objective validity of science, strengthen it; therefore if science can be universalized to the maximum, it is because simple natures are no more than "the general terms of the difficulty."[100] The singularity that the understanding apprehends is therefore that of its most profound reasons, for this singularity allows the understanding to grasp in its simplicity by one and only one formula the law governing a multitude of other single reasons whose domain is more limited.

According to whether we are considering *what* the idea represents, or the *idea,* insofar as it is in me, essences are understood either as delivering to us the structures and universal relations from which the things are woven— they *are,* in this case, *real beings*—or as *ideas* that resist my thought, being indeformable, etc.—they are, in this way, *recognized* as *real beings*.[101] But in any case, since essences are only abstract beings in me, they do not exist outside of me in the isolation they have in my thought, except in the case in which I perceive a real distinction between them. Most of the time, in things, they are not separated from a multitude of other essential beings that my thought sets aside when considering them each at a time. There is therefore some contrast between the complexity of things really existing outside of me and the simplicity of these abstract natures. Often we convert abstract beings that only my thought separates into things really separated existing outside us, and we thus convert into a real opposition between things the opposition of the abstract and the concrete that merely translates the real distinction between my thought and things: "For arithmetic and geometry, even though they are the most certain of sciences, deceive us in this respect, for what arithmetician does not think that his numbers have been abstracted from any subject by the understanding, but that also we must distinguish them truly by the imagination?"—meaning what arithmetician does not think that they are outside of him, as things really existing without subject?[102] Similarly, geometers consider lines as without width but construct real bodies from them by engendering surfaces by their movements.[103] Thus we are easily led to take as existing things, really separated from others, abstract beings that are constitutive characters of these things, but that are not in themselves separable, and that have not been separated except by and for my understanding. These abstract beings, converted into substantial things outside of me, then enter into conflict with the things really existing outside of me.[104] That is what is produced, for example, when one opposes space to the proper extension of the body occupying the space, or extension *(corpus geometricum)* to matter *(corpus physicum)*, or even the number numbering to things numbered.[105] It happens, in fact, that when transforming these abstract beings into things existing outside of me, we exclude from them the real substantial things outside of me (the only things which these are) or their characteristic properties, for example, when we say that *extension is not body,*[106] or that *the numbering number excludes the numbered thing.*[107] In this respect, imagination can be a great help, for it allows us to conceive that what is not included in the abstract being, isolated from the thing by my thought alone, is not isolated from the thing itself, on that account, and that if this abstract being does not account for some aspects of the thing, we have to avoid denying them.[108] This recourse to imagination is particularly pressing for physicists, who must retain from all mathematical distinctions only the ones that have a real foundation in things.[109] But this recourse is necessarily defective with respect to metaphysical concepts[110] like those of existence and essence, and their distinction of reason.

Thus essences cannot be distinguished in themselves from existences outside of me, except by an abstraction of our mind that really separates the essence that has become *idea* from the thing itself. That is why, even though essences constitute the basis of things, the distinctions established by our thought between the ideas that express them—with the simplifications that result from this, and that the conditions internal to our science require in order to promote evidence and certainty in our souls—are thus not always real and do not exist as such in the things outside of me. There is an elaboration of essences that occurs only in my understanding in search of a science. Many basic errors of pre-Cartesian science are due, according to Descartes, to the confusion between the concepts issued from the needs of our knowledge and the real articulations of things. We have already seen—and we shall see—that many aberrant interpretations relative to Descartes' doctrine arise from an often unconquerable confusion between what he has carefully distinguished, namely, the *veritas rationum* and the *veritas rei,* the necessary requirements in me in order that I reach clear and distinct ideas, and the necessary requirements in themselves for the thing or actual essence outside of me.

17. Replies to Two Difficulties; Suppression of the Intelligible World and Rational Positivism

These two fundamental theses, that essence distinguished from existence is nothing more than the idea in me of the nature of the thing existing outside of me and exists nowhere other than in my understanding, and that existence and essence are absolutely identical in themselves, appear to raise several difficulties.

1) Descartes conceives that physics must have recourse to experience in order to know which, among the possible combinations that mathematics uncovers, are those that God has realized in fact.[111] The world of possibles is therefore more vast than the world of existences. How can one admit this if essences and existences are one and the same thing? It is that the world of possibles resides in my understanding, where essence, as an idea, is dissociated from the existence outside of me. God has placed in me the clear and distinct idea of extension. My understanding perceives by means of this idea that the modes of extension and their combinations are indefinite in number. Moreover, God has only realized some of the combinations outside us. He could have made another world with extended substance; he did not make it, and experience teaches us that. But it is not necessary, in order to conceive that he could have realized other possibilities, to admit essences or possibles in themselves outside us that are distinct from existing things. These possibilities were included in the very being of the extended essence that God has posited in actuality. However, in order to choose from these possible combinations, did not God have knowledge of as many as possible, prior to the existence of the things he wished to create? That would be to presume that understanding is prior to will in God. And that would be to contradict the fundamental thesis of the free creation of eternal truths. The creative act belongs completely to the incomprehensible mystery of divine nature.

2) If essences are only ideas, how can one explain that elsewhere idea is so distinguished from essence that one can establish the difference between the a posteriori proof and the a priori proof of the existence of God with respect to this distinction? If all essences are identical to existences, how can Descartes establish in the a priori proof that God's essence is the only essence to be identified with its existence?

As for the first point, idea differs from essence insofar as essence is the idea clothed with its objective validity guaranteed by divine veracity. Thus, I know that what I know by means of my idea is the necessary nature of the possible thing, meaning that it is the structure that God wills immutably as the condition of the thing. Thus essence does not lose its character of being *a parte rei*, a condition of possibility of the existence of the thing, from the fact that it is conceived as being merely a pure and simple idea of my mind when it is conceived apart from existence; and this is less so to the degree that this idea testifies by its immutable nature that it is God himself who has implanted it in me. Moreover, the idea does not lose its character of mode of my thought from the fact that it is cloaked by divine veracity with an objective validity that allows it to be recognized indubitably by myself as an essence of the possible existing thing. As long as I do not know whether this idea possesses an objective validity, I cannot conclude anything from it relative to what is outside of me—from which arises the necessity for the a priori proof. Once I know that this idea is objectively valid, I can be assured that what I see clearly and distinctly in the idea must belong to it necessarily—from which arises the possibility and legitimacy of the a priori proof.

As for the second point, it is quite true that, *outside of me,* the essence of triangle cannot be without its existence and vice versa, but it does not result from this that in itself the triangle exists necessarily, for that is a property that does not belong to its nature. On the other hand, it belongs to God's essence to exist necessarily. If I situate myself, not from the point of view of things *(extra cogitationem nostram),* but in myself, in which essence is an idea separate from the existence of the thing, I see in consulting this idea that, with respect to a triangle, its essence is in me and it reveals its immutable nature to me, and that, however, the triangle can "not exist in nature": from this point of view, essence is separate from existence. With respect to God's essence, I see that it implies that the thing exists necessarily and that the essence I perceive in me cannot not be without a real existence, meaning an actual existence, outside of me. Thus, among all the essences, it is the only one, for me, that cannot be separated from its existence.

And since in themselves *(extra cogitationem nostram) essences are always and in all cases identical to existences,* we can see that, once I know that God exists necessarily and eternally, because of his nature or essence, I know ipso facto that his essence is itself necessary and eternal, for the necessity that this essence is, can only be necessary existence and reciprocally; however, once I know that the existence of any finite thing whatever—for example, the existence of a triangle—is created and contingent, I know ipso facto that the essence of the triangle is itself created and contingent. Since, on the other hand, it represents to me, in virtue of divine veracity and immutability, the eternal structure of the thing that can exist, I see that it is an eternal truth.

Consequently, I conceive that this truth is eternal and that I must have been created contingently by God. Thus it is sufficient that I consult the essence of a finite thing in me in order to read in it its own contingency as an eternal truth from the fact that the existence of the thing of which it is the essence is contingent; it is even sufficient that I consult the essence of the infinite in order to read in it its necessity to be uncreated, from the very fact of the necessary existence it entails.

Thus, as a result, a doctrine much like Malebranche's, who holds the essence of created, finite, and contingent things to be uncreated, infinite, and eternal, is, for Descartes, radically unthinkable and even scandalous. It assumes, in fact, that outside our thought there is a real difference between the essential nature of the thing and its existence, to the extent that esence is in itself *(extra cogitationem nostram)* real, while the existing thing whose nature it constitutes might not be. There would be in this, according to Descartes, a conversion of a distinction of reason to a real distinction, of universals into things, of abstracts into concretes.

Nothing is more contrary to Cartesianism than the realism of Platonic ideas and the exemplarism of essences. If one is allowed to speak of the realism of essences, it is to the extent that, within my mind, clear and distinct ideas are presented as realities against which my own thought cannot do anything, since it is powerless to annihilate them or to modify them—in brief, it is to the extent that they are true and immutable natures, implanted in me by God. If we are allowed to speak of exemplarism, it is to the extent that God is *instar archetypi* with respect to the idea that we have of him—in brief, it is to the extent that his existence is the model of this idea and it is its copy. This exemplarism reverses Plato's exemplarism, in which the model is the idea and the existing thing its copy, in which existence is a defect with respect to idea, while for Descartes, "ideas can, in truth, easily become defective with respect to the perfection of things from which they are derived."[112] But at the same time, existence is nothing more than the very being of the essence outside of me, such that exemplarism, which makes my idea of God the reflection of his existence, makes it, in this way, the reflection of his essence.

Descartes annihilates the concept of a world of intelligible things governing the world of existences by means of this radical identification *a parte rei* of essences and existences. For him, only existences remain—existence of God, existence of souls, existence of body—and these existences are nothing more than their essences. If we wish to conceive outside my thought the essences that are located there as clear and distinct ideas, either they would be merely pure beings of reason, in the case in which we conceive them as really separated in themselves from existences, or else if we renounced this absurd separation, they would be the existing things themselves taken in what constitutes the whole of their being. In this way we would be affirming Descartes' positivism: outside of me, with the exception of God and the minds he has created, there is nothing other than matter, no ideal reality, no intelligibles; and we would also be affirming his rationalism, for there is nothing more in this existing matter than its essence, the object of clear and distinct knowledge. The combination of this positivism and this rationalism engenders the reduction of physics to a mathematics of geometrical extension and of movement geometrically defined.[113]

This rational positivism, which admits nothing more than the infinite power of the creative God above the world of things reduced to the reality of their essential nature, contrasts vividly with the doctrines of Saint Augustine and Saint Thomas, who profess that essence is in itself before existence,[114] by putting in God the ideas of existences susceptible to be created. Descartes' opposition to the general doctrine of the major Cartesians, who all admit an intelligible world or its equivalent, is no less radical: for Malebranche, ideas are eternally real outside of us, independently from created things; for Spinoza, there is outside my thought, in God, an eternal essence of body distinct from its temporal existence and an eternal essence of soul preceding its existence; for Leibniz, essences are in themselves proper beings prior to their existence and attain existence by an intelligible mechanism of reciprocal exclusion, by the agreement that rules the calculus *de minimis et maximis*.[115] In this affirmation of a world of real essences outside me and outside existing things, Descartes could only see (using his language and speaking strictly) a "pure tautology," meaning an illusory doubling of concrete reality to which we superimpose the abstraction of our mind, converted into beings, but which are only *beings of reason.*

Notes

Notes

Unless otherwise indicated, all references to Descartes' works are to Charles Adam and Paul Tannery's edition, *Oeuvres de Descartes* (Paris: Cerf, 1897-1913; new revised ed. Vrin, 1964-74), in 11 vols. Cross-references within this text are designated with "see above" or "see below" (e.g., "see below, vol. II, chap. x, sec. 3).

Introduction

1. (Paris: Aubier, Editions Montaigne, 1952); 2d ed., 1968; in 2 vols.: vol. I: *L'âme et Dieu*, 390 pp.; vol. II: *L'âme et le corps*, 339 pp.
2. "Descartes selon l'ordre des raisons, d'après M. Gueroult," *Revue de Métaphysique et de Morale* 60 (1955): 417.
3. *Meditations*, Preface, VII, pp. 9-10.
4. "De la méthode prescrite par Descartes pour comprendre sa philosophie," *Archiv für Geschichte der Philosophie* 44 (1962): 172-73.
5. Ibid.
6. *Revue Philosophique de la France et de L'étranger* 145 (1955): 329-39.
7. *Revue de Métaphysique et de Morale* 59 (1954): 231-32.
8. Ibid.
9. "The History of Philosophy as a Philosophical Problem," *The Monist* 53 (1969): 563-87; and "Le problème de la légitimité de l'histoire de la philosophie," *Archivio de Filosofia* 1 (1954): 39-63.
10. "The History of Philosophy as a Philosophical Problem," p. 574.
11. Margaret Wilson, *Descartes* (London: Routledge & Kegan Paul, 1978); also Edwin Curley, *Descartes against the Skeptics* (Cambridge: Harvard University Press, 1978), and some of the articles in Michael Hooker, ed., *Descartes, Critical and Interpretive Essays* (Baltimore: Johns Hopkins University Press, 1978).
12. (The Hague: Martinue Nijhoff, 1964), p. 38.
13. "Expérience ontologique et déduction systèmatique dans la constitution de la métaphysique de Descartes," *Cahiers de Royaumont* (Paris: Editions de Minuit, 1957), p. 28.
14. "Note sur l'interprétation de Descartes par l'ordre des raisons," *Revue de Métaphysique et de Morale* 61 (1956): 418.
15. *Etudes sur Descartes, Spinoza, Malebranche et Leibniz* (Hildesheim: Olms, 1970).
16. *Nouvelles réflexions sur la preuve ontologique de Descartes* (Paris: Vrin, 1955).
17. *Dynamique et métaphysique leibniziennes,* (Paris: Les Belles-Lettres, 1939; 2d ed., Aubier, 1967).
18. *Malebranche* (Paris: Aubier, 1955-58); in 3 vols.: vol. I: *La vision en Dieu;* vol. II: *Les cinq abîmes de la Providence,* A. *L'ordre et l'occasionalisme;* vol. III: *Les cinq abîmes de la Providence,* B. *La nature et la grâce.* Also *Etendue et Psychologie chez Malebranche* (Paris: Les Belles-Lettres, 1939).
19. *Spinoza* (Paris: Aubier, 1968-74); in 2 vols.: vol. I: *Dieu;* vol. II: *L'âme.*
20. *Berkeley* (Paris: Aubier, 1956); *La Philosophie transcendentale de Salomon Maimon* (Paris: Presses Universitaires de France, 1931); *L'Evolution et la structure de la Doctrine fichtéenne de la science* (Paris: Les Belles-Lettres, 1930), 2 vols.
21. There is very little of the massive Gueroult corpus in English; aside from the couple of articles Gueroult wrote in English ("The History of Philosophy as a Philosophical Problem," and "Substance and the Primitive Simple Notion in the Philosophy of Leibniz," *Philosophy and Phenomenological Research* 7 (1946): 293-315), there is very little in translation. Translated articles are "Spinoza's Letter on the Infinite," in *Spinoza, A Collection of Critical*

Essays, ed. Marjorie Grene (New York: Anchor Books, 1973), pp. 182-212; "The Metaphysics and Physics of Force in Descartes," in *Descartes: Philosophy, Mathematics, and Physics,* ed. Stephen Gaukroger (Sussex: Harvester Press, 1980), pp. 196-229; and "Space, Point and Void in Leibniz's Philosophy," in *Leibniz, Critical and Interpretive Essays,* ed. Michael Hooker (Minneapolis: University of Minnesota Press, 1982), pp. 283-301.

Preface

1. *Revue de Métaphysique et de Morale,* abstracts of thesis defences (1950), p. 435, col. b.
2. *To Voetius,* VIIIB, p. 41.
3. The phrase, "to split hairs" *(épiloguer),* is Descartes', or at least, his translator's, Clerselier, who is rendering the Latin expression *in singulas tantum clausulas argutari (Meditations,* Preface, VII, pp. 9-10).
4. *Rules,* Rule 2, X, p. 363.
5. *Meditations,* Preface, VII, pp. 9-10. "We would not wish for more in a topic of philosophy than to be able to give it a mathematical demonstration." *To Mersenne,* 30 August 1640, III, p. 173, ll. 15-19. "Everything must be deduced with such evidence that it can be counted as a mathematical demonstration" to the degree that he "assumes that those who will read his works . . . at least . . . have a mental aptitude for understanding mathematical demonstrations." *Principles,* II, art. 64.
6. Our emphasis.
7. *To Mersenne,* 24 December 1640, III, pp. 266-67.
8. *Discourse on Method,* 6th pt., VI, p. 67.
9. *To Elizabeth,* 6 October 1645, IV, p. 305.

Chapter I. Cartesian Metaphysics and the Order of Reasons

1. "There is nothing more useful to inquire about than the nature and limit of human knowledge. . . . Nor should it appear to be a tedious or difficult task in dealing with what we sense within ourselves, *to define the limits of the mind"* (our emphasis). *Rules,* Rule 8, X, pp. 397-98. "And lest we should remain forever uncertain as to what our mind can encompass, and lest it should make ill-advised and foolish efforts, we must, for once in our lives, before setting ourselves to discover particular truths, make careful inquiry into what knowledge the human reason is capable of discovering." Ibid., pp. 396-97. Compare with Locke: "After we had a while puzzled our selves, without coming any nearer a Resolution of those Doubts which perplexed us, it came into my Thoughts, that we took a wrong course; and that, before we set our selves upon Enquiries of that Nature, it was necessary to examine our own Abilities, and see, what Objects our Understanding were, or were not fitted to deal with [. . . .] The Understanding, like the Eye, whilst it makes us see, and perceive all other Things, takes no notice of it self: And it requires Art and Pains to set it at a distance, and make it its own Object." *Essay,* [the Epistle to the Reader and] bk. 1, chap. 1.

The primacy of self-reflection, established in a methodological principle for the determination of the limits of our faculties, marks the impregnation of empiricism by Cartesianism. One ought to note the contrast between this and the empiricism of a Gassendi: "Even though they [corporeal things—M. G.] are external to you, it is by no means strange that you could know and comprehend them more distinctly than yourself. But you ask how is it possible that I conceive something foreign to me better than myself? I reply that in the same way the eye *sees other things but does not see itself"* (our emphasis). Gassendi, *Objections V,* VII, p. 268. Compare also with Kant: ". . . to submit reason in the whole extent of its power to critical examination" and "to determine the limits of its possible knowledge," *Critique of Pure Reason,* A761, B789 et passim. This subordination of the whole philosophical enterprise to the determination of the power of our understanding and its limits is not to be found in the philosophy of the great Cartesians: Spinoza, Malebranche, and Leibniz.

2. *Rules,* X, p. 395, ll. 17-24. "And although many things can often be proposed to him, the investigation of which is forbidden by the present rule, he will nevertheless not consider himself more ignorant, because he clearly perceives that those same things exceed the capabilities of the human mind. The very fact that he knows that the matter under inquiry can be known by no one, will, if he is sensible, abundantly satisfy his curiosity." *Rules,* X, p. 396, ll. 19-25. This is a mathematical idea according to which, to demonstrate that a problem is insoluble for our understanding, or that our capacity to know has limits, is not something negative, but a positive acquisition, a science: *the science of limits.* Cf. Kant: "The former knowledge of our ignorance, which is possible only through the critique of reason itself, is *science." Critique of Pure Reason,* A758, B786; cf. also the *Prolegomena,* sec. 57-59.

3. *To Mersenne,* 15 April 1630, I, p. 144.

4. Ibid., p. 145: "What easily leads one to error here is that the majority of men do not consider God as an incomprehensible and infinite being." *To Mersenne,* 6 May 1630, I, p. 150.

5. *Replies to Objections I,* VII, p. 113; *Replies to Objections V (to Gassendi),* VII, p. 368.

6. *To Mersenne,* 6 May 1630, I, p. 149.

7. "They ought to judge . . . since God is a cause whose power surpasses the *limits of the understanding* and since the necessity of these truths in no way exceeds our knowledge, that they are some lesser thing subject to this incomprehensible power." Ibid., p. 150. Concerning God, Free Creator of the good, the true, and the order, cf. *Replies to Objections VI,* VII, sec. 8.

8. *The Search after Truth,* X, p. 503, ll. 8-23.

9. And doubtless from 1628. By boldly affirming that the real interest for mathematics resides in its method, once one has set aside its disguise, Descartes indicates as early as the *Rules* his disdain for mathematical puzzles (the problem of the cycloid, for example) that the learned men of the period dared each other to solve. He attributes to them no greater importance than what we today would attribute to crossword puzzles: "I would not think much of these rules if they were of no greater use but for the solution of these empty problems that the arithmeticians and the geometers play with when they wish to occupy their time, for in that case, I would have succeeded only in solving trifles with perhaps more subtlety than others do." *Rules,* Rule 4, X, p. 374.

10. *To Mersenne,* March 1636, he announces his plan to publish the *Discourse* under the title *Project of Universal Science which may Elevate our Nature to its Highest Degree of Perfection,* together with the *Dioptrics,* the *Meteors,* and the the *Geometry,* "in which the most curious topics have been chosen in order to prove the universal science . . . explained in such a way that even those who have not studied them can understand them." I, p. 339.

11. *Treatise on Light,* chap. 7, sub finem, XI, p. 48. The spirit of the *Geometry* is the same: "I maintain . . . that one ought to persuade oneself that our descendants would not be able to find anything within this topic that I could not just as easily have discovered, had I wished to take the trouble to do so." *To Mersenne,* December 1637, I, p. 480. Cf. also *To Mersenne,* 12 September 1638: "I would tell you that it is not my style to stop at minor geometrical demonstrations, which can easily be discovered by others, and which those who know me would not be able to judge that I am ignorant of." II, p. 361.

12. *To Mersenne,* 10 March 1642, III, p. 544. Cf. "For truth consists in what is indivisible." *Replies to Objections VII,* VII, p. 548, l. 19. "All my opinions are joined together in such a way and so strongly dependent on one another that one could not appropriate any for oneself without knowing all of them." *To R. P. Vatier,* 22 February 1638, I, p. 562. Cf. also III, p. 379. Alquié, in *La Découverte métaphysique de l'homme chez Descartes* (Paris, 1950), p. 5, wrote that "we do not think that Descartes has a system"—Descartes thinks the opposite.

13. *Rules,* Rule 1, X, p. 361.

14. Ibid., p. 360.

15. *To Gibieuf,* 19 January 1642, III, p. 478.

16. *Replies to Objections II,* IX, p. 121.

17. *To Mersenne,* 24 December 1640, III, pp. 266-70.

18. Cf. below in vol. II, Conclusions, sec. 4.

19. *Replies II*, pp. 121 seq. Concerning the impossibility, according to Descartes, to understand his doctrine if one does not first deal with the *seriem et nexum mearum rationum,* cf. Preface to the *Meditations*, VII, pp. 9-10, and *Replies to Objections V*, VII, pp. 378-79, texts that we have cited in our preface, p. 10.

20. *To Mersenne*, 24 December 1640, III, pp. 266-67.

21. This is a Kantian designation that prevails. The Cartesian designation is "a priori proof" (cf. *Entretien avec Burman*, V, p. 153) because of its opposition to the proof drawn from effects, a posteriori, or *ab effectu;* this is in conformity with medieval tradition.

22. If Descartes is obliged to "disavow completely" Regius, who in his *Fundamenta Physicae* "seems to have stated nothing about physics and medicine that he had not drawn from my writings, as he asserted it," doubtless, it is because "he denied some metaphysical truths upon which all his physics depended," but above all because "he transcribed badly and changed the order." *Principles,* Preface IXb, p. 19, ll. 15-25. *To Elizabeth,* March 1647, IV, p. 625, ll. 24-29.

23. In any case, Descartes admits only experience according to the order determined and indicated by reason: it is experience "according to the truth," meaning experience rectified and disclosed by the linkage of reasons *(Principles,* II, art. 24, 25; III, art. 4, 5; *Rules,* Rule 12, X, pp. 431 seq; *Discourse,* IV, p. 64). It is from this that he draws his repeated assertions that experiments are only useful when one possesses true principles and that the most specific are mostly "false and superfluous, if one does not know the truth of the matter before making them" *(To Mersenne,* 23 December 1630, I, p. 196). It is also from the above that he draws his critique of experiments: "As for Galileo's experiments, which you have submitted to me, I deny them all" *(To Mersenne,* April 1634, I, p. 287). In fact Galileo was wrong, according to Descartes, to neglect the resistance of air. Descartes' opposition to the experimental method is that he does not draw from the experiment itself, but from mathematics, a priori, the principles that ought to explain it. Experiments can serve to verify, but not to suggest hypotheses. That is why experiments have a discriminatory role to play with regard to the various principles reason furnishes and among which God has chosen to realize this universe, rather than any other *(Principles,* III, art. 46). This rational and mathematical origin of principles is, in any case, what Descartes opposes to Scholastic physics, which rests on common experience *(Principles,* II, art. 37), by virtue of the principle that "the sequence of being to knowledge is proper."

The rejection of common experience for the rational is, let us note, the indispensable postulate of real experimental science, which discovers hypotheses and invents experiments that are often denied by empirical appearances. Galileo himself pits mathematical conceptions with experiments without any particular experiment necessarily disabling the theory; he also institutes experiments constructed by reason, "the experiments of reason" (cf. Koyré, *Etudes Galiléennes* [Paris: Hermann, 1939; available as *Galileo Studies* (Atlantic Highlands, N. J.: Humanities Press, 1978)]). Scientific progress has consisted of the substitution of the rational and real for experience in general (G. Bachelard, *le nouvel esprit scientifique* [Paris: Alcan, 1934], p. 4). It tends to reject as illusory any experience that contradicts the rational language of mathematics. Thus the objection, "this contradicts experience," which Leibniz often addresses against Descartes (for example, with respect to the laws of motion), is not decisive by itself. One needs to know *which experience* is contradicted. If common experience is contradicted, one can note that Leibniz himself contradicts it just as often.

24. *Replies to Objections II,* IX, pp. 121-22.

25. Ibid., p. 121.

26. Ibid., pp. 122-23.

27. "One can name it *Meditationes de prima philosophia,* since I do not merely treat the topics concerning God and the soul in it, but in general those concerning all the first things that can be known by philosophizing in order." *To Mersenne,* 10 November 1640, III, p. 239.

28. "Foreseeing the difficulty that many would have in conceiving the foundations of metaphysics, I have tried to explain the principal points in a book of *Meditations,* which is not very large, but whose volume has been increased and whose matter has been much illuminated

by the objections that certain very learned men have sent me in their regard and by the replies that I have made to them. . . . In order that it [the first part of the *Principles*—M. G.] may be properly understood, it is advisable to read beforehand the *Meditations* that I have written on the same subject." *Principles,* Introduction, IXb, p. 16.

29. See the *Letter to Clerselier* of 15 April 1649.

30. *Replies to Objections II,* IX, p. 121. *Synopsis of the Meditations,* VII, pp. 12-13; IX, p. 9.

31. That is Bréhier's hypothesis in *La Philosophie et son passé* [Paris: Alcan, 1940], p. 104.

32. Bréhier rightly remarks that Descartes' thesis differs from Duns Scotus' because Duns Scotus' God does not create the possibles and his will is limited by the contradictory (ibid., p. 112); but one may doubt that this difference was sufficient to affect theologians profoundly. Moreover, Bréhier links up in Cartesian philosophy the concept of eternal truths with that of the evil genius (pp. 113 et seq.), a linkage that cannot be accepted and that seems contrary, as we shall see, both to the spirit and to the letter of the Cartesian texts. This linkage confers to God's will an anarchical omnipotence that Descartes himself refuses him; in fact, there is an order of impossibility to which this omnipotence can be radically subordinated, which is the set of what contradicts the concept of omnipotence itself. Thus it is God's omnipotence that renders impossible *for God himself* that he is a great deceiver.

33. Bréhier, ibid., p. 116.

34. "I tried as much as possible to follow this order in my *Meditations.*" *Replies to Objections II,* IX, p. 121. "I tried to write nothing in all this treatise for which I did not have extremely exact demonstrations. I saw myself as obligated to follow an order similar to that which the geometers make use of, which is to begin by putting forward all the things upon which the propositions we seek depend." *Synopsis of the Meditations,* VII, pp. 12-13; IX, p. 9. "And now, in order to have the opportunity to examine this question without interrupting the order of meditation I set for myself, which is to pass by degrees from the notions that I find to be the first in my mind to those that I can discover afterwards, I should here, etc. . . ." *Meditation III,* IX, p. 29. "As for me, I only followed the analytic path in the *Meditations* because it seems to me the most true and the most appropriate for teaching." *Replies to Objections II,* IX, p. 122. "Thus I judge that it is not proper nor even possible to insert into the *Meditations* the replies to the objections one can make to them, since that would interrupt the whole sequence." *To Mersenne,* 24 December 1640, III, pp. 266-67. Concerning not "perverting the order" of the *Meditations,* cf. *To Mersenne,* 31 December 1640, p. 272.

35. Concerning the analogies that Descartes established between his *Metaphysical Meditations* and the demonstrations of Apollonius, cf. Baillet, *La Vie de M. Descartes* (1691), VI, chap. 1, p. 101. See also below in vol. II, chap. xiv, sec. 12; chap. xxi, sec. 5.

36. *Rules,* Rule 12, X, p. 418.

37. "The first principle is the *existence of our soul* because there is nothing that is more easily known to us. I also add that this is not a condition that ought to be required of the first principle, that it be such that all other propositions can be reduced and proven by it; it is sufficient that it be useful toward proving several and that there be no other upon which it depends nor that can be found before it, for it may be the case that there is no principle in the world to which all things can be reduced. Moreover the way in which one reduces all propositions to '*impossibile est idem simul esse et non esse*' is superfluous and of no use; on the other hand it is extremely useful that one begins to assure oneself of the *existence of God* and then of the existence of all other creatures by the *consideration of one's own existence*" (meaning by the consideration of the existence of one's own self). *To Clerselier,* June-July 1646, pp. 444-45.

38. *Replies to Objections II, Geometrical Summary,* corollary to prop. III: "God has created heaven and the earth and all that is contained in them, and in addition, he can make everything we clearly conceive be exactly as we conceive them." This corollary serves as lemma to demonstrate prop. IV.

39. That is why Descartes can stipulate that one must suppose some order even between things that do not precede each other naturally *(Discourse,* VI, pp. 18-19). In the *Rules,* he

states more precisely that the order of the method is that of the production of our knowledge insofar as it is certain and necessary, and not the order of things: "This proposition . . . shows that things can be arranged into different series, not indeed insofar as they are referred to particular classes of entities, as philosophers have divided them into categories, but so that the knowledge of some *can flow from the knowledge of others* in such a way that, whenever some difficulty arises, one can immediately notice whether it will be worthwhile to examine some other propositions first, and which ones, and in what order." *Rules*, Rule 6, X, p. 381.

40. Cf. below, vol. II, chap. xiii, sec. 3; chap. xiv, sec. 12.

41. Commenting on this fragment of Descartes' manuscript published by Baillet, Gilson wrote not unjustly: "Descartes' aim is not uniquely or principally to invent new ideas, because the whole originality, even the whole fecundity of his ideas stems from the place they occupy in the deduction, not from their content considered in isolation." *Commentaire du Discours de la Méthode* [Paris: Vrin, 1925], p. 172. From this we can draw the conclusion, which is no longer entirely Gilson's, that everything in Descartes' philosophy is new, even what appears to be old.

42. *Entretien avec Burman,* V, p. 165.

43. Ibid.: "That is a most desirable occupation for man to pursue, because it is what can yield all the abundant benefits for life."

44. *To Elizabeth,* 28 July 1643, III, pp. 692-93; *To Chanut,* 26 February 1649, V, p. 291, ll. 20-21.

Chapter II. Doubt and the Evil Genius

1. *Rules,* Rule 12, X, pp. 421-22.

2. *Descartes Erkenntnistheorie, Eine Studie zur Vorgeschichte des Kritizismus,* (Marburg, 1882).

3. Natorp's error, and generally the school of Marburg's error, stems from a bias contrary to any sane historical method, which consists in interpreting at whatever cost every philosopher, whether prior or posterior to Kant, through the perspectives of Kantian philosophy, metamorphosing the former into precursors, who are more or less unconscious [of what they are doing], and the latter into disciples, who are more or less unfaithful. Moreover, it happens that, in this case, in opposition to what Natorp thinks, the *Meditations,* more than the *Rules,* is the means by which one can compare Descartes to Kant, since it is the *Meditations* that rises to a point of view comparable to the *Critique* by proposing to establish the objective validity of our knowledge, a problem that the *Rules* ignores.

4. *Meditation I,* VII, p. 18, ll. 6-14; IX, pp. 13-14. In general we give references to both the Latin and French texts of the *Meditations.* Baillet *(Vie de M. Descartes* [1691], bk. VI, chap. 9, p. 172) believes that the French translation, which was reviewed by Descartes, is even preferable to the original, since Descartes, wishing to "illuminate" some Latin passages that were not clear enough "for many people," made "some small changes" and "corrected himself." However the reasons Baillet gives for his preference are not very convincing a priori. If the French version is better, it is because the translators, for reasons of elegance, have removed some, if not all, the "philosophical jargon" that even in Latin already seemed rough and barbaric. If Descartes did not want to change the style of his translators, it is because "his modesty and the esteem he had for them . . . make him think their style better than his." In truth, it often happens that the French translation weakens the rigor and concise precision of the Latin. In addition, with respect to technical and scientific philosophy, Descartes seems more at ease with the Latin. How many times does it happen that he interrupts a letter begun in French in order to express himself in Latin when he wishes to be precise! However, since Descartes, by editing the translation, has sometimes added or revealed in French some nuances that the Latin version kept hidden, we must conclude that one has to consult both versions in order to be able to choose from each the most expressive or the most precise formulations.

5. *Meditation I,* VII, pp. 16-20; IX, pp. 13-15; *Rules,* Rule 2, X, p. 365.

6. *Meditation I*, VII, p. 20, ll. 7, 11, and 12.

7. The distinction between primitive intellectual notions, which are in themselves simple or unbreakable (extension, mathematical essences, the intellect, etc.), and sensible primitive notions, which, although composite in themselves, are simple and unbreakable for us (sensations), ought to be related to the Leibnizian distinction between the simple natures, *in themselves* unbreakable, which are the ultimate elements of analysis, and are mental entities *(primitivae simplices)*, and the simple natures that are unbreakable *for us*, which are sensible entities *(confusa sensuum):* "Sunt etiam privitivi simplices omnia phaenomena confusa sensuum, etc. . . ." "Colores, sapores, etc." Leibniz, *De analysi notionum et veritatem*, in Couturat, *Opuscules et fragments inédits de Leibniz* [Paris, 1903], p. 360, and also pp. 38, 219, 512, etc. The obscurity and confusion of sensible entities are however different in Cartesian philosophy, since they arise out of the effective mixture of two incompatible natures, whereas in Leibnizian philosophy, they only arise from the incapacity of our mind to attain an infinitely small constituent. Although stemming from a composition, the sensible element is however unbreakable in itself. The confusion and obscurity of sensation are therefore, in Cartesian philosophy, intrinsic characteristics, and not extrinsic characteristics, only relative to us, as they are in Leibnizian philosophy. On the first degree and second degree (congeniality) of innateness, see vol. II, chap. xiv, sec. 9.

8. *Meditation I*, VII, p. 20; IX, p. 16.

9. *Meditation V*, VII, p. 65; IX, p. 52.

10. *Meditation I*, VII, p. 13; IX, p. 16.

11. "What reason can anyone give to make me doubt them [the truths of geometry—M. G.]? Would it be that my nature is such that I am likely to be deceived? But I already know that I cannot be mistaken in the judgment for which I clearly know the reasons. Would it be that I considered many things as true and certain that I later recognized to be false? But I had not clearly and distinctly known any of these things." *Meditation V*, VII, p. 70; IX, p. 56.

12. *Meditation I*, IX, p. 16. Cf. *Discourse*, pt. IV: "If it happened that we had some very distinct idea, even in our sleep, as for example when a geometer dreams of some new proof, his sleep would not keep the proof from being true." VI, p. 39, l. 13.

13. Ibid., pp. 16-17.

14. *Principles*, 1, art. 6.

15. In the *Meditations*, will and freedom are only considered from the point of view of the conditions of the possibility of science (freedom to doubt, to pay attention, to avoid haste, to affirm only clear and distinct ideas, to avoid error, etc.). The moral point of view is almost absent. From the metaphysical point of view, the only problem is the reconciliation of the ill use of freedom of will, which entails error and sin, with the goodness and absolute veracity of the author of our origin. When, near the end of his life, Descartes considers the moral question, he places virtue and the supreme good under the good use of free will, under the firmness of will *when lacking anything better*, meaning lacking clear and distinct knowledge of what is good that is possible for us, meaning of what is in itself suitable to do in each occasion. In brief, lacking the good judgment that assumes the possession of the truth, excellence will be related to the will to judge well, which must be satisfied with being the will to bring forth the best judgments possible (cf. vol. II, chap. xix, "Some Consequences Concerning Medicine and Morality"). The problem of free will therefore seems for Descartes to be a second-order problem, no matter how important the role that free will plays in the discovery of truth and in moral action.

16. The comparison of radical doubt with the effort to straighten a bent stick by bending it in the opposite direction, gives the method the character of a spiritual exercise that relates it to the proceedings of religious elevation. Metaphysical and religious requirements intersect when they order a break with habits and a detachment with respect to the sensible. (With respect to the combination of the religious genre with the geometric genre, cf. below, vol. II, chap. xxi).

17. *Replies to Objections V*, VII, p. 349. Compare with the *Rules*, Rule 12, X, p. 417, ll. 16-27, in which Descartes, commenting on Eudoxus of Cnidus' formulation *(sozein ta*

phainomena), indicates the need for methodological assumptions that can be more or less fictive (like the imaginary circles of the orbits of Aristotle's or Ptolemy's planets), but that are necessary in order to distinguish simple and composite things, and in order to see, with respect to one and the other, where error may reside; these are the notions that can be known certainly, in order that we may apply ourselves to them alone.

18. "But it is useful not to accept any belief without considering on what title or for what cause one accepts it." *To Mersenne,* 16 October 1639, II, p. 598. "To examine its certificate of believability" will be one of the favorite formulas of Kantianism.

19. *Meditation II,* VII, pp. 24-25; IX, p. 19.

20. *Replies to Objections II,* IX, p. 114.

21. Cf. Régis, *Réponse au livre qui a pour titre P. Danielis Huetiis censura philosophiae cartesianae* [Paris, 1691], pp. 3 and 5.

22. *Meditation VI,* VII, p. 89, l. 19; IX, p. 71; *Replies to Objections IV,* VII, p. 226, l. 18; IX, p. 176.

23. *Meditation VI:* "And to these reasons for doubting I have since added two other very general ones." VII, p. 77, l. 7.

24. *The hyperbolic doubts based on natural reasons for doubt* are in opposition to the *metaphysical doubt* (hyperbolic doubt based on the hypothesis of the evil genius). The expression, *natural doubt,* in the final analysis, is suitable only for nonhyperbolic doubts, meaning true and nonfictional doubts.

25. That is the thesis defended by Gouhier, *IX Congrès* international de philosophie (1937), I, pp. 69 seq., and Bréhier, *La Philosophie et son passé* [Paris: Alcan, 1940], pp. 113-16.

26. Gouhier, ibid., p. 72.

27. That is the thesis we have upheld in "Descartes au Congrès Descartes," *Revue de Métaphysique* 45 (1938): 122 seq.—see also vol. II, chap. x—and also defended by Jean Laporte in *Le Rationalisme de Descartes* (Paris: Presses Universitaires de France, 1945), p. 171.

28. *Replies to Objections VI,* IX, p. 230.

29. *Meditation IV,* IX, p. 43; *Principles,* I, art. 29.

30. "Malice is not compatible with supreme power." *Entretien avec Burman (Meditation I),* V, p. 147. "*I am supposing that there is some deceiver who is extremely powerful and, if it is permissible to say, malicious and clever. . . .* A restriction is added here because there would be a contradiction in the language of the author if he said 'supremely powerful and malicious,' since omnipotence and maliciousness are incompatible. That is why he adds *if it is permissible to say (si fas est dicere)."* Ibid. *(Meditation II),* V, pp. 150-51. In opposition to the hypothesis of the free creation of eternal truths, the hypothesis of the evil genius is a supposition in the category of impossible or absurd suppositions.

31. "Not yet knowing, or rather pretending not to know, the author of my being." *Meditation VI,* VII, p. 77, l. 15.

32. *Discourse,* VI, pp. 38-39. Since God is the Supreme Being, he is also necessarily the supreme good and the supreme truth, and hence, it is contradictory that something proceeds from him that positively tends toward falsity." *Replies to Objections II,* IX, p. 113. "That every deception depends on some defect is manifest to me by the light of nature, because a being in which there is no imperfection cannot tend toward nonbeing, that is, cannot have nonbeing, or nongood, or nontruth as its end or purpose—for these three things are the same. It is manifest that in every deception there is falsehood and that falsehood is something nontrue, and consequently a nonbeing and a nongood." *To Clerselier,* 23 April 1649, V, p. 357. "Evil comes from any defect." *To Elizabeth,* January 1646, IV, p. 354. Cf. also IV, p. 308; V, p. 8.

33. One must distinguish between the true God, clearly known, and false gods, for once the true God is clearly known, not only is it not permissible, is it not possible that man attribute anything false to him. . . . But to attribute to the false gods . . . and even to the true God when he is known only confusedly, something false as a hypothesis, can be either good or bad, depending upon whether the purpose for which one framed such a hypothesis is good or bad— for what is thus feigned and attributed by hypothesis is not itself affirmed as true by the will,

but merely proposed for examination by the understanding. . . . Thus the case of someone who imagines a deceiving God (or even the true God, but not yet clearly enough known to himself nor to the others [for whom he frames this hypothesis]) and who does not make use of this fiction for any evil purpose . . . but only to enlighten the understanding further, and to know for himself or to bring others to know more clearly God's nature, such a person, I say, etc. . . ." *To Buitendick,* 1643, IV, p. 64.

34. "Infixa quaedam meae menti vetus opinio." *Meditation I,* VII, p. 21; IX, p. 16. "The preconceived opinion of God's supreme power" and "on this opinion." *Meditation III,* VII, p. 36; IX, p. 28.

35. "Principally because we have been told that God who has created us can do anything he pleases. . . ." *Principles,* I, art. 5. To this opinion is opposed the knowledge of a true God, whose omnipotence is incompatible with deception. This opinion is "without reason": "I have no reason to believe that there is a God who is a deceiver. . . . The reason for doubt that depends only on this opinion is very tenuous, and so to speak, metaphysical." *Meditation III,* ibid.

36. *Objections II,* IX, p. 99; *Objections VI,* IX, p. 220.

37. *To Mersenne,* 6 May 1630, IX, p. 150.

38. *Replies to Objections VI,* IX, p. 230; *Meditation I,* IX, p. 17; *Principles,* I, art. 5.

39. "For I can persuade myself that I was so made by nature that I could easily make mistakes, even in those matters that I believe I understand with the greatest of evidence, especially because I remember having judged many things true and certain, which later other reasons compelled me to consider false." *Meditation V,* VII, p. 70.

40. "Could God have ordered one of his creatures to hate him, and thereby made this a good thing to do?" Reply: "God could not do this now; but we simply do not know whether he could have done it. And why could he not have been able to give such an order to one of his creatures?" *Entretien avec Burman,* V, p. 160; Adam's trans. [Paris: Boivin, 1937], p. 53.

41. "And certainly there is no doubt about whether God was unable to create me such that I would never be mistaken; it is also certain that he always wills that which is best. Is it therefore a better thing to be able to make a mistake than not to be able to do so?" *(Anne ergo melius est me falli quam non falli?).* *Meditation IV,* VII, p. 55.

42. Gouhier [above, n. 25], pp. 72-73.

43. The two reasons are distinct in reality, even though Descartes subscribes to the theory of transcendentals, and identifies *ens, verum,* and *bonum;* cf. the letter to Clerselier cited above, n. 32, and *Replies II:* "Since God is the Supreme Being, he is also necessarily the supreme good and the supreme truth." IX, p. 113.

44. See below, vol. II, chap. xv, sec. 7 and 9.

45. See above, nn. 30 and 32.

46. See vol. II, chap. x.

Chapter III. The Cogito: Knowledge of My Existence and Knowledge of My Nature

1. *Discourse,* VI, p. 33, l. 20; *Meditation III,* VII, p. 35; IX, p. 27.

2. See the appendix at the end of vol. II. This principle is expressed in the first person in the *Meditation,* in conformity with the requirements of the reflective process of the I on itself: "Let him deceive me as much as he wishes, *he* [*God*—M. G.] *can never make it be that I am nothing, as long as I am thinking that I am something"* (our emphasis). IX, p. 19. I therefore experience in myself that there is an impossibility for God himself there. The principle, "In order to think one must exist," therefore appears to me free from the grasp of the evil genius. Moreover, this principle is an axiom that Descartes uses here and there under various forms, for example, when he states that being and reason are contemporaneous in man "even though being is a condition of reason," as light *(lux)* is contemporaneous with the light *(lumen)* of which it is the cause *(To Morin,* 13 July 1638, II, p. 209). That which here thus appears to me necessarily ("he

senses in himself that it cannot be that he is thinking without existing," VII, p. 140) as being an impossibility in itself, even for God, will ultimately be explained from the point of view of *God in himself.* Cf. below, chap. x, *The General Theory of Possibility.*

3. Cf. to the appendix of vol. II, for my note to the International Congress of 1937, "Le Cogito et la notion 'Pour penser il faut être' " *(Actes du Congrès,* fasc. I, pp. 53 seq.), and the discussion of this thesis by H. Gouhier, "Les exigences de l'existence de la métaphysique de Descartes," in *Revue Internationale de Philosophie* (April 1950), n. 12, and G. Dreyfus, "Discussion sur le Cogito et l'axiome 'Pour penser il faut être,' " same *Revue* (January 1952), n. 19.

4. VII, p. 145; IX, p. 114 (our emphasis).

5. ". . . It is impossible for us never to think of something without having at the same time the idea of our soul as something capable of thinking everything we are thinking." *To Mersenne,* July 1641, III, p. 394. One ought to relate this with the Kantian *Ich denke:* "It must be possible for the 'I think' to accompany all my representation, for otherwise something would be represented in me that could not be thought at all, and that is equivalent to saying that the representation would be impossible, or at least that it would be nothing to me." *Critique of Pure Reason,* "Analytic of Concepts," sec. 16, ed. B.

6. *The Search after Truth,* X, p. 521.

7. *Rules,* Rules 6 and 12, X, pp. 383, 418, 422; *Principles,* I, art. 53; *To Elizabeth,* 21 May 1643, III, p. 665; *To Gibieuf,* 19 January 1642, III, pp. 475-76; *Replies to Objections I,* IX, pp. 94-95; *Replies to Objections IV,* pp. 174-75. Cf. Laporte, "L'idée de liaison nécessaire chez Descartes," *IX Congrès international de philosophie* (1937) II, pp. 9-14.

8. Laporte, ibid. In his *Le Rationalisme de Descartes,* [Paris: Presses Universitaires de France, 1945], p. 97, n. 4, Laporte, our friend whom we miss, has reproached us for having transformed into a modal distinction the distinction of reason that Descartes established between substance and its principal attribute (in "Descartes au Congrès Descartes," *Revue de Métaphysique* (1938), pp. 116 seq.). But we wished to demonstrate, on the contrary, as does Laporte, that by making the Cogito into a personal concrete self, one is forced to establish a modal distinction between substance and its principal attribute, in opposition to what Descartes teaches. J. Laporte adds that, by opposing *"thought* as impersonal attribute with a *personal* subject" we went against Descartes' language, which says *Cogito (my* thought) and not *Cogitatur.* However, in this case we were aiming at Laporte's expressions, and not Descartes'; Laporte wrote: *"Thought,* restricted to itself, remains something abstract . . . and it cannot be fully conceived except under *the concrete form of a personal reality."* J. Laporte, "L'idée de liaison nécessaire," in *Actes du Congrès Descartes* (Paris, 1937), II, p. 14. This terminological question matters little, in any case. For what does Descartes mean? He simply means this: What do I know if I am not deceived when I believe myself to be Descartes? Do not madmen believe themselves to be gourds, Louis XIII, or the Cardinal? Cannot the evil genius deceive me about my own individuality? Did not Mercury succeed, for an instant, in having Socius doubt his personal identity? But in order to be deceived in this case, I must at least be thinking; and since I am thinking, I exist, for in order to think one must exist. In brief, in order to be deceived about myself, it is not necessary that I be Socius, Descartes, the Cardinal, nor any such individual, nor even an individual or a person in general, but simply that I be "a thinking thing," meaning a self, or thinking subject in general—any kind of thinking essence, whatever.

9. *Replies to Objections I,* IX, pp. 95-96; *Replies to Objections II,* p. 104; *Replies to Objections IV,* pp. 171 seq.; *Meditation VI,* p. 62, etc. There is no other concrete self for Descartes than the self that is united substantially to the body. And the Cogito is the self conceived without the body; this self can only be a pure intelligence. And pure intelligence is the same in all of us.

10. "Since extension, which constitutes the nature of the body, differs greatly from the various shapes or modes of extension that it assumes, so thought, or the thinking nature, in which I believe the essence of the human mind consists, is far different from this or that particular act of thought. . . . Therefore by thought I do not mean something universal, which

includes all modes of thinking, but a particular nature that takes on these modes, just as extension is a nature that takes on all sorts of shapes." *To Arnauld,* 20 July 1648 (trans. by Clerselier [1668], letter VI of vol. II), V, p. 221, ll. 21-25.

11. "Of all the attributes I bestowed upon myself, only one remains for me to examine . . . it is the only one [thought—M. G.] that I cannot separate from myself." *Search after Truth,* X, p. 521. "It alone cannot be detached from me." *Meditation II,* VII, p. 27, l. 8; p. 29, l. 3. "Furthermore, I find in myself various faculties of thinking that have their own particular characteristics, such as the faculties of imagination and of perception, without which I might conceive myself clearly and distinctly as a *whole* being." *Meditation VI,* VII, p. 78, l. 21.

12. *Replies to Objections IV,* IX, p. 172.

13. *Replies to Objections IV,* IX, pp. 171-72; *Principles,* I, art. 11.

14. "There is a real difference between them [between *distinguere* and *abstrahere*—M. G.], for in distinguishing a substance from its accidents, we must consider the one and the other, which helps greatly for getting to know substance. Instead, if one separates the substance from its accidents only by abstraction, meaning if one considers it alone without thinking of them, one cannot know it well, because the nature of substance is manifested by its accidents." *To Clerselier,* IX, p. 216. In truth the distinction introduced because of the modal distinction is that of *the principal attribute* (by which the essence of substance is known to me) and of its particular modes. As for the distinction between the principal attribute and substance, it belongs only to pure reason. It confers to thinking substance nothing that can be defined other than by thought. The principal attribute is only what is assigned as the substratum of modes in complete substance. It is thought itself that is substance and is manifested as such once I know it as depending only on itself; substance is the principal attribute taken in its own being. There is no real difference between them. They are in themselves completely identical, and they correspond with two different ways of perceiving the same thing, according to whether I reflect on it as what it is as *thought,* or what it *is* as thought. They are "two names for the same thing," as the mountain and the valley, action and passion. *Principles,* I, art. 52-53, 63-64. That is how one ought to interpret Descartes' reply to Burman (V, p. 156): It is as impossible to conceive thought without its substantial subject as it is to consider the mountain without the valley, the mountain and the valley being but a single and same slope expressed with respect to two different points of view.

15. "I have not abstracted the concept of wax from that of its accidents, but rather I have tried to show how its substance is manifested by its accidents and how its perception, when it is rendered manifest, differs from that of the vulgar and confused. . . ." *Replies to Objections V,* VII, p. 359. Cf. Burman's objection: "But it appears that he abstracted when he taught, in this very same Meditation, that the accidents are separable from wax and that thus [stripped bare— M. G.] the body of the wax itself, or its substance, remains. Reply: Nonetheless, the author has not abstracted; for although he conceded and stated that these accidents, such as hardness, coldness, etc., are removed from the wax, he also stated and expressly remarked that other accidents always succeed and replace them, so that wax is never without accidents. Thus he has never abstracted wax from all accidents." *Entretien avec Burman,* V, p. 151. The accidents are contingent with respect to the substance, but not with respect to accidentality: "Thus shape and movement are modes, properly speaking, of corporeal substance, because the same body can exist at one time with one shape and at another time with another shape, sometimes in motion, and sometimes not, while on the contrary, neither *this* shape nor *this* movement can be without this body." IV, p. 349, ll. 3-8.

16. *Principles,* I, art. 61. By opposition to the modes whose ideas are rendered incomplete by the abstraction of our mind . . . "the idea of a substance . . . is complete because I can conceive it alone and deny of it everything else of which I have an idea." *To Gibieuf,* 19 January 1642, III, p. 475.

17. "Those things that God can separate or preserve one without the other are really distinct." *Principles,* I, art. 60. *Replies to Objections I,* VII, p. 120, ll. 15 seq.; *Replies to Objection IV,* VII, p. 253, ll. 19-28; *Replies to Objections VI,* VII, p. 434, ll. 23-27; *To Gibieuf,* 19 January

1642, III, pp. 474-75; *To the Abbot of Launay,* 22 July 1641, III, pp. 420-21.

18. IV, p. 350; *Replies to Objections I,* IX, pp. 94-95; *Principles,* [I], art. 62. Cf. Laporte, *Le Rationalisme de Descartes,* pp. 92 seq.

19. *Rules,* Rule 9, X, p. 418, ll. 13-19.

20. *Meditation I,* VII, p. 20, ll. 24-27; IX, p. 16.

21. III, p. 665.

22. *Summary of the Meditations,* VII, p. 12, ll. 13-15; IX, p. 9.

23. *To Silhon,* March 1637, I, p. 353, ll. 20-25.

24. "As for myself, I have never presumed that my mind was in any way more perfect than those of common people; I have even often wished to have as quick a wit, or as clear and distinct an imagination, or a memory as ample and ready as other people. And I know of no other qualities that contribute to the perfection of the mind, because as far as reason or sense is concerned, it is the only thing that makes us men and distinguishes us from the animals, and I wish to believe that it is whole in each of us. I follow in this the common opinion of the philosophers, who say that there are differences in degree only among the *accidents,* and not for the *forms* or *natures* of *individuals* within the same *species.*" *Discourse,* pt. I, IV, p. 2, l. 20, to p. 3, l. 2. On the soul as the "principal form" of man, cf. VII, p. 356.

25. *Meditation VI,* VII, p. 78, l. 21.

26. *Replies to Objections VI,* VII, p. 380, ll. 14-16.

27. Cartesian generalization is mathematical in nature; mathematical generalization is possible and justifiable only by the discovery of higher reasons allowing "a more evident and more distinct knowledge of things." *Rules,* X, p. 458. For example, by meditating on the nature of the right triangle, we discover in the nature of the triangle in general a higher *ratio* of the characteristic property of the right triangle relative to the square of the hypotenuse. This property appears then as the limiting case of two contrary series: when the angle at the apex is acute, the sum of the squares of the sides of the angle is greater than the square of the base; when the angle at the apex is obtuse, the sum is smaller; when the angle is neither acute nor obtuse, but a right angle, the sum is equal: we then have Pythagoras' theorem. Cf. Clavius, *Elementa* (of Euclid) (Frankfurt, 1607), vol. I, prop. 47, theorems 33-34, pp. 147-48; vol. II, prop. 12-13, theorems 11-12, pp. 192-302. About Clavius, see below, vol. II, chap. xxi, sec. 4. Thus from the intuitive knowledge of the right triangle in general, we can arrive at the intuitive knowledge of the triangle in general, in which we discover the internal reasons of the properties of right triangles as well as those of acute and obtuse triangles (oxygons and amblygons). By a new process in the meditation (Clavius' book having been for Descartes, as well as for Leibniz, a real resource), analytic geometry, constantly varying the angle at the apex from extreme acuteness to extreme obtuseness, will translate the variation relative to the squares of the sides of the angles to the square of the base by a curve (whose formula will be given by analytic geometry), the property of the right triangle having been determined as a critical moment in that curve. That is why Leibniz makes of the right triangle the most perfect triangle, since it is the most determined triangle and since it is the only triangle within an infinity of triangles to have that property. In the same way, for Descartes, equal is the absolute nature for unequal, and horizontal is the absolute nature for oblique *(Rules,* X, p. 382). And similarly, the intuition of the intellectual nature in general, which is an *ens reale* given through the intuition of the intellectual nature of my finite self, allows me to understand and reduce to the unity of a single reason the properties of the finite intellectual nature in general and the infinite intellectual nature in general.

28. "Thus all the demonstrations of mathematicians deal with true entities and objects, and the complete and entire object of mathematics and everything it deals with is a true and real entity; this object has a real and true nature, just as the objects of physics do." *Entretien avec Burman (Meditation V),* V, p. 160.

29. "I do not see that you needed all this apparatus, when you had other grounds for being certain, and it was true that you existed." *Objections V,* VII, p. 259, ll. 1-3; IX, p. 18.

30. *Meditation I,* VII, p. 23, ll. 9-10; IX, p. 18.

31. Ibid., VII, p. 23, ll. 10-13; IX, p. 18.

32. *Replies to Objections V*, VII, p. 352.

33. Thévenaz, "La question du point de départ radical chez Descartes et Husserl," in *Problèmes actuels de la Phénoménologie* (Brussels, 1952), p. 24.

34. *To Elizabeth*, 28 June 1643, III, pp. 691-92; *Replies to Objections II*, IX, pp. 122-23; *Principles*, III, art. 45.

35. *Rules*, X, p. 360.

36. Cf. below, [chap. viii], n. 24.

37. VII, p. 27.

38. *Principles*, I, art. 53 and 65. Representation can be without judgment, will, desire, passion, but not vice versa, because these faculties only add something to the idea. Cf. *Meditation III*, IX, p. 29.

39. "I show that a man who thus doubts everything material cannot for all that doubt his own *existence:* from this *it follows* that he, meaning his soul, is a being or substance that is not at all corporeal, whose nature is only to think." *To Silhon*, I, p. 353, ll. 16-18 (our emphasis).

40. "By a reflection of the human mind on itself *(mens humana in se conversa)."* *Meditations*, Preface, VII, p. 7.

41. *Meditation II*, IX, p. 21.

42. "Since I have supposed these things to be nothing." VII, p. 27.

43. Ibid.

44. *Meditation II*, IX, pp. 21-22.

45. Ibid., p. 22 (our emphasis). The French text is more explicit than the Latin text, which purports to eliminate from the mind only imagined things: "Mentemque *ab illis* diligentissime esse advocandam." VII, p. 28, ll. 17-18.

46. "I am a thing that thinks, that is, a mind, or a soul, or an understanding, or a reasoning being, words whose meaning was previously unknown to me." VII, p. 227, ll. 14-16. The word *mens* is sometimes translated by soul, sometimes by mind. The word *mind* designates the soul in its Cartesian sense of incorporeal thing, a pure principle of thought, excluding the *anima* understood as principle of life; the word *soul* refers to the common use of the notion, not specified by philosophical analysis. This brings about two further specifications: 1) the soul is by nature mind, meaning it is excluded from anything corporeal (hence excluded from *anima);* the soul is by nature a pure intelligence, meaning it excludes imagination and sensation. On *anima* and *mens*, cf. *Replies to Objections V*, VII, pp. 355-56, and Clerselier's translation contrasting "soul" to "mind," Descartes, *Oeuvres philosophiques*, ed. L. Aimé Martin [Paris, 1839], p. 198a-b.

47. "The faculties of understanding and imagining do not differ only with respect to degree, but as two completely different modes of operating." *Replies to Objections VI*, VII, p. 385.

48. *Principles*, I, art. 53.

49. *Replies to Objections I*, VII, pp. 120-21; *Replies to Objections IV*, VII, pp. 219-22; *Principles*, I, art. 60-63; *To Gibieuf*, 19 January 1642, pp. 474 seq.

50. *Meditation II.* "Is there nothing in all that which is not just as true as it is certain that I am and that I exist, even though I were always asleep and even though the one who has created me directed all his efforts to deluding me? Which one of these attributes can be distinguished from my thinking? And which can be said to be separable from my nature?" VII, p. 28-29. This segregation proceeds from the mathematical spirit, which is the inspiration of the rules that have presided over the reform of algebra. We ought to relate this to the *Rules*, Rule 12, X, p. 417, ll. 3-8 and 16-27, a rule that allows us to attain a distinct intuition of each thing in spite of there being a plurality of things: "Reject from the ideas we have of things everything that does not require one's present attention, in order to more readily keep the rest in our memory." The problem of the distinction between simple natures and composite natures stemming from the combination of simple natures is symmetric to the one that the algebraists posit when they have to express and represent simple terms, whether known or unknown, and to distinguish them from the relations that unite them (additions, substractions, multiplications, divisions).

51. "Since I have supposed these things to be nothing and since, without abandoning this supposition, I find that I do not cease to be certain that I am something." Ibid., VII, p. 27.

52. *Meditation II*, VII, p. 29; IX, p. 23. Cf. VII, p. 145, ll. 21 seq.

53. ". . . Because up to now we have had no ideas of the things belonging to the mind that have not been extremely confused and mixed up with the ideas of sensible things, and this was our first and principal reason why none of the ideas asserted about God and the soul could be understood with sufficient clearness, I thought that I would not be doing little if I showed how one must distinguish the properties or qualities of the mind from the properties or qualities of the body, and how one must recognize them. For although many have already said that in order to conceive immaterial or metaphysical things well, one must separate one's mind from one's senses, nevertheless *no one, as far as I know, has yet shown how this can be done. And the true, and in my judgment, the only way to do this is contained in Meditation II. . . ." Replies to Objections II*, IX, pp. 103-04 (our emphasis).

54. "You thus conclude: 'I am precisely a thing that thinks, meaning a mind or soul, or an understanding, or a reasoning being.' Here I recognize that I have been deceived, for I thought that I was addressing a human soul, or this internal principle by which man lives, senses, moves, and understands, but instead I was speaking to a pure mind, since I see that you have not only divested yourself of your body but also of part of your soul." *Objections V*, VII, p. 263. "But you ask, 'what then am I?' A thing that thinks? You mean by that a thing that doubts, understands, affirms, denies, that also imagines and senses. You say many things here; I will not stop at any of them, but only at your statement that you are a thing that senses. For truly this surprises me, inasmuch as you have already asserted the opposite." Ibid., p. 268.

55. *Replies to Objections V*, [VII], p. 356, ll. 12-22; *Meditation VI*, VII, p. 86, ll. 7-10; *Rules*, Rule 12, X, p. 416.

56. "I see no difficulty in understanding that the faculties of imagination and sensation belong to the soul because they are kinds of thought, and yet they belong to the soul only as joined to the body, because they are of a kind of thought without which one can conceive the soul as entirely pure. . . ." *To Gibieuf*, 19 January 1642, III, p. 479. That is what *Meditation VI* confirms using the language of essence: "This ability to imagine that I possess insofar as it differs from the power of conceiving, is in no way necessary to my essence, that is, to the essence of my mind, for even if I did not possess it, there is no doubt that I would always remain the same person I am now—from which it seems that one can conclude that it depends on something that differs from my mind." *Meditation VI*, IX, p. 58. "From the very fact that I know with certainty that I exist and that yet I find nothing else belonging necessarily to my nature or essence, except that I am a thing that thinks, I readily conclude that my essence consists solely in being a thing that thinks. . . . In addition, I find in myself various faculties of thought that each have their own particular characteristics; for example, I find in myself the faculties of imagination and sensation, without which I might no doubt conceive myself clearly and distinctly as a whole being; but I could not reciprocally conceive them without me, meaning without an *intellectual substance* to which they are attached or to which they belong, for in the notion we have of these faculties . . . they embrace some type of intellection. From this I conceive that these faculties are as distinct from me as modes are distinct from things." Ibid., p. 62.

57. *Meditation VI*, VII, p. 78; ll. 2-6; IX, p. 62.

58. VII, ibid., ll. 21-28; IX, ibid.

59. VII, p. 73, ll. 8-9; IX, p. 58.

60. VII, p. 78, ll. 28-30; p. 79, ll. 1-6.

61. Cf. also *Principles*, I, art. 65.

62. But he does not hesitate to specify in his reply to Mersenne of 27 April 1637 (I, p. 363), dated approximately May 17 by the editors of Mersenne's correspondence [Paris, 1945-70] (VI, p. 260): "Willing, understanding, imagining, sensing, etc., are only various ways of thinking that all belong to the soul."

63. *Passions of the Soul*, [I], art. 17.

64. *To Regius,* May 1641, III, p. 372, ll. 9-11 ["Willing and understanding differ only as the activity and passivity of one and the same substance"].

65. *Principles,* I, art. 32; *Passions,* [I], art. 17.

66. *To Regius,* May 1641, III, p. 372, ll. 11-16.

67. *Passions,* [I], art. 19.

68. *Meditation VI,* IX, p. 45.

69. *Principles,* I, art. 6.

70. Ibid., art. 7.

71. Ibid., art. 39.

72. "There can be no doubt that I am, if I can be deceived." *Meditation II,* VII, p. 25, ll. 7-8; IX, p. 19; *Meditation III,* VII, p. 36, ll. 15-16; IX, p. 29. *Discourse,* pt. IV, VI, p. 32, ll. 15 seq.: "It must necessarily be that I who was thinking it [that everything was false—M. G.] am something."

73. *Search after Truth,* X, p. 515.

74. *Principles,* I, art. 53.

75. Ibid., art. 7.

76. *Objections V,* VII, p. 259, ll. 1-5.

77. *Replies to Objections V,* VII, p. 352, ll. 6-11.

78. *Passions,* [I], art. 19.

79. "The idea I have of a thinking substance is complete in that I have no other idea preceding it in my mind." *To Gibieuf,* 19 January 1642, p. 475, ll. 22-25. And this notion of will is preceded in my mind by the idea of a faculty of knowledge, or *intellectus.* Moreover, one must here distinguish between several points of view: 1) the intellect really conditions the will, because thought, or consciousness of will supposes thought (a demonstration that will not be achieved until the certainty of the objective validity of my clear and distinct knowledge is acquired); 2) will conditions (through attention) the *exercise* of my thought, which leads one to say that thought supposes will, but in another sense than when I say that will supposes thought—for the condition for exercising and the condition for possibility are two completely different conditions.

80. Compare with Malebranche, *Recherche de la Vérité* available as *The Search after Truth* (Columbus: The Ohio State University Press, 1980), III, pt. 1, chap. 1

81. "Substantia intelligens." *Meditation VI,* VII, p. 78, l. 25. "Intellectionem enim nonnullam in sua formali conceptu includunt." Ibid., ll. 25-27. Cf. also *Meditation II,* VII, p. 29, ll. 9-11.

82. "Thinking is [an attribute that belongs to me]; only it cannot be detached from me. I am now admitting nothing that is not necessarily true. I am therefore, speaking precisely, only a thinking being, that is a mind, or soul, or an understanding, or a reasoning being. . . ." *Meditation II,* VII, p. 27, ll. 13-14.

83. This second *quid* is introduced at VII, p. 27, l. 18: "Quid praeterea?"

84. Ibid., p. 28, ll. 20-23. Cf. *Replies to Objections II,* VII, p. 160, ll. 7-13; *Principles,* I, art. 9 and 65.

85. *Principles,* I, art. 53.

86. *Meditation II,* VII, p. 29, l. 20.

87. O. Hamelin, *Le Système de Descartes* [Paris: Alcan, 1911], p. 150.

88. See the end of vol. II, Appendix, n. 2.

89. *Meditation II,* VII, p. 31, ll. 7-8, 9; p. 32, l. 12; p. 34, l. 5 etc.

90. Spinoza will push far the introduction of this necessity, understood by the intellect, in the mechanism of the perception of existing things. Cf. *Ethics,* II, prop. XVII; V, prop. VII. Leibniz will also do the same by means of the intermediary of the intellection of incompossibility.

91. Léon Brunschwicg subtly and rightly remarks that he has even introduced subtlety of mind in geometry.

92. "When I was young, if interesting discoveries were presented to me, I sought to discover them myself without having recourse to their author, and then, little by little, I came to note

that I was using some determined rules in this discovery." Descartes, *Opuscula* (1619), X, p. 214, ll. 1-3.

93. Husserl, *Logische Untersuchungen* [Halle, 1900-1901], I, chap. 7, pp. 123, 128, etc.

94. *To P. Mesland,* 2 May 1644, IV, p. 120, ll. 16-20.

95. *Reply to Objections VI,* IX, p. 225.

96. "I am now admitting nothing that is not necessarily true. I am therefore, speaking precisely, only a thinking being, that is, a mind or soul, or an understanding, or a reasoning being. . . ." *Meditation II,* VII, p. 27, ll. 12-14.

97. "But is it perhaps true that those same things that I suppose not to exist because I do not know them are really no different from the self that I do know? I do not know; I am not disputing this question at the moment, since I can only pass judgment on things that are known to me." VII, ibid., ll. 24-28.

98. *Objections IV,* VII, p. 201; IX, p. 157.

99. Ibid., VII, pp. 201-2; IX, pp. 157-58.

100. *Replies to Objections IV,* VII, p. 220; IX, p. 171; *Entretien avec Burman,* V, p. 151; *Replies to Objections II,* VII, p. 129, ll. 21, 24-28. Descartes even doubts that anyone can ever grasp everything intelligible in anything whatever, "no matter how small it is." Cf. *Replies to Objections V:* "A concept adequate to things, such as no one possesses, not only in the matter of the infinite, but even with respect to anything, however small" VII, p. 365, ll. 3-5. Compare with Leibniz, *Meditationes de Cognitione,* etc. (1684), Leibniz, *Philosophische Schriften,* ed. Gerhardt [Berlin, 1875-90], IV, p. 424.

101. *Replies to Objections IV,* VII, pp. 220 seq.; IX, pp. 174 seq.

102. VII, pp. 220-21; IX, pp. 174 seq.

103. *To Mesland,* 2 May 1644, IV, p. 120.

104. Ibid.

105. *To Gibieuf,* 19 January 1642, III, pp. 475-76. "It is certain that after having arrived at the knowledge of the nature of our soul by degrees, as I have just done, and after having known in this way that it is a spiritual substance . . . one did not need to be a great philosopher to conclude as I did that it is therefore not corporeal." *To Mersenne,* July 1641, III, p. 396.

106. *Rules,* Rule 12, X, p. 420.

107. This original distinction between what is valid "for me" and what is valid "in itself" belongs to the critique. Nevertheless the opposition between Descartes and Kant is manifested here. Although for Kant the "I think," insofar as it is given as the condition of all possible knowledge, immediately brings me the certainty that I exist *(quod),* it could never furnish me the knowledge of what I am *(quid)* and the way in which I represent myself to myself, in contrast to what Descartes affirms: "In the synthetic original unity of apperception, I am conscious of myself, not as I appear to myself, nor as I am myself, but only as I am." *Critique of Pure Reason,* sec. 25 [B157]. The thinking self, as condition of all knowledge, is in fact, a simple form; its representation is only a *thought,* and not an *item of knowledge,* whether it is a substantial reality captured by an intellectual intuition (Descartes), or whether it is a phenomenon arising out of the synthesis of a varied reality, determinable in the intuition of an inward sense upheld by that of a permanent spatial reality (Kant). The Fichtean position, on the other hand, is closer to Descartes', for it suffices that I know *that* I am *(dass)* in order to know *what* I am *(was). (Grundlage der gesamten Wissenschaftslehre* [1794], S.W., I, pp. 96-97). Fichte, like Descartes, will seek to establish the nontemporal validity of this knowledge realized in the course of time. He even goes beyond Descartes in opposing Kant, since he entirely reduces the thing itself *(was)* to the thing for oneself *(für),* meaning he reduces it to the activity of the self that posits its being. He thus suppresses from the beginning the distinction that Descartes introduces provisionally between the nature of my self in itself and the subjectively certain representation that I give myself of this nature. Fichte had only a vague awareness of his affinities, on this point, with Descartes, whom he knew rather badly *(Grundlage,* pt. 1, sec. 1, S.W., I, pp. 99-100). In the final phases of his philosophy, Fichte will reintroduce the Cartesian distinction between the immediate certain knowledge of what I am for myself and the being of

this self in itself: the object of his ascending dialectic will be the one Descartes pursued in his *Meditations,* namely, the establishment, in some mathematical fashion, of the perfect coincidence between the certain subjective representation that I give myself of the nature of my self, by means of intellectual intuition (for oneself), and nature (in itself) of this self, which is in itself really for oneself *(reines Für).*

108. *Replies to Objections V,* VII, p. 357, ll. 26-28, trans. Clerselier, ed. Louis Aimé Martin, p. 199a. Cf. also the letter of August 1641, n. 3, III, p. 425.

109. VII, p. 27, ll. 12-13; IX, p. 21.

110. VII, p. 25, ll. 21-24; IX, p. 20.

111. VII, p. 27, l. 26.

112. VII, p. 27; IX, p. 21.

113. *Replies to Objections V,* VII, p. 357.

114. *Letter on Objections V,* IX, p. 215.

115. The text just cited at first seems to contradict the texts we cited before, since it talks about *abstraction* in opposition to *exclusion,* and the latter talks about *exclusion* in relation with *abstraction.* In fact, the difficulty is insoluble as long as one does not distinguish between the point of view of the truth of science and the point of view of the truth of the thing. From the point of view of the truth of science, exclusion is the act of rejecting what does not belong to a complete idea, in order to obtain it in its clarity and distinction; abstraction is the act of arbitrarily considering only a part of this idea and of obtaining from this part considered apart only an inadequate and confused knowledge. From the point of view of the truth of the thing, exclusion is the act of rejecting from the thing itself what we have legitimately rejected from its idea. And, as long as I do not know whether the necessity of the idea expresses the necessity of the thing, I must refuse to exclude from the thing the element I have excluded from my idea; it is in this sense, meaning with respect to the thing, that there is no "complete exclusion and negation," but a simple abstraction of this element. In brief, exclusion outside a clear and distinct idea, which is opposed to *abstractio intellectus* in the sphere of science, is simple abstraction with respect to the truth of the thing, as long as nothing allows us to exclude from the latter what one has excluded from the clear and distinct idea.

116. IX, p. 155.

117. *Objections IV,* VII, p. 199; IX, p. 155.

118. "But first I come to the place where I began to prove that, from the fact that I knew nothing else belongs to my essence—meaning to the essence of my mind—beyond the fact that I am a thing that thinks, it follows that there is nothing else that belongs to it in fact *(revera).* That was the same place in which I proved that God is or exists, the God who can accomplish everything I conceive clearly and distinctly to be possible." *Replies to Objections IV,* IX, p. 170; VII, p. 219; and ibid., IX, pp. 175, 176; VII, p. 225, l. 26, p. 226, l. 26. "The first [objection—M. G.] is that it does not follow from the fact that the human mind, reflecting on itself, does not know itself to be other than a thing that thinks, that its nature or its essence is only to think, in the sense that this word *only* excludes all the other things that might be said to belong to the nature of the soul. To this objection I reply that it was not my intention here to exclude these according to the order of the truth of the thing (which I was not then treating), but only according to the order of my thought; thus my meaning was that I knew nothing pertaining to my essence except that I was a thing that thinks or a thing that has in itself the faculty of thinking. But I shall show further how, from the fact that I know nothing else pertaining to my nature, it follows that there is nothing else that belongs to it, in fact." *Meditations,* Preface, VII, p. 7.

119. *Replies to Objections II,* IX, pp. 102 seq.

120. "For example I do not yet know that the mind has the power to move the body, or to be united substantially with it." *Replies to Objections IV,* IX, p. 171.

121. *To Gibieuf,* 19 January 1642, III, p. 478.

122. Ibid., *Replies to Objections IV,* VII, p. 221, ll. 6-8, 11-14.

123. *To Mersenne,* 31 December 1640, III, p. 274, ll. 16-19.

124. *Replies to Objections IV,* VII, p. 219, ll. 17-28; *Replies to Objections V,* IX, p. 213; *To Gibieuf,* 19 January 1642, III, p. 478.

125. *To Gibieuf,* ibid.

126. *Meditation II,* IX, pp. 21-22.

127. *Meditations,* Preface, VII, p. 7, etc.

128. *To Arnauld,* 27 July 1648, V, p. 221, ll. 6-9.

129. *Rules,* Rule 9, X, pp. 400-401.

130. *Entretien avec Burman,* V, p. 149.

131. *Entretien avec Burman,* V, p. 148. The manuscript has a marginal note referring one to the *Dioptrics* (ed. 1644), p. 148; VI, p. 163.

132. *Dioptrics,* VI, p. 163. The example that Descartes gives to Burman illustrates this observation marvelously well, for if when I am conceiving and thinking, I am also conscious of speaking and eating, then this latter consciousness is rather obscure and confused, and if I render it clear and distinct by bringing my attention to the act of speaking and eating, the consciousness I would then have of my former conception would become less clear and distinct.

133. *Rules,* Rule 9, X, pp. 400-401.

134. Malebranche, *Recherche de la Vérité* [above, n. 78], VI, pt. 1, chap. 5. Cf. Gueroult, *Etendue et Psychologie chez Malebranche* [Paris: Les Belles-Lettres, 1939], pp. 14-15.

135. Since my existence is reduced to my thought, there will therefore be as many separate moments of my existence as there are instantaneous intuitions of singular things: "We can understand clearly that it is possible for me to exist at this moment, while I am thinking of *one thing,* and yet not to exist at the next moment, when I may think of *something different,* if I happen to exist" (our emphasis). *To Arnauld,* 4 June 1648, V, p. 193, ll. 18-21.

136. *Rules,* ibid. That is why the whole effort to know simple natures consists in "distinguishing them from one another and intuiting each one separately by a firm mental glance." Rule 12, ibid., p. 425.

137. Ibid., pp. 401-2.

138. Ibid., pp. 402-3.

139. Ibid., Rule 11, p. 407.

140. *Rules,* Rule 6, p. 381, ll. 19-22, et passim.

141. *Rules,* Rule 7, X, pp. 387 seq.

142. *Rules,* Rule 1; *To Mersenne,* 10 March 1642, III, p. 544; *Replies to Objections VII,* VII, p. 548, l. 19.

143. *Rules,* Rule 11, pp. 407-8; Rule 6, pp. 383 seq.

144. ". . . by entrusting *almost* no part of the process to memory, I *seem* to intuit the whole series at once" (our emphasis). *Rules,* Rule 7, X, p. 388.

145. See below, chap. vi, sec. 10-11.

146. "We should note that those who truly know recognize the truth with equal ease, whether they have derived it from a simple subject or from a confused one, for they comprehend each truth by a similar, but unique and distinct act, as soon as they have reached it; but the whole difference is in the path of reasoning, which certainly must be longer if it leads to a truth farther removed from the first and most absolute principles." *Rules,* X, p. 401.

147. *Replies to Objections VII,* VII, p. 559, ll. 16-20.

148. Spinoza, *De Intellectus Emendatione,* sec. 27; *Ethics,* II, prop. 21, Scholium; Fichte, *Versuch einer neuen Darstellung der Wissenschaftslehre* [1797], I, pp. 525-30. Cf. also Plotinus, *Enneads,* II, 9, 1, ll. 23 seq. Aristotle presents two solutions: 1) for God, which is the actual identity of the thought with the thought of the thought *(Metaphysics,* XII, 1074b seq., and 2) for man, in which there is a passage from potency to actuality. The infinite process of thought seeking to think itself supposes a stopping place in a principle that is no longer thought, properly speaking *(Eudemian Ethics,* VIII, 14). This solution with respect to potency and actuality opens the path of unconsciousness, which will be the path of Leibniz, Schelling, etc. The Platonic discussion never raises the question at the level of the thought of the thought *(Meno,* 80e-86c, and *Theatetus,* 188a seq.).

149. This is what Bourdin does, in another way, by putting the whole difference between soul and body in that the soul considers that it thinks, while the body does not: "By removing the true and very intelligible difference that exists between corporeal things and noncorporeal things, namely, that the former think and that the latter do not, and by substituting another that cannot have an essential character in its place, namely, that the latter consider that they think while the former do not consider this, he also prevents one from understanding, as much as possible, the real distinction between the soul and body." III, p. 559, l. 23, p. 560, l. 1.

150. *Entretien avec Burman,* V, p. 149.

151. *Discourse,* pt. III, VI, p. 23, ll. 21-24.

152. *To Dinet,* VII, p. 580, ll. 19-25.

153. *Replies to Objections VII,* VII, p. 464, ll. 17-23.

154. "The distinction of reason, *which is created by thought." Principles,* pt. I, art. 60-62; IX, 2, pp. 51-53.

155. See above [in sec. 10] and below in [sec. 11].

156. *Replies to Objections VI,* VII, p. 422; IX, p. 235.

157. II, p. 72; *Principles,* pt. II, art. 24, 39; pt. III, art. 63 seq; *The World,* XI, p. 45. See below, chap. vi, sec. [II] on the idea of time.

158. See below, ibid.

159. *Rules,* Rule 3, X, p. 370; Rule 11.

160. "That is why 'my own existence' . . . does not depend on a series of causes." *Replies to Objections I,* IX, p. 85.

161. *Principles,* Preface, IX, 2, p. 14, ll. 15-19.

162. *Principles,* I, art. 60; VIII, p. 28, ll. 25-31.

163. Ibid., ll. 20-21.

164. *Principles,* I, art. 64; VIII, p. 31, ll. 15-21.

165. In order to attain it, we would have to stop placing the numerical invariant in the subsistence of a certain volume; that is how one can explain a number of Cartesian assertions, for example: "I think that the stone is a substance or something capable of existing by itself." *Meditation III,* IX, p. 35. "If you remembered what was said at the end of *Meditation II* about wax, you would know that bodies themselves are not properly speaking known by the senses, but only by the understanding; so that there is no difference between sensing something without another, and having the idea of something and understanding that this idea is not the same as the other. And that cannot be known except from the fact that one thing is conceived without the other. And that cannot be known certainly unless one has a clear and distinct idea of both things." *Replies to Objections II,* IX, pp. 104-5. "All the small parts of bodies are substances." *Principles,* II, art. 55. A result of this is that the various physical substances are *aggregates of substances.* The thesis of the numerical invariant conceived as the subsistence of the same total volume through the various deformations applies only to aggregate substances, which are alone visible, in any case—for example, it applies to this piece of wax or this piece of iron. In fact, each corpuscle or molecule of a given body retains both its volume and its form. The numerical invariance of the aggregate substance is only the subsistence in it of the same molecules in the same quantities, whatever the shapes and states of this substance, as long as this substance is not destroyed. When a body dilates or contracts under the influence of any physical agent whatever, it always preserves the same volume of matter and the same quantity of molecules, even though this volume appears diminished or augmented. The explanation is that the intervals between its molecules have shrunk or enlarged, being filled by other bodies, as one can understand through the example of the sponge *(Principles,* II, art. 5-6; IV, art. 31, etc.). The numerical invariant of the aggregate is not a direct function of the numerical invariant of the molecule or the corpuscle. A large corpuscle contains more matter (more volume) than a smaller corpuscle. But if the form of large corpuscles is such that they cannot be squeezed tighter against each other in the aggregate, for the same apparent volume, the aggregate of large corpuscles will always hold less matter, meaning real volume, than an aggregate of small corpuscles that can be squeezed tighter to one another.

166. *Principles,* I, art. 64.
167. *Principles,* I, art. 51.
168. *Principles,* I, art. 60; VIII, p. 28, 1. 31, p. 29, ll. 1-6 (our emphasis).
169. *Principles,* I, art. 63-64.
170. *Meditation II,* IX, 1, p. 24. What remains in this case is clearly not just extension in general, which is *the same for all bodies,* but a certain invariant of extension, which is *only the same for wax.*
171. *Summary of the Meditations,* IX, i, p. 10.
172. *To Silhon,* March 1637, I, p. 353.
173. *To Mesland,* 2 May 1644, IV, p. 113. The whole paragraph develops the comparison at length: "Just as it is not an action, but a passion of wax to receive various shapes, so it seems to me that it is a passion in the soul to receive this or that idea, and that only volitions are actions. It receives its ideas partly from objects touching the senses, partly from impressions in the brain, and partly from the preceding dispositions in the soul itself, and by the movements of the will. Similarly, a piece of wax receives its shapes partly from the pressure of other bodies, partly from the shapes or other qualities present in it—such as whether it is more or less heavy or soft, etc.—and partly from its movement, when, having been pushed, it still has the power to continue moving."
174. *Principles,* II, art. 5, 6, 7; IV, art. 31.
175. *Rules,* Rule 9, X, pp. 400-1.
176. *Discourse,* beginning of pt. I: "Reason is the same by nature in all men." "I wish to believe that it [reason or good sense—M. G.] is fully present in each one."
177. Descartes has not treated the problem of the individuation of minds. If he had treated it, he could have combined the individuation by means of the body with which I am substantially united (and individual differences would arise from the differences of the constitution of this body) with the individuation by means of the intelligent substance (and individual differences would arise from the difference of intellects— if one admitted such a difference—whose invariable quantity of thought could be greater or lesser, depending on the substances). One cannot see how these differences could arise from volition, since it is identical in all these substances, being infinite in each as it is in God. The first individuation would correspond with individuation by matter; the second, with individuation by form. But at the start of the *Discourse* Descartes is categorical about this: all human understandings are the same; they therefore have the same finitude and the same quantity of thought. Individual differences could not arise from the form (the soul alone, understanding and will) but from accidents (therefore they arise from the fact that we are united with a body).
178. *Summary of the Meditations,* VII, pp. 13-14; IX, 1, p. 10.
179. *To Mesland,* 9 February 1645, IV, p. 167; *To Mesland,* 1645-46, IV, p. 346; *Rules,* Rule 12, X, p. 411, 1. 17; *Replies to Objections V,* VII, p. 374, ll. 20-23.
180. *Principles,* I, art. 60. The texts of the *Principles* that we have just explained allow us to respond to a question Berkeley addresses to Descartes in his *Common Place Book:*
"In *Meditation III* Descartes calls himself a thinking substance and calls a stone an extended substance; he adds that the two agree in that they are substances. But in the following paragraph he calls extension a mode of substance." *Common Place Book,* n. 785, ed. Luce [London: Thomas Nelson, 1948-57]. This observation concerns VII, p. 44, ll. 21-28, and p. 45, ll. 2-8. According to what we have stated above, *extension* (with *figura, situs, and motus)* is related to a body as its mode insofar as its three dimensions can vary indefinitely within the limit of an invariable quantity of extension that specifies the body. Thus this invariable quantity is a substance with respect to the variations of extension, while itself being a mode of the universal extended substance, from another point of view.

Berkeley poses another question with respect to the piece of wax: "In *Meditation II* Descartes states that the notion of this particular wax is less clear than the notion of wax in general; in the same *Meditation,* a little before, he refuses to consider bodies in general, because (he states) these general notions are ordinarily confused." *Common Place Book,* n. 784 (ed. Luce). This concerns VII, p. 30, ll. 5-7, p. 31, ll. 18-19. There Descartes wishes to take a concrete example, something that we see and feel. And we do not see or feel bodies in general; we have only a general concept of them, which is confused for common sense, and upon which disagreement reigns. On the other hand, everyone is in agreement with the perception of the piece of wax. Once it is demonstrated that the particular piece of wax is knowable only through an idea of my understanding, a fortiori it will be evident that that follows for wax in general, common sense itself no longer contesting that the passage from the particular to the general is accomplished by the understanding. Moreover, at that time, we would also have acquired, by means of the analysis of the particular piece of wax, a clear and distinct concept of the substance of bodies in general (geometric extension).

Chapter IV. The Cogito: Priority of Knowledge of Soul over Knowledge of Body

1. "When I first concluded, following the reasons contained in my *Meditations,* that the human mind is really distinct from the body and was more easily known than it, and other things treated there, what compelled me to assent to this was that I noticed nothing in these arguments that was not coherent and nothing that was not drawn from evident principles according to the rules of logic.* But I confess that I was not thereby wholly *persuaded (plane persuasum fuisse)* and that I almost had the same experience as the astronomers who, after having been *convinced* by many proofs *(postquam evicerunt rationibus)* that the sun was many times larger than the earth, could not prevent themselves from judging that it was smaller than the earth when viewed with their eyes. But when I proceeded further and, relying on the same principles, I considered physical or natural things, first by examining the notions or ideas I had in me of each thing, and then by distinguishing carefully the one from the other in order that my judgments be fully harmonious with them, I recognized that nothing belonged to the nature or essence of body, except that it was a substance extended in length, width, and depth, . . . and that the colors, odors, tastes, and other similar things were merely sensations that have no existence outside my thought, . . ." *Replies to Objections VI,* VII, p. 440; IX, p. 238.

*We are concerned here with "true logic" such as Descartes has defined it in VII, p. 107. The Latin text of *Meditation II* opposes *Nec possum abstinere quin putem,* l. 21, to *quod verum est,* ll. 26-27; VII, p. 29; the translation, "the truth of which I was persuaded *(la vérité desquelles je suis persuadé)"* allows a nuance of the Latin to escape, a nuance that is underscored in the *Replies to Objections VI.*

2. Persuasion and conviction are opposed in Descartes' philosophy somewhat as *peitho* and *bia* are opposed in Plato's philosophy. The first is a deep agreement and close acquiescence, either with sensations or habits, or with the fundamental requirements of our mind; the second is an external constraint in which will, far from being seduced, sees its consent torn from it by the force of reasons. When conviction encounters a persuasion opposed to it, it can be brought to move against itself with difficulty. That is the case here. When a persuasion, which is established spontaneously in the nature of our understanding, is produced in ignorance of the reasons that in themselves justify it, it can be shaken up by contrary suppositions. For example, those who spontaneously believe in the truth of the conclusions drawn from clear and distinct ideas possess only a persuasion from these ideas, which can be shaken up by the hypothesis of the evil genius, as long as they do not have the proof of the existence of God and that he is not a deceiver. The demonstration that God exists and is veracious adds a scientific conviction to it that renders it unshakable: which is why I distinguish the two [science and persuasion]." *To Regius,* 24 May 1640, III, pp. 64-65. A persuasion based only on will and grace, which has no support from our passions, is most strongly reinforced by our rational conviction, which, in this case, touches us more than what is taught to us by our faith: "I must confess a weakness in myself that is, I think, common to the majority of men, namely, that however much we wish to believe, and even however much we think we do firmly believe all that religion teaches, we are not commonly so *touched* by things that only our faith teaches us and that our reason cannot

attain, as when we are *persuaded* by very evident natural reasons." *To Huyghens*, 13 October 1642, IV, p. 180. For Descartes persuasion is not the privilege of sensation; pure reason is by itself also capable of sometimes engendering it by means of conviction. This is a point on which Descartes is in disagreement with Pascal. With respect to this see the subtle remarks of L. Prenant on the role of intellectual sensation in evidence. "Le Sentiment de l'Evidence," pt. 1, p. 104, in the *Revue Philosophique* (April-June 1951).

3. *Letter to Elizabeth*, June 1643, III, pp. 691-92.

4. *Principles*, I, art. 9, p. 71; *To Mersenne*, July 1641, III, p. 314.

5. "Common sense, as it is called, or the imaginative power." *Meditation II*, IX, p. 25. "I am nearly deceived by the terms of ordinary language; for we say that we see the same wax if it is present, and not that we judge that it is the same wax . . . ; from this I would conclude that one knows the wax by means of eyesight and not by the simple inspection of the mind." IX, p. 25. *Principles*, art. 72.

6. *Meditation II*, IX, p. 23.

7. Ibid., pp. 23-25.

8. On this confirmation by physics, refer to n. 1 of this chapter.

9. *Meditation II*, IX, p. 24.

10. Ibid., VII, p. 34; IX, p. 26.

11. "Because our soul has no color, smell, or taste, nor anything that belongs to body, it is not possible to imagine it or form an image of it. But that does not make it any less conceivable; *on the contrary*, since it is by means of it that we conceive all things, it is itself more conceivable than all other things put together. . . ." *To Mersenne*, July 1641, III, p. 394 (our emphasis).

12. *Meditation II*, IX, p. 26.

13. *Replies to Objections V*, VII, p. 360; *Principles*, I, art. 11; *To Mersenne*, July 1641, III, p. 394, ll. 22-31.

14. *Replies to Objections II*, IX, p. 103.

15. *Rules*, Rule 7, X, p. 395.

16. "Juxta leges verae Logicae de nulla unquam re quaeri debet *an sit*, nisi prius *quid sit* intelligatur." VII, p. 107, ll. 26-27. "Omnino a nosse ad esse consequentia valet." *Replies to Objections VII*, VII, p. 250, l. 5. About true logic, cf. III, p. 272, and *Replies to Caterus*, IX, pp. 85-86.

17. "I know that I exist and I am seeking to discover what I am, the I that I know to be." *Meditation II*, VII, p. 27, ll. 28-29; IX, p. 21.

18. VII, p. 25, l. 15; IX, p. 19.

19. "Our method for investigating truth, which bids us to reject everything as uncertain and, beginning with the knowledge of our existence, proceeds to the examination of our nature, that is, of the thing which we already know to exist." *Replies to Objections VII*, VII, p. 514, ll. 1-5.

20. *Replies to Objections VII*, VII, p. 519, l. 26; p. 520, ll. 5-10.

21. That is the meaning of Descartes' reply to the dull and tiresome Bourdin: "That is as if no new knowledge of existence could be acquired and as if the absence of this precluded all acquaintance with the essential nature of things." VII, p. 514, ll. 20-22.

22. *Letter to Elizabeth*, 21 April 1643, IV, p. 665, ll. 1-4; and 28 June 1643, p. 693.

23. "They join here my physics with pure mathematics, which I would wish above all they would resemble." *Letter from Descartes to Clerselier on Objections V*, IX, pp. 212-13. "My whole physics is nothing more than geometry." *To Mersenne*, 27 July 1638, II, p. 268, l. 13. It is distinguished from geometry properly speaking in that the latter is abstract and occupies only the mind, while it is a concrete geometry and it attempts to explain the phenomena of nature (ibid.)

24. Cf. vol. II, chap. xv, sec. 3.

25. "Painful and laborious undertaking." *Meditation I*, IX, p. 18; *Replies to Objections II*, IX, pp. 104, 122-23; *Replies to Objections V*, VII, p. 349; *To Elizabeth*, 28 June 1643, p. 693; *Principles*, I, art. 71; *To Mersenne*, III, p. 394, etc.

26. *To the Marquis of Newcastle*, March-April 1643, V, pp. 136-39.

27. *Replies to Objections II,* IX, p. 103.

28. *Meditation II,* IX, pp. 24-25 (our emphasis).

29. "Rejecting everything that does not belong to the wax, we see what remains; certainly nothing is left but what is extended, flexible, and moveable." *Meditation II,* VII, p. 31, ll. 1-3. Cf. also the example of the stone, *Principles,* II, art. 11.

30. Cf. above, chap. iii, sec. 11.

31. *Meditation II,* IX, p. 24.

32. *Meditation II,* VII, p. 31, ll. 23-28; IX, pp. 24-25.

33. Ibid., VII, p. 32, ll. 6-12; IX, p. 25.

34. *Meditation II,* IX, p. 25; VII, p. 32, l. 12. "Nec ex eo percipi quod tangantur aut videantur, sed tantum ex eo quod intelligantur." VII, p. 34, ll. 3-5.

35. *Meditation VI,* VII, p. 81, ll. 20-21, p. 83, ll. 6-12; IX, pp. 64, 66.

36. "We do not discover the nature of anything by means of the senses, but by means of our reason when it intervenes there. . . ." *Principles,* I, art. 73, sub finem; cf. *Replies to Objections II,* p. 103.

37. [*"Quid* erat igitur in ea quod tam distincte comprehendebatur? Certe nihil eorum quae sensibus attingebam. . . . Superest igitur ut concedam, me nequidem imaginari *quid sit haec cera,* sed *sola mente percipere.''*] *Meditation II,* VII, p. 30, ll. 21-22, p. 31, ll. 16-18 (our emphasis).

38. This concerns the conditions of representation as such. Descartes expressly states this when he replies to Gassendi: "You argue in passing that, while not admitting the existence in myself of anything except mind, I nonetheless speak of the wax that I see and touch, which I could not do except by using my hands and eyes. But you ought to have noticed that I expressly pointed out that I did not then deal with sight or touch, which are realized by means of corporeal organs, but only with the thought of seeing and touching, which has no need of these organs, as we experience every night in our dreams." VII, p. 360, ll. 20-27.

39. Kant, *Critique of Pure Reason,* "Transcendental Aesthetics," ed. Hartenstein [Leipzig, 1853], sec. 3, p. 63, and sec. 8, pp. 74, 77-78.

40. This concerns the first qualities of the *phenomenon,* of which matter and its first qualities (movement, principle of impenetrability and force) constitutes only one part, and space constitutes the other part.

41. This is Jean Laporte's interpretation in *Le Rationalisme de Descartes* [Paris, 1945], pp. 128 seq.

42. "If you remember what was said about wax at the end of *Meditation II,* you would know that bodies themselves are not, properly speaking, known by the senses, but only by the understanding. . . ." *Replies to Objections II,* IX, p. 105.

43. *Replies to Objections VI,* VII, p. 440; IX, p. 238; *To Elizabeth,* June 1634, III, pp. 691-92; *Principles,* I, art. 71.

44. *Replies to Objections II,* IX, p. 122.

45. *To Mersenne,* July 1641, III, p. 395.

46. *Meditation VI,* IX, pp. 57-58.

47. *To the Marquis of Newcastle,* V, p. 136.

48. *To Mersenne,* ibid.

49. "The faculties of understanding and imagining differ, not so much with respect to more and less, but as two completely different manners of acting." *Replies to Objections V,* VII, p. 385.

50. J. Laporte, *Le Rationalisme de Descartes,* p. 128.

51. One must "know what is meant here by the word idea . . . ," which is "the thing conceived in thought, insofar as it is objectively in the understanding in the manner in which objects are commonly there." Thus the idea of the sun is not "the sun insofar as this external denomination is in it . . . but the sun itself existing in the understanding, not as a formal truth, as the sun exists in heaven, but objectively, meaning in the manner in which objects commonly exist in the understanding. . . ." *Replies to Objections I,* VII, pp. 102 seq.; IX, pp. 81 seq. "Among my

thoughts some are like images of things, and it is to these that the word *idea* properly applies."
Meditation III, IX, p. 29. "Ideas are in me as pictures or images." Ibid., p. 33.

52. *Replies to Objections V,* VII, p. 385, ll. 9-13.

53. "Natural light makes me recognize clearly that ideas are in me like pictures or images." *Meditation III,* VII, p. 42, ll. 11-15; IX, p. 33.

54. *Principles,* I, art. 10; *Search for Truth,* X, pp. 523-24.

55. This is a problem that will be dealt with, for the first time, according to the perspectives of subjective idealism by Fichte. The analysis of the piece of wax, by indicating that the idea of the understanding is a necessary condition of the representation of things, is a first step in this direction, but the initial positing of the idea as representation of an object remains a "primitive fact" in Descartes' philosophy (as in Reinhold's philosophy), for which Descartes reserves the name "first notion" in his terminology.

56. *Replies to Objections V,* VII, p. 385.

57. *To Regius,* January 1642, II, p. 493, ll. 10-17.

58. Nothing is more decisive, with respect to this, than the text to which J. Laporte himself refers, namely, axiom 5 of the *Geometrical Summary* of *Replies II.* This text proves that the objective reality at stake is not the reality of the idea of extension seen by the understanding, for this idea is "inherent" in it, but the idea of the image depicted in fantasy: "Where does the knowledge that heaven exists come from? Is it because we see it? But this vision does not touch the mind except insofar as it is an idea, an idea, I say, inherent in the mind itself, and not an image depicted in fantasy. But in virtue of this idea we cannot judge whether heaven *exists,* unless we assume that every idea must have as cause of its objective reality some thing that is really existing; and this cause we judge to be heaven itself, and so forth for the other causes." In this way it is demonstrated that the principle of causality applied to the objective reality of ideas is a condition for the positing of the existence of all things, *sensible* as well as insensible. Applied to the contents of the ideas of the understanding alone, it refers to God, as eminent cause; applied to the content of sensations, it refers to existing bodies as formal causes. That is why Descartes replies to Hyperaspistes that if the idea of extended things does not allow one to conclude that extended things exist, because it is inherent in the mind, then the *existence* *("rerum naturalium existentia")* of these things is not impossible to prove, insofar as these ideas of these *existing* things do not come from ourselves, but from elsewhere. . . . *Reply to Hyperaspistes,* August 1641, III, p. 428-29.

59. Cf. vol. II, chap. xiii, sec. 3.

60. *To Gibieuf,* 19 January 1642, III, p. 479, ll. 10 seq.

61. *Meditation III,* IX, p. 31.

62. "We must know that, since every idea is a work of the mind, its nature is such that it does not itself require any other formal reality than what it receives or borrows from thought or mind, of which it is only a mode, meaning a way or manner of thinking. In order that an idea contain an objective reality rather than another, it should no doubt obtain it from some cause in which there is at least as much formal reality as the idea contains objective reality." Ibid., IX, p. 32; VII, p. 41, ll. 15-20.

Chapter V. The First Proof of God's Existence by Effects

1. "In order to move the earth from its place and transport it to another place Archimedes required nothing more than a fixed and sure fulcrum. In a similar manner I would have the right to entertain high hopes, if I were fortunate enough to find a single certain and indubitable thing." *Meditation II,* IX, p. 19. It is Epicharmus' trope, *dos moi pe sto, kai kineso ten yen,* that Jacobi will apply to belief, instead of to intellectual evidence (Jacobi, epigraph of *Ueber die Lehre des Spinozas* [Breslau, 1785]).

2. *Meditation III,* IX, p. 34.

3. *Meditation III,* IX, p. 28.

4. Ibid., p. 17. "Quoties a me profertur." VII, p. 25.

5. *Meditation V,* VII, p. 69, l. 16; IX, p. 55. Cf.: "I experience in myself this weakness of not being able to fix my mind continually on the same thought." *Meditation IV,* VII, p. 62, l. 2; IX, p. 49. From which stems the process Descartes recommends in order to remedy this deficiency: "it is necessary for me to go over them in thought again and again, until I pass from the first to the last so quickly that I seem to perceive the whole series simultaneously while entrusting hardly any parts of it to memory." *Rules,* Rule 11, X, p. 409, ll. 5-8. This process is only an approximation *(videar, fere).*

6. See above, chap. i, sec. 10.

7. Cf. the interesting analyses of Lachièze-Rey on this point: "Réflexions sur le Cercle Cartésien," *Revue Philosophique,* August 1937.

8. "I cannot help believing them true *while* I am conceiving them clearly and distinctly." *Meditation V,* VII, p. 65, ll. 6-9; IX, p. 52.

9. *Letter to Clerselier on Objections V,* IX, p. 205, ll. 11-25.

10. *Meditation V,* VII, p. 66, l. 21, p. 67, ll. 5 seq.; IX, p. 53.

11. "Thus I recognize very clearly that the certainty and truth of all science depends solely on knowledge of God, so that before I knew him, I could not have known any other thing." *Meditation V,* IX, p. 56.

12. *Replies to Objections II,* VII, p. 141; *Replies to Objections V,* VII, p. 384; *Replies to Objections VI,* VII, p. 428. *Principles,* I, art. 13. *Entretien avec Burman,* V, p. 178.

13. *Meditation II,* IX, p. 27.

14. VII, p. 36, l. 30, p. 37, ll. 1-3; IX, p. 29.

15. VII, p. 40, ll. 5-8; IX, p. 31.

16. VII, p. 37; IX, p. 29.

17. This objective reality is none other than the authentic representative content, that is, once we have abstracted away the judgments that can be added on it.

18. Cf. Laporte, *Le Rationalisme de Descartes,* Paris, 1945, pp. 123-25; G. Lewis, *Le Problème de l'Inconscient et le Cartésianisme* (Paris: Presses Universitaires de France, 1950), pp. 74-76.

19. "Since ideas are like images, there can be none that do not seem to represent something to us." VII, p. 44, l. 4; IX, pp. 34-35.

20. *Meditation IV,* VII, p. 57, ll. 13-15; IX, p. 45. Laporte's thesis suffers mostly from a lack of clarity, in this case. On the one hand, he rightly notes that "my sensation of freedom entails the idea of infinity" *(Le Rationalisme,* p. 123) and that "it entails and places in contrast two disproportionate terms: my imperfect being that desires and the idea of the perfect to which desires are suspended" (p. 124). But instead of drawing, in conformity with the order, the conclusion that the idea of the infinite is, in me, the condition of the consciousness of my freedom as infinite, he seems to lean to the opposite conclusion, namely, that the experience of my freedom as infinite is, in me, the condition or the source of the idea of infinity: "the idea of the infinite does not have to 'come to us from elsewhere.' A simple reflection on myself discovers for me two primitive notions within the depth of my will, *free will* and *infinity,* which indeed, make up a single notion" (p. 125). Now, of course, the idea of infinity comes from *ourselves,* but is this "ourselves" my will or the objective reality of an idea? The texts—and the order—prove that the answer is the objective reality of an idea. G. Lewis unambiguously favors the answer that, it seems, must be excluded: "The source of the idea of infinity is therefore not some abstract notion, deposited mysteriously in the mind at birth, but a concrete experience in which the mind experiences the fullness of this 'positive power to determine oneself' independently from any foreign determination." *Le Problème,* pp. 74-75. "The dissociation in man, of an infinite will and a limited intellect, is a fact of experience, and from this contrast arises the ideal of a totally achieved and actual perfection. . . . The objective reality that allows consciousness to grasp the idea of God, is our being itself insofar as it is the reflection of the Supreme Being" (pp. 75-76). We will finally note that God, in the first proof by effects, is discovered by causal action on us. The proof is therefore possible only through the *passion* resulting in us from this action. Nothing *active* in us would enable us to prove God's existence. That is why, from the start of *Meditation III,* Descartes eliminates everything that, in the mind,

constitutes "an action adding itself on ideas," ideas being precisely pure passion alone, cf. *Treatise on the Passions*, [I], art. 1 and 17.

21. VII, p. 37, ll. 13-20; IX, p. 29.

22. VII, p. 37, ll. 20-28; IX, ibid.

23. VII, p. 37, ll. 13-20; IX, p. 29.

24. *Meditation IV*, VII, p. 57, ll. 12-15; IX, p. 45.

25. Thus, as we have seen above, one of the differences between *Meditation II* and *Meditation III* is that the second deals with the form of consciousness and the third with its contents.

26. Cf. *Entretien avec Burman*: "*Et quia nullae ideae nisi tantum rerum* [or *rei*—M. G.], esse possunt" (the text of the *Meditations* has "*tanquam rerum*"). Burman objects about the idea of nothingness. Descartes replies that it is a negative idea and that one can barely *(vix)* call it an idea. Descartes means *idea* in its strict and proper sense here. No doubt we have ideas of common notions, which properly speaking are not things. Ideas are then taken in a wider sense. V, p. 153. Moreover, these ideas are no less in the mind as images of relations belonging to beings.

27. VII, p. 37, ll. 22-28; IX, p. 29.

28. Descartes attributes by extension the qualities of *truth* and *falsity* to ideas not having objective validity that, in virtue of their constitution as ideas, refer to an object outside of us, of whom they would be a copy. That is material falsity, in opposition to *true and formal falsity*, which concerns judgment. But as long as judgment does not allow itself to be carried away by this aspect of the idea, there is no falsity in actuality; there is nothing more than the objective reality of the idea, posited in us, escaping error, even though it can incite our judgment in some measure ("they can barely give us the occasion to fail").

29. *Replies to Objections II*, VII, p. 130, ll. 10-16; IX, p. 103.

30. VII, p. 37, l. 22; IX, p. 29.

31. VII, p. 37, l. 29, p. 38, ll. 1 seq.; IX, p. 29.

32. VII, p. 38, ll. 8-10; IX, p. 30.

33. VII, p. 38, l. 11, p. 39, ll. 1-14; IX, pp. 30-31.

34. "For while each person commonly persuades himself that the ideas we have in our thought are completely similar to the objects of which they proceed, I see no reason to assure us that that is so, but I note several experiences that must make us doubt it." *Treatise on Light*, XI, p. 4.

35. VII, p. 39, ll. 15-29; IX, p. 31. Cf. in the *Treatise on Light* the well-known example of the policeman, XI, p. 6.

36. Ibid.

37. Liard, editor of the *Principles* [Paris, 1891], p. 102. Hamelin, *Le Système de Descartes* [Paris: Alcan, 1911], p. 198. Descartes' point of view is comparable to Kant's in this respect: "What is truth? The nominal definition of truth, that it is the agreement of knowledge with its object, is assumed as granted; the question asked deals with the general and certain criterion of truth of any and every item of knowledge. To know what questions may reasonably be asked is already a great and necessary proof of sagacity and insight. . . . If truth consists in the agreement of knowledge with its object, that object must therefore be distinguished from other objects; for knowledge is false if it does not agree with the object to which it is related, even though it contains ideas that may be applicable to other objects. Now a general criterion of truth must be such that it would be valid in each and every instance of knowledge, however their objects may vary. It is obvious, however, that such a criterion [being general] cannot take into account the [varying] content of knowledge (relation to its [specific] object). But since truth concerns just this very content, it is quite impossible, and indeed absurd, to ask for a general test of the truth of such content. A sufficient and at the same time general criterion of truth cannot possibly be given. . . ." *Critique of Pure Reason*, "Transcendental Logic" [A58-59, B83]. Descartes perceived the difficulty in almost the same terms. However, his solution is different. Kant recovers a universal content by the pure a priori intuition of space and time, and

can thus discover a criterion of truth valid a priori for all possible contents of knowledge; he thus institutes a *transcendental logic,* or a science of the rules of the pure thought of an object. Descartes establishes the certain objective validity of a privileged idea, *distinguished from all others with respect to its object*—the idea of God—by proving its necessary conformity with the object it claims to represent. And he proves this by discovering in its *content* some characteristics such that this validity must be necessarily recognized for it. In this way he establishes a criterion of the truth of the contents that is both universal and sufficient in a twofold way: 1) by refuting the evil genius, which restores to clearness and distinctness their ability to testify as to the objective validity of ideas, an ability that our understanding naturally attributes to them; and 2) by discovering that the *indubitable presence of an (objective) reality* in the content of an idea necessarily entails its truth. And this presence is immediately certain for my understanding, with respect to clear and distinct ideas. And, on the contrary, it is uncertain with respect to obscure and confused ideas. Cf. below, chap. v, sec. 16.

38. *Meditation III,* VII, p. 37, ll. 23-25; IX, p. 29.

39. "Natural light allows me to know evidently that ideas are in me as pictures or images, . . ." *Meditation III,* VII, p. 42, ll. 11-12; IX, p. 33. "And since ideas are like images, there can be none that do not seem to represent something to us." VII, p. 44, l. 4; IX, pp. 34-35. Cf. *Entretien avec Burman,* 16 April 1645, V, p. 153.

40. *Meditation III,* VII, p. 37, ll. 3-4; IX, p. 29.

41. *Meditation III,* VII, p. 40, ll. 6-7; IX, p. 31.

42. *Letter to Clerselier,* 23 April 1649, V, p. 354, ll. 8-18. Cf. below, n. 51. Cf. *Entretien avec Burman,* V, p. 160: "Everything that is able to be clearly and distinctly conceived in a chimera is a true entity. It is not fictitious, since it has a true [and immutable—M. G.] essence; and this essence comes from God as much as the actual essence of other things."

43. In conformity with the point of view of common consciousness, the word *adventitious* designates ideas imposed on me by a foreign corporeal cause. They come to me during the course of my life. The idea of God, insofar as it is produced in us by God, could literally be called adventitious, since it arises from a cause foreign to me. But it is an innate idea since it is always implanted in my understanding. The term adventitious concerns only the ideas that come to me during the course of my existence.

44. *Meditation III,* IX, p. 41.

45. "The true ideas that are inborn with me, of which the first and principal one is the idea of God." *Meditation V,* VII, p. 68, ll. 8-10; IX, p. 54.

46. "Haec non aliunde habere videor quam ab ipsamet natura." VII, p. 38, l. 3.

47. As a result there will be two extremely different degrees of this validity.

48. *"And since ideas are like images, there can be no ideas that do not seem to represent something to us,* and if it is true to say that cold is only the absence of heat, then the idea that represents it as something real and positive would not inappropriately be called false." VII, p. 44, ll. 4-8; IX, pp. 34-35.

49. "The second degree of sense." Cf. *Replies to Objections VI,* IX, pp. 236 seq. The first degree is corporeal, therefore still unknown to us for now.

50. "The third degree of sense." Ibid.

51. "My purpose was to derive a proof for the existence of God from the idea or thought we have of him, and so I thought that I was required first of all to distinguish all our thoughts into certain classes, in order to observe which are those that can deceive. By showing that not even chimeras contain falsity in themselves, I hoped to forestall those who might reject my reasoning on the ground that our idea of God belongs to the class of chimeras. I was also required to distinguish the ideas that are inborn with us from those that come from elsewhere, or are made by us, to forestall those who might say that the idea of God is made by us, or acquired by hearsay. Moreover, I insisted on our lack of certainty of what we are told by all the ideas we think come from the outside in order to show that there is no single idea that gives such certain knowledge as the one we have of God. Finally I could not have said 'there occurs another way . . .' if I had not first rejected all the others and thus prepared my readers to conceive better

what I was about to write." *To Clerselier,* 23 April 1649, V, p. 354.

52. *Meditation III,* VII, p. 40, ll. 7 seq.; IX, p. 31.

53. Ibid., VII, p. 36, ll. 26 seq.; IX, pp. 28-29.

54. VII, p. 40, l. 6; IX, p. 31.

55. VII, p. 42, l. 22; IX, p. 33.

56. IX, p. 36, l. 30; VII, p. 29.

57. IX, p. 29.

58. VII, p. 42, l. 9; IX, p. 33.

59. VII, p. 40, l. 6; IX, p. 31.

60. VII, p. 36, ll. 26-27; IX, p. 28.

61. VII, pp. 36-37; IX, p. 29.

62. *"Conformis,"* Replies to Objections IV, VII, p. 233, l. 18.

63. *Meditation III,* IX, p. 41; VII, p. 51, l. 20.

64. *Meditation V,* VII, p. 68, ll. 6-9; IX, p. 54.

65. *Meditation III,* VII, p. 52, l. 6; IX, p. 41.

66. Ibid., VII, p. 36, l. 26; IX, p. 28.

67. VII, p. 36, l. 30; IX, p. 29.

68. It is "in conformity" *(conformis)* with it. *Replies to Objections IV,* VII, p. 233, l. 18.

69. *Meditation III,* VII, p. 42, ll. 6 seq. Cf. *Principles,* I, art. 18.

70. *Entretien avec Burman,* V, p. 156.

71. Ibid.

72. *Meditation III,* VII, p. 51, l. 20; IX, p. 41 (our emphasis).

73. "Applicat solum activa passivis." *Entretien avec Burman,* ibid. Cf. *Objections VII,* [VII], and Descartes' replies to them.

74. Concerning the identification of any idea with a passion, see vol. II, chap. xiv, sec. 4.

75. *Meditation III,* VII, p. 51, ll. 18-21; IX, p. 41.

76. Ibid., VII, p. 41; IX, p. 32.

77. Ibid., p. 37, l. 22; IX, p. 29.

78. VII, p. 40, ll. 7-12; IX, p. 31.

79. *"Ad minimum,"* Meditation III, VII, p. 41, l. 14; "at least as much," IX, p. 32. This definition of causality is indispensable in order to safeguard in principle the possibility of the eminent character of divine causality. It has as its correlative the axiom: "Whatever can do the greater can do the lesser"; this axiom intervenes in the second proof by effects (VII, p. 48, ll. 16-24; IX, p. 38; V, p. 154). It therefore seems that the Cartesian principle of causality does not establish a strict equality between cause and effect as Hobbes or Leibniz do (equality between the *causa plena* and the *effectus integer*), but the relation, cause is greater than or equal to effect. In actuality, the axiom thus formulated does not seem to be applied to physical things, in which above all we are concerned "never to attribute to a cause any effect that surpasses its power" *(Principles,* II, art. 60), but only to metaphysical things. *To Arnauld,* 4 June 1648 (Clerselier trans. [1668], II, letter 4, p. 22), V, p. 193, ll. 22 seq. "The axiom *whatever can the greater can do the lesser* applies only in the same order of operations, or in things that require a single power." *To Mersene,* 21 April 1641, III, p. 362. Here the order of operation *(eadem ratio operandi)* is the act of real creation *(creare realitatem)* and presumes the homogeneity of both formal and objective reality *(realitas formalis* and *realitas objectiva).*

80. VII, p. 45; IX, pp. 35-36.

81. Cf. above, chap. v, sec. 2.

82. Cf. below, chap. vii, sec. 11.

83. VII, p. 45; IX, pp. 37-38.

84. IX, p. 41.

85. *Replies to Objections V,* VII, p. 365, ll. 9-18.

86. Ibid., p. 365, ll. 6-8; *Replies to Objections I,* VII, pp. 103 seq., 113-14.

87. VII, pp. 44-45; IX, p. 35.

88. *Replies I,* VII, pp. 103-4; IX, p. 83.

89. VII, p. 41, ll. 26-27, p. 42, l. 13, p. 103, l. 1; IX, pp. 33, 82.

90. *Meditation III,* IX, p. 32.

91. VII, p. 42, ll. 11-15; IX, p. 33.

92. "This manner of being objective belongs to ideas as part of their own nature." VII, p. 42, l. 4; IX, p. 33.

93. VII, p. 42; IX, p. 33.

94. VII, p. 42, l. 6; IX, p. 33.

95. VII, p. 40, l. 21; IX, p. 32.

96. VII, p. 42, l. 11; IX, p. 33.

97. Liard's edition of the *Principles,* p. 102.

98. Hamelin, *Le Système de Descartes,* p. 198.

99. *Replies to Objections II,* VII, p. 135, ll. 18 seq. "We see by means of this same [natural— M. G.] light that it is impossible for us to have the idea or image of anything whatever, unless there is in us or elsewhere an archetype that, in effect, includes all the perfections that are thus represented to us." *Principles,* I, art. 18. Cf. above all, axiom 5 of the *Geometrical Summary (Replies II),* IX, p. 128.

100. *Replies to Objections II, Geometrical Summary,* definitions 2 and 3, IX, p. 124. *Objections III* (Reply to Hobbes' Objection V), IX, p. 141. *Letter to Mersenne,* July 1641, III, p. 393. *Letter to Clerselier on Objections V,* IX, 1, p. 209, ll. 15-19.

101. *Replies to Objections IV,* VII, p. 233, ll. 6-16; IX, pp. 180-81.

102. See above, chap. v, sec. 9.

103. Sensible ideas insofar as they do not resemble the external things that cause them are proportionally deprived of objective reality; their objective reality is reduced to a *minimum.* Cf. below, chap. v, sec. 17.

104. IX, p. 31.

105. Equivalence *(adéquation),* understood here not in the Cartesian sense of *complete* knowledge, but in the ordinary sense of *conformable* knowledge. Cf. *Replies IV,* VII, pp. 220-21, 233, l. 18. Cf. Arnauld, *Des vraies et des fausses idées,* chap. 23, pp. 109 seq. in J. Simon's edition [Paris, 1843].

106. *Replies I,* IX, p. 82.

107. *Meditation III,* VII, p. 51; IX, p. 49.

108. One must "distinguish between intellection in conformity with our understanding, such as each recognizes himself as having with respect to the infinite, and the complete and perfect conception *(adaequatus conceptus)* of things, which understands everything intelligible in them, but is such that no one ever possesses it, not only for the infinite, but perhaps also for anything else in the world, however small." *Replies to Objections I,* VII, p. 365, ll. 1-5.

109. "Because the word *comprehend* signifies some limitation, a finite mind cannot comprehend God, who is infinite; but that does not prevent him from perceiving God, as one can touch a mountain while one cannot embrace it." *Letter to Clerselier on Objections V,* IX, p. 210, l. 10-15. Better yet, even though I cannot comprehend all of infinity, *by this very incomprehensibility* I have a true and complete idea of it, and not an altered and partial idea of it: *"The idea of infinity, in order to be true, cannot be comprehended* by any means, since this very incomprehensibility is included in the formal reason of infinity. Nevertheless, it is manifest that the idea we have of the infinite does not represent merely a part of it, but the whole infinite, such as it has to be represented by a human idea; although it is certain that another more perfect, that is, more accurate and more distinct idea, can be framed by God, or by any other intelligent nature more perfect than us. Similarly, someone ignorant of geometry, no doubt, has the idea of a complete triangle when he understands that it is a figure composed of three lines, although geometers can know several other properties of the triangle and discover a quantity of things in its idea that the beginner does not notice. Thus, just as it suffices to conceive a figure bounded by three lines in order to have the idea of a whole triangle, similarly, it is also sufficient to conceive a thing bounded by no limits in order to have a true and complete idea of the whole of infinity." Ibid., p. 368. These observations do no more than comment on the passage of

Meditation III that states that the idea of infinity is the clearest, most distinct, and truest of the ideas I have in my mind, on the condition that one conceives that it is in its nature to be incomprehensible to my limited mind and in its nature to have, formally or eminently, all the perfections that I can conceive and an infinity of others of which I am ignorant. This latter condition is related to the absolutely positive character of the infinite thing, in opposition to the negative character that renders it incomprehensible and concerns, not what it is in itself, but what it is necessarily for us (cf. *Meditation III*, vii, p. 46, ll. 22-28; IX, p. 37; cf. also *Replies I*, VII, pp. 113 seq.; IX, p. 90).

110. *Replies to Objections V*, VII, pp. 364-65. *To Mersenne*, May 1630, I, p. 151; January 1641, III, p. 284; July 1641, III, pp. 392-93. *Entretien avec Burman*, V, p. 154. *To Clerselier*, 23 April 1649, V, p. 356.

111. "Finally, neither is it true that God will mean something very little, unless he is greater than as conceived by us, for he is conceived as infinite, and nothing can be greater than the infinite." *Replies V*, VII, 365, ll. 18-21.

112. VII, p. 41, ll. 26-27, p. 42, l. 13, p. 103, l. 1.

113. Also nothing in the formal reality of God does not resemble the objective reality of our idea; for formal cause is also defined as cause similar to its effect: "In a similar or in an eminent way . . . in the cause." *Replies II*, VII, p. 135, ll. 11-12.

114. V, pp. 545-46.

115. Thus the negative aspect of incomprehensibility only concerns the relation of the objective infinite reality (of the idea) with the finite understanding itself, not the infinity of this reality, which is absolutely positive. That is why incomprehensibility, as the formal reason of *infinity*, refers to the *infinite thing* itself, as an absolutely positive being, of which a part of its intelligibility escapes our understanding: "Moreover, I distinguish between the formal reason of infinity and that which is infinite, since even though we understand infinity to have as much positive reality as might be, we understand it only in a certain negative fashion, namely, that we perceive no limitation in the thing; but the thing itself that is infinite is positively understood, but not adequately—that is, we do not comprehend all of what is intelligible in it." *Replies I*, VII, p. 113; IX, p. 90. The French translation considerably weakens the Latin text.

116. Kant, *Critique of Pure Reason*, [A592, B620 to A603, B631].

117. IX, p. 33.

118. Ibid.

119. IX, p. 82.

120. Ibid.

121. "We ought at least to note that there are no images that must wholly resemble the objects they represent; for otherwise, there would be no distinction between the object and its image." *Dioptrics*, 4th Discourse, VI, p. 113, ll. 1 seq. It is true that in this case Descartes is concerned with sensible images, but the remark has an absolutely general scope.

122. It seems to us that Descartes' expression, "the thing insofar as it is in the mind in the way things commonly are, meaning objectively or by representation," does not contradict the conception of the idea as image of the object, as Wahl thinks ("Notes sur Descartes," in *Revue Philosophique*, 1937, p. 370; *Tableau de la philosophie française* 1946, p. 229). The expression consists in giving a definition of representation: it is the thing itself, but under the form of image, the only way in which it can be in us.

123. IX, p. 33.

124. "There is an equivocation here in the word *idea*. For it can be taken materially as an operation of my understanding, and in this sense it cannot be said to be more perfect than myself; or it can be taken objectively, *for the thing that is represented* by this operation, which, even though we do not suppose that it exists outside my understanding, can nevertheless be more perfect than myself with respect to its essence." VII, p. 8, ll. 20-28. The expression "the thing represented" constitutes the whole equivocation, since that thing is *in us* only as the objective reality that is lacking in the perfection of *formal existence*.

125. IX, pp. 81-82.

126. Cf. above, chap. v, sec. 11. *Objections III* (Descartes' Reply V), IX, p. 141. *To Mersenne,* II, p. 393.

127. *Passions of the Soul,* I, art. 17, 19. *To Mesland,* 2 May 1644, IV, p. 113, l. 24. *To Regius,* May 1641, III, p. 372, etc.

128. *Rules,* Rule 4, X, p. 376.

129. *Meditation III,* VII, p. 35, l. 30. Cf. with respect to this subject, Gouhier's correct observation, in "Les exigences de l'existence dans la métaphysique de Descartes," in *Revue internationale de philosophie,* April 1950, p. 5.

130. *Replies to Objections I,* VII, p. 102; IX, pp. 81-83; *Replies to Objections IV,* VII, p. 233; IX, pp. 180-81.

131. One can find the same dual aspect in Kantian philosophy. On the one hand, mathematical concepts appear to have objectivity insofar as, rendering experience possible, they guarantee that we will find possible objects corresponding to them in this experience; on the other hand, they possess an intrinsic objectivity, which is independent of experience (their transcendent reality), from which experience seems to draw its own reality, which it derives from the universal structure they impose upon it. It is the same for Malebranche: on the one hand, mathematical ideas have an intrinsic objectivity as intelligible realities in God, and on the other hand, an extrinsic objectivity insofar as, serving God as archetypes in his creation of existing things, we are assured of seeing them expressed in those things—meaning we are assured of being able to apply them to the world of experience whose possibility they condition, in the same way that they condition in us the possibility of the representation of these things.

132. Arnauld, *Des vraies et des fausses idées.* Malebranche, *Réponse à la dissertation de M. Arnauld sur un Eclaircissement du Traité de la Nature et de la Grâce, Recueil des Réponses du P. Malebranche,* 1 (Paris, 1709), pp. 365-68.

133. "And since ideas are like images, there can be none that do not seem to represent something to us, and if it is true to say that cold is only a privation of heat, the idea that represents it to me as something real and positive would not inappropriately be called false, and so forth for similar ideas." *Meditation III,* IX, pp. 34-35. *Replies to Objections V,* VII, p. 232, ll. 21 seq.

134. *Meditation III,* IX, p. 34.

135. *Replies to Objections IV,* VII, p. 233, ll. 6-16; IX, pp. 180-81.

136. *Meditation IV,* VII, p. 81, ll. 17-22, p. 81, ll. 6-16; IX, p. 64, sub finem, p. 66.

137. *Meditation III,* VII, p. 40, ll. 7 seq.; IX, pp. 31-33.

138. Ibid. IX, pp. 32 seq. And one has to explain by another cause why an idea contains such objective reality rather than another: VII, p. 41, ll. 20-24; IX, pp. 32-33.

139. VII, pp. 41-42; IX, pp. 32-33.

140. *Meditation IV,* VII, p. 62, ll. 15-17; IX, p. 49.

141. *Meditation III,* p. 44, ll. 10-14; IX, p. 35: "We cannot say that this idea of God is materially false and . . . that it is in me insofar as I am deficient, as I have said about the ideas of heat and of cold." VII, p. 46, ll. 5-9; IX, p. 36.

142. *Replies to Objections IV,* VII, p. 234, l. 19 to p. 225, l. 4; IX, pp. 181-82. Material falsity of sensations residing in their representative character, which Descartes thinks is inherent to them, disappears in Malebranche's philosophy, in which the representative character is removed from them. And this character is removed from them at the same time that they are stripped of the *minimum* of objective reality that Descartes allows them, since they are converted into affections of the soul explained by the soul alone, and not by its substantial union with the body. In Malebranche's philosophy, by themselves with respect to existing bodies and their biological relations with my body, sensations do not have the proper objective validity that Descartes grants them because of the fact of the intrinsic nature of their content, which they derive from the substantial union, but which they acquire only extrinsically from the fact that God, through the free institution of the laws of the union of soul and body, invests them externally with a constant signification relative to the modifications occurring in my body through the action of surrounding bodies.

143. This series is not continuous, as it is in Leibniz's philosophy. There is, on the other hand, a solution of continuity between the region of the infinite, the region of the finite, and the region of the infinitely small.

144. *Meditation III,* IX, p. 29.

145. Ibid.

146. "Those that represent substances are undoubtedly something more, and contain in themselves, so to speak, more objective reality (meaning they participate by representation with a higher degree of being or perfection) than those that represent only modes or accidents. Moreover, the one by which I conceive a supreme God, eternal, infinite, immutable, omniscient, omnipotent, and the universal creator of all things that exist outside himself, that idea, I say, has certainly more objective reality in itself than those by which finite substances are represented to me." IX, pp. 31-32. Cf. also axiom 6 of the *Geometric Summary of Replies II,* VII, pp. 165-66. This determination of degrees of being as a function of a hierarchy of notions founded on the inequality of their dignity, leading up to the Perfect Being existing by itself, belongs to the Augustinian-Platonic tradition of Saint Anselm. Cf. *Monologion,* chap. 4.

147. They are judgments about quantities (quantity of objective reality) that, however, to some extent, entail judgments of validity, for the *quantity* is evaluated here by means of *degree of perfection.* Descartes does not yet distinguish clearly between judgments of truth and of reality and judgments of validity, of perfection—which is something Malebranche begins to perceive.

148. I, p. 353.

149. *Meditation III,* VII, p. 46, l. 5: IX, p. 36. Cf. Hennequin, *Etudes d'Histoire des Sciences et d'Histoire de la Philosophie* (Paris, 1908), I, pp. 244 seq.

150. The last vestige of the Cogito as a principle of order in *Meditation III* can be found in the classification of the various thoughts with the view toward giving ideas priority in the investigation. This classification agrees, as we have seen, with the conception of the essence of the soul as pure intellect, and with the relation of substance and its modes, doctrines that derive from the Cogito alone. But this classification belongs only to the preamble to the demonstration and has only an eliminative function. The inquiry, properly speaking, according to the degrees of order, begins only with the methodical examination of the quantity of perfection of objective realities, an examination conditioned by the preliminary—at least implicit—positing of the idea of the perfect.

151. *Discourse,* pt. IV, VI, pp. 33-34.

152. "I see manifestly that there is more reality in infinite substance than in finite substance, and yet that I have in some way in me a notion of the infinite that is prior to my notion of the finite—that is, the notion of God is prior to the notion of myself. For how would it be possible that I can know that I doubt and that I desire—that is, that I lack something and that I am not perfect—unless I had in me an idea of a being more perfect than me, by comparison to which I might know the defects of my own nature." *Meditation III,* IX, p. 36. "Explicitly, we can know our imperfection before knowing the perfection of God, because we can attend to ourselves before we attend to God, and we can conclude that our being is finite before arriving at divine infinity. However, implicitly, knowledge of God and his perfections must always precede knowledge of ourselves and our imperfections. For, in reality, God's perfection is prior to our imperfection, the latter being a defect and a negation of divine perfection, and every defect and every negation presupposes the thing of which it is a defect, a negation." *Entretien avec Burman,* V, p. 153.

153. "Like the idea of myself, it [the idea of God—M. G.] is born and produced with me from the moment I was created." *Meditation III,* IX, p. 41.

154. VII, p. 51, ll. 20 seq.; IX, p. 41.

155. VII, p. 51, ll. 29-30 and p. 52, ll. 1-2; IX, p. 41.

156. *Rules,* Rule 12, X, p. 422; *Meditation IV,* VII, p. 53, ll. 6-15. Cf. Laporte, "L'idée de liaison necéssaire chez Descartes," *IX Congrès international de Philosophie* [1937], II, p. 14; *Le Rationalisme de Descartes* [see above, n. 18], pp. 98-99.

157. Cf. above, chap. v, sec. 16.

158. Cf. above, n. 151.

159. *Meditation V,* VII, p. 71, l. 3; IX, p. 56. Cf.: "And although, in order to conceive this truth thoroughly, I have had to make a great mental effort, nevertheless, I find myself at present not only as certain of this as of everything that seems to me most certain, but moreover, I notice that the certainty of all other things depends upon this so absolutely that, without this knowledge, it is impossible ever to be able to know anything perfectly." *Meditation V,* VII, p. 69, l. 10; IX, p. 55. In fact, it is because of God that I can know that the science I had of myself in *Meditation II* has an objective validity—in brief, that I have effectively the nature I conceived myself as having. The thinking self therefore appears at two moments of the chain: as Cogito or subjective certainty *(Meditation II),* and as essence having objective validity and ontologically expressing a substance *(Meditation VI).*

160. *Replies to Objections V,* VII, p. 384.

161. *Replies to Objections IV,* IX, pp. 171-72; *Replies to Objections V,* VII, pp. 359-60; *Principles,* I, art. 11.

162. *Meditation IV,* VII, pp. 52-53; IX, p. 42.

163. *Meditation V,* VII, p. 69, l. 4; IX, pp. 54-55.

164. *To Mersenne,* 21 January 1641, III, p. 284, ll. 3-11: "We cannot embrace by means of words, nor even comprehend by our mind, all the things that are in God, and thus God is ineffable and incomprehensible. However, in reality, many things are in God, or are referred to God, that we can grasp by the mind and express by words. There are even many, many more things there than anywhere else. Thus, God is the most knowable and distinguishable of all beings *(ideoque est maxime Cognoscibilis et Effabilis)."*

165. *Meditation IV,* VII, p. 53, ll. 5-17; IX, p. 42.

166. *Meditation III,* VII, p. 40, ll. 7-11; IX, 1, p. 31.

167. *Objections II,* VII, p. 124, ll. 29 seq.; *Objections IV,* VII, p. 214, ll. 17 seq.; *Objections V,* VII, pp. 405 seq.; *Replies to Objections II,* VII, p. 140, l. 12; *Replies to Objections IV,* VII, p. 245, ll. 25 seq., p. 246, l. 9. Cf. Hamelin, *Le Système de Descartes* [above, n. 37], pp. 138 seq.; Gilson, *Commentaire du Discours de la Méthode* [Paris: Vrin, 1925], pp. 360-62, 484: Lachièze-Rey, art. cit. [above, n. 7].

168. Cf. above, chap. i, sec. 2. We have already resolved part of the problem (cf. chap. v, sec. 1 and sec. 19): the problem of the relation between divine veracity and remembering evidence.

169. Hamelin, *Le Système de Descartes,* p. 142; E. Baudin, cf. Gilson, *Discours, Commentaire,* p. 484; Gilson in his commentary on the *Discourse* (ibid.) abandons a formula proposed by him in "Descartes et la Métaphysique scolastique," *Revue de l' Université de Bruxelles,* 1923-24. However, this formula was excellent: "It is one thing to have the certainty of an evident truth, and another to have the certainty that the evident truths are true." The whole problem is located there—to discover by metaphysics a certain foundation for the certainty of clear and distinct ideas that the nature of my mind imposes upon me without reflection. Failing this discovery, the atheist cannot preserve the certainty that the evident truths are true and that the certainty he has of their truth is legitimate.

170. "Ex magna luce in intellectu magna consecuta est propensio in voluntate." *Meditation V,* VII, p. 59, ll. 1-3; IX, p. 47.

171. *Discourse,* pt. IV, VI, p. 76, ll. 6-28.

172. *Principles,* IV, art. 205.

173. Descartes distinguishes degrees of absolute certainty; the lowest degree of this certainty (for example, the certainty of the existence of bodies, *Summary of the Meditations,* VII, p. 16; IX, p. 12) always differs by nature from the highest degree of moral certainty *(Principles,* IV, art. 205-6). The distinction of degrees in the absolute is natural for a philosophy in which natures that are absolute with respect to the series they govern can at the same time be relative with respect to another more absolute term, which does not depend on any other term. For example, God is absolutely absolute, in opposition to thinking and extended substances, which are relative absolutes and could not exist without him. We can find this conception of degree of

absolute in Leibniz: *"Magis absoluti,"* cf. *Die Philosophischen Schriften von G. W. Leibniz*, ed. Gerhard (Berlin, 1875), IV, p. 397.

174. Régis, *Réponse au livre qui a pour titre P. D. Huet, "Censura Philosophiae Cartesianae"* (Paris: Jean Cusson, 1691), p. 106.

175. "I am not free to conceive a God without existence." *Meditation IV*, IX, p. 53. "It is not in my power to diminish it, or to add anything to it." *Meditation III*, IX, p. 41; *Meditation IV*, IX, p. 54. Cf. below, chap. viii, sec. 6.

176. *Meditation V*, IX, p. 53.

177. See below, vol. II, chap. x, "The General Theory of Possibility."

178. *Rules*, Rule 12, X, p. 422; *Meditation IV*, VII, p. 53, ll. 6-15.

179. *Replies to Objections II*, VII, p. 138.

180. *Meditation V:* "Supreme and Perfect Being, in whose idea alone necessary or eternal existence is included." IX, p. 55. *Principles*, I, art. 14.

181. J. de Tonquédec, *La Critique de la Connaissance* (quoted by Bréhier, *La Philosophie et son passé* [Paris: Alcan, 1940], p. 29).

182. "Since we have considered the *immense and incomprehensible power* contained in his idea, and we have recognized that it is so full and abundant that in fact it is the true cause of why he is and always continues to be, and that there can be nothing else besides it, we say that God exists per se, and no longer negatively, but on the contrary most positively." *Replies to Objections I*, VII, p. 110 (our emphasis).

Chapter VI. The Second Proof of God's Existence by Effects

1. *Meditation III*, VII, pp. 47-50; *Replies to Objections II*, VII, p. 136; *Replies to Objections V*, p. 270; *To Mesland*, IV, p. 112. Cf. Koyré, *Essai sur l'idée de Dieu chez Descartes* (Paris, 1922), p. 190; Gilson,*Etudes sur le rôle de la pensée médiévale dans la formation du système cartésien* ([Paris: Vrin], 1930), pp. 210 seq.

2. *Replies to Objections I*, VII, p. 106.

3. Cf. Brunschwicg: "As for me, I would hesitate to emphasize at all costs the external and accidental elements of Cartesian metaphysics. In his writing of 1637 Descartes seems to me less bent on gaining the interest of the Scholastic reader . . . than seeing clearly his own thought, not departing in any way from the doctrine of 'the order of reasons' in which reasons depend on one another. That is why, after he has derived the divine infinity of the *Cogitatio* from the *Cogito*, he turns toward the *sum,* in order to derive from it the absolute divinity of being." "Mathematique et Métaphysique chez Descartes," *Revue Métaphysique*, 1927, p. 304.

4. *Meditation III*, IX, p. 39; *Replies to Objections I*, VII, pp. 111, 112.

5. VII, p. 47, l. 24, p. 48, ll. 1-6; IX, p. 38.

6. VII, p. 47, ll. 7-28, p. 49, ll. 1-20; IX, pp. 38-39.

7. VII, p. 49, l. 21, p. 50, ll. 1-10; IX, pp. 39-40.

8. VII, pp. 50-52; IX, pp. 40-41.

9. Gilson, *Commentaire du Discours de la Méthode* [Paris: Vrin, 1925], pp. 331-333.

10. *Meditation III*, VII, p. 51, ll. 24-26; IX, p. 41; *Replies to Objections II*, axiom 7, VII, p. 166, ll. 3-7; *To Mersenne*, 25 December 1639, II, p. 268, ll. 3-9.

11. *Replies to Objections II*, VII, p. 133; *To Clerselier*, 23 April 1649, V, p. 357.

12. Cf. below, vol. II, chap. x.

13. *Meditation IV*, VII, p. 57.

14. It is also a common notion that is the object of an axiom. Cf. *Replies to Objections II*, axiom 6, VII, p. 165, ll. 29-30.

15. VII, p. 48, ll. 7-9. Cf. *Discourse*, pt. IV: "I would have been able to get from myself, for the same reason, all the surplus I recognize to be lacking in me, and thus become infinite, eternal, immutable, omniscient, omnipotent, and finally possess all the perfections that I can notice in God." VI, p. 35, ll. 2-6. And *To Mersenne*, 25 December 1639, II, p. 628, ll. 3-9.

16. Notice Arnauld's astonishment, 3 June 1648, V, p. 189, l. 22.

17. *Entretien avec Burman,* V, pp. 154-55.

18. "That is why, when one asks whether something can give itself existence, this must be understood merely to mean whether anything has a nature or essence such that it does not need to have any efficient cause in order to be or to exist. And when one adds 'if something is such it will give itself all the perfections of which it has an idea, if it is true that it does not yet have them,' one means that it is impossible that it does not have in actuality all the perfections of which it has ideas; for by natural light we can know that the thing whose essence is so immense that it does not need an efficient cause in order to exist, does not need to have all the perfections of which it has ideas, and that its own essence gives it eminently everything that we can imagine given to other things by an efficient cause. And these words, 'if it does not have them, it will give them to itself,' are merely explanatory; for the same natural light that allows us to know the thing cannot at the present moment have the power and will to give itself something new, allows us to know that its essence is such that from all eternity it has everything we can now think it would bestow upon itself, if it did not have it already." *Replies to Objections IV,* VII, pp. 240-41; IX, p. 186.

19. *Replies to Objections I,* IX, pp. 85-86. Caterus' objection (VII, p. 94, ll. 15-23; IX, p. 76) falls under the Kantian critique of the Transcendental Dialectic, according to which any proof by effect, assuming that it can establish the existence of a necessary being, could not prove that this necessary being is God. The Cartesian proof escapes the objection. Cf. Kant, *Critique of Pure Reason,* A603, B631 seq.

20. V, p. 189.

21. *To Arnauld,* 4 June 1648 (Clerselier trans., II [1667], letter 4, p. 22), V, p. 143, ll. 22 seq. (our emphasis).

22. *Discourse,* pt. IV, p. 35, ll. 14-15. *Principles,* I, art. 20. "Nec dubitarem, nec optarem." VII, p. 48, l. 7.

23. *Principles,* I, IX, 2, p. 34.

24. VII, p. 166.

25. *To Mersenne,* 21 April 1641, III, p. 362.

26. Cf. Gilson, *Commentaire,* pp. 340-41.

27. Cf. below, chap. vi, pt. II, on the discontinuity of time, sec. 9-12.

28. Cf. IX, p. 88, note a. "Moreover, I did not seek what is the cause of my being insofar as I am composed of body and soul, but only and precisely insofar as I am a thing that thinks. . . . Thus . . . I was able to hold for certain that nothing can be in me of which I do not have some knowledge." IX, p. 85.

29. *Replies to Objections I,* IX, pp. 85, 88.

30. *Replies to Objections V,* VII, p. 370, ll. 15-18.

31. "I do not see that this succession of causes could lead me elsewhere than to allow me to know the imperfection of my mind, in that I cannot understand how an infinity of such causes have so succeeded one another from all eternity, and that there has not been a first." *Replies to Objections I,* IX, p. 85. Cf. *Entretien avec Burman,* V, p. 155.

32. *Replies to Objections I,* IX, p. 88.

33. Gilson, *Etudes,* pp. 209 seq.

34. *To Mesland,* 2 May 1644, IV, p. 112, l. 1, to p. 113, l. 4.

35. Gilson, ibid. Gilson observes that by denying the infinite progression of causes *in esse* in the instant and that by admitting the progression *in fieri* in time, Descartes agrees with Saint Thomas, even though he expresses himself as if he were unaware of—or he contested—this agreement; Gilson also notes that Descartes disagrees with Saint Thomas by admitting, in his physics, a infinite progress of causes *in esse* in the instant. This latter theory would ruin the basis of the Cartesian argument, according to Gilson.

36. Descartes does take sun and light as an example of a preserving cause that must be simultaneous with its effect, which proves that in the physical order, division to infinity does not exclude the simultaneous presence of cause and effect. But we are concerned here with only a comparison intended to render *sensible* the difference between causes *in esse* and causes *in*

fieri. For in reality, sun and light at an instant are one and the same effect, whose founding cause, or conservative cause at the actual instant, is the act of divine creation. And this relation of the creative divine act to the existing thing is derived by hypothesis by means of the condition requiring the effect to be fragmented to infinity in the plenum, since matter itself is founded by divine action. We should note, in addition, that if each elementary movement depends only on the divine creative act founding it, and does not in itself depend on what precedes it, no more than the next movement depends on it, each instant of movement in its founding action no more depends on a series of causes than the self does. There is therefore only a small step to take in conferring substantiality to each elementary movement, thus ending up with a Leibnizian doctrine. The indivisibility of divine creative action and the absolute independence that it confers to each created moment of movement is therefore, in Descartes' philosophy, the substitute for what in Leibniz's philosophy becomes force or the monad, meaning the indivisible of hyperphysical and metaphysical nature that is beyond local movement but is its independent source.

37. "Moreover I will add . . . that we cannot arrive merely at a secondary cause [Aristotle's moved motor—M. G.], but that the cause that has enough power to preserve something outside of it must with all the more reason preserve itself with its own power, and thus it exists by itself." *Replies to Objections I*, IX, p. 88.

38. "That is why I prefer to support my reasoning with my own existence, which does not depend on a series of causes and which is so well known to me that nothing can be better known; and about myself I do not so much ask what was the original cause that produced me, but what is the present cause that preserves me, in order to disentangle myself from all series and succession of causes." IX, p. 85. Physics will also conceive each elementary (instantaneous) movement as in itself not depending on any series of causes. Cf. below, chap. vi, on the discontinuity of time.

39. *To Arnauld*, 29 July 1648, V, p. 221.

40. *Principles*, I, art. 51.

41. *Entretien avec Burman*, V, pp. 154-55.

42. Ibid.

43. Cf. above, chap. vi, sec. 3.

44. Cf. vol. II, chap. xvii, sec. 5.

45. *Meditation III*, VII, p. 51; IX, p. 41.

46. *Entretien avec Burman*, V, p. 156.

47. Ibid., cf. above, chap. iv, sec. 3.

48. *Meditation III*, VII, p. 51, ll. 18-20; IX, 1, p. 41.

49. Ibid., VII, pp. 51-52; IX, 1, p. 41.

50. Cf. above, chap. v, sec. 14.

51. *Meditation III*, VII, p. 49, ll. 12-20; IX, 1, p. 39.

52. Cf. *Replies to Objections I*.

53. Axiom 5, governed by axiom 4, *Geometrical Summary of the Meditations, Replies to Objections II*.

54. *Replies to Objections II*, IX, p. 107.

55. *Replies to Objections I*, VII, pp. 108-9; IX, p. 86; *Replies to Objections IV*, VII, p. 244, ll. 5 seq.; IX, p. 188.

56. *To Mesland*, 2 May 1644, IV, p. 112, ll. 23-26.

57. *Replies to Objections IV*, VII, pp. 240-41, 243, ll. 20-25; IX, p. 186.

58. "Those who follow the guidance of natural light alone spontaneously form here a concept common to efficient and formal cause, participating in both. Hence when something exists by another it exists as if from an efficient cause, and when something exists by itself it exists as if by a formal cause—meaning it is of such nature that it has no need of efficient cause." *Replies to Objections IV*, VII, p. 238, ll. 22-28; IX, p. 184. "I think we must show that between the efficient cause properly speaking and no cause, there is something in the middle, namely, the positive essence of the thing." Ibid., VII, p. 239, ll. 15-18; IX, p. 185.

59. *Objections I,* IX, p. 76; *Objections IV,* pp. 162-66.

60. *Notes on a Program,* VIII, p. 368. *Replies to Objections I,* VII, p. 108; IX, p. 86; *Replies to Objections IV,* VII, p. 24, ll. 10-11; IX, p. 185.

61. *Replies to Objections I,* VII, p. 110, ll. 21-32; IX, pp. 88-89; *Replies to Objections IV,* IX, pp. 182-83.

62. Ibid., VII, p. 111, ll. 2-8; IX, p. 88.

63. *Replies to Objections I,* VII, p. 11; IX, p. 88; *Replies to Objections IV,* VII, p. 241; IX, pp. 185-86.

64. Ibid., VII, pp. 240-41, 243, ll. 20-25; IX, p. 186.

65. Ibid., VII, p. 239, ll. 18-23; IX, p. 185.

66. Ibid., VII, p. 243, ll. 23-26; IX, p. 188.

67. Cf. vol. II, chap. X, "The General Theory of Possibility."

68. Cf. above, chap. v, sec. 12.

69. VII, pp. 238, 239; IX, pp. 184, 185.

70. "But it seems to me to be self-evident, and not needing a proof, that everything that exists is either by a cause or by itself considered as a cause." *Replies to Objections I,* IX, p. 89. "But we cannot make use of this [the consideration of efficient causes in order to prove the existence of God—M. G.] unless we give license to our mind to seek the efficient causes of all things in the world, without making an exception of God. For by what reason would we except God from this inquiry before having proved whether he exists." *Replies IV,* IX, p. 184. "For how could those who do not yet know God seek the efficient cause of all other things, in order thus to arrive at knowledge of God, if they did not think that it was possible to seek the efficient cause of everything? And how could they stop at God as the first cause and make him the end of their inquiry unless they thought that the efficient cause of each thing must be distinct from the thing itself?" Ibid., p. 189.

71. "And even if it is admitted that there is a first cause that concerns me, I cannot say that it is God, unless I truly have the idea of God." *To Mesland,* 2 May 1644, IV, p. 112, ll. 23-26.

72. *To Mersenne,* 11 March 1640, III, p. 36, ll. 7-10.

73. *Principles,* II, art. 35.

74. I, pp. 72, 88, 89; VII, pp. 48-49.

75. *Principles,* III, art. 63; VIII, p. 115, l. 9, art. 111, p. 159, l. 14.

76. *Entretien avec Burman,* V, p. 148.

77. Laporte, *Le Rationalisme de Descartes* [Paris, 1945], pp. 158-60, 256 seq.

78. Light as cause *(lux)* and light as effect *(lumen)* are contemporaneous as are the movements of the extremities of a stick, or being and reason in man, even though being is a condition of reason *(To Morin,* 13 July 1638, II, p. 209).

79. "That by which we intuit what is nonexistent, or instantaneous, or motionless, is no less true knowledge than that by which we understand what is existence or duration or movement." *Rules,* Rule 12, X, p. 420, ll. 2-8.

80. Bergson, *L'Evolution créatrice,* 1st ed. [Paris, 1907], pp. 295, 356 seq., 370, 373.

81. VII, pp. 48-49. "Considero temporis partes a se mutuo sejungi posse." *Replies to Objections I,* VII, p. 109, ll. 9-10.

82. *Principles,* II, art. 36.

83. *Principles,* III, art. 63, 111.

84. Bergson, *L'Evolution,* pp. 373-74.

85. "The duration of each thing is a mode or a way in which to consider this thing insofar as it continues to exist." *Principles,* I, art. 55. Cf. *To Clerselier,* 23 April 1649, V, p. 355.

86. *Principles,* ibid., art. 57.

87. Even though Descartes uses this argument *(Principles,* II, art. 20, for example), he does not use it alone.

88. *Replies to Objections I,* VII, p. 112-13; *Principles,* I, art. 26, 27; *To Mersenne,* 31 December 1640, III, p. 273; *To Chanut,* 6 June 1647, V, pp. 51-52; *Entretien avec Burman,* V, p. 167.

89. *To Mersenne,* 30 September 1640, III, p. 191, ll. 20-23.

90. *To Morus,* 5 February 1649, V, p. 273, ll. 7-12; *Principles,* II, art. 20.

91. *Principles,* II, art. 39; *The World,* VI, p. 45.

92. II, pp. 72; III, p. 173; II, p. 163; *Principles,* III, art. 55-59.

93. *Principles,* II, art. 25; IV, p. 187.

94. II, p. 72, 363; III, p. 193; *Principles,* II, art. 32; III, art. 55-59; III, p. 176. "But this tendency to move must follow the same rules as local movements." II, p. 143. "It is therefore identified with movement because the action includes not only the power or tendency to move, but also the movement itself." II, pp. 203-4.

95. *Olympica,* X, p. 218, ll. 10-11, quoted by Wahl, in *L'idée de l'instant dans la philosophie de Descartes* (Paris, 1920), p. 40.

96. Even though the *conatus* is defined as the tendency to move, even though we have to concern ourselves with it only at the beginning of a descent, and even though equilibrium is conceived as infinitely slow movement, Descartes does not attain the notion of virtual work, but that of elementary work. Cf. Gueroult, *Dynamique et Métaphysique leibniziennes* [Paris: Les Belles-Lettres, 1939], pp. 67-70.

97. *Principles,* II, art. 24, 25.

98. *To Mersenne,* 18 November 1640, [III], pp. 245-46.

99. *To Morin,* 12 September 1638, II, p. 363; cf. also II, pp. 143, 295.

100. *Dioptrics,* Discourse I, VI, pp. 83-84; *To Morin,* 12 September 1638, II, p. 370. Cf. also I, pp. 307-8; II, pp. 42, 72; XI, pp. 90 seq.; *Principles,* III, art. 62, 63, 77, 79, 87, 111.

101. *Entretien avec Burman,* V, pp. 163-64.

102. *Principles,* II, art. 36, 39, 42; III, art. 57; *The World,* XI, pp. 44-45.

103. *To Mersenne,* 11 March 1640, III, p. 36, ll. 7-10; III, pp. 176, 619.

104. *Principles,* III, art. 63, 111.

105. "You try in vain to evade [what I have explained about the independence of the parts of time—M. G] by proposing the necessity of the series between all the parts of time considered abstractly, of which we are not concerned here, since we are concerned with the time or duration of the thing itself, about which you could not deny that the movements cannot be separated from those immediately following." *Replies to Objections V,* VII, pp. 370-71.

106. *Principles,* I, art. 57.

107. *Principles,* II, art. 55, 56.

108. *Entretien avec Burman,* V, pp. 148-49; *To Chanut,* 6 June 1647, V, pp. 52-53.

109. *Principles,* II, art. 36; IX, p. 39.

110. *To Morus,* 15 April 1649, V, p. 343, ll. 1-12.

111. "Conservationem sola ratione a creatione differe." *Meditation III,* VII, p. 49, ll. 9-11; IX, p. 39. Continuous creation is not contínous production: "God does not preserve himself in the sense in which conservation means the continuous production of a thing." VII, p. 243, l. 5.

112. As the polemic against Morus demonstrates, the rejection of empty duration is the correlative of the rejection of material void. Cf. *Letter from Morus to Descartes,* 5 March 1649, V, p. 302, ll. 10-19; *Descartes to Morus,* 15 April 1649, V, p. 343, ll. 1-7.

113. "Actually it is quite clear to all who attend to the nature of time that a substance, to be preserved at every moment it endures, needs the same power and the same action that would be necessary to produce it and to create it anew if it did not yet exist." *Meditation III,* [VII], p. 49, ll. 6-9. "If he thinks that the several parts of time do not depend upon one another, and that he has supposed that his body has existed up to the present time by itself—meaning without causes—it does not follow that he must exist in the future, unless he has in him some real and positive power, which so to speak will reproduce him continuously." IX, p. 87.

114. *Principles,* II, art. 39.

115. *Entretien avec Burman,* V, pp. 148-49.

116. "Nullus motus fiat in instanti." *Principles,* II, art. 39; VIII, p. 64, l. 2. However, we break up movement into instants of movements that are necessarily rectilinear: "Only the straight line is completely simple and has a nature that is understood in an instant, for in order to conceive

circular movement, or something else, which may or may not exist, we must consider two of its instants, or rather two of its parts and the relation between them." *Treatise on Light,* XI, pp. 44-45. "Movement that is not movement, which is beyond movement, but is however already *'rectilinear,'* an instant of movement that is 'part' of movement": we see that the notion of *conatus* is already extremely near to the notion of differential; but it does not end up as that, as we will soon confirm.

117. *Olympica,* X, p. 218, ll. 10-11; cf. above, n. 95. Cf. *To Arnauld,* 4 June 1648, V, p. 193, ll. 18-21.

118. *Principles,* II, art. 33, 39.

119. *To Mersenne,* 30 September 1649, III, p. 193, ll. 9-11.

120. *Principles,* II, art. 33, 39.

121. III, p. 176; *Principles,* III, art. 55-59, etc. Cf. Gueroult, *Dynamique et Métaphysique leibniziennes,* pp. 73-75.

122. "An infinity cannot be greater than another. Why not? Where is the absurdity? Especially if it is only greater by a finite ratio *(in ratione finita),* as in this case multiplication by 6, a finite ratio, in no way affects the infinity." *To Mersenne,* 15 April 1630, pp. 146-47. The different infinite speeds are precisely greater or lesser *in ratione finita.*

123. Actually Leibniz does not at all end the primacy of discontinuity. In fact, the principle of sufficient reason equally requires the principle of continuity and the principle of indiscernibles, which is its negation. The former posits that differences must vanish at the limit, the equal must be identified with the unequal, the oblique with the horizontal, the curved with the straight, the polygon with the circle, etc. The latter posits that differences are always irreducible in the final analysis. No doubt the distinction between the ideal and the real appears to resolve this conflict—the principle of continuity governing in the former and the principle of indiscernibles in the latter, but the principle of sufficient reason continues to require its dual contrary requirement in both worlds. And in the higher actual world, it is the principle of indiscernibles that wins, and the reconciliation of the two requirements ends up with only a relative continuity of the discontinuous, such that basically things are constituted by the discrete, the disparate, and that continuity, which is always apparent, but never real, remains an unsatisfied requirement of reason.

124. "What you then propose about duration and time rests on Scholastic opinions, with which I strongly disagree, that the duration of movement is of a different nature than the duration of things that are not moved, as I have explained it in article 57 of the first part of the *Principles.* Even if no bodies existed, it could still not be said that the duration of the human mind was entirely like the duration of God, because we manifestly know of succession in our thoughts, which cannot be admitted for God's thoughts. We conceive clearly that it is possible for me to exist at this moment, while I am thinking of one thing, and yet not exist at the next moment, when, if I do exist, I may think something quite different." *To Arnauld,* 4 June 1648, V, p. 193. This text proves that we cannot attribute to the duration of the created thing the character proper to the duration of the Creator and that the character of spiritual duration is the same as that of corporeal duration.

125. That is what Bergson notes when criticizing Descartes, *L'Evolution* above, n. 80, p. 374.

126. Vigier, "Les idées de temps, de durée, et d'éternité chez Descartes," *Revue Philosophique,* 1920.

127. J. Wahl, *L'instant chez Descartes.*

Chapter VII. Of the True and of the False

1. *Meditation III,* IX, pp. 34-35.

2. VII, p. 37, ll. 25-28; IX, p. 29; VII, p. 43, ll. 26 seq.; IX, p. 34. *Notes against a Program,* VIII, p. 363.

3. *Meditation IV,* VII, p. 62, ll. 20-25; IX, p. 50.

4. *Rules,* Rule 8, X, p. 397.

5. VII, p. 368, etc.

6. However little objective reality "the idea of heat or of stone" contains, "we cannot say that this way or manner of being is nothing." *Meditation III*, VII, p. 41, ll. 27 seq.; IX, p. 33. That is the small amount of reality whose efficient cause will be sought in *Meditation VI*, VII, p. 79, l. 15; IX, p. 63.

7. To these two limits: the absolute limit of my faculty of knowledge, or of my intellectual nature in general, and the limit separating within this faculty the pure understanding (place of clear and distinct ideas) from sensible knowledge (place of obscure and confused ideas), correspond two kinds errors: the error that consists in affirming what we do not know absolutely and the one that consists in affirming what we do not know sufficiently: "And this indifference extends not only to things with which the understanding has no knowledge, but also generally to all those that it does not know with sufficient clarity at the moment when the will is deliberating." VII, p. 59, ll. 15-19. But we must add that all false affirmation of things known imperfectly always entails the conversion of nothingness into being. That is what constitutes its formal falsity.

8. From which results the restriction of science to within a purely subjective certainty.

9. "Divine warrant could cover the whole proof for the existence of bodies in Cartesianism under one condition only: that the production of sensations by geometric extension was itself a clear and distinct idea." Gilson, "Spinoza, Interprète de Descartes," in *Etudes sur le rôle de la pensée médiévale dans la formation du système cartésien* [Paris: Vrin, 1930], p. 311.

10. *Discourse*, VI, p. 40.

11. Ibid., pp. 38-39.

12. III, p. 259; *Principles*, I, art. 39.

13. "First I recognize that it is impossible that I ever be deceived, since in all fraud and deception, there is some kind of imperfection." *Meditation IV*, VII, p. 53, ll. 23-29; IX, pp. 42-43. "Since God is supremely perfect, he cannot be the cause of any error." Ibid., VII, p. 62, l. 18; IX, pp. 49-50.

14. VII, p. 55, ll. 15-26; IX, p. 44.

15. *Meditation IV*, ibid.

16. *Meditation IV*, VII, p. 55: "And this reason alone is sufficient to persuade me that all causes of the type we call final are useless in physical matters," I, pp. 23-25; IX, p. 44; *Entretien avec Burman*, V, p. 158; *To Hyperaspistes*, III, p. 431, l. 14; *Replies to Objections V*, VII, p. 374, l. 20; *Principles*, I, art. 28, etc.

17. Ibid., VII, p. 54; IX, p. 43.

18. *Meditation IV*, IX, p. 43; *To Clerselier*, 25 April 1649, sec. 8: "That every deception depends on some defect is manifest to me by the light of nature. . . ." V, p. 357, l. 10.

19. VII, p. 57; IX, pp. 45-46.

20. *Meditation IV*, VII, p. 55, ll. 1-2; IX, pp. 43-44.

21. Even though Descartes intentionally sets aside the case of sin *(Summary of the Meditations*, VII, p. 15, ll. 6-12; IX, p. 11; *Replies to Objections II*, VII, p. 149; IX, p. 116; *Replies to Objections IV*, VII, p. 247, l. 25, p. 248, ll. 1-10; IX, p. 191), the case of sin and error are of the same order in this case, as is proven by the following remark: "For privation, in which the formal reason of error and sin consists. . . ." *Meditation IV*, VII, pp. 60-61; IX, p. 48. "[Will—M. G.] chooses the false for the true and the evil for the good; that is what leads me to err and sin." VII, p. 58, ll. 24-25; IX, p. 46.

22. VII, p. 61, l. 4; IX, p. 48; *Replies to Objections V*, VII, p. 376, ll. 1-14.

23. "That does not yet completely satisfy me." VII, p. 54, l. 31; IX, p. 43.

24. VII, p. 54, l. 31, p. 55, ll. 1-26; IX, pp. 43-44. Cf. above, chap. vii, n. 16.

25. That is the doctrine developed by Dirois, in *Preuves et préjugés pour la religion chrétienne et catholique contre les fausses religions* (Paris, 1683), and criticized by Leibniz in his *Theodicée*, II, sec. 197. The incomprehensibility of God, allowing one to admit an imperfect work, will allow me to grant the world indefiniteness only, and not infinity. Cf. *To Chanut*, 6 June 1647, V, p. 52. Cf. also *Principles*, III, art. 2.

26. *To Mesland,* 2 May 1644, IV, p. 113, ll. 5-11.

27. "In considering the nature of God, it does not seem possible that he should have endowe'l me with any faculty that is not perfect in its kind, meaning that lacks some perfection that it is due. For, if it is true that the more expert the artisan, the more perfect and accomplished are the works produced by his hands, what thing could have been produced by the Supreme Creator of the whole universe that is not perfect and entirely complete in all its parts?" VII, p. 55, ll. 27 seq. Compare with *Principles,* III, art. 1.

28. Cf. vol. II, chap. x, "The General Theory of Possibility."

29. VII, p. 55, l. 27, to p. 56, l. 8; IX, l, p. 44. "Through ceaseless ages, God, whose purpose brings/to birth whate'er on land or in the sea/ is wrought, or in high heaven's immensity; / Save what the sinner works infatuate. / Nay, but thou knowest to make crooked straight: / chaos to thee is order: in thine eyes / the unloved is lovely, who didst harmonize / things evil with things good, that there should be / one word through all things everlastingly. Cleanthes, *Hymn to Zeus,* in Arnim, *Stoicorum veterum fragmenta* [Leipzig, 1903-24], I, n. 537, p. 112, ll. 11 seq.

30. VII, p. 55, ll. 14-27; IX, p. 44.

31. This formal reason is just the negative aspect of infinity itself, which is something very positive (the perfect). *Replies to Objections I,* VII, p. 113, ll. 9 seq.; IX, p. 90.

32. Ibid.

33. Cf. above, chap. v, n. 163. By referring the condition rendering possible the knowledge of my finiteness to my knowledge of the infinite, and by using certain aspects of the Kantian theory of practical and theoretical ideas toward this end, the Post-Kantians returned to Descartes' position.

34. VII, p. 55, ll. 12-16; IX, p. 44.

35. Saint Paul, *To the Romans,* XI: 33. Saint Augustine, *Reply to Saint Prosper and to Hilaire,* I, *On the Predestination of Saints,* chap. 9, trans. Estienne (Paris, 1715), p. 57. "A particular disposition of God's wisdom that knows how to derive good from evil." Saint Augustine, ibid., chap. 16, p. 77. Malebranche, *Réponse à la dissertation de M. Arnauld sur un Eclaircissement du Traité de la Nature et de la Grâce, Recueil des Réponses du P. Malebranche,* II (Paris, 1709), pp. 437-38; *IX Entretien sur la Métaphysique et la Religion,* ed. Cuvillier [Paris: Vrin, 1941; available as *Dialogues on Metaphysics* (New York: Abaris Books, 1980)], pp. 26-28: *VIII Méditation chrétienne,* sec. 21-23; *Traité de la Nature et de la Grâce,* I, art. 43-46; *III Eclaircissement de ce Traité,* sec. 24-25. "To say with Saint Paul, *'O altitudo divitiarum et sapientiae,'* is not to give up reason, but rather to use the reasons that we know (for they teach us the immensity of God, about which our apostle speaks) and to confess our ignorance about the facts. Moreover, it is to recognize, before seeing it, that God has made everything as well as possible, according to the infinite wisdom that regulates his actions." Leibniz, *Theodicée,* pt. II, sec. 134; *Discours de Métaphysique,* chap. 30.

36. An interpretation that also has numerous texts testifying for it: "That his judgments are incomprehensible and that his means are impenetrable." Saint Paul, *Romans,* XI: 33, "He who has predestined us . . . according to the designs of his will." *Ephesians,* I: 5; ". . . the mystery of his will." Ibid., v. 9; "As his will wishes it," Saint Augustine, *On Predestination,* chap. 19, p. 85. "According to the counsel of his will," ibid; "the mystery of his will." Ibid., p. 84. Cf. *Dissertation de M. Arnauld,* etc.; also François Dirois, *Preuves et préjugés pour la religion chrétienne et catholique contre les fausses religions* (Paris, 1683).

37. That are both found confusedly in the writings of Saint Paul and Saint Augustine.

38. "When one considers carefully God's immensity, one sees clearly . . . that there is no order, no law, no reason of good and truth that does not depend on it. . . . For if any reason or appearance of good had preceded his preordination, it would have determined him to do what is best; but on the contrary, because he determined himself to make the things that are in the world, for that reason, as it is said in Genesis, 'they are very good,' meaning that the reason for their goodness depends on the fact that he wished to make them so." *Replies to Objections VI,* VII, p. 435, ll. 22 seq.; IX, p. 235. "There being no idea representing good or evil . . . that can

have been the object of divine understanding before its nature had been constituted as such by his will." VII, p. 432, ll. 1 seq.; IX, p. 233.

39. VII, p. 55, ll. 6-26.

40. Cf. above, chap. ii, sec. 6.

41. VII, p. 55, ll. 26 seq.

42. VII, p. 61, ll. 20-26.

43. *To Mesland,* 2 June 1644, IV, p. 119, ll. 6-14. The reconciliation of the absolute freedom of God and the necessity that he acts in virtue of the principle of the best is effectively accomplished by Descartes by means of the identification of God's will and understanding in the *Entretien avec Burman:* "Even though God is indifferent with respect to all things, however, he necessarily made the decrees he did because he necessarily willed the best, even though the best is so by his own will. We should not separate necessity and indifference in God's decrees here, and although his actions were supremely indifferent, nevertheless he acted at the same time with supreme necessity. . . . In reality, these decrees could not have been separated from God, and are not posterior to him nor distinct from him, since God could not have existed without them. One sees clearly enough how God accomplishes all by a single act. But these are not reasonings that can allow us to know these matters; we must never allow ourselves the indulgence of trying to submit the nature and the operations of God to our reason." V, p. 166.

44. "In order that this conclusion [that God can never deceive us—M. G.] be true, it is not necessary that we can never be deceived (for on the contrary I have frankly admitted that we are often deceived), but only that we are not deceived when our error would make it appear that God is willing to deceive, which cannot be." *Replies to Objections IV,* IX, p. 152.

45. VII, p. 56, l. 30, p. 57, ll. 1-15; IX, p. 45.

46. By the same means of evaluation, by means of the idea of the infinitely perfect, I discover the limitation of all my other faculties—memory and imagination—that, if they existed in God (which they certainly could not since memory, properly speaking presupposes time, and the imagination presupposes the union with a body) they would be infinite in him. Similarly I discover that my will, though infinite in some respects, is finite in some others. VII, p. 57, ll. 15-20. It is useless to emphasize again the error of those who see the source of the idea of infinity for Descartes in the experience of my will, for the latter is not infinitely infinite, and we can only judge its infinity or degree of infinity by means of the idea of the infinitely perfect, which is given first, by which we are taught that God's will, in relation to ours, is *major absque comparatione.* VII, p. 57, l. 16.

47. VII, p. 58, ll. 20-25; IX, p. 46.

48. VII, p. 376, ll. 1-14.

49. VII, p. 61, ll. 4-9; IX, p. 48.

50. VII, p. 60, ll. 11-19.

51. Ibid., ll. 10-25.

52. VII, p. 60, ll. 5-6.

53. VII, p. 60, ll. 6-10.

54. Ibid., p. 60, ll. 26-31; IX, pp. 47-48.

55. "Errors are not things or substances that require the actual participation of God in order that they occur; thus, with respect to God they are only negations, while with respect to us, they are defects or imperfections." *Principles,* I, art. 31.

56. *Meditation IV,* VII, p. 60, l. 31, to p. 61, ll. 1-4; IX, p. 48. "Here you are guilty of the false assumption of taking as a *positive imperfection* the fact that we are liable to err, since it is principally with respect to God the negation of a greater perfection in creatures. . . ." *Replies to Objections V,* VII, p. 376, ll. 1-4. The term "principally" *(praesertim)* indicates that, even with respect to ourselves, error, insofar as it is referred to our *substance,* is not a positive imperfection, since it is neither a substance nor a real mode of that substance. That is one of the origins of the Malebranchian conception of freedom as a moral form (moral intention) not constituting in itself a physical reality.

57. *Meditation IV*, VII, p. 62, ll. 11-20; IX, pp. 49-50. Cf. *To Clerselier*, 15 April 1649, sec. 8 (our emphasis).

58. *Meditation IV*, VII, p. 62, ll. 22-26; IX, p. 50.

59. *Discourse*, pt. IV, pp. 38-39 (our emphasis). In the *Discourse*, the universality of doubt is not obtained by means of the evil genius, but by the dream argument by which I can transform everything into a universal illusion. But this argument can only strike at the certainty of existences, and not the certainty of essences, for whether I dream or I am awake, essence always preserves the same intrinsic rational properties. In opposition to the argument of the evil genius, this argument concerns only the realm of the senses and the imagination, but not the realm of the understanding. The appeal to a perfect God in order to establish the perfection or truth of what, being real, is necessarily true and perfect—since it can have no cause other than a perfect God—can also guarantee the truth of essences against illusions concerning only existence (dreams), which its intrinsic truth has in contrast to a supposed positive falsity, measured against the hypothesis of the evil genius.

60. *Meditation IV*, IX, p. 48.

61. *Meditation IV*, VII, p. 61, ll. 9-19; IX, pp. 48-49.

62. "All the reasons that prove the existence of God and that he is the first and immutable cause of all effects that do not depend on human free will prove similarly that he is also the cause of all those that do so depend." *To Elizabeth*, 6 October 1645, IV, p. 314. "The better this infinity (of God) is known to us, the more certain we are that it extends even to the most particular actions of men." Ibid., p. 315. Cf. also *To Elizabeth*, 3 November 1645, IV, p. 333.

63. VII, p. 55, ll. 27 seq.

64. *Replies to Objections V*, VII, p. 376.

65. *Meditation IV*, VII, p. 61, ll. 19-23; IX, p. 49; *To Mersenne*, May 1630, I, p. 153, ll. 31 seq.

66. Cf. on this latter point the penetrating article of Laporte, "La finalité chez Descartes," in *Revue d'Histoire de la Philosophie*, 1927, pp. 366 seq.

67. IX, pp. 49-50.

68. *Meditation V*, IX, p. 50.

69. *Meditation IV*, IX, p. 49.

70. *Discourse*, pt. III, VI, p. 28, l. 9.

71. See above, chap. vii, n. 21.

72. See above, ibid.

73. *Principles*, Introduction, IX, 2, p. 16.

74. *To Elizabeth*, 28 June 1643, III, pp. 691-92.

75. *Principles*, I, art. 35.

76. *To Mersenne*, 25 December 1639, II, p. 628, ll. 3 seq.

77. *Meditation IV*, IX, p. 40.

78. *Meditation IV*, IX, p. 45. Malebranche will push this analysis of the various aspects of will farther. Cf. Ginette Dreyfus, "Les différents aspects de la liberté chez Malebranche," *Revue Métaphysique*, April 1947, pp. 142-65; July 1947, pp. 239-58.

79. Ibid.

80. *Meditation III*, IX, p. 41.

81. "By God I understand an infinite, eternal, immutable, independent, omniscient, omnipotent substance, by which I and everything existing (if it is true that there are existing things) have been created and produced. . . ." VII , p. 45, ll. 9 seq.; IX, pp. 35-36. "The unity, simplicity, or inseparability of everything in God is one of the principal perfections that I conceive to be in him, and certainly the idea of this unity and the assemblage of all the perfections of God cannot have been placed in me by any cause from which I have not received the ideas of all the other perfections. For nothing can have allowed me to understand them together and inseparably, without having gotten me to know in some way what they are and that I know them all in some way. . . ." VII, p. 50, ll. 16-24; IX, p. 40.

82. *Meditation IV,* VII, p. 58, ll. 16-17.

83. *Meditation IV,* VII, p. 58, ll. 20-25; IX, p. 46.

84. VII, p. 57, ll. 15-21; IX, p. 46.

85. VII, p. 58, ll. 23-25; IX, p. 46. "And this indifference does not merely extend to things about which the understanding has no knowledge, but generally also to those that it does not uncover with great clarity at the moment when the will deliberates about them." VII, p. 59, l. 15; IX, p. 47.

86. *To Mesland,* 2 May 1644, IV, pp. 117-18.

87. *To Mersenne,* 27 May 1641, III, p. 379, ll. 17-25. "I do not deny that the will has this positive faculty. Indeed I think it has it not only with respect to those actions to which it is not pushed by any evident reasons on one side rather than another, but also with respect to all other actions; so that when a very evident reason moves us in one direction, although morally speaking, we can hardly move in the contrary direction, absolutely we can. For it is always open to us to hold back from pursuing a clearly known good, or from admitting a clearly perceived truth, provided we consider it a good thing to demonstrate the freedom of our will by doing so." *To Mesland,* 9 February 1645, IV, p. 173, ll. 17-24. The French translation of this Latin text was inserted into vol. III, p. 379, ll. 17-25, as belonging to a letter for Mersenne of 27 May 1641. That is what Adam and Tannery observe on IV, p. 72.

88. *"Perexiguam et valde limitatam," Meditation IV,* VII, p. 57, l. 4.

89. Our emphasis.

90. *To Mersenne,* 1 July 1641, III, p. 395, ll. 12-19.

91. "Unde ergo nascuntur mei errores? Nempe ex hoc uno, cum latius habeat voluntas quam intellectus, illam non intra eosdem limites contineo." VII, p. 58, ll. 20-22.

92. IX, pp. 57-58.

93. "Our knowledge seems to be able to grow by degrees to infinity, and since God's knowledge is infinite, his is the goal to which ours strives." *To Chanut,* 1 February 1647, IV, p. 608, ll. 16-19. "While my knowledge can be augmented more and more, nevertheless, I do not conceive that it can be actually infinite, since it can never attain so high a degree of perfection that it is not capable of acquiring still some greater increase." *Meditation III,* VII, p. 47, ll. 15-18; IX, l, p. 37. *Rules,* Rule 9, X, pp. 400-401: "How the intuition of the mind should be used can be learned. . . ."

Chapter VIII. Essences (of Material Things and of God)

1. *Meditation V,* IX, 1, p. 50 (our emphasis).

2. *Meditation V,* VII, p. 65; IX, p. 52; VII, p. 69, l. 16; IX, p. 55.

3. Ibid., IX, pp. 50-51.

4. *Meditation V,* VII, p. 65, ll. 2-6; IX, pp. 51-52.

5. Ibid., VII, pp. 65-66; IX, p. 52.

6. VII, p. 65, ll. 16 seq.; IX, p. 52.

7. Ibid.

8. *Meditation V,* VII, p. 65, l. 26, to p. 66, l. 1; IX, p. 52. Brunschwicg gives an interpretation incompatible with the order of reasons to the text: "It happens that once the progress of the analysis has reached the summit of intuitive unity, the philosopher can and must consider this absolute truth as self-sufficient and independent from the movement by which the human mind has achieved this intuition." "Mathématique et Métaphysique chez Descartes," *Revue Métaphysique,* 1927, p. 313. In this case we are not concerned with the positing of the infinite Being himself, which is realized in the second proof by effects, but with the identity of the case of mathematical demonstrations and the case of the ontological proof. And in all these cases, "the nature of my mind is such that I could not prevent myself from thinking them true while I conceive them clearly and distinctly." The preceding *Meditations* had no object other than to establish the validity of this natural judgment. And even if what the *Meditations* has established is not true, this natural judgment would subsist nevertheless, but remaining exposed to

metaphysical doubt. Thus the ontological proof would be at least as certain as mathematical demonstrations. But we would not be able to assure that it could be much more certain.

9. The *"preceding Meditations"* refers especially to *Meditation III,* which establishes, by means of the veracious God, the objective validity of clear and distinct ideas, but it also refers to *Meditation I* and *II* insofar as they condition *Meditation III;* finally, *Meditation IV* confirms the objective validity of clear and distinct ideas by demonstrating, in another fashion, that their reality allowed them to escape error. We ought to note the two *now's* (IX, pp. 50, 52) that emphasize the dependence as mathematical truths of the ontological proof with respect to the preliminary demonstration of the validity of clear and distinct ideas that was accomplished in the preceding *Meditations.*

10. *Meditation V,* VII, p. 66, ll. 23-28, p. 67, ll. 1-3; IX, p. 54 (our emphasis).

11. On 25 November 1630, Descartes wrote to Mersenne: "I can boast of having found one myself that satisfies me completely and that makes me know *that there is a God, with more certainty than the truth of any proposition of geometry. . . ."* I, pp. 181-82. This is the proof by effects that is the "principal proof"; the ontological proof is only "at least *as certain"* as a geometrical truth. The "at least as certain" that is attributed to it hesitantly over geometric truth arises from the fact that it is the clearest and most distinct of all essences. The same expression, "at least as certain," attributed to the ontological argument is also found in the *Discourse,* VI, p. 36, ll. 30-31.

12. *Meditation V,* VII, p. 68, ll. 23 seq.; IX, p. 54.

13. *Meditation V,* VII, p. 68, ll. 6-9; IX, p. 54.

14. *Meditation III,* VII, p. 46, ll. 15, 18; IX, p. 36; VII, p. 46, ll. 27-28; IX, p. 37.

15. *Replies to Objections II,* IX, pp. 122-23.

16. *Meditation V,* VII, p. 69, ll. 5-9; IX, pp. 54-55.

17. *Replies to Objections II,* VII, p. 130, ll. 11-16; IX, p. 103.

18. Hamelin, *Le Système de Descartes,* pp. 201-2, n. 1 of p. 202.

19. *Replies to Objections II,* VII, p. 155, ll. 22-24; IX, p. 121.

20. *To Mersenne,* 24 December 1640, III, pp. 266-67.

21. In opposition to Hamelin, who states, "it is completely independent of the other. . . ." Ibid.

22. *Replies to Objections IV,* VII, p. 238, ll. 11-14; IX, p. 184; *Replies to Objections I:* "The principal reason . . ." VII, p. 101, l. 17; IX, p. 81. *Summary of the Meditations:* "The principal argument . . ." VII, p. 14, ll. 18-20; IX, p. 11.

23. That is Brunschwicg's belief: it would be "the absolute truth that is self-sufficient and independent from the movement by which the human mind has achieved this intuition." Cf. above, n. 8.

24. "But after having recognized that there is a God, and having recognized at the same time that all things are dependent upon him, and that he is not a deceiver, I can judge as a consequence that everything that I conceive clearly and distinctly cannot fail to be true; and even if I am no longer thinking of the reasons why I have judged this to be true, provided I only remember having understood it clearly and distinctly, there can never be a contrary reason that can make me consider them doubtful. Thus I will have a true and certain science. And this same science extends also to all things that I remember having formerly demonstrated, such as the truths of geometry and other similar truths." *Meditation V,* VII, p. 70, ll. 10 seq.; IX, p. 55.

25. *Principles,* I, art. 5, 13, 14.

26. VII, p. 70, ll. 10 seq.; IX, pp. 55-56.

27. VII, p. 65, l. 4: "Hence it is quite evident that everything that is true is something; and I have already amply demonstrated that everything I recognize clearly and distinctly is true," etc., until "and this appears true even though I must admit that it does not at first appear entirely obvious," etc., p. 66, ll. 1-2.

28. VII, p. 68, l. 21: "For the rest, whatever argument or proof I use, I must always return to this conclusion: that it is only the things that I conceive clearly and distinctly that have the power to convince me completely. . . ."

29. VII, p. 69, l. 26: from "Thus, for example, when I consider the nature of a triangle . . ." etc., to "it may easily occur that I come to doubt its truth, if I do not know that there is a God"; p. 70, l. 4: from "For I can persuade myself," etc., ibid., to p. 70, l. 18.

30. "And, as for the question of God" etc., to "And although" etc., p. 69, l. 10.

31. *Meditation V*, VII, p. 64, ll. 10-11, p. 68, ll. 18-20; IX, pp. 51, 54; *Replies to Objections I,* VII, p. 117, ll. 9 seq.; IX, p. 92. Cf. *Meditation III*, VII, p. 51, ll. 10-12.

32. *Meditation V*, VII, p. 67, ll. 5-13; IX, p. 53. Cf. above, chap. v, n. 174.

33. M. Gueroult, *Nouvelles réflexions sur la preuve ontologique* [Paris: Vrin, 1955].

34. *Replies to Objections II*, VII, p. 130, ll. 11-16; IX, p. 103.

35. To Mersenne, 24 December 1640, III, pp. 266-67. Cf. chap. i, sec. 2, for a fuller quotation.

36. "I believe that it is in conformity with Cartesian thought to add that the a posteriori proof and the a priori proof lose their ability to demonstrate when they are considered in isolation from each other." Brunschwicg, "Mathématique et Métaphysique chez Descartes," in *Revue Métaphysique*, 1927, p. 312. It would be better to say that "the a priori proof would lose its ability to demonstrate when taken in isolation from the a posteriori proofs"—the a priori proof is no help to the a posteriori proofs.

37. *Replies to Objections V*, VII, pp. 149-50; IX, p. 117; *Replies to Objections II*, VII, p. 11, ll. 22 seq. to p. 116, ll. 1-7; IX, pp. 91-92.

38. Brunschwicg, "Mathématique et Métaphysique chez Descartes," *Revue Métaphysique*, 1927, p. 310.

39. *Discourse*, pt. IV, VI, p. 36, ll. 18-21.

40. "And just as it perceives that it is necessarily involved in the idea of a triangle that its three angles are equal to two right angles, it is absolutely persuaded that the triangle has three angles equal to two right angles; similarly, from the fact that it perceives that necessary and eternal existence is comprised in the idea that it has of an absolutely Perfect Being, it must clearly conclude that this absolutely Perfect Being is or exists." *Principles*, I, art. 14.

41. *Replies to Objections I*, IX, p. 91; *Replies to Objections II*, IX, p. 128.

42. *Replies to Objections II*, VII, p. 164, ll. 2-5, p. 167, ll. 5-7; IX, pp. 127, 129.

43. "Whenever I choose to think of a first and Supreme Being, and to derive, so to speak, the idea of God from the treasure house of my mind, it is necessary that I attribute to him all kinds of perfections, even though it does not occur to me to number all of them and to apply my attention to each of them at a time. And this necessity is sufficient to conclude afterwards (as soon as I have recognized that existence is a perfection), that this first and Supreme Being truly exists." *Meditation V*, IX, p. 53.

44. *Replies to Objections II*, VII, pp. 166-67; IX, p. 128.

45. Ibid., VII, p. 166, ll. 14-18; IX, p. 129.

46. *Replies to Objections II*, VII, p. 164, ll. 2-5; IX, pp. 126-27. Cf. also *To Mersenne*, July 1641, III, p. 396.

47. Alquié, *La découverte métaphysique de l'homme chez Descartes* [Paris, 1950], p. 226.

48. *To Gibieuf*, 19 January 1642, III, pp. 476 seq.

49. *To Arnauld*, 29 July 1648, V, p. 223.

50. *To Gibieuf*, ibid., III, p. 477.

51. Descartes distinguishes between two degrees of imagination: the higher degree, or imagination of geometrical ideas *(ideae intellectae)*, and the lower degree, which is based on adventitious ideas *(ideae sensu perceptae)*. *Meditation VI*, VII, p. 73, ll. 18-20; IX, p. 58. And the mountain and valley are adventitious ideas.

52. *To Arnauld*, 29 July 1648, V, p. 223.

53. *Replies to Objections II*, VII, p. 164, ll. 2-5, p. 167, ll. 5-7; IX, pp. 127-29.

54. *Letter to the Marquis of Newcastle*, March-April 1648, V, pp. 136-37.

55. Ibid.

56. The terms *analytic* and *synthetic* are used by Descartes only to characterize the two kinds of orders in the chain of reasons of his system, not to characterize the various modes of presentation of his proofs for the existence of God. The use of these terms for that is

Brunschwicg's: the ontological argument is called analytic when it is presented as the immediate apperception of the necessary property of an essence, and synthetic, when this property is referred to it as outside of it, in virtue of a syllogism based on a universal major premise.

57. "By their nature they [the first notions of metaphysics—M. G.] are not less clear, and even often are more clear than those considered by geometers." *Replies II*, VII, p. 157, ll. 8-10; IX, p. 122.

58. "The other proof in *Meditation V* proceeds a priori, and not from effect to cause. In the *Meditations* it comes after the proofs in *Meditation III*, because the author has discovered these two proofs in such a way that the proof by effects precedes the proof he has deduced in *Meditation V*, and this latter succeeds it. But in the *Principles*, he placed the latter first, because the method and the order of discovery differ from the method and the order of teaching; and in the *Principles*, his purpose is teaching and he proceeds synthetically." *Entretien avec Burman*, V, p. 153. Adam's translation of this passage is defective and should be corrected as follows: "Cette autre preuve dans la Ve *Méditation* procède a priori, et ne va pas de l'effet à la cause. Dans les *Méditations*, elle vient après les preuves de la IIIe parce que l'auteur a découvert ces deux preuves de telle sorte que la preuve par les effets précède celle qu'il a déduite dans la Ve, et que cette dernière lui succède. Mais dans les *Principes*, il a mis celle-ci d'abord, parce que la méthode et l'ordre d'invention diffèrent de la méthode et l'ordre de l'exposition: or, dans les *Principes*, il expose et procède synthétiquement."

59. "I have followed the analytic path in the *Meditations*, because it seems to me the truest and most proper for teaching." *Replies to Objections II*, IX, p. 122. But in the *Entretien avec Burman* (V, p. 153), Descartes characterizes the synthetic order as suitable for teaching. How can one reconcile these two assertions? There are two kinds of teaching: 1) Lofty teaching that is addressed to "those who wish to take the trouble to meditate with me and to consider things with care." It aims at obtaining a perfect intellection from the reader, one as perfect as if he himself had discovered it; it emphasizes the true difficulties, the internal linkage of notions, and glosses over the minor difficulties—it is addressed more to the person who wishes to comprehend than to apprehend. 2) Vulgarization, or the abridged and synoptic exposition of results set out in an order that calms one's memory and attentiveness: it is the manual or Scholastic treatise, "the summary." Moreover, this summary can include lengthy discourses and reasonings, which the *Meditation* dispenses with, because, while addressing weak minds, the philosopher is required "to distinguish as many various propositions as there are things to note in the proposed difficulty," in order that "they be able to stop separately at each of them and so that we can cite them afterwards and point out for them which of the propositions they have to think about." From this results the use of definitions, demonstrations, reasonings, syllogisms, etc. But this method, which permits an extrinsic knowledge, imposes such a knowledge in spite of the prejudices, rather than dispelling them; it therefore exposes us to contradictions. Moreover, it is also inappropriate to metaphysical matters, in which the unsuitability of notions with the senses arises from prejudices of which the geometer is ignorant. This opposition between the two kinds of teaching is clearly indicated in the *Replies to Objections II*: "Analysis shows the true way by which the thing is discovered *methodically*, and shows how effects depend on causes; so that, if the reader wishes to follow it and look over carefully what it contains, he will understand the thing thus demonstrated no less perfectly and will render it no less his own than if he himself had discovered it. But this kind of demonstration is not suitable for convincing opinionated and unattentive readers, for, if one allows the least thing it proposes to escape without taking notice of it, the necessity of its conclusions would not no longer appear. And we are not accustomed to expressing amply the things that are clear enough by themselves, even though they are normally the ones we have to guard ourselves against. Synthesis, on the contrary, employs a different path, as it were from effect to causes (even though the proof it contains is often from causes to effects),* and demonstrates the truth contained in its conclusions very clearly. It employs a long series of definitions, postulates, axioms, theorems, and problems, so that, if someone denies one of its consequences, it may be shown to be contained in the antecedents. Thus the reader, as obstinate and opinionated as he

may be, has his consent compelled from him. But this method is not as satisfactory as the other method for the reader who wishes to understand, because it does not teach the method by which the thing is discovered. . . . I have followed only the analytic path in my *Meditations* . . . but as for synthesis . . . although it is suitable after analysis with respect to the things treated in geometry, it is not as suitable, however, to matters belonging to metaphysics . . . ," etc., to the end of *Replies to Objections II*, IX, pp. 121-22.

*For example, the proof of God's existence by effects, which takes place after the proof by essence in the synthetic order. God's essence is in itself effectively first with respect to the idea of God impressed in our mind. In themselves, essence and existence precede this impression.

60. *Principles*, I, art. 16.

61. *Replies to Objections II, Geometrical Summary*, end of prop. I.

62. Cf. vol. II, chap. x, "The General Theory of Possibility."

63. Kant, *Critique of Pure Reason:* "The unconditioned necessity of judgments is not the same as an absolute necessity of thing." A593, B621.

64. *To Mersenne*, 6 May 1630, I, p. 150.

65. *Meditation V*, IX, p. 53.

66. Cf. vol. II, chap. x, "The General Theory of Possibility."

67. We have seen that this question was linked with the concept of existence as a perfection, which, lacking to the idea, renders it with respect to the thing it represents, into a defective being.

68. Cf. chap. viii, sec. 13.

69. "Even though he [God—M. G.] acts with supreme indifference, he nevertheless acts at the same time with supreme necessity. . . . We see . . . well enough how God has created everything by a single act. But it is not our reasonings that can allow us to know these things; let us not be proud, we ought never allow ourselves to submit the nature and operations of God to *our* reasons." *Entretien avec Burman*, V, p. 166 (our emphasis).

70. *Objections V*, VII, p. 323. That is also Leibniz's thought. Perfection is not contained in the raw fact of existence, otherwise, a stone's existence would entail perfection over a merely possible man, and a present pain would entail a perfection over an absent pleasure; perfection is a virtue of being: *non esse, sed bene, esse perfectio est.* Cf. Leibniz, *Die Philosophischen Schriften*, ed. Gerhardt (Berlin, 1875), I, pp. 213-15; IV, p. 359, etc. Kant, *Critique of Pure Reason*, A599, B627.

71. *Replies V*, VII, p. 382, ll. 25-27 to p. 383, ll. 1-5.

72. Hegel, *Encyclopadie der Philosophischen Wissenschaften*, Introduction, sec. 51.

73. Cf. above, chap. v, n. 42.

74. "Existence is not distinguished from essence in God." *Replies IV*, IX, p. 188.

75. Kant, *Critique of Pure Reason*, ibid., A597-98, B625-29.

76. *Entretien avec Burman*, V, p. 164. "We think of the essence of a thing in one way when we abstract from whether it exists or not, and in a different way when we consider it as existing." IV, p. 349, ll. 13-15.

77. In Latin up to here.

78. IV, pp. 349-50.

79. *Principles*, II, art. 10, 11, 15.

80. Ibid., art. 22, 64.

81. *Principles*, I, art. 55, 57, 58, 59; II, art. 25, 27.

82. Ibid., art. 59.

83. Ibid., art. 59.

84. *Objections V*, VII, p. 321, ll. 6 seq.

85. *Replies to Objections V*, VII, p. 380, ll. 14 seq.

86. Ibid., p. 381, l. 22 to p. 382, l. 3.

87. Ibid., p. 382, ll. 3-24.

88. *Rules*, Rule 12, X, p. 418.

89. *Principles,* I, art. 59; *Rules,* Rule 16, X, p. 458, ll. 20 seq.

90. Ibid., Rule 13, X, pp. 430 seq.; Rule 5, 6, 7.

91. Ibid., Rule 12, p. 429, ll. 26-27.

92. Ibid., p. 418, ll. 13-19.

93. V, p. 221.

94. *Rules,* p. 418, ll. 13-19.

95. Ibid., ll. 27-29, p. 430, ll. 1-2. That is also the case with the thinking self such as it is detached in the Cogito: its simplicity engenders its generality, meaning its capacity of being discovered in all the most complex thoughts.

96. Ibid., p. 418, ll. 13-19.

97. Ibid., Rule 16.

98. Ibid., p. 456, ll. 1-5, p. 457, ll. 13 seq.

99. *Rules,* Rule 4, p. 374, ll. 6-7.

100. *Rules,* Rule 16, pp. 457-58.

101. *Entretien avec Burman,* V, p. 160. From which we see that if essence, insofar as it is in itself distinguished from existence, is an abstraction *with respect to existence,* as an object of my thought, it is not an abstract thing, since it is the only *real* and *direct* object of my thought.

102. *Rules,* Rule 14, p. 446, ll. 15-20.

103. Ibid., ll. 20-26.

104. Ibid., pp. 442-43.

105. Ibid., pp. 443 seq.

106. Ibid., pp. 445-46.

107. Ibid., p. 444.

108. Ibid., p. 442, ll. 22-30, p. 443, ll. 1-10, p. 445, ll. 13-23.

109. Ibid., p. 448, ll. 20-21. The importance of this control by imagination (meaning by experience) for physics is as great as the importance of mathematics in order to engender the abstract beings that mathematics treats, or to link them together in a way satisfactory to the requirements of the intellectual subject, that is, the conditions of human evidence and certainty—the invention of genetic processes, of entirely fictitious hypotheses, the supposition of order where there is none, etc. The physicist himself is required to comply with these requirements of reason in me, and to invent fictions also—equator, zodiac, polar axis, etc. (VII, p. 350, ll. 1-14), to employ divisions without any real foundation, such as the division of days into hours and minutes (in contrast with the division of a century into years and days, which is based on the real, on the complete revolutions of the earth around the sun and on its own axis). *Rules,* ibid., ll. 15-18.

110. *Replies II,* IX, pp. 122-23.

111. *Principles,* II, art. 46.

112. *Meditation III,* IX, p. 33. It is only within and for my consciousness that something remains of Platonic exemplars, since clear and distinct idea is conceived as not arising from sensible images, and since it is the perfect innate model to which the latter are compared in order that their imperfection is judged, and since it renders "universals" possible. Cf. *Replies V,* VII, pp. 381 seq.; *Entretien avec Burman,* V, p. 162.

113. It is the same with respect to my soul: its existence is no more than the actuality of its essence, its creation is no more than the creation of its essence, which God has willed imperishable like the existing essence—or actual essence—of bodies. The terrestrial life of the soul in principle has no connection with the institution of essence, or rather with a perishable mode of an other imperishable actual substance—geometric extension.

114. Saint Augustine, *Questions,* bk. 83, quest. 46; *Soliloquies,* I, 2, chap. 18, etc.; Saint Thomas Aquinas, *Summa Theologiae,* pt. I, quest. 14, art. 6, quest. 15, art. 2.

115. Malebranche, *Entretien sur la Métaphysique,* I, and elsewhere; Spinoza, *Ethics,* V, prop. 22, 23, scholium of prop. 29; Leibniz, *De rerum originatione radicali,* ed. Gerhardt [Heidelberg, 1925], VII, pp. 303-4, and elsewhere.

Martial Gueroult (1891-1976) was a professor at the Collège de France. His work centered on seventeenth-century European philosophy and included major studies of Leibniz and Spinoza. Translator *Roger Ariew* is assistant professor of philosophy and humanities at Virginia Polytechnic Institute and State University. *Alan Donagan,* who reviewed the philosophical aspects of the translation, is Phyllis Fay Horton Professor of the Humanities and professor of philosophy at the University of Chicago. *Robert Ariew,* assistant professor of French at Pennsylvania State University, checked the translation for linguistic accuracy.